D0388821

H.G. WELLS
ANOTHER KIND OF LIFE

By the same author

Macmillan / St Martin's Press
(as Michael Draper)
Modern Novelists: H.G. Wells

Oxford University Press
The Country of the Blind and Other Stories *by* H.G. Wells (editor)

Penguin
A Short History of the World *by* H.G. Wells (editor)

H.G. WELLS

ANOTHER KIND OF LIFE

MICHAEL SHERBORNE

PETER OWEN
London and Chester Springs PA, USA

Peter Owen Publishers
73 Kenway Road
London SW5 0RE

Peter Owen books are distributed in the USA by
Dufour Editions Inc., Chester Springs, PA 19425-0007

First published by Peter Owen Publishers 2010

ISBN 978-0-7206-1351-3

A catalogue record for this book
is available from the British Library

Printed and bound in Great Britain by CPI Antony Rowe

For Marianne,
with love and gratitude

ACKNOWLEDGEMENTS

My debt to previous biographers of Wells is evident throughout. I have particularly drawn on the work of Geoffrey West, Vincent Brome, Lovat Dickson, Norman and Jeanne MacKenzie and my old friend David Smith who, sadly, died while this book was going to press. Editions of Wells's correspondence by David and others proved to be equally valuable.

Drafts of this book have been read by 'intellects vast, cool and [not entirely] unsympathetic' – namely, Robert Crossley, John Hammond, Patrick Parrinder and John Partington. Their advice and otherworldly facility in spotting errors has been invaluable. I am also grateful for the positive feedback received from Sylvia Hardy and from Chris and Liz Rolfe.

A Velde Research Fellowship from the University of Illinois enabled me to spend a month in the summer of 2006 carrying out research in the Wells Archive, held in the Rare Book and Manuscript Library of the University of Illinois at Urbana-Champaign. Thanks are due to Dennis Sears, Valerie Hotchkiss and everyone else who helped out during my stay, not forgetting the Catholic anarchist ladies who took me out for a Thai lunch. Above all, my thanks are due to Gene and Margaret Rinkel, who not only helped me in my research, but also housed, fed and entertained me for the duration with a hospitality I shall always fondly remember.

Much of the basic research for the book was carried out on weekend visits to the British Library, whose staff courteously supplied me with many – often obscure – books. I also received helpful advice when consulting the Wells Collection at Bromley Central Library and sessions papers in the East Kent Archives Centre.

For permission to quote or reproduce written material I acknowledge and thank the relevant copyright holders, most of all A.P. Watt on behalf of the literary executors of the estate of H.G. Wells for permission to quote extensively from his published and unpublished writings and from the letters of Amy Catherine Wells. Quotations from the letters of Amber Blanco White née Pember Reeves appear courtesy of Dr Dusa McDuff, and those of Annajane Davis née Blanco White appear courtesy of 'AJ' herself and her son Michael, who also supplied helpful information on the Wells family tree. Helen Alexander and Tim Suter kindly gave permission to use the quotations from Moura Budberg. The extract from the letter by Christabel McLaren is reproduced with the gracious permission of Mr Christopher McLaren. The extract by Rebecca West from *Henry James*

(© Rebecca West, 1916) is reproduced by permission of Peters, Fraser and Dunlop on behalf of the estate of Dame Rebecca West. The extracts from Rebecca West's letters, taken from Victoria Glendinning's *Rebecca West: A Life*, published by Weidenfeld and Nicolson, are included by kind permission of David Higham Associates. The extracts from articles by George Orwell (© George Orwell 1941 and 1946) are reprinted by permission of Bill Hamilton, as the literary executor of the estate of the late Sonia Brownell Orwell, and Secker and Warburg. The quotations from T.S. Eliot appear courtesy of the Estate of T.S. Eliot and Faber and Faber. The extract from the diary of Edie Rutherford, preserved in the Mass Observation Archive at the University of Sussex, is reproduced by permission of Curtis Brown Group on behalf of the Trustees of the Mass Observation Archive (© the Trustees of the Mass Observation Archive, 2004). Quotations from the diary of Beatrice Webb are reproduced with the kind permission of the London School of Economics and Political Science. Quotations from the writings of Virginia Woolf are reprinted with the permission of the Society of Authors as the literary representative of her estate.

The front cover photograph and the 1934 portrait of Wells are reproduced with permission of the National Portrait Gallery, London. The image of the Fabian stained glass window on the rear cover was supplied by the London School of Economics and Political Science and is reproduced with the permission of the Beatrice Webb Memorial Trust. The picture of Wells on the set of *Things to Come* appears by permission of ITV Global Entertainment. Getty Images supplied the photographs of Rebecca West, Wells with Lenin and Wells in his study at Hanover Terrace. The photograph of Wells aged ten was supplied by Bromley Public Library, the picture of Wells with Elizabeth von Arnim by the Huntington Library, San Marino, California, and the picture of Martha Gellhorn by the Franklin D. Roosevelt Presidential Library, New York. All the remaining illustrations are reproduced courtesy of the University of Illinois.

Andrea Lynn, who has literally written the book on Wells's later love affairs, was kind enough to respond to my request for contact details of a number of copyright holders. I apologize if, through my oversight, any permissions have been accidentally omitted. If so, both I and publisher will be happy to make amends in future editions.

On the subject of publishers, enormous thanks are due to Antonia Owen, Nick Pearson, Simon Smith, Michael O'Connell and all at number 73 for their expertise and faith. My thanks also go to Charles Phillips for the copy-editing.

Last, but never least, I must thank my family – Marianne, Ella and Isabel – and my colleagues at Luton Sixth Form College, particularly the stalwarts of the English and Humanities Department, who have had to endure several years of my Wells obsession. I hope they will consider the outcome worth while.

FOREWORD BY CHRISTOPHER PRIEST

Of all the writers I have known or have known about, the one I really wish I had met is H.G. Wells. The chances of that were always slim. I was born three years before he died, which allows me in my more hubristic moments to think of myself as his contemporary, but, in reality, I don't think our paths ever crossed. By every account, including Michael Sherborne's in this excellent new book, he was the best company in the world – for a time, at least.

Wells's life is full of friendships, and nearly all of them were meant intently and passionately, pursued in an open and thoroughgoing manner, and often, when some friendship did end, Wells would add a touching or generous footnote: quietly donating money to help with children's education or medical bills. He befriended great men – fellow authors (including Gissing, James, Shaw, Bennett, Crane, Conrad, Gorky) and presidents (both Roosevelts as well as Stalin) – and he was the lover of many beautiful and intelligent women: his two wives, Isabel and Jane, as well as Rebecca West, Elizabeth van Arnim, Amber Reeves, Martha Gellhorn, Dorothy Richardson, Moura Budberg, Odette Keun and literally dozens more because he was an ardent adulterer. Women were drawn to him – one said his body smelled irresistibly of honey. His friendships with women did tend to end differently from the fall-outs he sometimes had with men, but once the emotions calmed down Wells seems to have made few bitter or long-lasting women enemies. Even his endlessly betrayed wives either stuck by him or supported him, and both remained friends with him.

The Swiss governess of his children between 1908 and 1913, Mathilde Meyer, wrote a charming and intimate memoir of life with the Wells family, as she remembered it (*H.G. Wells and His Family*). She describes the summer weekend parties, notably at Easton Glebe in Essex, when two days of energetic games confronted visitors. They had to endure violently contested hockey, charades (which often led to broken furniture), the smuggling game devised by Wells (this involved gumboots, a pond and a ball), vigorous dancing in the barn. Even card games were intimidating: Wells liked the fearsome Demon Patience. Yet friends and literary colleagues flocked to these exhausting events, over which Jane presided with a cool charm.

One of my favourite stories about Wells is told by Colin Middleton Murry (son of the critic John Middleton Murry). In *One Hand Clapping* he describes how, as small children, he and his sister were taken by their father to a house somewhere in London and left to fend for themselves in a large room where toys were scattered on the floor. Just then a plump-faced man with bright blue eyes rushed noisily into the room on his hands and knees and immediately organized them into a frantic game of toy armies, model trains and cannons that fired pencils. He played with them until they were completely absorbed in the game then slipped away. When their father came back to collect them, the man gave them each signed copies of *Floor Games* and *Little Wars*. It was only many years later that Colin Murry realized that this had been the author of one of his favourite novels, *The War of the Worlds*.

Somehow, among all his many love affairs – which produced at least two illegitimate children – and between his travels around the world to consult with statesmen and amidst his feuds with other writers, his properties overseas, his weekend parties, H. G. Wells managed to write books. An amazing number of books. He wrote nearly fifty full-length novels and about eighty short stories. This output alone would make him an extremely prolific writer, but, in addition to that, there is a mountain of non-fiction: essays, polemics, speculation, social criticism, letters, argument, histories, film scripts, pamphlets of every kind. I am only a modest collector of Wells's books, but I have accumulated more than 130 volumes. Most of these are, of course, by Wells himself, but there is another shelf with many more books about him.

We are now roughly a hundred years past the period when Wells was in his prime, and it is possible to understand the consensus view that Michael Sherborne adumbrates in his introduction to this book, that these days Wells is best remembered for his early scientific romances, his quarrels with people such as Henry James and George Bernard Shaw and a general suspicion that a thinker who spent much of his career being ahead of his time ended up behind the times. The rest of the book sets about correcting this.

Wells's work has been out of fashion for many years. After the glorious effulgence of books in the last decade of the nineteenth century and in the first of the twentieth, more and more of his novels had an undisguised message: they banged on about things, they set out to defend a position over which the author had got himself into hot water. By way of example, the novel *Ann Veronica* (1909) is a good one, but his over-publicized affair with Amber Reeves gave it an element of kiss-and-tell that perhaps was present but which distracted from the quality of the fiction. H.G. Wells always had a popular constituency, and for many years he was the most famous and well-liked author in Britain. Though these days his later fiction is little known, some of his best work came comparatively late, in particular *Mr Britling Sees It Through* (1916) and *Christina Alberta's Father* (1925).

Interestingly, Michael Sherborne points out how the literary historians who identify modernism as the form that replaced the Victorian novel, and thereby created the idiom of the modern literary novel, always manage to sideline Wells's writing. This is undoubtedly because his work was so original it could not be pigeonholed. Here was a man who foresaw the military possibilities of nuclear fission about thirty years before Project Manhattan, who warned against foreign powers that might build armadas of warplanes, who envisaged a European union, who supported women's liberation even before they had the vote, who promoted a league of all nations, who predicted a capitalistic world economy run by investment bankers who were underpinned by socialistic state bail-outs, and much more and yet who could write such charming Dickensian novels as *Kipps* (1905) or *Tono-Bungay* (1909). It's ironic that the same literary sidelining goes on today: if Wells were still around they'd call him a 'sci-fi' writer and phone him up for a sound bite on the Large Hadron Collider or the latest high-concept Hollywood film and still believe that the work of 'real' novelists is to do with middle-class angst.

Wells was a great writer, and he left us dozens of great works. He was also an interesting man, a decent man, and an honest one. He worked hard.

Christopher Priest
Hastings, January 2010

CONTENTS

ILLUSTRATIONS BETWEEN PAGES 224 AND 225

Unless stated otherwise, all pictures are reproduced courtesy of the University of Illinois.

Wells in 1934, portrait by celebrity photographer Howard Coster; © *National Portrait Gallery, London*

Wells on the set of *Things to Come* with Pearl Argyle and Raymond Massey, 1935; © *ITV Global Entertainment*

Anthony West, Wells's son by Rebecca West, who became a novelist in his own right

Martha Gellhorn, travel writer and war correspondent, who Wells claimed had been his lover, pictured in Spain in 1937; *Franklin D. Roosevelt Library, New York*

Wells in his study at Hanover Terrace, London, 1940; *Kurt Hutton/Hulton Archive/Getty Images*

Wells at his final photoshoot, in March 1945, cursing his neighbour's sycamore tree and 'all the smart Alecks of Reaction'

For the normal man, as we have him to-day, his personal unity is a delusion. He is always fighting down the exposure of that delusion. His first impulse is to rationalize his inconsistencies by telling himself fanciful stories of why he did this and that. The tougher job, which all men and women will ultimately be educated to undertake, is to recognize the ultimately irreconcilable quality of these inconsistencies and to make a deal between them.

H.G. Wells, *Experiment in Autobiography*

INTRODUCTION

A sudden gust of air delivers an invisible man amidst a whirl of metal struts. The outline wobbles, sighs, grows three-dimensional and textured. The noise ceases. The man, a short, slightly tubby figure in a woollen suit, clambers from the bicycle-like structure and peers with curiosity around the room into which he has materialized. His eyes are a piercing blue. He strokes his small moustache and seems pleased, though not surprised, to find he is in a library after closing hours.

He begins to leaf briskly through the twenty-first-century newspapers and reference books. He is delighted by what he learns of women's liberation, globalization and scientific progress, taking particular pleasure in television, space travel, lasers, atomic power and the growth of the ecology movement. He nods as he reads of the wars and religious upheavals that have run alongside these developments. It is all much as he expected. 'I told you so,' he chuckles, 'you damned fools!'

He is visibly disappointed, on the other hand, to find so little progress has been made towards a socialist world state. He shakes his head, murmuring, 'What on earth are those Chinese up to now?'

Struck by an afterthought, he locates the literature section and looks himself up in a reference book: Herbert George Wells, 1866–1946. He reads the key phrases aloud, as if to convince himself that they really say what they do, occasionally pausing to snort with derision. 'Left school at fourteen; later studied under T.H. Huxley under whose Darwinian and agnostic influence he always remained; best writings are science-fiction stories; attempts to produce more serious fiction relied on a crude "saturation method"; was uncomprehending of the literary giants of his time such as Henry James and James Joyce; a Fabian socialist, he believed in inevitable progress to a Utopia run by a scientific elite; his many polemics on politics and society are marred by anti-Semitic and eugenic ideas; at the end of his life he seems to have seen through his own naïve optimism and died in despair. His books, popular in their day, were condemned by more discerning readers, with whom posterity has largely agreed.'

Wells shuts the book, curses comprehensively, then erupts into laughter, perhaps because he genuinely does not care for his posthumous reputation, perhaps because so many of the comments he has read are demonstrably untrue. He replaces the book on the shelf, is about to climb back on to the saddle, then changes his mind and makes for the door. Having read about the prevalence of casual sex in the twenty-first century, he has decided it is his duty to investigate.

His footsteps echo down the corridor. The man is gone, the machine remains, the saddle temptingly empty. If we want to know the complex, interesting, perhaps more positive, truth about H.G. Wells, we have only to climb on and adjust the chronometer. How far shall we go?

I
FAMILY AND CHILDHOOD
1851–1880

Night follows day like the flapping of a black wing, the surface of the earth swirls and a series of images races past almost too fast to be registered. A scattering of ashes lifts from a choppy sea, swirls together and dives into an upturned jar. Stalin shakes his head, Roosevelt beams, Lenin points a finger. A fire of wood burns with little blue flickerings of flame. A naked woman smiles menacingly and holds up a razor. A passenger gasps in exhilaration as a primitive aircraft plunges and rises. A figure stands defiantly on a balcony, steeling himself not to flinch as bombs fall all around. Kisses, quarrels, charades, parlour games. Interlocked bodies move to and fro on the floor of a church. A tandem hurtles along a suburban road, carrying a laughing couple. A goddess steps out of a Botticelli painting and into a Thames-side pub. A little boy is flung into the air, lands on a tent peg and lets out a brief yell like a birth cry.

The machine shudders and, with the dial showing a date somewhere in the middle of 1851, we are at the edge of London's Hyde Park. On the face of it this is an unfavourable time and place to seek H.G. Wells – he will not be born for another fifteen years and, when he is born, it will not be in a public park – but something is certainly happening. A huge crowd is converging on a gleaming glass and iron building. Almost lost in the throng, a small, animated woman in her late twenties cranes her neck for a glimpse inside.

With more than a hundred thousand items to see at the Great Exhibition, most visitors prioritized the mechanical exhibits: machines for manufacturing cotton, machines for making cigarettes, locomotives, microscopes, cameras, a Singer sewing machine – even a Colt revolver. Thomas Carlyle, one of the Exhibition's most scathing critics, had declared back in 1829 that the world was being taken over by machinery.[1] Here was cast-iron proof.

The Great Exhibition marked Victorian Britain's confidence about its leading role in what would later be called globalization. Though it may be hard to believe today, in the 1850s Britain owned half the ocean-going ships in the world and half the railway lines; it was producing five times as much iron as the USA, ten times as much as Germany. But its supremacy would not last for ever. The American Colt revolver was designed to be made quickly and cheaply from standard components; British guns were still being made one at a time by craftsmen.

If the writing was on the wall for Britain as the world's dominant power, it was not apparent to the visitors walking the aisles, including at various times Queen Victoria, Prince Albert, the Duke of Wellington, Charles Dickens, Charles Darwin and, less important in the general scheme of things but much more significant for us, the woman we glimpsed as we arrived, a lady's maid named Sarah Neal – later to be Mrs Sarah Wells. We rightly think of her youngest son as a figure of the early twentieth century, but his formative years were Victorian and his life was shaped by many of the forces that the exhibition put on display.

International competition driving the growth of education would give Wells the chance to break out of his servant-class background and equip him with a distinctive, science-based world-view. His imagination would be fired by awareness that the future would be excitingly different from the present but that some aspects of it might be foreseeable. Globalization and its consequences would become a central concern of his thinking. The unprecedented mingling of social classes at the exhibition prefigured the shifting class balance of society, which he would try to match with political and artistic innovations. The existence of the British Empire would shape Wells's vision of a unified world. Even the futuristic appearance of the Crystal Palace prefigured the exotic, utopian settings of some of his stories. Many events had to take place, however – generally highly unwelcome ones for his mother – before Herbert could make his entry into her life.

Sarah had been born on 10 October 1822 in Chichester, where her parents ran the Fountains Inn. In her late twenties she had worked as a lady's maid to an army officer's wife, travelling around England and Ireland. In 1848 when her younger sister died, she quit to look after her mother, who was suffering from long-term ill health. By then the Neals had moved to Midhurst to run the New Inn and, after a couple of years in this pleasant West Sussex town, Sarah found a new appointment. However, the household was too High Church for her ('almost Roman Catholic'[2]) and after three months she moved to Uppark, a country house on the South Downs eight miles from Midhurst. Here she became a trusted upper servant, attending to the needs of Lady Fetherstonhaugh's younger sister, Frances Bullock. In June 1851 the Uppark gardener left and, fatefully, was replaced by one Joseph Wells.

Joe was almost six years younger than Sarah, having been born on 14 July 1828 on the Redleaf estate in Kent, where in 1843 he began his gardening career, though his lifelong passion was not gardening but cricket. He played for the nearby Penshurst club from 1842 to 1847, at which time the owner of Redleaf died and the estate was sold. Over the next four years Joe drifted through a number of gardening jobs. Like many other people in that period of severe economic difficulties, he thought about emigrating to the gold fields of the USA or Australia. Instead he found his way to Uppark.

It was not love at first sight – not for Sarah, at least: 'thought him peculiar', she wrote in her diary. Joe was a restless personality who would occasionally lie at night on the Downs, wondering. He was extrovert, widely read and not afraid to speak up for himself. People tended to recollect him as a large man, though he was actually around five foot eight inches tall. Sarah, in contrast, was small, quiet, tightly self-controlled and conservative in her views. She felt at home kneeling in the church, within whose beliefs and rituals she found reassurance, not sprawled out on the bare ground beneath the stars. But perhaps one thing these two individuals in their twenties did share was a desire to find some personal relation to the cosmos – and some doubt about what that relation might be. It is easy enough to see the differences between Sarah and Joe. Their common assumptions, compatible roles and mutual humour are the kind of information that evaporates from history.

Whatever the details, the two evidently came to enjoy each other's company. There were weekly get-togethers in the Servants' Hall, where the concertina and the fiddle played country dances by candlelight; there were chances to talk in the procession to and from South Harting Church every Sunday. Joe presumably took advantage of these opportunities to overcome Sarah's initial aversion. In a letter written to patch up a quarrel, he baulks at her view of original sin, with its implication that a child might be consigned to Hell for the sins of its parents.[3] Yet he rejects the belief with tact and professions of love and faith, assuring Sarah of his willingness to study the Bible with her in the years to come.

Their prospects as a couple must have seemed promising. While the recent past had been a nightmare of poverty for many people – Dickens's *Hard Times*, Gaskell's *North and South* and Mayhew's *London Labour and the London Poor* all appeared in the first half of the 1850s – Sarah and Joe were not uneducated manual labourers but skilled workers in a prestigious service industry. Moreover, though they could not know it, the economy was about to enter on a quarter-century of general growth. Unfortunately, the secure life on which they seemed to be set at Uppark was about to come to an end.

In April 1853 the health of Sarah's mother again became critical. Sarah resigned from her post and returned home to what seemed likely to be her mother's deathbed. Determined not to lose her, Joe resigned from Uppark a month later, pursued Sarah to Midhurst, confirmed their engagement and secured her father's blessing, before relocating himself to the Gloucestershire farm of his brother Charles.

In the event it was Sarah's father who died. After his sudden collapse in late August, Mrs Neal became deranged. She attacked her daughter and accused her of having her husband imprisoned. Even when her reason returned, she remained terminally ill, and the shocked and bereaved Sarah had to nurse her, waiting miserably for the end, while her father's creditors circled. Mrs Neal died on 5 November.

Immediately after her funeral Sarah was informed that all of her family's possessions had been seized. The next day the brewers who owned the inn gave her twenty-four hours to vacate the premises.

It had been Sarah's intention to find another job as a lady's maid, but Joe, supported by one of her aunts, insisted that immediate marriage was the best option. A special licence having been obtained, the ceremony took place on 22 November 1853 at St Stephen's Church, Coleman Street, in the City of London. Sarah's summary of the occasion in her diary, written on the tenth anniversary of the event, recalls a major disaster from which her life had yet to recover:

> no preparation . . . alone at the Altar . . . no bridesmaid . . . the sombre dress of black cast off for one hour . . . we parted a few hours after . . . no more to meet that year . . . I in as much confusion as ever. Oh could I have followed and carried out my own plans, how different our lives might have been!!!

Joe had managed to find himself a new gardening job at Trentham, a palatial mansion outside Stoke-on-Trent that boasted one of the largest formal gardens in England but did not run to married quarters. 'Saddie', as he had nicknamed his wife, had to billet herself on various relatives for the next five months, merely paying him occasional visits.

In April 1854 Joe moved on to a well-paid job as head gardener with a staff of ten at Shuckburgh Park, near Warwick, and this time the job came with an attractive tied cottage. Nine months later, on 20 January 1855, Sarah gave birth to a girl whom they named Frances after her former employer but who was known familiarly as Fanny or Possy. Having almost died at birth, Fanny remained prone to illness and was a constant concern to her mother. She was not the family's only worry. The assertive Joe did not get on with his employer, and in July he was dismissed; in August the family had to leave the cottage. While Joe again set off in search of employment, Sarah and her baby daughter were taken in by some of his relatives.

No gardening jobs were forthcoming, so Joe turned his hand to a new line of work in order to support his family. Two of his cousins, Thomas and George Wells, were shopkeepers in Bromley, Kent. Tom ran a grocer's, George a china and crockery shop. George offered to let Joe have his lease and stock for £50 down, plus £100 from his father's inheritance; Tom agreed to help out with the groceries. The family moved in October. 'How sad to be deceived by one's relations,' commented Sarah in her diary only two weeks later. 'They have got their money and we their old stock.' In fairness, even if the shop never prospered, it had stayed open for eleven years and, thanks to the economic upturn, it would remain in business for another thirty-one. After a successful career in service, however, Sarah was never able to reconcile herself to the dull grind that would be her lot as a shopkeeper's wife in

Bromley. Her diary is a record of depression and despair, relieved only by love of her children.

The coming of the railway in 1858 would shortly begin Bromley's transformation into an outer suburb of London, but in 1855 it was a small town with a population of around 5,000, where horse-drawn coaches stopped on their way up to the capital. The inns at which they stopped were the White Hart and the Bell, the latter recommended by no less a personage than Lady Catherine de Burgh in *Pride and Prejudice*.[4] Just over the road from the Bell, in a terrace of tall, brick buildings, was the family's shop, 47 High Street, also known as Atlas House after a lampstand in the form of the Greek god Atlas carrying the globe, displayed in the small right-hand window of the shop.

Behind the shop was a parlour from which a narrow staircase led to the basement. The front of the basement was occupied by the kitchen, which received daylight from a grating at street level; the back was the scullery. As the shop was built on a slope, it was the scullery that gave access to the yard behind the house. This yard measured about thirty feet by forty and contained the well from which the family pumped their water and, disquietingly close to it, the 'closet', a cesspit covered by a brick outhouse. Taking the stairs up instead of down led to two bedrooms and, above these, to two attic rooms, the front one designated the children's bedroom.

As we have seen, Sarah took a dim view of her new home. Shortage of space meant the place was cluttered up with stock. Coal could be got to the hole under the stairs only by lugging it through the building, leaving a trail of gritty black dust; the smelly contents of the brick dustbin in the yard had to make the reverse journey. Lack of money meant dingy, second-hand furniture and bare boards; and there was a constant disgusting battle with cockroaches. This was not the lifestyle Sarah had expected when she agreed to marry Joe. She felt badly betrayed.

While Sarah was trapped in Atlas House, her husband had the opportunity to pursue a more satisfying mode of life. Though he still talked of emigration, this time to New Zealand, his practical strategy was to use the shop as a day job and earn as much as possible from his hobby of cricket. From the 1860s to the 1880s the barbarities of cockfighting, bare-knuckle prizefighting and free-for-all football were being superseded by organized modern sport, and, though he could never be among the wealthy gentlemen amateurs who ran the game, Joe was determined to play his part in this cultural crusade. In 1856 he helped revive the Bromley Cricket Club.

The same year he shot off part of a thumb while hunting rabbits, but fortunately the injury did not affect his skills as a round-arm bowler. In 1857–69 he played as a professional for Kent, and in 1862, playing for them against Sussex at Hove, he became the first man in first-class cricket to take four wickets with four successive balls. Encouraged by this moment of glory, he began to sell cricketing equipment from the shop. It was obtained from a cousin whose life Joe had once saved in a swimming incident and who was willing to let him have extended credit.

For Sarah, cricket was 'low, useless, merely for amusement'. It gave her husband an excuse to be away from home for days at a time, leaving her to mind the shop, do the cleaning and the needlework and look after their growing family. In 1857 there came a son, Frank, and in 1862 a second son, Freddy, also known as Fuss or Fussy.

Having escaped his home all day playing cricket, Joe would vanish in the evenings to the Bell or the Duke's Head and play cards. His vow to Sarah during their courtship that they would read the Bible together by the fireside proved so wide of the mark that now he even refused to attend church on Sundays. Sarah's exasperated diary entries show how keenly she felt her husband's neglect and how exploited she felt herself to be ('Still I am not *appreciated*! What can man expect of woman'), but protest did her little good. William Baxter, local historian and friend of Frank Wells, recalled Joe as 'a dictatorial, over-bearing man, over-awing his delicate lady-like wife'.[5] Joe generally spoke of the world around him with a humorous 'mixture of derision and impatient contempt'.[6] In less humorous moments, his temper was liable to flare out at anyone and everyone, often in language that later, when his geniality returned, he regretted.

At the beginning of 1864 the underlying unhappiness of the Wells's marriage was overtaken by outright tragedy when Fanny developed appendicitis. She suffered three days of agony and died in her mother's arms shortly before her ninth birthday, leaving – in Sarah's painful words – only 'toys & little clothes lying about' as a mark of her unique existence.

Less than two years later, at the age of forty-three, Sarah became pregnant once more, presumably hoping that a new baby might do something to assuage her loss. She may even have been hoping for another daughter. However, on 21 September 1866, around 4 p.m., she gave birth to a boy.

Would Sarah have conceived him so late in life if she had not lost Fanny? It seems unlikely. Looking back in his autobiography, the late arrival's own view of the matter is plain: he had been created to replace his sister. He resented and rejected this role of substitute. Not only had Fanny been a girl, but she was one with a similar temperament to her mother, ready to share Sarah's interests. He, on the other hand, was a high-spirited, self-assertive boy who inherited many of his father's qualities. His mother's attempts to fit him into the terrible void left in her life by Fanny inevitably led to 'a process of severance and estrangement'.[7]

His official name was Herbert George Wells, but he was more often known as 'Bertie', 'the Buzzwhacker', 'Busswuss' or simply 'Buss'. From the first he seems to have been demanding: 'never had so tiresome a baby as this one', Sarah wearily noted in her diary. On 15 January 1868 he struck out and gave his mother a black eye. On 28 April he fell out of bed on to his glass feeding-bottle and received a cut over the right eye which required stitches and left a permanent scar.

As he grew out of babyhood and began to investigate his surroundings, the newcomer found himself in the kitchen, scullery and yard of Atlas House. Even sixty years later he could recall every detail of the yard, such as the convenient dust-bin from which eggshells, tins and boxes could be retrieved and arranged into a miniature world of his own.

Beyond the back fence he could hear, and presumably smell, the premises of John Covell the butcher. It was occasionally possible from the top floor of the house to glimpse pigs rooting about in the carcasses of slaughtered animals. During the night the pigs, sheep and cattle awaiting slaughter could sometimes be heard crying out and struggling to free themselves. Still more alarming than the world beyond the back wall was the world within Bertie himself, which also manifested itself at night. In a recurring 'geometrical nightmare', he later wrote, it seemed 'as if a mad kaleidoscope charged down upon me, and this was accompanied by intense distress'.[8]

Bertie spent most of his early years close to his mother. He was a sickly child, given to headaches and bilious attacks, and he was also her precious substitute for her lost daughter. A picture taken at about the age of three and a half shows him dressed in a unisex frock and positioned awkwardly on a photographer's chair, as if ready to twist to one side, slip to the floor and make off out of the picture. His brother Freddy stands beside him with one hand on his shoulder, partly in fraternal reassurance, partly as if to prevent escape.

Sarah took Bertie to church every Sunday, read the Bible with him and taught him to recite the Catechism, but it seems she had mellowed from the militancy that had disturbed Joe back in the Uppark days. In one of her religious books she papered over the illustrations of Hell to spare her son from seeing the distressing scenes they depicted. A curious child, he held the page up to the light and took a good look.

And what was his response to his religious instruction? In his autobiography he assures us that he was a 'prodigy of Early Impiety', but we should not take the claim too literally.[9] It is easy enough to believe that he was less inclined to devotion than his sister had been, that he was bored by much of what he was required to learn and that, as he grew older, he became impatient with his mother's preaching – the more so in that she seems to have lost some of her conviction with the death of Fanny. Yet if in the long term Bertie's understanding was resistant to Christianity, his imagination retained the impression of it deeply.

Even after he had consciously rejected the Christian faith, something he did not do until well into his teens, a love-hate obsession with religion persisted, and he continued to carry the stories and images of the Bible in his mind. He would later note, 'I write in phrases that the evangelical Christianity of my childhood made familiar to me, because they are the most expressive phrases I have ever met for the psychological facts with which I am dealing.'[10] In particular, the events of the apocalypse – the destruction of this world through a series of miraculous happenings and the establishment of a new, perfect order of things in which an elite group of believers was exalted – maintained a lifelong hold on him.

While Bromley remained stubbornly untransfigured, the earthly paradise of Uppark was tantalizingly present less than fifty miles away. Perhaps even more than Joe, Sarah dreamed of escaping from her home and family. She remained in touch with her former employer, Frances Bullock, and must often have thought longingly of her former life, far from the depression and exasperation of Atlas House. Her nostalgia for this past, and her resentment of her husband, encouraged her devotion to the cult of the widowed Queen Victoria, and, as Bertie grew older, Sarah took him on expeditions to Windsor and Chislehurst to see Her Majesty go past.

Even if under present conditions she could not rejoin the world of the upper classes, Sarah was determined to impress upon her sons a conviction that they were better than their immediate environment. They were not to mix with common children who might teach them swear words. They were discouraged from mixing with any local people who seemed rough in their manner or unorthodox in their religion.

Sarah was also mindful of 'the three Rs'. She pasted up a display in the kitchen from which Bertie learned the alphabet and numerals. He learned to recite up to one hundred and to read and write, tracing his first written word ('butter') from her handwriting. Around the age of five he was sent to a small 'dame school' in South Street, kept by a Mrs Knott and her daughter Miss Salmon, for further basic training in literacy and numeracy. Bertie was escorted to and from the school by Freddy, who was sufficiently close to him in age to share in storytelling, the double act of Fuss and Buss developing a long-running series of tales about a character called Puss the Cat. (Bertie would prove a lifelong cat lover.)

Bertie's other brother, Frank, nine years older than he was, had inherited his father's love of the outdoor life and with it a disposition to follow his own path regardless of others. He had a knack for using machinery that he employed to engineer spectacular mischief for a gang of admirers. He let off a home-made bomb in an elm tree next to the cricket field, rode a shunting engine along the railway line at Windsor and wired up the bells in his 'uncle's' hotel so that when one was pressed they all rang simultaneously. He was, in Sarah's indulgent words, a 'dreadful tease'.[11] About the time Bertie was starting at Mrs Knott's, Frank was made a reluctant apprentice of Crowhurst the draper in the Market Square.

As for Bertie, if he lacked his father's outdoor qualities he inherited his aggressive temperament. The runt of the Wells pack, a sickly child who could easily have been dominated by his older brothers and other children, he quickly learned the importance of sticking up for himself. In disputes with his brothers over who owned what, he would scratch, kick and bite, and he once threw a fork at Frank that stuck in his forehead and left a mark for over a year. On another occasion, he flung a wooden horse that missed its intended target, Freddy, but smashed a window. Bertie was always able to take advantage of his youth and poor health in fights with his brothers, knowing that his yells of distress would cause his mother to intervene on his side. His brothers eventually came up with a solution. When provoked, they would corner him in the attic and suffocate him with pillows.

Others proved more appreciative. He had a gift for drawing comical sketches (the 'picshuas' that enlivened his correspondence all his life) and a retentive memory that was well suited to recitation. Those lacking in physical power often cultivate their intellectual and verbal strengths, and Bertie was a natural performer whose precociousness made him especially popular with his girl cousins at Tom Wells's. His father, too, recognized that his son had talent. His period with Kent having come to an end, Joe had found himself a couple of two-year appointments, first with Bickley Park (1870–2), then Chislehurst (1873–4). By the time of the Chislehurst matches, Bertie at six or seven was old enough to accompany his father, and on one occasion he decorated some tree trunks with chalk drawings, winning the praise of one of the Chislehurst gentlemen. Perhaps remembering how his own youthful talent for writing and drawing had come to nothing, Joe began to make a point of commending his son for his wit and flair.

It was at a home match, however, that Bertie found himself violently redirected towards the republic of letters. Still aged seven, he was playing outside the scoring tent when the grown-up son of the landlord of the Bell seized him and began playfully throwing him up and catching him. When he missed, Bertie came down on a tent peg and broke his leg. He was carried home to have the limb set between two splints. The operation proving unsuccessful, the tibia had to be rebroken and reset. Frank later recalled that Bertie's cries during this process were 'terrific'.[12] Seventy years later the victim could still feel where the break had been.[13]

Retrospectively, his agonizing injury proved to be a stroke of good fortune. First, the landlady of the Bell, Mrs Sutton, was so anxious to make amends that she was willing to supply Bertie with any food he wanted. Used to a meagre diet dominated by cabbage and potatoes, he now found that he could order himself a nourishing alterative of brawn, chicken, jellies and fruits. Second, he had the time and opportunity to acquire the habit of reading.

Bertie seems to have had limited interest in fiction at this stage, preferring true-life accounts of foreign lands and their fauna, which he enjoyed chiefly as backdrops for his adventure fantasies. He also read enthusiastically about warfare, especially the campaigns of the Duke of Wellington against Napoleon and the battles of the American Civil War. He took a further interest in American history through the writings of Washington Irving. Later he moved on to fictional treatments of the Wild West, the cattle noises from Covell's yard presumably providing a suitable accompaniment to his reading.

After his leg had healed, his mother and father encouraged Bertie to resume playing with other boys, feeling that such prolonged immersion in books could not be healthy. Their protests were a waste of breath. A sensitive child, he knew full well that his parents were unhappy with their lot in life, especially each other. Now another member of the Wells family had found a better world than the emotional slough of Atlas House.

In the years that followed, Bertie seems to have been a voracious reader. There were bound volumes of *Punch* on which he modelled comic sketches of his own, Captain Cook's *Travels*, an eighteenth-century atlas showing many unexplored regions and the poetry of Sir Walter Scott. (Bertie's recitations from memory included passages from Scott's 'Marmion' and 'The Lady of the Lake'.) On Sundays he was required to read the Bible. Further devotional reading his mother prescribed included Clarke's *New Testament* and Sturm's *Reflections on the Works of God*. At one point Sturm directs his readers' attention to the Moon. 'Can it be supposed,' he asks, 'that the surface of a body some thousands of square miles in extent should be destitute of living creatures?'[14]

The exotic places and thought-provoking questions Bertie encountered in his reading gave him a temporary release from Atlas House. They may also have provided some welcome refuge from the less pleasant aspects of school life when, in the summer of 1874, aged seven and three-quarters, he began his formal education. There was an Anglican National School in Bromley, which, thanks to the Education Act of 1870, was now the local branch of a growing system of state elementary education. Like his brothers before him, Bertie was not sent here, but to Morley's Academy, a little way down the High Street from Atlas House. The National School was intended for the lower classes. To go there would have been an acceptance of social inferiority.

Morley's Academy may have sent its pupils out into the world unable to undertake such basic tasks as writing a formal letter or multiplying fractions, but because it charged fees and recruited from the lower middle classes it at least had a respectable status. Bertie's separation from the lower orders was confirmed by the feuding between the two schools, which would occasionally flare into tribal battles on Martin's Hill, fought with wooden clubs and stones wrapped in scarves.

Thomas Morley's teaching took place in a wooden extension built out over his scullery, a single room accommodating between twenty-five and thirty-five boys between the ages of seven and fifteen. About half the boys were boarders living at the school. From nine to twelve in the morning, then from two to five in the afternoon, Morley would attempt to educate his wide range of clients 'like some very ordinary chess player who has undertaken to play thirty games of chess simultaneously'.[15] Whole-class teaching was impractical, so Morley generally set individual or group tasks. The curriculum included accounting, French, geography, geometry, mathematics and, when Morley had been provoked by the morning paper, expositions of his liberal political views: essentially, reduce public spending on the royal family and the armed forces.

At a time when the central theme of British domestic politics was the middle classes' struggle against vested interests in the name of free competition, Morley's mission was to equip his pupils to make their way in the world as self-reliant individuals – once, that is, they'd left his charge. Until then he kept order by beating them with a cane, hooked conveniently over the gas bracket next to his desk, or, failing that, with anything else that came to hand, and by making them hold heavy objects at arm's length. Morley also subjected the boys to fierce verbal abuse. In order to avoid swearing, he would resort to such odd terms as 'wobblers,' 'chumblep*um*pennies' and 'hounds'. When Morley withdrew behind his desk, left the room or just dozed off after lunch, the boys would abandon work to talk, play games, fight or generally misbehave until order was violently restored.

At the age of eight, Bertie developed his first strong friendship, with a Londoner named Sidney Bowkett. The two boys shared a quick intelligence and imagination that set them apart from their fellows, the kind of qualities that might be expected to isolate youngsters as 'swots' or 'teacher's pets', particularly when combined with the aggressive favouritism practised by Morley.

Though Wells's autobiography tends to emphasise his boisterousness, William Baxter recalled Bertie as a 'meek and mild' type, the kind of lad who would be regarded by his schoolfellows as a 'mother's boy' and whose polite manners made him a favourite with Morley's wife and daughter. Bertie and Freddy were certainly jeered at for a time because of their home-made clothes, and Bertie sometimes resorted to buying acceptance from others through his access to cricket equipment.

With Bowkett, however, he was able to form a secret society of two that deliberately excluded others. They had their own initiation ceremony, which involved putting a forefinger in a burning gas jet. They had a secret language, a defensive pact against larger pupils and an exciting fantasy life. They took over the Puss the Cat saga, borrowed the disreputable anti-hero Ally Sloper from the comic papers of the period and made Bert Wells and the Boker Boy heroes of Jules Verne-style expeditions to exotic parts of the globe, equipping themselves with imaginary hot-air balloons and diving suits.

To pal up with someone else in order to deter bullies is a classic way for a child to cope with low status. Sociologists have a name for it: 'reciprocal altruism'. Other tactics frequently adopted are academic achievement and an escape into compensatory daydreams. Bertie was a good student, and he habitually relieved his frustrations through fantasies, picturing himself as a great general whose armies fought in the countryside around Bromley. Most often they clashed on Martin's Hill, site of the real-life battles between Morley's Bull Dogs and the National School Water Rats, battles in which an undernourished swot, however inwardly heroic, could not be expected to cut a martial figure. In the world of the imagination, everything could be transformed.

Predictably, heroic warfare was not the only type of fantasy that Bertie found himself experiencing in adolescence. The political cartoons he saw in *Punch* and *Fun* sometimes personified nations as female figures: Britannia, La France, Erin and so on. In contrast to the figure-concealing garments worn by the actual women of Bromley, the diaphanous robes of these divinities revealed perfect female bodies as envisaged by male cartoonists like Tenniel. At night Bertie's pillow embraced him in the shape of their glorious breasts and arms. In the daytime, ashamed because his mother had taught him that the nude body was sinful, he still found his eyes dwelling on revealing prints and statuettes of women and men in shop windows; and on visits to Crystal Palace, matrix of the Great Exhibition, now resited as an entertainment complex at Sydenham, he saw plaster casts of Greek statues that were equally arousing.

Bertie soon learned from other boys at school the forbidden words and biological facts his parents had concealed. One of Morley's pupils was given to exposing himself. Some of the boarders who slept two in a bed practised mutual masturbation. Bertie himself experienced some homosexual feelings up to the age of thirteen or so, but his sexuality developed in private. A 'one-sided love affair with the bedding' grew naturally into solitary masturbation, but his pursuit of this pleasure was severely inhibited by the widespread claim that it was medically damaging and, worse still, constituted the unforgivable sin that would lead to automatic damnation.[16]

A photograph of Bertie aged nine or ten, none the less, shows a boy whose fears and fantasies are well under control. Posed before an open book, arms folded on the table, he presents a confident face to the camera. This could be a boy with a lot to say for himself: a gust of chatter filled with awkward questions and sardonic observations. Once again there is an impression of a figure arrested in flight. He looks likely to spring up as soon as the picture has been taken and dash away in search of something to investigate or someone to impress.

Though he had few dealings with girls of his own age, he was lucky enough to find more female relatives to augment Tom Wells's daughters as an audience on whom he could practise his charm. Another 'Uncle' Tom – Thomas Pennicott, Sarah's second cousin – ran a riverside inn at Clewer near Windsor called Surly

Hall. (His previous venture, the Royal Oak, was the one that had had its bells mischievously rewired by Frank.) Pennicott was a widower with two daughters in their twenties, Kate and Clara. They and the chief barmaid, Miss King, enjoyed fussing over the quick-witted youngster, encouraging his repartee and pretending to flirt with him. Thanks to an annual invitation, between the ages of eleven and thirteen Bertie was able to have a summer break far from the pressures of home and school.

Even those three young women were overshadowed, however, when one summer, probably in 1878, there appeared on the lawn at Surly Hall 'a delightful vision in fluttering muslin, like one of the ladies in Botticelli's *Primavera*'.[17] It was the famous actress and beauty Ellen Terry, who had come to the inn to study a part. She became the leading lady of Henry Irving at the Lyceum around this time, and when Irving came to visit her both stars were happy to talk to Bertie. Better still, he was allowed to 'punt the goddess about' on the Thames. Back at home, walking along the Bromley footpaths, he liked to imagine – as his creation Wallace was to do in 'The Door in the Wall' – that he might one day turn a corner and find himself back with the beautiful girl in the garden.

One of Wells's distinctive characteristics all his life would be his dependence on female attention. Without a woman to stimulate him with her observations and behaviour, and encourage him with her interest in his work, his life swiftly drained of much of its meaning. Conversely, part of his attractiveness to women must have been his evident appreciation of them and their ideas, in a society where men still often assumed the gentle sex to be feather-headed. These features of Wells's character seem to have been established early on, probably as compensation for the attitude of his mother who, while she certainly did not reject him, was evidently unable to conceal her disappointment that he was not as companionable and supportive for her as Fanny had been.

Bertie's summer holidays afforded not only female company but also intellectual stimulation. Kate Pennicott encouraged his drawing and reading, and though 'Uncle' Tom was illiterate the family had a complete illustrated edition of the works of Dickens, together with a bound copy of the *Family Herald* containing a translation of Eugène Sue's underworld melodrama *The Mysteries of Paris*. Bertie also delved into J.G. Wood's *Natural History* and encountered a frightening picture of a gorilla that lodged in his mind, to emerge at unfortunate moments when he was passing shadowy corners.

But what was Bertie himself writing and drawing in these formative years? From somewhere in the period 1877–80, a short book called *The Desert Daisy* survives to offer engaging glimpses of things to come. It is a work of exuberant parody, its story about war-mongering kings, dishonest bishops and idiotic generals showing a thorough contempt for Establishment figures. In a more genial assault on his elders, Bertie compares himself to historic authors such as Shakespeare and Homer. 'Beats *Paradise Lost* into eternal smash!' enthuses an imaginary reviewer.

How deeply Bertie had read Homer, Shakespeare or Milton is another question. At this stage of his career his chief model seems to have been Heinrich Hoffmann, whose *Struwwelpeter* was the only children's book he possessed. Hoffmann's book was a forerunner of the modern comic strip, and its playful blend of text and illustration seems to have encouraged Bertie to parody the form of conventional books. *The Desert Daisy* not only imitates the appearance of a published volume but claims to be a second edition, with quotations from reviews and a preface explaining that several passages have been deleted because their pathos had caused swooning among lady readers.

In a striking glimpse ahead to one of Wells's later narrative techniques, the book claims to have two authors: Wells and Buss. The illustrations are in two styles, depending on which author supposedly drew them. Buss takes responsibility for most of the writing, while Wells contributes the preface revealing that Buss has now retired to Colney Hatch lunatic asylum where he is forbidden to write. Since Wells's parents accused him of spending too much time with books, this device may be a way of distancing himself from his subversive imagination. We may also suspect that the division between Buss and Wells reflects some conflict between being Joe's son and Sarah's.

Joe offered a role model that was aggressively humorous and oriented towards pleasure; Sarah valued respectability, conformity and hard work. In writing *The Desert Daisy* Bertie seems to be enjoying releasing his imagination as Buss, his father's son, then distancing himself from frivolity by a swift morph into Wells, the upright young man his mother wished him to be. The identification is supported by his parents' letters, his mother always addressing him as 'Bertie', which happened to be the Queen's nickname for the future Edward VII, while his father usually preferred 'Buss'. Of course, the sustained care with which *The Desert Daisy* was produced is a reflection of Sarah's temperament. Bertie's challenge would not be to choose between the two sides but to achieve a productive mix of them. His parents would be the *yin* and the *yang* by which his life was shaped.

The development of an adult identity would become crucial when he had to start earning a living, and there were signs that the fateful day would not be long in coming. His periods of escape into the world of the imagination and the world of Surly Hall were all the sweeter because the income and lifestyle of the Wells family had recently taken a severe turn downwards. One Sunday in October 1877 Sarah and Bertie returned from church to find Joe lying in the yard groaning in pain. They fetched their neighbours from the shops either side and carried the injured man upstairs to his bedroom. Apparently, in an attempt to prune the upper shoots of a grape vine on the back wall, Joe had balanced a couple of ladders on top of a table and clambered up the unsteady scaffolding, only to tumble and fall to the hard ground beneath.

A suggestion that this might have been a failed suicide attempt sounds improbable but is by no means out of the question.[18] As we shall see, Joe would later threaten to kill himself. *The History of Mr Polly*, which is about a bankrupt unhappily married shopkeeper who attempts suicide, perhaps recalls family history, and its author himself was prone to suicidal thoughts in later years.

There is a further theory. Wells tells us that his father had 'a kind of attractiveness for women' and seemed to be aware of his effect on them, but he doubts whether his father was ever unfaithful 'beyond a light flirtation – in Bromley at any rate'.[19] Eliza Hopton tells a different story. The Hoptons were greengrocers and coal merchants with a shop opposite Atlas House. According to Eliza,

> Old Joseph used to have a lady friend in on Sunday mornings when Mrs Wells had taken the boys to church. On this particular Sunday, the church bell to show the service was over started ringing earlier than usual. There was no time to let the lady out by the shop door so he helped her over the back yard wall. Old Joseph came a cropper and broke his thigh.[20]

Were the table and ladders conveniently present in the yard, then, to create an alibi? Like the suicide theory, this account is certainly not impossible, though the official version of events is more straightforward.

Whatever the cause may have been, the consequence of the injury was clear enough. While he would in time be able to play cricket again, Joe's days as a money-earning player were over. A job coaching at Norwich Grammar School had lasted from 1873 to 1875, but he seems to have had no regular cricketing jobs thereafter. Now the Wells family's income was permanently slashed and there were doctors' bills to pay – and this at a time when the business faced increasing competition. The opening of a second railway station in Bromley in 1878 accelerated the process of suburbanization that had tripled the town's population since the Wells's arrival. Customers would be ever more likely to go to London to do some of their shopping, and the retail practices of the big city had started to come to them in the form of home deliveries from chain stores.

In the past Sarah had sometimes been able to hire the services of a charlady, Betsy Finch, to help around the house. That was no longer an option. Conditions grew worse. The family's diet deteriorated, potatoes more and more often replacing meat. When Frank, now living in at the drapery, offered Sarah half a sovereign to buy Bertie some boots she cried with gratitude.

It was during this critical period that Bertie experienced a dream which first terrified, then transformed him. In his own words:

> I feared Hell dreadfully for some time. Hell was indeed good enough to prevent me calling either of my brothers fools, until I was eleven or twelve. But one night I had a dream of Hell so preposterous that it blasted that undesirable resort out of my mind for ever. In an old number of *Chambers' Journal* I had read of the punishment of breaking a man on the wheel. The horror of it got into my dreams and there was Our Father in a particularly malignant phase, busy basting a poor broken sinner rotating slowly over a fire built under the wheel. I saw no Devil in the vision; my mind in its simplicity went straight to the responsible fountain head. That dream pursued me into the day time. Never had I hated God so intensely.
>
> And then suddenly the light broke through to me and I knew this God was a lie.[21]

If this reaction is anything to go by, Sarah Wells was wise to cover up the pictures of Hell in her book. Wells is again exaggerating the finality of his response, but at the age of eleven or twelve his anguish over this dream certainly constituted a key moment in his life.

As he entered adolescence and became more self-aware, Bertie observed his family sliding down through poverty towards bankruptcy and loss of status, carrying his future with them. He had been brought up to believe that all events happened due to the will of an all-powerful God who had placed the people Buss thought laughable – monarchs, bishops, generals and politicians – at the top of society and people like the Wells family dangerously near the bottom. Religion divided people into the saved or damned; the social system divided people into winners or losers. If God existed, He was a puppet master controlling these two parallel systems. Wells casually assumes this parallel in his autobiography:

> Just as my mother was obliged to believe in Hell, but hoped that no one would go there, so did I believe there was and had to be a lower stratum, though I was disgusted to find that anyone belonged to it.[22]

At eleven or twelve Bertie could not have explained his developing world-view in abstract terms any more than he could have explained that writing enabled him to bring conflicting aspects of his kaleidoscopic personality into harmony, but he sensed that the world of creativity, learning and adventure that he longed to enter was going to be denied him, and in its place he was going to be allotted poverty, obedience and self-denial. But suppose one entertained the shocking possibility that God did not exist? Then the future might still be open. Poverty, obedience and self-denial could be fought.

By 1879–80 Sarah and Joe could not afford to pay Bertie's school fees. He was spared an immediate introduction to the world of work only because Morley, conscious of his abilities, deferred the charge. The teacher's faith in his pupil proved justified when, in the College of Preceptors' examinations, Bertie came national joint-first for book-keeping and obtained distinctions in several other subjects. It was to no avail. Much as Bertie would have liked to continue with his education, his family could not afford to support him. In June 1880, at the age of thirteen, he was forced to leave school.

Bertie knew exactly what was in store for him. Frank had been a draper for nine years. Freddy had now been one for four, having been apprenticed in 1876 to Sparrowhawk's. Bertie could remember Frank playing a last game of marbles with him before putting away childish things and going off to his fate. He knew that both his brothers worked long hours, doing interminable chores under close supervision, that they received no pay for the duration of their apprenticeships and that they had to live almost like prisoners in their places of employment, with little free time in which to be themselves:

> Now it was my turn to put the things away, put the books away, give up drawing and painting and every sort of delight, stop writing stories and imitations of *Punch*, give up all vain hopes and dreams, and serve an employer.[23]

Frank and Fred Wells had been relegated to the humble station in life that society deemed suitable for them. Herbert Wells was about to go through the same process, and no amount of talent, intelligence or silent thinking of blasphemous thoughts would enable him to escape into another kind of life. Or so, for a little while longer, society could assume.

2
FIVE FALSE STARTS
1880–1884

The downturn of Bertie's fortunes coincided with his mother's moment of triumph. On the death of Lady Fetherstonhaugh, her sister Frances had taken over the family name and estate. She needed someone trustworthy to assist her in running Uppark and wondered if her one-time lady's maid might be induced to come back as housekeeper. Presented with her wildest dream come true, Sarah did not need to be asked twice. At last she could walk out of Atlas House, leave her cricket-crazed husband to his own devices and attempt to resume her former life.

The only issue to be decided was what to do with the youngest of her children. The answer was to apprentice him to a respectable trade, with a trial month to ensure both parties were satisfied, then make a payment from the family's hard-earned savings to cover the board and training he would receive. His brothers had been apprenticed to drapers satisfactorily – in her view, if not theirs – and there seemed to be no reason to abandon a successful formula. Since she would no longer be on hand to watch over Bertie in Bromley, she sought out a suitable position close to her relatives at Surly Hall. In the summer of 1880 the Pennicotts' dog-cart dropped the boy and his portmanteau outside the drapery of Messrs Rodgers and Denyer in Windsor High Street.

That it was a prestigious establishment, patronized by the Royal Family, cut no ice with Bertie. He hated it even before he saw it. The prospect of a twelve- or thirteen-hour day from 7.30 a.m. – dusting, window-cleaning and working at the cash desk, then reporting to the dormitory in time for lights out at 10.30 p.m. – was not one that had the slightest appeal to him, and he set about his tasks with a lack of enthusiasm that made his father's labours at Atlas House seem positively Stakhanovite.

He shirked his duties, read books or did algebra problems under the cash desk, got into a fight with a junior porter that resulted in a black eye and, despite his superlative certificate in book-keeping, constantly failed to make the cash sheet tally with what was in the till. Resentful colleagues had to stay late every night and recalculate the figures, speculating as they did that Bertie might be pilfering the money. His only bright moments that July came on Sundays and early closing days when he could flee to the Pennicotts. Unfortunately, reaching Surly Hall entailed a long, dark walk along the Maidenhead Road, made especially alarming by mischievous talk of a panther having escaped from a nearby riverside house.

Bertie must have been relieved when, at the end of his trial month his policy of non-cooperation paid off and Rodgers and Denyer rejected him.

What now? Sarah's scheme to get him off her hands was in ruins, and there was as yet no Plan B. While Bertie laid low at Surly Hall, Joe tried to use his cricketing connections to get his son a placement as a bank clerk but without success. Tom Pennicott had better luck with his brother-in-law, Alfred Williams, formerly a teacher in Jamaica, more recently a school desk manufacturer in Clewer.

Spending too freely had reduced Williams to a clerk in his own factory, but he had recently relaunched himself as teacher at a National School in Somerset. He was prepared to let Bertie, a bright lad with a well-attested ability to pass examinations, work under him as an 'improver'. The exact nature of this post is unclear. If Bertie was a registered teacher-pupil, then he would be paid by the state and would follow a course of instruction delivered by Williams that led to an entrance examination for teacher-training college. Given Williams's inexperience, however, it is quite possible that the job was actually for a 'monitor', a teaching assistant who received a lesser payment and no recognized instruction and whose career prospects were less certain.

From Windsor to Wookey is over one hundred miles, and, for a boy just turned fourteen, boarding a train to a place where he knew no one, to teach in the kind of lower-class school his parents would not let him attend as a pupil, the departure must have been an unnerving one. That October he found himself positioned alongside his unknown 'uncle', sometimes with a curtain to divide their pupils into two classes, teaching whatever occurred to him – much of it, presumably, recalled from Morley. Some of his pupils were as big as he was. When they scorned his instruction or mocked his accent, which they must have done all too frequently, the fourteen-year-old was reduced to a desperate imitation of Morley's disciplinary methods:

> I fought my class, hit them about viciously and had altogether a lot of trouble with them. I exacted a full performance of the penalties I imposed and on one occasion pursued a defaulter headlong to his home, only to be routed ignominiously by his indignant mother and chased by her and a gathering rabble of variously sized boys back to the school house.[1]

This description from Wells's autobiography distances the incident by applying the terms of knockabout comedy ('routed ignominously', and so on), but it is safe to assume it would not have felt comical at the time. An insight into Bertie's true state of mind at Wookey can be glimpsed in an aside from another book, where he recalls how, on the first evening, his uncle told him about some unpleasant spiders before placing him in a dark, unfamiliar bedroom and he disgraced himself by screaming the house down.[2] Many years later the nightmare would be profitably converted into a short story, 'The Valley of Spiders'. For now his only solace was the company of his new employer and youngest daughter Edith – the rest of the Williams family having remained in Clewer. Both were notable characters.

One of Williams's arms was a stump ending in a piratical hook, which he unscrewed at mealtimes and replaced with a fork. Over meals he would deride religion and mock society as a laughable pretence. After his mother's piety, Bertie found this attitude refreshing. Williams would become something of a role model for him, and he would later make his 'uncle' with his chin 'like the toe of a hygienic slipper' the inspiration for the philosophical confidence trickster Chaffery in *Love and Mr Lewisham.*[3]

Edith, at twenty-one years of age, was stimulating in a rather different way, and on recreational walks about the vicinity she pressed her fourteen-year-old relative to assist her in exploring sex. Quite how far her investigations went is unclear. Wells simply records that it was 'hot, uncomfortable, shamefaced stuff'. Edith's curiosity may have been more scientific than lustful, as she went on to become a nurse.[4]

The time spent in Wookey must have been distressing for Bertie in several respects, but it was, as they say, 'character building', and he certainly found it more rewarding than life at the drapery. However, for better or worse, Plan B did not last. By November the school inspectors had realized that Williams's West Indian credentials were not all that he had claimed them to be, and in December he was dismissed.

Bertie was put on the train back to Windsor via an overnight stay in the Temperance Hotel, Maidenhead. Perhaps influenced by the free-spending style of his 'uncle', he unwisely devoted the final part of his travel allowance to a set of photographs of himself and to a Bath bun, so was unable to afford his second train and had to painfully lug his portmanteau the four miles to Surly Hall.

What he found there came as a shock. Miss King had departed. Kate was threatening to leave. Clara had taken to drink and run off with a lover who would ultimately leave her to drown herself. Off-season the pub was dark and empty, and 'Uncle' Tom was not only maddened by his daughters but oppressed by debts. Any early signs of all this breakdown had passed over Bertie when he was a child, but he had returned from Wookey with an older head on his shoulders and was beginning to understand such adult matters.

Fortunately for Bertie, his destiny did not tie him to Surly Hall. He had an invitation to Uppark, and he arrived on 20 December 1880, just in time for Christmas. His mother must have been exasperated at his double failure to make a start in life but must also have been pleased to have him home. Snowed in for almost a fortnight, he amused himself by producing a daily newsletter, *The Up Park Alarmist,* and putting on a shadow play for some of the domestic staff in a home-made miniature theatre.

Since Bertie would visit Uppark many times during the following decade and it would exert considerable influence on him, it is worth pausing to reflect on this unusual reference point in his life. The house had been built in the early 1690s for the third Lord Grey, an aristocratic traitor to King James II who, by paying hefty fines and incriminating his friends, rose to be an earl. One of his sons sold the 5,000-acre estate to Sir Matthew Fetherstonhaugh, a Fellow of the Royal Society whose many interests included politics and the visual arts as well as science. In time Bertie would emerge as Sir Matthew's spiritual heir.

His immediate heir, however, had been his son, Sir Harry Fetherstonhaugh, who clearly knew what was expected of a Regency aristocrat. He gambled, hunted, rode and entertained the Prince Regent, his guests on some occasions reputedly so stupefied by alcohol that they were pushed home in wheelbarrows. He took as his mistress fifteen-year-old Emma Lyon (later Nelson's Lady Hamilton), who is said to have danced naked on his dining table; he later discarded her, pregnant. After about 1810, however, Sir Harry fell out with the Prince and adopted a comparatively sober way of life – until 1825, that is, when, aged seventy-one, he showed something of a return to earlier form by marrying one of his dairy maids, twenty-year-old Mary Ann Bullock.

By the middle of the century, at Uppark as elsewhere, the public tone was being set by the rising professional classes, and Regency scandal had given way to Victorian respectability. The former dairymaid became the widowed Lady Fetherstonhaugh until her younger sister Frances inherited the title.

Whatever Bertie knew about the history of Uppark, at least three aspects of the place must have begun to affect him quite early on. One was the simple existence of this alternative reality: beautiful parkland, an elegant red-brick building with stone facings, large rooms full of paintings and hand-crafted furniture. Shuttling between the world of work with its limited facilities and low aspirations and the contrastingly expansive world of Uppark, Bertie could never become wholly subdued to his everyday environment. Like his parents, he could not forget that behind his dull surroundings, and not many miles behind, there existed a better kind of life, and this knowledge fuelled his discontent just as it had theirs.

A second aspect of Uppark, reinforcing his discontent, was the fact that his mother now lived there permanently. She had not simply failed to take her youngest son along with her but dispatched him to a succession of unwelcome apprenticeships in order to set herself free. Every visit to Uppark would have reminded him of the dramatic contrast between his own life near the bottom of the social ladder and his mother's position. Bertie may well have been able to appreciate the logic of her decisions, but emotionally he must have burned with resentment.

He already sensed that he had been created as a substitute for his dead sister and had begun a lifelong rebellion against his mother's wish for him to be like her. Now he had a second reason for hostility. Everything Bertie came to stand for entailed a systematic reversal of his mother's conservative views. His scepticism about religion, the monarchy and the class system must have been strongly reinforced by the position in which he found himself.

The third aspect of Uppark to affect him was Sir Harry's cultural legacy. In an attic next to his bedroom Bertie found volumes of engravings of the Vatican paintings of Raphael and Michelangelo (highly stimulating to an adolescent boy – not only great art but great art in the form of naked bodies) and a box of mysterious brass objects that he eventually succeeded in assembling and discovered to be a telescope and tripod. One night, hearing the bedroom window open, Sarah investigated the noise and discovered her son, like her husband thirty years before, gazing in wonder at the night sky above Uppark – in Bertie's case through the eyepiece of the reconstituted telescope. Later, the books from Sir Harry's library would feed his questing mind still further.

For now, though, the educational legacy of Uppark could be explored only fleetingly. Sarah had been casting about for a plausible Plan C, and on 15 January 1881, the holiday over, Bertie was dispatched to her old home town of Midhurst, where Samuel Cowap the pharmacist required an assistant. Once more the apprentice did not last the trial month.

In his autobiography Wells speaks fondly of Midhurst and the chemist's shop, lovingly recreated in the pages of *Tono-Bungay*, and claims that he left the job on his own initiative when he realized that the cost of becoming a qualified dispenser was more than his mother could afford. Yet it is hard to believe that she had not already checked the figures. Wells passes somewhat rapidly over a broom fight with an errand boy that resulted in the smashing of a dozen soda-water siphons and fails to mention prescribing unfortunate medication for a customer while left alone in the shop. All factors considered, Cowap and Bertie agreed that he was not the right lad for the job.

Once he could no longer count on the payment for Bertie's apprenticeship, Cowap insisted his failed assistant quit the premises immediately to make way for a replacement. Until Sarah could come up with a Plan D, her son became a temporary boarder at the local grammar school, a passing expedient that would turn out to be a crucial step in his destiny.

Bertie had already been sent to the school for a few hours' initial grounding in Latin, needed to handle prescriptions, and he had made a favourable impression on the teacher there. Horace Byatt had recently presided over the reopening of the school and was looking for good results to build its reputation and his income. Bertie was a natural assimilator and, whatever his deficiencies in the retail trade, an able and well-motivated student. Byatt was therefore happy to take Bertie on as pupil number thirty-three and accommodate him in his house along with a few other boarders.

Between 23 February and 14 April Bertie amused himself by writing comic stories, sketching in the other pupils' schoolbooks and initiating the annual founder's day paper chase but devoted the bulk of his time to studying evening-class subjects. If he passed, he would get certificates; Byatt would get payments. Unsurprisingly, Byatt was keen for Bertie to come back in May to sit the examinations, which he did.

In that same month, however, he also commenced his next and longest apprenticeship. Sarah had sought advice from a hard-headed, practical man, Sir William King, the Uppark agent, who found a suitable placement for the boy at the Southsea Drapery Emporium, Portsmouth, on the coast directly south of Uppark. Perhaps he had a word with the proprietor, Edwin Hyde, and advised him that his charge was a bright lad but rather a handful, needing to be supervised strictly if he was to stay the course. Certainly this time we hear nothing about fights with porters and irresponsible behaviour towards customers, even though Bertie looked no more favourably upon this job than he had the similar one in Windsor. He promised his weeping mother that he would try harder this time but went reluctantly. Left alone in the upstairs dormitory upon arrival, he sat stunned with dismay at what had happened to him.

The trial month came and went without incident. In June the fee was paid and the four-year articles of apprenticeship were signed. Days became weeks, weeks became months, the months grew into a year; Bertie remained locked into the thirteen-hours-a-day drapery routine.

The facilities were excellent. Hyde even supplied his workers with a reading room of several hundred books. There are people in Britain today doing worse drudgery for longer hours, and in the 1880s it would have struck many people as a solid start to a respectable career, but Bertie wanted to lead a creative life, not devote his existence to pins and packages. The drapery assistant Minton in *Kipps* is undoubtedly speaking for the author when he sums up the draper's career in a despairing image of claustrophobia and waste: 'We're in a blessed drainpipe and we've got to crawl along it till we die.'[5]

As at Windsor, Bertie longed for his Sundays and early closing days. On bank holidays he could take the train to Godalming, Surrey, for hilarious times with Frank, who was still a draper but who now lived out in lodgings. At other times he would receive invitations to Uppark, where he could throw off his petty workaday self and peer through his telescope like a modern Galileo, transcending his constricted existence and seeing life from a liberating perspective. Even the chalk hills under his feet, he realized, had once been at the bottom of a prehistoric sea.

Returning to the drapery, Bertie resumed his old practice of neglecting his duties in favour of reading, concealing himself behind cotton goods to tackle a Latin primer or the Social Darwinist philosophy of Herbert Spencer. In these stolen moments he must have begun to acquire the skills of time management that would later enable him to cram several lifetimes into one. He also acquired a view of human nature rooted in biological evolution, initially in the crude formulation that life is a ruthless struggle between individuals, classes, nations or races. Though he would soon come to realize the limitations of this outlook, he would not fully free himself from its influence until after 1900.

He kept a notebook in which he broached such topics as 'What is matter?', 'What is space?' and, a strong indication of his frustrations, the ethics of suicide. In his quest for wisdom he bypassed the fiction books in the drapery library and concentrated on the encyclopaedias and reference books, judging that what he needed most urgently was information and ideas. It is hard to disagree with the conclusion, but the long-term effect was to reinforce the exaggerated split between the creative and reasoning aspects of his mind, already visible in *The Desert Daisy.*

Further useful books came from the library of the Young Men's Christian Association in nearby Landport. The YMCA reading room hosted one of the many mock parliaments of the time, which tracked national political controversies and allowed contributors to practise their formal debating skills – for Bertie was by no means alone in his aspirations to better himself. Large numbers of people who, a century later, would have gone to college or university were trapped in unfulfilling jobs by the limited educational opportunities and social mobility of Victorian Britain. In attending the YMCA, Bertie was tapping into a vigorous culture of mutual improvement. In later years such thwarted individuals would make up a considerable part of his readership. For now, though confused by the procedures and topics of the debates, he began to develop some interest in political discussion.

His presence at the YMCA was not simply opportunistic. While Bertie had taken on much of the scepticism of 'Uncle' Williams and evidently enjoyed shocking others with his radical ideas, he naturally retained many of his mother's attitudes. So much is suggested by the low value he put on fiction – a traditional, if old-fashioned, Nonconformist view. His closest friends at the drapery, two office clerks named Field and West, were committed Christians. West was as reluctant a draper as Bertie but dreamed of escape to a church career.

Bertie spent his Sunday evenings attending churches of various denominations with his two friends and, accompanied by a 'sisterly' costume-room assistant, even sampled a revivalist mission at the Portsmouth Roman Catholic Cathedral. A shared seriousness and culture drew him into the Christian community, but the questionable arguments he heard there, and the Catholic preacher's lurid threats of hellfire, fuelled his rationalist scepticism. As well as the churches, he made a point of visiting a secularist society.

On his lunchtime expeditions for materials that the workroom did not have in stock, he came across a newspaper shop that sold two radical journals: the recently launched atheist weekly, the *Freethinker,* and the slightly more established birth-control monthly, the *Malthusian*. He took copies back to the drapery to shock his peers. The *Malthusian* provided him with thought-provoking articles on how greater use of contraception might affect such phenomena as poverty and prostitution. The *Freethinker* aimed to dispel superstition, particularly belief in the Bible as divine revelation, using on the one hand scholarship and learning and on the other ridicule and sarcasm – it even had a 'Profane Jokes' section.

To an admirer of 'Uncle' Williams this must have been appealing, but, as the autobiography notes, Bertie found the *Freethinker* rather narrow in its appeal: 'It left me altogether at a loss for some general statement of my relation to the stars.'[6] Atheism did away with the divine scheme but was essentially a negative doctrine that failed to provide the young rebel with a replacement set of beliefs that could inspire him, direct his action and legitimize his aspirations. With the Uppark telescope, in contrast, he was able to contact 'the starry heavens in a state of exaltation'.[7] The stars he saw were not just data to be rationally understood but a vision that lifted him out of himself and placed him within a cosmic order. At such moments the world-view of science felt like a possible replacement for the world-view of religion.

While, as Sarah's son, Bertie passed his evenings at Field's house, singing hymns, praying and borrowing religious books, as Joe's son he was mentally undressing the girl apprentices and the sisterly costume-room assistant. On one occasion he even had to go to Sarah 'flushed and shrill-voiced' to ask for money to pay off a debt incurred playing cards.[8] The implicit challenge facing Bertie was to find a self-conception that would not only make convincing sense of his place in the cosmos but let him integrate these two sides of his personality, the devout and the down to earth, or at least enable them to pull in roughly the same direction.

In his letters he could do it stylistically, using pious biblical language with comic irony – to Frank, for example:

> Now my brother it occurreth unto me that I should feel great joy in coming unto thee at Godalming this Sunday which is to come and if thou canst send unto me the money I will come unto thee & with thee will I spend the two nights and one day (which providence hath ordained unto me) in grave & serious discourses.
>
> Now my brother will I cease this letter for the night cometh when *no man* can work much more write letters to damned brothers who ain't a going to write back.[9]

In the second year of Bertie's apprenticeship a new junior replaced him at the bottom of the hierarchy – later a model for the fictional Artie Kipps – and he graduated to a black morning coat with tails, but he did not relish either of these signs that he was progressing ever further towards an adult identity that he loathed. Soon it would be too late to escape. At the age of sixteen he was old enough to be solicited in the street by prostitutes, and one Christmas in his teens he experienced the excitement of being unexpectedly kissed by an Uppark kitchen maid called Mary. As with many another youngster, growing sexual frustration must have given further force to his rebellion against his parents and those in authority over him.

Before long he was passing from slacking and wilful incompetence to outright confrontation. When his mother expected him to be confirmed as a member of the Church of England and his employer dispatched him to the Vicar of Portsmouth to be prepared, Bertie proclaimed that he could not accept the literal truth of Christian doctrine. With his mother he was bolder still and reduced her to tears by describing himself as an atheist. She consoled herself that at least he hadn't turned Catholic.

Bertie's dissidence was, once again, part of a larger movement. By the late nineteenth century the credibility of many traditional religious assumptions had been damaged by the accumulated findings of geology, biblical scholarship, comparative anthropology and evolutionary biology. Some sceptics were taking a militant stand against the Establishment. In particular, the republican and birth-control champion Charles Bradlaugh was repeatedly prevented from taking his seat in Parliament because, as an unbeliever, he refused to swear an oath on the Bible. On one occasion he was even imprisoned in the Big Ben clock tower. On 7 February 1882 he turned up at the House with a petition signed by more than 240,000 people but was thrown out once more.

The following Christmas the staff of the *Freethinker* were prosecuted for printing blasphemous cartoons, and the editor, Bradlaugh's protégé G.W. Foote, was sentenced to twelve months' hard labour. ('Thank you, my lord,' he responded coolly, 'the sentence is worthy of your creed.') By defying his mother, the Vicar and Mr Hyde, Bertie was affirming his solidarity with these contemporary secularist heroes.

And he had not finished rebelling yet. After consulting his brother Frank and his friend West, he had written to Horace Byatt, probably late in 1882, asking whether there was any chance of returning to Midhurst Grammar School as an usher (assistant teacher). Byatt remembered the talented youngster well, having apparently derived some income from his examination results, and replied favourably. When Bertie passed the news to Sarah, however, her reaction was not encouraging. She had already paid £40 to Hyde for Bertie's apprenticeship, which was still less than halfway through, and she was committed to paying another £10. He should remain in his post and pray for God's help, she told him. Joe Wells couldn't decide whom to support, initially sympathizing with Bertie but changing his mind when he realized the financial implications.

Some biographers have judged Bertie's parents to be selfish, but they merely lacked the advantage of hindsight. Based on the experience of their own and previous generations, they assumed that a basic education and an apprenticeship were what a lower-middle-class child needed. Having made that assumption, they tried hard to find a high-quality placement for their son. In contrast, the career path of a teacher, let alone a writer, must have seemed mysterious and uncertain. The expansion of the education system was a recent phenomenon that might not last, but it was clear to them that people would always need drapers.

Bertie, on the other hand, knew where his interests and abilities lay and may also have sensed that, in the modern, more socially mobile world, education was becoming a route into professional society in a way that it had not been for earlier generations. None the less, faced with the intransigence of his parents, the most obvious course for him would have been to give up.

It is instructive here to consider the fates of the three Wells brothers. Fred, who inherited his mother's conformist temperament, remained a draper. Frank, who took after his father, rebelled against his job but without any alternative goal in life. Bertie, combining his father's restless assertiveness with his mother's seriousness and determination, was capable of sustained, purposeful action and in the course of this youthful rebellion began to find the strengths of his personality.

In the spring of 1883, having borrowed money for his train fare, he paid Byatt a visit in Midhurst. Byatt gave him dinner, showed him round the new school-house and discussed his prospects. At sixteen Bertie was already too old to enter the teaching profession as a pupil teacher in an elementary school, but Byatt would be prepared to take him on as an assistant from September. There would be no pay for the first nine or ten months while he was learning the job, but he could share lodgings with an existing usher (assistant teacher). Bertie wrote to his mother, estimating his likely overheads as £35 for the first year. He told her he would leave the matter in her hands but of course did nothing of the sort.[10]

A family row blazed through the summer. Joe threatened to kill himself if they wasted any more money on their youngest son. Bertie threatened to do the same if he was left in the drapery, meditating on the gloomy depths of the sea near his workplace, not entirely in jest. One Sunday, summoned by his employer to be reprimanded for some act of disobedience, he stormed out of the shop before breakfast and set off across the Downs for Uppark to confront his mother. Exhausted and sick with hunger after hours of walking, he presented himself to her as she returned up Harting Hill from the church service, ready to argue his case for the umpteenth time. His situation looked desperate, but it was becoming clear whose will was the strongest.

It was not just a matter of Bertie's intransigence, however. Recollecting his star pupil's facility for passing lucrative examinations, Byatt was moved to raise his offer to £20 for his first year at the school and £40 thereafter. This shifted the financial argument significantly in Bertie's favour, and his parents at last wearily capitulated. Bertie's desire for more education became, finally, Plan E.

The outcome was not only a change in Bertie's circumstances but in his self-belief. Previously he had been on the receiving end of others' decisions; now, approaching the age of seventeen, he had discovered a power in himself to make events go the way he wanted, bringing a ferocious self-assertion to bear against the visible worlds of his job and his family and the less tangible worlds of class, respectability and religion. Oscar Wilde would write that children start by loving their parents but eventually come to judge them and then rarely forgive them. Wells's letters of 1883 show that he had reached the tipping point in this painful yet painfully elating process. In one he even instructs Sarah to threaten Joe with bankruptcy, an interesting reflection not only of Bertie's conviction that he had to drill sense into his errant parents but his awareness of their estrangement.[11]

Bertie insisted on leaving the drapery emporium as soon as possible – summer sale or no summer sale – in order to prepare himself for school adequately and, perhaps more importantly, once and for all, to escape from a role in life he hated. However, even though he got his way on this point, he did not get it on everything.

In order to conform to the school statutes, he was compelled to go back on his previous stand and allow himself to be confirmed as a member of the Church of England. Byatt arranged a crash course with the Midhurst curate. Bertie went through the motions as ungraciously as possible, asking pointed questions about the scientific evidence related to biblical chronology and the exact nature of transubstantiation. That the Church of England was unable to answer his questions to his satisfaction, and was prepared to receive him even though he clearly did not believe a word of its dogma, only confirmed his view of it as a repository of dead traditions and without integrity or conviction. He endured confirmation at Midhurst parish church in March 1884, then gave a repeat performance at Harting so Sarah could watch the ceremony.

Though smarting over his lost honour, Bertie had the pleasure of finally putting shop dormitories behind him. He rented a shared bedroom above a sweetshop, along with the existing usher, Harris, with whom he soon became friends, and he was delighted to find that the owner, Mrs Walton, supplied much more enjoyable food than either his mother or the emporium had done. His agreeable accommodation would be celebrated in *The Wheels of Chance* and *Love and Mr Lewisham.*

Crowned with a mortar board, he now worked in the main classroom of Midhurst Grammar School alongside Byatt, rather as he had done with Alfred Williams in Wookey, except that Byatt was a professional teacher who was able to give him plenty of practical advice on how to deal with the pupils. He naturally encouraged young Wells to teach in the classic 'chalk and talk' style of the time but tried to restrain the pace of his teaching and his impatience, which often expressed itself in the shoving of pupils. After his wasted years, Wells was hungry to learn; he found it difficult to make allowances for children whose motivation was considerably less than his own, especially after what he had endured from his pupils in Wookey. Looking back towards the end of his life, one of his few regrets was the aggression and 'actual cruelty' he had fallen into as a schoolteacher.[12]

Like his creation Mr Lewisham, whose early teaching experiences are based on this period in Midhurst, young Mr Wells placed a 'schema' on the wall of his lodgings, mapping out a future career of strenuous activity. The day's teaching over, he did not stand down from his labours but resumed his old role of evening-class student. Byatt chose subjects that the Education Department was willing to fund, handed Wells the most suitable textbooks he could obtain and for the most part let him get on with it. Driven by an urgent desire to catch up on his education, Wells soon had a basic grounding in physical and biological science. The results of the May examinations, when they came, would be more remarkable than either he or Byatt had envisaged.

For now, Wells must have been highly pleased with his position. He was developing into a promising young teacher with good career prospects and had a pleasant environment in which to continue this development. In the autumn of 1883 he and Byatt would sometimes take a turn in the garden before supper and admire the spectacular sunsets caused by the eruption of Krakatoa. Wells acquired friends with whom he could walk or go boating on the Rother – until they broke an oar, which had to be paid for in painful instalments. He occasionally joined in with local football and cricket matches. He even kept up with his old school pal Sidney Bowkett, who at about this time did what Joe had never got round to and went off to seek his fame and fortune in the USA. It would be more than ten years before Bert Wells and the Boker Boy met up again, during which time both would experience enormous changes.

Between his labours and his recreation, Wells also found the time to write a couple of illustrated comic stories and made his first contribution to journalism with a letter to the *Midhurst Times*, warning of the dangers of alcohol but prophesying that its abuse would diminish as social conditions improved. This pronouncement probably reflects his worries about his father's boozing but is also symptomatic of Wells's developing ideas. Like many another radical, his interests were moving on from secularism to the newly revived notion of socialism.

With his colleague Harris rushing to keep up with him, Wells stalked impatiently about the lanes of Midhurst, expounding on how the world might be changed for the better. In a local newspaper shop he had bought a cheap copy of Henry George's controversial bestseller, *Progress and Poverty*, a book that had already converted many to socialism, among them Tolstoy and Shaw. George, a crusading American journalist, argued for the replacement of all existing taxes by a single tax on the rental value of property. This, he argued, was the only effective way of transferring wealth from the privileged landowners to the majority, ensuring justice and encouraging enterprise.

Wells found the concept attractive. It was neat, technical and argued with apparent logic, all of which appealed to his rational, scientific outlook, but it also had a visionary aspect, for George envisaged the consequence of his tax policy to be a perfect world, and at key moments he broke into unrestrained apocalyptic hyperbole:

> It is what he saw whose eyes at Patmos were closed in a trance. It is the culmination of Christianity – the City of God on earth, with its walls of jasper and its gates of pearl! It is the reign of the Prince of Peace![13]

Wells did not need much convincing that present social arrangements were less than ideal. After all, Uppark was there to instruct him. When visiting his mother, he could hardly fail to notice the contrast between the lives of the Wells family and that of the landowning Fetherstonhaughs and their circle. The point was given almost diagrammatic form by the fact that the Uppark servants' quarters were located in the basement of the house, with underground tunnels running to various satellite areas such as the stables and dairy.

That Sarah's personal rooms were located above stairs complicated the diagram somewhat. Evidently society was not a simple conflict between a ruling class and its hired labour. There was a range of middle-class groups also, from which Wells himself came, even if he did not feel unqualified allegiance to their assumptions. He knew that their lifestyle would have been accounted luxury by those at the very bottom of society, trapped, several people to a room, in insanitary, disease-ridden slums.

From Sir Matthew's library at Uppark Wells obtained further critiques of class society to set alongside that of Henry George. First, there were *The Rights of Man* and *Common Sense* by Thomas Paine, whose eloquent defence of the American and French revolutions was still considered extreme one hundred years after they were written. In the 1880s few were yet ready to endorse Paine's vigorous advocacy of graduated income tax, old age pensions and maternity benefit, let alone his double-barrelled blasts at the class system and traditional religion as mutually supporting frameworks of superstition.

Second, and even more importantly for Wells, there was Plato's *Republic*, which he read one summer lying on a grassy slope at Uppark, enthralled that such a highly revered author could be so subversive. While scholars regarded Plato's philosophy as speculative and theoretical, for Wells it was virtually a manifesto. Plato's hero, Socrates, undertakes to explain the nature of justice by mapping out what a just society would be like. It would still be a class society, but exceptionally gifted children from the lower class would be secretly admitted to the ruling elite, the Guardians. The appeal to Wells of this meritocratic notion is obvious. The family and sexual relations would be organized in a rational manner, with private property abolished and wives and children held in common. Most of Plato's readers have found such notions repugnant, but to a young man who felt let down by his parents and who was growing up in a society where sex was concealed behind walls of silence, it was all deeply exciting.

A critic would later complain that in his utopian speculations, 'In place of the family unit, with its emotional context, Wells offers the omnipotent state, with its rigid and intellectual context.'[14] This mindset came from his youthful sense that his own family was deficient and from the seemingly empowering ideas of Plato. As is suggested by his reading of the *Malthusian* back in Southsea, Wells was eager to get at the facts about sex in a clear, rational way. Under Plato's influence, he began to imagine sex without the kind of marriage commitment that had anchored his father to Atlas House, encounters with 'free, ambitious, self-reliant women who would mate with me and go their way'.[15] Unfortunately, such women did not seem to be living in Midhurst.

Wells's first biographer tells us that in this period 'he had himself well in hand' sexually, a phrase that is probably more true than intended.[16] Wells later admitted that his lack of a sex life was due to want of opportunity and that a semi-innocent scuffle with one of his landlady's daughters left him aroused and fantasizing.[17]

His career, at least, was offering him some satisfaction. When in July 1884 his examination results arrived, he had achieved first-class passes in Human Physiology, Physiography, and Magnetism and Electricity, and seconds in Mathematics and various arts subjects. Byatt was delighted. But Wells also received something else in the post which, for the time being, he chose to conceal from Byatt: a 'blue paper' inviting him to apply for a teacher-in-training scholarship to study at the Normal School of Science in London.

The government was aware that, since the days of the Great Exhibition, when Britain was the chief workshop of the world, other countries had become serious rivals. In particular Germany – under the control of Prussia since the Seven Weeks' War in the year of Wells's birth and enlarged at the expense of France in the war of 1870 – was clearly aiming to become a Great Power. It had already overtaken Britain in technical education. The retaliatory desire to improve the standard of science teaching that had led to Byatt's evening-class payments had also prompted a scheme to recruit science students.

The straightforward course of action for Wells would have been to show the scholarship offer to Byatt and seek his views. However, Byatt might have forbidden him to apply, insisting that, since he had invested in Wells, the latter must fulfil his side of the bargain. He therefore filled in and posted his application secretly. No doubt he felt some guilt at deceiving the man who had engineered his escape from the drapery, but his struggle to get out from under the low aspirations of his mother and his employers had taught him the ways of the world. If he did not put himself first, no one else would. Byatt was offering a full-time teaching post with a pay increase at the end of the first year plus up to £25 for teaching science classes – an opportunity that would only recently have seemed like a dream come true – but the alternative was a second-class railway ticket to London, a guinea-a-week maintenance grant and the chance to study under the great T.H. Huxley.

Thomas Henry Huxley was one of the leading scientific figures of the Victorian era. He had championed the cause of science teaching and working-class education in articles, lectures and royal commissions. His greatest fame, however, was, in his own phrase, as 'Darwin's bulldog', the man who had publicly argued the case for the theory of evolution, seeing off Bishop Wilberforce in a historic debate at the British Association for the Advancement of Science in 1860.

When Wilberforce had asked whether Huxley claimed descent from a monkey through his grandfather or through his grandmother, Huxley had muttered, 'The Lord hath delivered him into mine hands', and delivered his crushing retort:

> If . . . the question is put to me, would I rather have a miserable ape for a grandfather or a man highly endowed by nature and possessed of great means of influence and yet who employs these faculties and that influence for the mere purpose of introducing ridicule into a grave scientific discussion, I unhesitatingly affirm my preference for the ape.

There are actually several accounts of the clash and this particular version of Huxley's riposte, which he provided in a letter, seems to have been polished up in retrospect, but here it is the legend that counts.[18]

For Wells, the choice between being a provincial schoolteacher and a student of this plain-speaking champion of reason and truth was no contest at all. When the confirmatory letter came, he none the less had to explain his decision to Byatt. Not unreasonably, Byatt was furious. Why hadn't he had the decency to discuss the matter before he posted the application? How could he treat his benefactor in this cavalier way? It was a *fait accompli*, however, and Byatt was a reasonable man whose job, after all, was to help young people in their progress through life. After a couple of days he reconciled himself to the decision and gave Wells his blessing.

The would-be science student probably had more work to do reconciling his mother to what was in effect his sixth start in life in just four years. Though she tried her best to be happy for him, she must have had serious doubts by now about his capacity to stick at any occupation. Moreover, she was aware of Huxley's reputation as an irreligious man, coiner of the word 'agnostic'. Wells fobbed her off with the argument that Huxley was the dean of the college, and surely a dean must by definition be a religious man.

Before heading off to London – perhaps no longer entirely comfortable at the school after his treatment of Byatt – Wells went to Uppark, then over to Bromley to stay at Atlas House. This was probably the time at which he was closest to his father. Joe was running the shop on a token basis, occasionally selling sporting equipment at cricket matches but mostly reading and looking at nature. He was full of admiration for his son's academic achievements and keen to hear about what he had learned. The green fields around Bromley were vanishing beneath housing estates, erasing the world of Wells's childhood, a process that would be vividly recalled in *The New Machiavelli*. Joe, now supporting himself with a stick, took him on expeditions to see exactly what was being lost.

A year previously his father had been an obstruction to his career, to be threatened with bankruptcy, but that crisis was now history. Wells was coming to admire Joe for his capacity to go on learning and thinking throughout his life (contrasted with Sarah, whose views, in his opinion at least, had rigidified upon leaving school), and for his ability to live one day at a time, indifferent to the world of competition and getting on. Wells's own course was set to a different star. He had the spirit, ambition and formal qualifications to challenge the modern world on its own terms.

In the four years since he had left school Wells had learned to adjust rapidly to new places and new people and to stand firmly on his own feet. He had discovered that his father's determination to please himself, coupled with his mother's capacity for sustained application in a greater cause, gave him a formidable ability to overcome obstacles. With the opportunity of a science degree before him, he now had everything he wanted. It must have seemed that nothing could go wrong.

3
STUDENT
1884–1887

It was a slightly nervous Herbert Wells who emerged from lodgings in the Edgware Road one September morning in 1884 and set off south across Kensington Gardens for his first day at college. Over a hundred years later entering higher education might be a daunting experience, but it would be normal for a bright teenager to leave his or her home town, go off to university and take a degree. In 1884 Wells was exceptional in taking a degree at all (that year less than two thousand students were beginning degrees at Oxford and Cambridge) and even more exceptional in taking a government-sponsored science degree. Though several alternative routes to higher education had been developed over the previous half-century, the stereotypical university student still came from a wealthy family and proceeded via an exclusive school to an Oxbridge college. In following a meritocratic, government-initiated route, Wells was ahead of his time – a position he would in due course make his own.

Having crossed the park, he entered Exhibition Road, South Kensington, an area of London developed, as its name suggests, with proceeds from the Great Exhibition. Several museums and libraries of national importance had been sited there. Just along from them stood the Normal School of Science, created three years previously through a merger of the Royal College of Chemistry and parts of the Royal School of Mines. The institution would become regal again in 1890 as the Royal College of Science – appropriately enough, the republican Wells was there during the interregnum – then expand wider still to become Imperial College, part of the University of London.

Passing through the wrought-iron gates, Wells entered the five-storey red-brick and terracotta building that housed the Normal School and was steered by the hall porter through noisy groups of returning students to a hydraulic lift, which took him, very slowly, to the top floor. His first-year course, Elementary Biology and Zoology, would be taught here from 10 a.m. until 5 p.m. each day. Wells's degree would be made up of three one-year courses, with successful completion of each required before he could proceed to the next.

Having emerged from the lift, he wandered mistakenly into a prep room from which he was briskly ejected. He then found his way to the laboratory – a high, narrow room of deal tables, microscopes, sinks, taps and blackboards – where he watched other students arrive, then took delivery of the twitching corpse of a rabbit. This seems to have been his first dissection, and the act of pushing the blade through the warm fur and flesh cannot have been entirely easy.

As he worked, gamely but inaccurately, at the carcass, a pair of spats moved into his field of vision. He looked up and found himself confronted by the formidable gaze of Professor Huxley. Immediately he lowered his eyes and hacked still more determinedly, severing the main branch of the portal vein, which unhelpfully began to squirt blood. When he looked up, the great man had moved on. Wells never did speak to Huxley, except for a brief 'Good morning' while holding open a door, but he attended his lectures with great enthusiasm and felt a lifelong pride in having studied under such a historic figure.

As a state-sponsored 'paid student', Wells knew that he hadn't had it as easy as some of the 'paying students' who were working around him in the laboratory, and his comparative poverty would surely be a handicap, but the presence of Huxley demonstrated that he had at last got a foothold in that world of learning to which he aspired, and he was determined now to get all that he could from it:

> For a year I went shabby and grew shabbier, I was under-fed and not very well housed, and it did not matter to me in the least because of the vision of life that was growing in my mind.[1]

'Not very well housed' bears some elaboration. Sarah had found him his first accommodation, which was certainly well positioned for the college and ought to have been a respectable establishment, as the woman who ran it was the daughter of one of Sarah's old acquaintances in Midhurst. The daughter had not, however, maintained her mother's high religious tone. Her chief amusement was hunting the streets for flirtatious men, accompanied by a similarly minded housewife who lodged on the ground floor.

The house was quite crowded and probably quite smelly, as it had no bathroom and the inhabitants would have had to take turns at a tin bath. Eight people lived there, including Wells. He worked at his studies in a little gas-lit living-room while the landlady's two sons messed around over their homework at the same table. He was soon drawn into the sleazy weekend rituals of the household, which on Sundays meant he was assigned to the landlady's sister-in-law and spent the afternoon on the sofa with her 'attempting small invasions of her costume and such like gallantries'.[2] On one occasion he attempted to invade his landlady's costume, too, when she left her blouse provocatively unbuttoned.

After some weeks he was able to escape from this 'simmering' environment, thanks to a niece of Joe's, Janie Gall, who worked at Derry and Tom's department store in Kensington. She occasionally went for Sunday walks with Wells and, picking up his hints that his present accommodation was not entirely suitable, suggested he might be better off with his Aunt Mary at 181 Euston Road.

Aunt Mary was the widow of one of Joe's brothers who had failed as a draper and died in the workhouse, a fate that must surely have steeled his nephew's resolve to reject drapery as a career. Aunt Mary now ran a down-at-heel lodging house with her sister, Arabella Candy, and here Wells based himself for the rest of his student days, in winter working by candlelight with his feet wrapped in underwear and thrust into a drawer to escape draughts.

A third member of the family also lived at number 181: Mary's daughter Isabel, a dark-eyed, beautiful girl the same age as Wells. Inevitably it was not long before Wells became sexually fixated upon his cousin. His skinny physique and shabby clothes could not hide his dynamism and charm, which he was soon employing in courtship, much as Joe had brought the force of his personality to bear on Sarah more than thirty years before.

Despite the disapproval of Aunt Bella, the couple soon became unofficially engaged. Most weekdays on his way to college Wells escorted Isabel to and from her job, retouching photographs in Regent Street. Sometimes he would pick her up from her evening class at the Mechanics' (later Birkbeck) Institute. At weekends they walked in Regent's Park and visited art galleries, churches and public meetings. Dressed as a respectable Victorian in the top hat and the tail coat he had acquired at the Southsea drapery, his poverty none the less hinted at by a reusable collar of discoloured indiarubber that had to be scrubbed nightly with a toothbrush, Wells expounded his views much as he had done previously when pounding the lanes of Midhurst.

Wells's social life as a student was not confined to escort duties with Isabel. He soon befriended a slightly older student, also in his first year, called A.V. Jennings, who was the son of a London schoolteacher. Jennings appreciated Wells's iconoclastic humour but was quite prepared to stand up to him and challenge his radical views. On one occasion, realizing that Wells's weekly maintenance allowance had run out, as it often did, leaving him unable to afford a midday meal, Jennings insisted on treating him to meat and two veg, jam roly poly and beer. Wells accepted the offer only once but remembered it with appreciation for the rest of his life.

Wells's commitment to his studies precluded further close friendships in his first year, but he got himself elected to the Debating Society committee, and over the next two years developed several acquaintances through this group, remaining in touch with some of them for decades: notably William Burton, Arthur Morley Davies, Elizabeth Healey, Tommy Simmons and Richard Gregory. With these and other friends, Wells exchanged books, visited art galleries, attended Gilbert and Sullivan operas, watched Sir Frederic Leighton painting frescoes at the Museum of Ornamental Art (later to become the Victoria and Albert Museum) and pooled money to buy magazines featuring articles by Huxley.

The students made expeditions across London to political meetings, seeing the Liberal Prime Minister Gladstone, one of the great orators of the age, speaking on the Irish Question, presumably during the 1885 election campaign when he announced his dramatic conversion to Home Rule. They also saw Charles Bradlaugh around about the time he was finally allowed to take his seat in the House of Commons. However, their curiosity seems to have been most aroused by the various socialist groups.

Socialism, then as now, was a single name for a range of political philosophies, the common core of which was the belief that the existing distribution of wealth and power was so irrational that it needed to be radically altered before the majority could achieve fulfilment. Early versions of socialism had sprung up in the turbulent, criss-crossing wakes of the French Revolution and the Industrial Revolution. By the middle of the nineteenth century these naïve attempts to change the world through utopian communes and general strikes had run their course.

The mid-century radicals, the Chartists, accepted the capitalist system, as it seemed to be capable of delivering prosperity but wanted to make it more accountable, principally by extending the vote to all adult men. Once the Chartist movement had failed, many people who were discontented with British society gave up the struggle as hopeless and emigrated to the USA or the colonies. The political initiative was left to the rising middle classes with their liberal view, as expounded by Thomas Morley back in Bromley, that the way to make society more just and efficient was gradually to whittle away aristocratic privilege and allow the fittest to prevail.

By the last quarter of the century even mainstream liberal opinion (inside and outside the actual Liberal Party) was beginning to accept that removing impediments to competition was insufficient – not least because the pre-eminence of Britain was being challenged by foreign states like Germany, prepared to invest seriously in education, welfare and the armed forces. Government intervention for the common good, paid for by income tax, had come to stay. The overlapping movements of New Liberalism and socialism could be seen as a logical extension of the state's expanding role, a shift of emphasis from reluctant intervention to thoroughgoing reconstruction and control from above, but there were several other reasons for their emergence at the time that Wells was a student.

From the mid-1870s to the mid-1890s the Liberals' free trade policy resulted in cheap food imports that satisfied consumers but devastated British agriculture. Because of the fall in prices, people who were in work tended to become better off, though their employers often responded to the squeeze on their profits by trying to speed up work. The increased wealth and the friction with employers both helped strengthen the trade-union movement. Meanwhile, the plight of the large numbers who were unemployed or trapped in low-paid jobs stood out more clearly. Unskilled workers began to fight for a better deal in what became known as the 'New Unionism'.

Their poverty was evident to many well-off town-dwellers and, where it could not readily be seen with the naked eye, the growth of investigative journalism brought it to light in exposés such as Andrew Mearn's *The Bitter Cry of Outcast London* and George Sims's *How the Poor Live*, both published in 1883. In this context, the writings of thinkers such as Henry George, and the as yet lesser-known Karl Marx stimulated the growth of several socialist groups in London, a network of three thousand or so dissidents who proceeded to argue among themselves about how the world could be changed for the better.

In 1884 the Fabian Society was founded, and later in the year the designer and poet William Morris seceded from the Marxist Social Democratic Federation to set up his own Socialist League. As beneficiaries of state involvement in education, some of the grant-receiving science students were drawn to socialism, but it is not clear whether at this stage they gave their allegiance to any one group in particular. They seem to have gone to all the main groups but most often took the Underground railway to Hammersmith for Sunday-evening sessions at Morris's London residence, Kelmscott House.

The speakers here included two men who would later be close to Wells. One was Graham Wallas, a Classics teacher who had just repudiated Christianity and resigned from his school post. Wells later recalled how presciently Wallas had attacked Marxists for their failure to plan for the consequences of revolution.[3] The other was George Bernard Shaw, at that time an unemployed and unpublished novelist. Wells and his friends Burton and E.H. Smith were sufficiently enthused by what they heard to start sporting red ties as a symbol of their revolutionary sympathies.

Though Wells began developing political interests in his first year at college, he was most committed to them in his second and third years. During 1884–5 his main concern was his studies. At Christmas 1884 he got a first-class pass in Biology and in February a second in Botany. When he went off to Uppark for the summer he must have been fairly confident of doing well. In the event, despite his disappointment that Huxley had fallen ill towards the end of the Biology course and handed over the teaching to a demonstrator, G.B. Howes, Wells was still one of only three students to score more than 80 per cent in the summer examination of 1885 and earn First Class Honours. His jubilation is evident in a letter to his brother Fred in which he mentions the possibility of achieving a doctorate by 1900.[4] The highly promising student then returned to South Kensington and set about destroying the very prospects he cherished.

Wells's autobiography puts forward the standard excuse on which derelict students have always relied. It was poor teaching that was to blame. He was taught Physics by two extremely distinguished scientists: Professor Frederick Guthrie, ill with undiagnosed cancer, whom he found too slow, then his assistant Charles Boys, whom he found too fast. Though Wells was not alone in his criticisms of their teaching, his excuse deserves the equally standard reply: how was it that, despite their defects, most of the other students managed to pass the course?

Guthrie's teaching was none the less a factor, as it required the students to spend a great deal of time making apparatus. Wells not only considered this pointless, he was very bad at it. Attempts to construct barometers and millimetre rules left him with little to show but painfully burned fingers and acid-stained trousers. Rather than admit to failure, he retaliated by deliberately mocking the tasks set him – refusing, for example, to construct anything in the shape of a cross because he was not a Christian – and eventually producing a device to measure sound waves that was so outstandingly bad that it was preserved in a cupboard for several years. To Wells, Guthrie's tasks were frustrating chores, comparable to those imposed upon him in his drapery days, and he responded to them in the same way, by shirking, confronting his supervisors and defiantly going off to read. When reprimanded for missing lab sessions, he turned up at the college bearing Latin and German textbooks that he used to pass a London University matriculation examination in January 1886.

Wells had left the drapery precisely in order to escape from manual labour. What had motivated him in his first year as a student was evolution as an alternative account of why human beings existed and how the world worked, founded on hard evidence and so capable of blasting away the ancient biblical myths. Wells's understanding of the Christian world-view was that it was a closed one in which God sent people to a predetermined fate. In the contrasting vision of science, the evolving human race was beginning to uncover its true place in a comparatively open universe, one that might permit it to secure some control of its destiny. This was the liberating vision that had stimulated Wells's imagination and led him to South Kensington in the first place, though we should note that Huxley himself thought of the evolutionary process as predestined.

In the Newtonian physics taught in the second year the universe was certainly not open and evolutionary; it was a collection of atoms that moved according to mathematical laws. Eventually, when the atoms had expended all their energy, the history of the universe would be over. The physicist's vision of life, in other words, was an even more dispiritingly closed system than the religious one – as Wells clearly saw. He kidded Jennings and others that he was working on a 'Universal Diagram'. If you could input the first ever movement by an atom, it would trace how the knock-on effects brought the whole of the present world into being. (This idea was not original to Wells, having been proposed as long ago as 1763.) If the universe was a closed system, its energy unwinding towards final 'heat death', there could be no room for human purpose and will. If Newton and Professor Guthrie were right, it was impossible for individuals to pursue their own destiny, let alone change the world.

This was the grim vision from which Wells walked away in his second year. And where did he go? To various libraries around the South Kensington complex to read about literature, history and religion – such names as Goethe, Shakespeare and the Buddha are mentioned in the autobiography – eventually devoting imprudent amounts of time on the one hand to *The French Revolution* by Thomas Carlyle, one of the most celebrated books of the nineteenth century, and on the other to the prophetic works of William Blake, who at that time was still something of a cult figure.

Wells seems to have embodied painfully in his own person the debate between Huxley and Matthew Arnold a few years earlier about the relationship between science and literature, knowledge and wisdom. His choice of authors tells us a great deal about the conclusions he was reaching. Carlyle and Blake both had lower-class origins and hated the class system, though Carlyle was emphatically no democrat. Both grew up in Protestant sects, later rejected conventional Christianity but remained champions of spiritual values and were fiercely opposed to scientific materialism.

Carlyle complained in his 1829 essay 'Signs of the Times':

> the Metaphysical and Moral Sciences are falling into decay, while the Physical are engrossing, every day, more respect and attention . . . men have lost their belief in the Invisible, and believe, and hope, and work only in the visible.

In Carlyle's view, scientific materialism revealed a limited truth. Accepted uncritically, it devalued spiritual awareness and encouraged materialism in the vulgar sense of the small-minded pursuit of wealth and status. Wells was so impressed by Carlyle that his prose style began to imitate that of his master. Fifty years later, in the autobiography, he describes himself at this period not only as a 'thoroughly detestable hobbledehoy' but as a 'philosophical desperado', pointedly echoing Arnold's jibe that Carlyle was a 'moral desperado'.[5]

Blake, very different from Carlyle in other respects, was in full agreement about science. He was scornful of the notion that the universe could be reduced to a collection of material particles. To Blake, the universe was not a fact to be measured but a complex experience that had to be actively construed by the imagination. A healthy mind would engage with it at many levels, not prioritizing material analysis. In a letter of 1802 he prays:

> May God us keep
> From single vision and Newton's sleep![6]

Wells's reading programme was not a rejection of science, only a recognition that science needed to be supplemented by the perspectives of humanistic disciplines. None the less, in addition to the ongoing struggle between his serious, idealistic side and his playful, self-assertive one, a related conflict in Wells's personality had now appeared between the role of scientist and that of artist.

At South Kensington he liked to think of himself as an artist among scientists; later, as a famous author, he would claim to be a scientist among artists. Writing creatively proved the most effective way to reconcile the two roles. In October 1885 Wells delivered a lecture to the Debating Society on 'The Past and Future of the Human Race', which allowed him to integrate scientific and imaginative perspectives, presenting ideas about the future evolution of human beings that he would later draw upon in *The War of the Worlds*.

If Wells's complaints about the quality of the teaching he received are suspect, he was on stronger ground when he complained about the nature of the course. He was training to be a teacher; where was the instruction on how to teach? He would be preparing his pupils for a visibly changing society; where was the social perspective? By listening to political theorists and reading outside his subject, Wells could plausibly argue that he was compensating for the failure of the authorities to give him a balanced education. This cannot, however, excuse such behaviour as making stupid noises in lectures by blowing down a rubber tube – conduct suggesting that taking on the role of teacher early in life had left him with a need to make up his immaturity quota.

A final contributory motive to be considered in accounting for Wells's self-destructive behaviour is resentment at having to compete with other students with more advantages. That Wells had such a chip on his shoulder is evident from a fight he had with the clerk who paid out the grant money every Wednesday. Apparently he had called out the names of the students in an insufficiently respectful tone.

Wells's second year as a student must have been an oddly mixed experience, then. His relationship with Isabel was steady, and up to a point fulfilling for him, but sexually frustrating as well. He no longer found his studies stimulating; instead they goaded him into unworthy behaviour. Reading and attending political meetings gave him food for thought and allowed him to escape into a bigger world, where his demotivation as a student seemed less significant. Perhaps his greatest fulfilment came from the Debating Society, where his shrill public-speaking voice did not prevent him from adroitly mixing ideas and entertainment and obtaining a gratifying audience reaction. On one occasion he was ejected from the basement lecture theatre for what were deemed to be blasphemous references to Jesus as 'a certain itinerant preacher' and the New Testament as a 'compilation'.[7] As he was carried out, with someone tugging at his hair, he relished his resemblance to Bradlaugh and the Irish nationalist MPs, people who were doing something to change the world.

His disappointing second year over, Wells spent most of the summer at his Uncle Charles's farm, the Elms, in Minsterworth, Gloucestershire, prudently placing himself at a distance from his mother in the waiting period for his examination results. When they arrived, they did not make comfortable reading. A first in Geometrical Drawing was the high point. In Elementary Physics and Geology Wells had got second-class passes, but he had failed Astronomical Physics, and his practical work in Physics, unsurprisingly, had been singled out as extraordinarily poor.

A letter written to Tommy Simmons shortly after the arrival of these results reveals his doubts about whether he would qualify for a third year of grant. He asks for the names of some teaching agencies and declares that if he could find a decently paid job he wouldn't return to the college even if he were permitted to do so.[8]

At the same period Wells sent Simmons a 'picshua' guying himself as a pretentious young man meditating on his future greatness. Manuscripts scattered around him include 'How I Could Save the World', 'All About God', 'Wells Design for a New Framework for Society' and 'Secret of the Kosmos'.[9] Whatever degree of irony was intended (and, since Wells would one day write books matching some of these titles, the irony has subsequently shifted direction), this is a strange set of ideas to be entertained by an informed follower of science. To Huxley, science was a force that would tend to erode empty authority, letting us look upon reality in a cautious, chastened way. Wells's cartoon shows how far he was from engaging with science as Huxley understood it. His attitudes were closer to the prophetic pronouncements of Carlyle and Blake, though with a saving consciousness of his own absurdity.

Despite his fears, Wells's grant was renewed. He could at this point have decided to recover the situation by knuckling down to his reading for Geology, but instead he threw himself into writing the speech on socialism with which he intended to open the autumn session of the Debating Society. His mind was still on student politics in September when, spending some time around his twentieth birthday with his father in Bromley, he wrote to Simmons with a humorous plan for the Debating Society members to take up key positions in the social order after their graduation, possibly a parody of the Fabian 'permeationist' approach to socialism. Wells himself would end up in the Church, a move calculated to do it permanent damage.[10]

For now, it was his own future that Wells seemed determined to wreck. Professor J.W. Judd's Geology course was his chance to redeem his scientific career, but it was a chance that he could not motivate himself to take. Though he discovered some interest in crystallography, most of the course bored him. There was, in his view, far too much note-taking and rote-learning. He would dutifully set out to spend a couple of hours organizing his notes in the Dyce and Foster Reading Room or the Art Library but find his attention distracted by the pictures and writings of Blake who seemed to have so much more to say.

On 15 October 1886 Wells delivered his long-gestated lecture on 'Democratic Socialism', which proposed that the state should take control of production and distribution and asserted that socialism was characterized by the merging of the individual in the state. This was an odd opinion to be voiced by someone who seemed incapable of merging himself into the state institution in which he was currently enrolled, even to the extent of carrying out his studies, but the great socialist state was a hypothetical ideal, whereas the college and its demands were all too present and mundane.

In December Wells came up with a new source of distraction for himself when he launched a student magazine, the *Science Schools Journal.* In addition to his reading outside the course, he had lately been putting a lot of effort into his writing. A letter to Elizabeth Healey at Easter had contained a lengthy reflective poem. At some point towards the end of his student days he earned a guinea by contributing a sentimental short story to the *Family Herald.* In the *Science Schools Journal* he could pursue topics that genuinely interested him. The first number, for example, contained a piece on Socrates. Because Socrates was rejected by his contemporaries and bravely submitted to their death sentence, he had tended to become the atheist's alternative role model to Jesus. Possibly Wells even felt himself to be something of a Socrates, challenging those about him from the purest of motives – the desire to make them examine their assumptions – only to be condemned rather than appreciated as a result.

One person who certainly did not appreciate his efforts was the college registrar, who, from April 1887, forbade him to edit the *Journal,* presumably hoping that he might instead devote the last months of his third year to study. Though William Burton replaced Wells as nominal editor, Wells continued to be the motive force, sometimes contributing articles under defiantly improbable pseudonyms. He had already featured as Walter Glockenhammer. In May, writing as Septimus Browne, he contributed 'A Tale of the Twentieth Century' and in June, reappearing as Sosthenes Smith, 'A Vision of the Past'. These two satirical pieces were strong hints about where his future as a writer lay. The former describes the disaster that ensues when a perpetual motion machine is applied to the London Underground railway (at that time still steam-powered, though due to start electrification in three years); the latter records an ironic conversation between extinction-bound dinosaurs who regard themselves as the noblest product of evolution, destined to progress to perfection.

Nor did Wells let up in his involvement with the Debating Society where, in addition to hearing a talk on time as the fourth dimension, which planted some important seeds in his mind, he gave at least two speeches of his own. One argued against the worship of great men. This was a slap at his guru Carlyle. Like most readers of Carlyle, Wells was more impressed by his diagnosis of modern ills than by his proto-fascistic advocacy of inspired leaders as the solution. None the less, Carlyle's elitism, and his belief that great writers constituted a kind of priesthood, left a lasting impression on Wells, chiming in with his interest in Plato's Guardians and in the Enlightenment aristocrats who had created Uppark.

More entertainingly, the South Kensington Socrates went on to deliver a mock scientific lecture on perpetual motion. The apparatus he had devised clearly outdid any of Professor Guthrie's workaday creations and, significantly enough, purported to defy the second law of thermodynamics, which condemned the closed universe to run down. It was a rod that constantly rotated without needing to be powered. When members of the audience heard a sound from under the table and alleged that an electromagnet was turning the machine, Wells dismissed the suggestion. On the contrary, he explained, his perpetual motion machine was itself generating electricity by induction and he was merely harnessing it to work a coffee mill, as he triumphantly demonstrated by reaching under the table and scooping up some freshly ground coffee. As the laughter and applause of his comrades showed, much as Wells may have aspired to be a hard-nosed revolutionary he was also what he had been since childhood, a gifted comic performer.

Behind the defiance and humour, however, lay an anxious young man who looked at himself in the mirror and despaired at what he saw – a diminutive weakling who had been stunted by his family's poverty. (Wells seems never to have faced up to the possibility that he also took after his mother in build.)

Thrusting aside self-doubts, he continued to court Isabel, but marriage required an income, an income required a job and, for someone who did not come from a privileged background, a job required qualifications. Wells made some effort to revise for his examinations that summer, but it was too little too late.

We have no record of his mother's reaction to the results, though we can reasonably infer that she would have been furious at the way he had spent his last two years at college and confirmed in her view that to give up his teaching job at Midhurst had been folly. Bertie's plan to become a learned man had proved to be just what she feared: another false start, another example of his failure to see things through. Since we do not hear of Wells going to Uppark in the summer of 1887 he presumably remained with Isabel and Aunt Mary, and they had to console him in his disappointment. Like many students before and since, Wells had managed to convince himself he would scrape through despite his follies. However, he did not. (Forty-five years later, in the autobiography, he still cannot believe the outcome and accuses Professor Judd of rigging the results.) He had retaken Astronomical Physics and raised it to a second, but he had failed Geology Parts I and II. There was no possibility now of his grant being renewed and therefore no way that he could retake these components or start on any others. His dreams of a career as a scientist were over.

4
'IN THE WILDERNESS'
1887–1890

The summer in which H.G. Wells failed to achieve his degree is better remembered by posterity as the summer of Queen Victoria's Golden Jubilee. To see the once unpopular monarch enthusiastically celebrated must have irritated the republican Wells no end, as it did many other radicals. When the Queen ventured into the working-class East End of London, she was greeted by a 'horrid noise' that proved to be booing from socialists and Irish nationalists.

Both groups were again evident on the streets in November of 1887, when ten thousand protesters, including the writers William Morris, R.B. Cunninghame Graham and George Bernard Shaw, marched to Trafalgar Square in central London to object to Britain's policy in Ireland. In what became known as 'Bloody Sunday' the clash between the protesters and the police left two dead and more than one hundred injured.

While the 'Irish Question' produced violent confrontation, the socialist movement itself was making visible progress. Over the next two or three years, strikes against poor pay and conditions would enable the gas workers, the London dockers and the Bryant and May match girls to achieve not only successful outcomes but massive public support. In 1889 a collection of *Fabian Essays*, written by Shaw and Graham Wallas among others, set out the case for comprehensive social reform, while the German chancellor, Bismark, was confirming the practicality of such ideas by stealing the socialists' clothes, introducing his own welfare programme of insurance benefits and old age pensions to win the support of the working class for his regime.

It might be expected that Wells would have followed these developments keenly, together with major scientific breakthroughs of the period such as the measurement of the speed of light and the discovery of electromagnetic waves, but he had little chance to engage with public affairs of any kind. Instead, as he later put it, he 'wandered in the wilderness of private school teaching'.[1]

His London University matriculation and his year's work at Midhurst qualified him for several available teaching posts, out of which he opted for a job as usher at the Holt Academy, near Wrexham in Wales. It seems odd that a secularist should choose a school that included a Methodist training college, but Wells thought the place might have counterbalancing advantages. For one thing, he would be able to mix with some students of his own age:

> I thought all Wales was lake and mountain and wild loveliness. And the Holt Academy had the added advantage of re-opening at the end of July and so shortening the gap of impecuniosity after the College of Science dispersed.[2]

Only on the last point did the Academy fulfil his expectations. He was repelled by the district ('its most prominent feature was a gasometer'), depressed by the buildings, disdainful of the pupils, regarded the head teacher as a verbose drunkard and had limited respect for his fellow teacher, a French 'cuckold maker' named Raut.[3] Wells was not pleased to find that his duties involved teaching scripture, nor that he had to share a bedroom with two of the three trainee ministers ('lumpish young men apparently just off the fields').[4] The pupils in turn resented being bossed about by a skinny college boy with an English accent, whose sense of his own superiority was probably quite evident to them. Wells realized that he would have to stick to the job for at least a year, using it as a chance to make some money while working at his writing, then see what further opportunities arose.

He found solace in penning letters to old student friends and flirting with a young woman named Annie Meredith, a schoolteacher at home on vacation. This was questionable behaviour in a man with a fiancée, as Wells admits in his autobiography, offering the excuse that Isabel's limitations as a letter-writer had allowed her to slip to the back of his mind.

On Monday 30 August, exactly a month after his arrival at the school, Wells took part in a game of rugby.[5] It gave the pupils a chance to revenge themselves on their puny new teacher. A boy called Dick Gratton fouled Wells, ramming him below the ribs with his shoulder and sending him sprawling. When Wells got up he was in too much pain to continue. Pursued by the jeers of the other players, he dragged himself back to the house, was violently sick, then lay down to recover. When he got up to relieve himself he found to his dismay that he was filling the chamber pot with blood.

Shock and fear were followed by a night of hallucinations. Next day the local doctor diagnosed a crushed kidney and prescribed bed rest and nourishment. By the following week Wells had recovered sufficiently to set out the gory details in a letter to his mother:

> I was hurt badly in the loin, my kidney was crushed, my liver bruised & my intestines & muscles between the ribs & the pelvis mashed up more or less. Consequently I was in danger of departing this life by one or two different ways. The kidney might inflame, or the bowels, or I might have stoppage – a delightful method of dying of which you have doubtless heard tell before – or I might get weakened by the bleeding.[6]

Reading this would surely have sent Sarah's thoughts straight back to the death of Fanny, as Wells must have been aware. Evidently he still wanted some of his mother's yearning for her lost daughter to be diverted his way.

In his sickness he would have liked to escape from Holt, but the only place he might have gone was Uppark, and Miss Frances was at present unwilling to have him. Relations between the increasingly deaf and crotchety Sarah and her similarly afflicted employer were deteriorating. Additionally, Sarah had recently been busy supervising the sale of Atlas House, the business having finally been declared bankrupt, and the relocation of her dependent husband to a cottage in the hamlet of Nyewood, near Rogate, about three miles from Uppark. Here Joe was joined by Frank, who had now given up drapery to become an itinerant clock repairman and watch seller. The thought of yet another lame-duck member of the Wells family moving into the vicinity to distract her housekeeper was too much for Miss Frances.

Wells spent his twenty-first birthday trapped in Holt. Apart from reading, his only relief was a visit at the end of September from his student friend William Burton, accompanied by the young woman he had recently married. Like Wells, Burton was a former pupil-teacher and assistant schoolmaster who had not completed his degree. Burton, however, had managed to get himself a good position at the Wedgwood Potteries in Stoke-on-Trent. The contrast between his flourishing career and Wells's must have been uncomfortably obvious. Wells tried to resume his teaching job, but his efforts to regain his independence were thwarted when he began to cough up blood. The Wrexham doctor wrongly diagnosed tuberculosis or, as it was then known, consumption.

Since consumption tended to be fatal, Miss Frances felt compelled to relent. Wells was able to quit his ill-starred post and travel by train to Uppark in November. Once at Uppark, installed in a room next to his mother's, he suffered his most serious haemorrhage yet. Fortunately a young doctor called William Collins was in the house, dressing for dinner after a day's shooting, and he quickly applied ice bags to Wells's chest to stop the bleeding.

Wells remained at Uppark for four months in a worryingly uncertain state of health. Collins dismissed the idea of tuberculosis but advised Wells that he had a dangerously damaged kidney, chronic dyspepsia, a weak lung and possibly diabetes. He might always be an invalid. After many years of trying to escape from his mother and her world, Wells was frustratingly dependent on both and could possibly be so for the remainder of a short life.

He turned with renewed determination to his writing, explaining in a letter that he would probably have to produce formula fiction for the market, though what he really wanted to do was give the world the benefit of his opinions through essays and criticism.[7] In the event neither approach would prove to be where his deepest strengths lay.

Remembering the story he had sold to the *Family Herald* during his student days, he produced another entitled 'The Death of Miss Peggy Pickerskill's Cat' and sent it off to the *Herald* and *Household Words*, both of which sent it straight back. A novel, *Lady Frankland's Companion*, which sounds as though it might have been based on his mother's experiences, was developed to 35,000 words but never finished. It was probably during this time, however, that Wells devised a far more promising project, a story about time travel called *The Chronic Argonauts.* Between attempts at the art of fiction, Wells kept up his letter writing, tried to learn shorthand and read widely. Burton and others sent him books, and he borrowed some fiction from the curate at Harting, the church where he had been sullenly confirmed just four years earlier.

Dr Collins, who took over his care, turned out to be an admirer of the French philosopher Auguste Comte, the founder of the positivist school of thought, which attempted to apply scientific methodology to social issues. The ultimate development of positivism was meant to be a perfect society, organized by an elite of scientists and engineers and inspired by a non-theistic faith. Like most British admirers of Comte, Collins did not take these utopian aspirations seriously and adopted only what was compatible with liberal individualism. This led to amiable disputes with Wells, whose ideas were much closer to Comte's. Exactly what kind of socialist Wells was at this time it is hard to say, however. We find him speaking equally warmly of Ruskin, Morris, Marx and the Fabians, the playful, constantly shifting tone of his letters making it difficult to tell whose ideas he found most persuasive.

By February 1888 Wells knew Collins sufficiently well to send him a letter seeking help in finding a job as a research assistant to an author such as Frederic Harrison (the leading British positivist), Shaw or one of the Huxleys. Though sympathetic, Collins was unable to help.

The Christmas festivities behind him, Wells entered into a period of virtual hibernation. The tone of his letters oscillates between self-pity and self-mockery, the two not always distinct. 'Today lungs positively *rustle* when I breathe,' he reported to Arthur Morley Davies. 'Air gurgles as it enters trachea. Cough up Swiss tinned milk in quantity. Expect to congest in a day or two. In which case, – farewell.'[8] The tone is flippant, yet Wells sounds genuinely worried about his prospects for survival. To Elizabeth Healey he was more openly morbid, though one cannot quite rule out a touch of hand-to-the-brow comic affectation:

> I shall never join the Marching Column again. My youth went long ago – my *life work* will be to give as little trouble as possible in an uncongenial universe while I stay therein and not to leave too big a hole in anybody else's world when my creation terminates.[9]

Wells longed to escape the monotony of Uppark by repaying Burton's visit, but not until the end of April 1888 was he well enough to set out for Stoke-on-Trent, staying two nights in London and visiting South Kensington on the way. His renewed cheerfulness at the prospect is evident in a letter to Healey:

> I am not a broken down invalid, I have merely had a revolution in my constitution – on the principle that a man who would revolutionize the World must first revolutionize himself.[10]

Once at the Burtons in Stoke, he enjoyed being with people of his own age who shared his interests. His imagination was stimulated by the landscape of the Five Towns district: the blazing iron foundries, the luridly smoky atmosphere, the canals running between piles of coloured clay. In the two months he stayed at 18 Victoria Street, Basford, he embarked upon a 'vast melodrama' set in the Potteries, rather in the style of the *Mysteries of Paris* that he had read long ago at Surly Hall, and was pleased to observe some improvement in the quality of his writing.[11] A fragment was later recast as 'The Cone', a story in which a character, cheekily named Raut after the 'cuckold maker' of Holt, is set upon by a wronged husband and horribly murdered.

In a letter written to Davies at this time, Wells lamented his lack of success as an author. His melodrama had reached 25,000 words but did not seem likely to earn him any money. He had burned several of his stories in despair. Most of the pieces he had sent to magazines had never even been returned. As for his desire to change the world,

> I am afraid the hungry maw will presently engulph [*sic*] the Prophet of the Undelivered Spell, and the unwarned world hurry on to damnation.[12]

He does not bother to mention *The Chronic Argonauts*, which had begun to appear in three parts in the *Science Schools Journal* that April, yet we know with hindsight that it was this unfinished, experimental piece that pointed the way ahead.

It tells the story of Moses Nebogipfel, a strange-looking scientist who takes up residence in a reputedly haunted house in Wales. He is hated and feared by the local people, who suspect he is a warlock and attack him. Nebogipfel is finally revealed to be a genius born ahead of his era who has invented a time machine in order to escape from the present to the more developed society where he believes that he belongs.

In its use of realistic descriptions the *Chronic Argonauts* is more like a novel than anything Wells had yet published, the realistic detail being used to make the fantastic events plausible. Competing explanations are also introduced to make the fantasy more believable yet more mysterious – a rhetorical move that Wells had learned from recent reading of Nathaniel Hawthorne and which would be fundamental to his mature science fiction.

From the biographical point of view, the most fascinating aspect of the *Chronic Argonauts* is that Nebogipfel is a caricature of his creator. In depicting a scientific outsider in Wales, said to have arrived by train from London, a genius born before his time who is misunderstood and attacked by moronic locals, Wells is evidently drawing on his own experiences. If he was conscious of this when he wrote the piece he had banished it from his thoughts by the time he wrote his autobiography, where he grumbles that the reference to Mount Nebo is irrelevant.[13] Nebo was the vantage point from which Moses, having led his people through the wilderness, looked ahead to the Promised Land that he could see but never enter.[14] It is actually a highly apt allusion since Moses Nebogipfel can glimpse the future but never reach it.

The same held true for Herbert George Wells, who saw himself as 'the Prophet of the Undelivered Spell'[15] and, in a letter the following year, as 'a dumb prophet like Moses'.[16] Wells feared he might soon die, long before the arrival of the just social order that was his dream. None the less, much as his mother had heaven as an ultimate goal to make sense of her life, so he was able to look to his socialist Utopia. A key difference between these two ideals was that his Utopia did not depend upon belief in the supernatural, so appeared to be compatible with science. Like Comte, Wells rejected Christianity but did not wholeheartedly reject religion.

After more than two months at the Burtons' house it was evident that Wells had outstayed his welcome. The hosts were tiring of their seemingly immovable guest with his constant arguments and sarcasm, and he in turn was bored by their company and perhaps jealous of their happiness. At the start of July he went for a walk in Trury Woods, lay down among the hyacinths to consider his position and came to the conclusion that he had been dying long enough. It was time for a new start. Among other considerations, he must have been aware that now was the season for teachers to be appointed.

To the poorly disguised relief of his hosts, he announced that he would be leaving for London the following day. His mother had sent him two halves of a five-pound note in separate letters in case of emergency which, reconstituted like Kipps's half-sixpences, would cover his immediate expenses. Having sent off some letters to teaching and employment agencies, he packed his portmanteau – the same one he had taken with him when he first left home for the drapery eight years before – and embarked on a train for the capital city.

He did not tell anyone he was coming, hoping that he could find a paying job before he revealed himself to his old acquaintances. His first night was spent in a cheap lodging house in Judd Street, just over the road from St Pancras Station. The following day he searched for digs and settled for a budget-price bedsitting-room, or more accurately part of a sub-divided attic, in Theobalds Road. He then settled into a routine of visiting teaching and employment agencies and leafing through want advertisements, eating – when he felt he could afford to – in local cafés.

In his autobiography Wells claims that he had begun searching too late in the year to get a permanent teaching job, yet his search took place at about the same time that he had had his pick of several jobs the previous year. Perhaps potential employers were put off by his poor health record. In the previous school year he had managed only a month's teaching, and there was no certainty that he was fit enough now to be a reliable employee. For whatever reason, the only work he could find was preparing an army applicant for science examinations.

The unemployed prophet had to spend many of his daylight hours wandering the streets, window-shopping and observing the passing crowds. On Sundays, when the shops were shut, he resorted to chapels and churches – in particular St Paul's Cathedral, which was big enough for a lone soul to sit musing without attracting attention. In the evenings he would return to his attic room and listen frustratedly to the intimate moments of a young couple on the other side of the thin partition. Naturally his thoughts began to turn to Isabel. She and Aunt Mary had quit the lodging-house business and moved to an apartment in 12 Fitzroy Road, Primrose Hill.

Despite his initial resolve, Wells was forced after all to seek help from old friends. Jennings, now a biology lecturer at the Birkbeck Institute and a junior demonstrator at South Kensington, threw him the lifeline he needed by paying him to make a set of biological diagrams. Wells got a ticket to the British Museum Reading Room, copied diagrams out of books there, then produced enlarged versions of them in a small laboratory Jennings shared in Chancery Lane. Wells was able to do some reading at the Museum, as well as at his old place of refuge, the Education Library in South Kensington.

Though he had not seen Isabel for more than a year, he still considered himself engaged to her. Back in Stoke, he had written a letter to Elizabeth Healey, voicing his concern over what would happen to Isabel if he died and asking her to befriend his fiancée.[17] Though he had been hoping to present himself to Isabel and her mother as a reinvigorated man with a respectable job and prospects, Wells swallowed his pride, contacted them and by the start of August had moved in. The move was eased by the absence of the sceptical Aunt Bella, who had left for a housekeeping job in Wiltshire.

Wells was now being supported by Isabel, who was earning a good wage as a photographic retoucher, but he did what he could to bring money into the household. He kept up his work for Jennings, did some more examination coaching and found an ingenious, if ethically suspect, source of extra income in submitting quiz questions to weekly magazines for half a crown a time, then sending in the winning answers under another name.

Wells disliked the concept of marriage. His early letters sneer at prospective couples and several times note the danger of a man marrying a woman who will not support him in his life's work. Indeed, in the ten-year falling out that followed his stay with the Burtons, he denounced their relationship to mutual friends in these very terms.[18] His own parents were not an encouraging example of wedded bliss, so it may be significant that it is in a letter written while staying with 'that alcoholic savage' his father at Nyewood in September that Wells sets out his views on the subject most bluntly, declaring most marriages to be failures and those that prove successful just as likely to be so if the couple had not gone through a marriage ceremony.[19]

If this is how Wells felt, then he might have been expected to try to escape from his commitment to Isabel. He did the opposite, working as hard as he could to make a career that would support them as a married couple. Like his father, who had become fixated on Sarah despite their incompatibility, Wells longed for intimacy with the woman he loved. The cynic within was unable to prevent nature fulfilling its course.

In the November and December issues of the *Science Schools Journal*, under the self-mocking name 'Tyro', Wells published a short story entitled 'The Devotee of Art' about an obsessive painter who neglects his dying wife. It begins in an appropriately arty style derived from Poe, then surprises the reader after several pages by a comical downshift in tone, culminating in a conclusion – it was all a dream – that does not adequately resolve the discord. The story is symptomatic of Wells's feelings at the time, as he was trying to persuade himself not to be a devotee of art. He was probably making a public declaration to his fiancée as well, since the wife in the story is named Isabel. In order to cherish the woman he loved, his ambition to be a writer would have to be sacrificed, at least for the short term, and he would have to put his energies into a full-time job that would enable him to build a nest-egg for their marriage.

The job had already been found. From January 1889 he was going to be a science teacher at Henley House School, three miles to the west of Primrose Hill, in Mortimer Crescent, Kilburn. As at Holt, the job entailed part-time teaching at a local girls' school. His new employer was a Scotsman named J.V. Milne. Among the pupils would be his son Alan, who would later find fame as A.A. Milne, the creator of Winnie the Pooh. The school magazine had been founded by Alfred 'the Dodger' Harmsworth, now a rising magazine proprietor, whom Wells would meet when Harmsworth returned to the school as an 'old boy'.

Though Milne was looking for a resident teacher, Wells wished to be close to Isabel and needed time to finish his degree, so he insisted on nine-to-five weekday attendance only. Remembering his experiences at Holt, he also specified he should not teach scripture. Impressed that Wells would risk losing the place over a matter of conscience, Milne appointed him.

Wells spent the Christmas break at Uppark but by now had had more than enough of the place or, rather, of the people there. Firing on all cylinders, ready to embark on a new phase of his life, he found the deferential country-house small talk maddening. ('They are *damned phonographs bloody old talking Dolls*.')[20]

It was with relief that Wells returned to London and reported for duty at the school where, thanks to hard work, he was soon settled in. Characteristically, he taught science without the use of experiments, preferring to demonstrate or write on the board. Guthrie's practical work had confirmed Wells's aversion to apparatus, and in any case he tended to think of teaching in terms of conveying information, not as guided exploration, with limited concern for the practical involvement of pupils. Clever boys thrived in his classes; the others tried his patience and often became targets for flying chalk.

During 1888 Wells had made occasional return visits to the South Kensington Debating Society, and in January 1889 he enjoyed a bout with his old friend Tommy Simmons, who had also become a schoolmaster. During the course of a debate on socialism, Wells defended Marxism as based on Darwinism, argued for the abolition of inherited wealth and maintained that the use of contraception should be discouraged. Wells's early socialism was evidently an extreme form of liberalism: Thomas Morley multiplied by Henry George.[21] Through abolishing private property and inheritance, the state could create a level playing field for competition between individuals. In this meritocracy, presumably, the Fetherstonhaugh family would fall and Bertie Wells would rise. Under present arrangements, however, the young revolutionary had been doing rather badly in the struggle for existence and had had to rely on the inherited wealth of Miss Frances to protect him, a state of affairs that probably made him all the more resentful of the system.

In May the engagement between Wells and Isabel was formalized, and, on the strength of Wells's new job, the household moved to more spacious apartments further up the street at 46 Fitzroy Road. Having studied intensively during the evenings, Wells took his Intermediate B.Sc. in July, passing with Second Class Honours in Zoology. During August he took a well-earned holiday with Isabel and Aunt Mary at Whitstable on the Kentish coast.

Wells kept himself hard at work studying several subjects for his finals and for a substantial teaching qualification, the College of Preceptors' Licentiateship, which he obtained through an examination shortly after Christmas 1889. He was the only candidate out of 108 to gain the full diploma, along with £20 in awards for his performance in Natural Science, Mathematics and the Theory and Practice of Education. At the end of the year he extracted a pay rise from Milne and, by threatening to take a job elsewhere, seems to have got his hours reduced into the bargain.

Amidst all this effort, there was little time for creative writing, yet when in

December his old friend Davies came to London to matriculate and they helped each other with their studies, Wells seems to have shown him a new draft of *The Chronic Argonauts*. Davies would see two different versions of the story over the next three years. Evidently Wells had recognized that his time machine idea had enormous potential, if only he could unlock it. It was a project too good to let go.

5
AN ATTEMPT AT CONFORMITY
1890–1893

Two of Wells's 'picshuas' of the early 1890s show him hard at work at his desk. In one an enormous quill pen wags over his shoulder, signifying his industry. To finance his marriage Wells had to maintain a punishing workload throughout 1890, teaching full-time while studying for the final stages of his B.Sc., a qualification that had recently acquired new significance.

Restless as ever, he had been looking round for alternative work, presumably through friends and agencies. In January the self-advertisement paid off when he found himself being headhunted by the University Correspondence College, an organization that offered tuition to people taking external examinations, mostly with the University of London. Its clients received lessons and practice questions by post, some face-to-face teaching in London or Cambridge and the opportunity to buy dedicated textbooks. In some respects a forerunner of the Open University, the college was especially valuable to women, who were still excluded from the more established universities but who could study as external students at London no matter where they lived. The college's biology tutor was quitting to become a professor in South Africa, and the proprietor, William Briggs, urgently needed a replacement, ideally someone with a good science degree that could be flagged up in the prospectus.

Science graduates were not easy to find in the 1890s, especially ones with teaching experience and a readiness to embark on an unorthodox career path. Briggs invited Wells to an expenses-paid interview at his office in Cambridge and, having looked him over, offered £2 per week in the first instance for marking practice questions. If Wells got his B.Sc., he could progress to a permanent job, the rate of pay depending on the class of the degree.

It was just the kind of opportunity Wells had wanted. He dutifully saw out his remaining two terms at Henley House School, but as early as February he was doing evening work for Briggs at 13 Booksellers Row, off the Strand in London. The College owned a laboratory over the premises of its publishing company, W.B. Clive, where tutors could demonstrate the skills needed for practical examinations.

Holding down two jobs while studying for a degree was stressful. Wells lamented the state of his 'poor little overcrowded brain' in a letter to Tommy Simmons, claiming that he was not so much 'worked out' as 'dead'.[1] Simmons was so alarmed that Wells had to send a follow-up letter explaining he had been exaggerating for comic effect, but it is easy to believe that he was often depressed and exhausted.

His reward came in January 1891 when he was awarded his Bachelor of Science degree with First Class Honours in Zoology and Second in Geology. At the age of twenty-four he had recovered from his undergraduate misadventures and become a certified man of learning. He had already taken out a subscription to the Royal Zoological Society, and in December 1891 he secured a further teaching qualification, Fellowship of the College of Preceptors with Honours, together with a Doreck Scholarship prize of £20.

Wells was now able to become a full-time employee of the University Correspondence College, working an average of nearly fifty hours per week. His students were self-motivated adults, pursuing their degrees through an arduous, alternative route to the traditional one of private school and Oxbridge, very different from the press-ganged schoolchildren Wells had been used to nagging and shoving in the past.

His comparative sympathy for his new charges is evident in a recollection by one of them, T. Ormerod, who describes Wells at this period as

> somewhat below average height, not very robust in health, with evident signs of poverty, or at least disregarding any outward appearance of affluence. In dress, speech and manner he was plain and unvarnished, abrupt and direct, with a somewhat cynical and outspoken scorn of the easy luxurious life of those who have obtained preferment and advantage by reason of social position or wealth . . . There were a real kindliness and a very evident sympathy towards his pupils, many of whom were struggling against poverty and disadvantage, to obtain a university degree.[2]

Wells's assistant, John Lowson, recalled

> a slim, fair, alert young fellow . . . with bright observant eyes, a thin wisp of a moustache, a quiet, easy, pleasant mode of speech . . . He was an excellent lecturer and demonstrator, genial and unaffected in his dealings with the students and always anticipating and ready to meet their difficulties.[3]

Lowson found Wells a sociable boss, happy to wind down at the end of the day over a pint of beer and give his assistant the benefit of his views on politics and society and to voice his literary ambitions before heading off to catch his train, often fitting in some last-minute marking on the journey home.

As a sideline to his new job, Wells found he was even able to do some paid writing. One of his colleagues at the college, Walter Low, edited the *Educational Times,* which was published by the College of Preceptors, the teachers' organization that had been figuring so helpfully in Wells's life ever since his first set of public examinations at the age of thirteen. Low received £50 for editing and writing the paper, plus a further £50 for paying the other contributors. He simplified his job considerably by passing the whole of the second sum to Wells, who as a result commented on educational issues frequently between 1890 and 1895. It was valuable journalistic experience; he credited Low with teaching him many tricks of the writer's trade.

In Walter Low, Wells seemed indeed to have found a soul mate: an intelligent young man, knowledgeable about literature and politics, eager to make something of his life, resentful of the prosperity around him, keen to grab some of it for himself, yet determined to do so on his own terms. Sadly, in five years' time Low would suffer the early death that Wells himself constantly feared.

Knowing his own frailty, Wells took the precaution of periodic health checks at a laboratory in South Kensington. He had a further haemorrhage at the end of the year, but Dr Collins assured him that his prospects for a long life were increasing. A period of rest at Uppark over Christmas would, none the less, be advisable. Compared to Wells's usual schedule, his Christmas 1890 visit to Uppark might have qualified as a rest, but it was a sufficiently active one to include the drafting of a significant pair of essays, 'The Universe Rigid' and 'The Rediscovery of the Unique'. In them, Wells got to grips constructively with his two rival visions of life.[4]

'The Universe Rigid' sets out his dread that, as physics and Christianity both seemed to imply, the cosmos is a closed, preprogrammed system. Seen by an omniscient observer, from a notional point outside space and time, it would be complete and incapable of change, devoid of any scope for free will.

In 'The Rediscovery of the Unique' he challenges that notion with an existentialist alternative, grounded in the evolutionary importance of variation within the species. Looked at in sufficient detail, every object that we can see turns out to be unique. Even two bullets, machine-made from the same mould, will have minute variations in texture and shape. If nothing is truly identical to anything else, perhaps all the way down to atoms, then logically no two events can be wholly identical. Two bullets fired from the same gun, one after another, may follow significantly different trajectories and have significantly different consequences. Life is therefore inherently unpredictable.

This view of life as a mysterious, individual adventure sides with Darwinian biology against Newtonian physics, and seems to be in line not only with human experience but with subsequent scientific ideas of indeterminacy and chaos. The 'Rediscovery' is argued with wit and verve and culminates in a peroration that fuses the religious and the secular, the prophetic and the scientific in a dramatic metaphor:

> Science is a match that man has just got alight. He thought he was in a room – in moments of devotion, a temple – and that his light would be reflected from and display walls inscribed with wonderful secrets and pillars carved with philosophical

> systems wrought into harmony. It is a curious sensation, now that the preliminary splutter is over and the flame burns up clear, to see his hands lit and just a glimpse of himself and the patch he stands on visible, and around him, in place of all that human comfort and beauty he anticipated – darkness still.

Here at last, with a little help from Walter Low, is the characteristic literary voice of H.G. Wells: the measured rhythms of the practised speaker, conceivably addressing a roomful of adult students, skilfully mixing general points with concrete examples, expanding and digressing yet always pacing himself so as to arrive in good time at a key phrase or image. And as he elaborates he drifts into something like a story. His voice fades to an almost subliminal prompt for our imaginations and we find ourselves picturing an anonymous explorer striking a match . . .

What the explorer sees would not materialize for another four or five years, but for a moment Wells had found the right path. He must have realized that the 'Rediscovery' was something of a breakthrough in his writing, as he at once submitted it to the *Fortnightly Review*, the organ of Victorian liberals and positivists, grown colourful and subversive under the editorship of Frank Harris who was already something of a notorious character, though not yet the author of the infamous *My Life and Loves*.

Wells was delighted when Harris accepted the essay, which appeared in July 1891. Shortly before publication he followed up his success by sending in 'The Universe Rigid' and was cautiously pleased when Harris summoned him to discuss it. Unfortunately, the reason Harris had sent for him was that, having read the piece in proof, he found it incomprehensible.

Not realizing what lay in store, the Fitzroy Road household prepared its champion for the literary summit. Wells donned his morning coat and took up his umbrella. It was a tatty umbrella, but it had a new elastic band and, provided it was not opened, looked respectable enough. His silk hat, apparently the same one he had acquired nine years previously at the Southsea drapery, was another matter. Aunt Mary would not let the rising author out of the house until its unhealthy texture had been attacked with a hard brush, a soft brush and repeated wiping with a silk handkerchief. Slightly flustered by the delay, Wells set off for the editorial office in Henrietta Street, where he was left to stew nervously for a while before being admitted to the presence of the formidable Harris and two assistants.

'I can't understand six words of it,' Harris told him bluntly. 'What do you *mean* by it? For Gahd's sake tell me what it is all *about*? What's the sense of it? What are you trying to *say*?' Drained of confidence, Wells made halting attempts to paraphrase, while Harris muttered, 'Gahd, the way I've been let in!' to the minions either side of him. The meeting culminated with the editor announcing the article would be pulled and the type dispersed.[5]

When he got home, filled with shame and anger, Wells took out his feelings on the hat, which, to the shock of his aunt, he proceeded to smash beyond repair. Its shabby finish seemed to him to sum up the lower-middle-class background that he had failed to rise above that day. He had intended to behave like a scientifically trained young man with the future in his bones; instead he had behaved like a servant summoned from below stairs.

Wells's literary prospects were not quite as bad as they felt, however, even if he had failed to capitalize successfully on his first major breakthrough. Being in the *Fortnightly* even once was an impressive addition to his CV. When the 'Rediscovery' appeared, many readers were impressed, including Oscar Wilde, who appreciated the gently subversive tone and paradoxical observations that to a degree resembled his own work and told Harris that he seemed to have found a writer of some potential.

Wells managed to place some scientific pieces with the *Gentleman's Magazine* during 1891–3. As well as his continuing work for the *Educational Times*, he began to receive payments for writing the College's newsletter, *The University Correspondent*. He maintained his presence in the South Kensington *Science Schools Journal* with 'Specimen Days', published in October 1891, an account of a cycle journey from Petersfield to Crawley made with Frank during July. By September he had even recovered sufficiently from his encounter with Harris to make a fresh attempt on him with a version of *The Chronic Argonauts*, suggesting that it was best to forget about 'The Universe Rigid'. Harris did forget the article; he also forwent the story.

As all these efforts at publication suggest, Wells had not entirely reconciled himself to a career teaching at the correspondence college. He felt some satisfaction at piloting his students past the gatekeepers of the Establishment, rejoicing in his first year that forty-nine of the college's students had passed the London University intermediate and preliminary science examination, the highest number ever reached by one institution, thirty of them taught by him, as against a mere nineteen taught by Jennings at Birkbeck. However, as time passed he could not, as an ambitious man, see any obvious career progression for himself and, as a socialist, he felt uncomfortable working for a profit-making company, however beneficial its effects on individuals' careers. He wanted to revolutionize the educational system, not drill people in how to produce exemplary examination answers without learning much actual biology. None the less, the probability was that Wells would gradually relinquish his literary and political ambitions and settle into the role of a college teacher with a sideline in educational and scientific journalism.

After a bout of flu in May 1891 had led to a further haemorrhage, Wells had to give up class teaching temporarily and confine himself to correspondence work from home. He looked around for alternative employment such as museum work but found no openings. The substitute college teacher was employed out of his salary, which had the drastic consequence that for the foreseeable future he could no longer afford to marry Isabel. Given his reservations about marriage as an institution and his awareness that he and Isabel were markedly different in temperament, this could have been a golden opportunity to break off the engagement with honour. But, while he seems to have entertained the idea, in the end it was out of the question for him:

> I wanted to marry; I had indeed a gnawing desire to marry, and my life in close proximity to my cousin was distressing and humiliating me in a manner she could not possibly comprehend.[6]

The jarring word 'humiliating' presumably suggests a forced dependence on masturbation. At some point in this period (Wells is vague about the date) he paid for sex with a prostitute:

> my secret shame at my own virginity became insupportable and I went furtively and discreetly with a prostitute. She was just an unimaginative prostitute.[7]

The mere act of sex was not, it turned out, what he wanted. In Isabel he had found a beautiful, companionable woman, and what he desired above all else was to possess her physically, to achieve shared fulfilment with her and to be carnally acknowledged as a man in his own right.

In due course Wells recovered sufficiently to resume his teaching duties. With his income restored, plus Briggs's agreement to pay for the writing of a textbook, he could press ahead with the marriage. He found a house to let at 28 Haldon Road, at the north end of Wandsworth. It was big enough to accommodate Wells, Isabel and Aunt Mary and was within walking distance of East Putney station, from which he could commute to Booksellers Row and, from December 1892, to better-equipped replacement premises in nearby Red Lion Square, Holborn. The house rented, the marriage took place at All Saints Church, Wandsworth, on 31 October 1891. Frank was there and wept, presumably overcome that his little brother had grown to be a man of such account: a graduate, a teacher, a journalist, a husband. If he had been able to look into his brother's heart he might have wept for other reasons too.

As an unbeliever, Wells would have much preferred to marry at a registry office or, better still, simply to have lived with Isabel. But as a respectable young woman, she could not countenance either of these options. One hundred years later, in the future that Wells would soon be struggling to foresee, things might have been very different. For a couple to live together without formal ties, or undertake a trial marriage, would become acceptable to respectable British society.

But that was not how it was in 1891, and Wells was therefore forced to marry against his convictions.

In this context the wedding night was nothing short of a disaster. He was 'avid' and fell upon her without any thought of foreplay. She was 'shrinking', passively 'submitted' and wept:

> I dried her tears, blamed my roughness, but it was a secretly very embittered young husband who went on catching trains, correcting correspondence answer books, eviscerating rabbits and frogs and hurrying through the crowded business of every day.[8]

The nearest thing to an explicit sex scene in Wells's fiction, written forty years later, depicts the first night of a similarly inexperienced couple. The man assails his wincing partner with 'insane energy', then, when he pulls himself out, is appalled to see blood on his penis. The only maidenhead he knew about was the one on the road to Reading. When he returns from washing himself, the woman angrily demands to know what he has done to her and points in horror at a 'dirty' condom he has left lying on the bed.[9]

How much this is a reflection of Wells's own experiences we cannot be sure. We are on safer grounds in saying that with two people who were fully committed to the marriage the failure of the wedding night would not have been significant. Since Wells had married to a considerable extent because he wanted to enjoy regular sex, Isabel's lack of response became a source of resentment that quickly poisoned their relationship. Wells felt that he had tried to conform to the expectations of society and had not received the satisfaction due to him.

Worse, once the lure of sex was past, their differences in temperament stood out more clearly. Biographers have tended to portray Isabel as placid and conventional, but what evidence we have suggests that she was a young woman of some initiative and enterprise with progressive views. However, she not only lacked the ready sexual passion on which Wells had been counting but was understandably reluctant to build their lives too firmly around the hope that her husband might write great books and change the world.

Part of Wells continued to love Isabel. They had, after all, been a couple for the best part of seven years and they had lived in the same house for nearly six. After something like two thousand nights lying in bed a few yards from her, wishing they were in one another's arms, he had built his emotional life around her to the point of obsession. Yet now another part of him, the part which was, to use his own word, 'embittered' by her lack of response, longed to punish her for the humiliation that she was nightly dealing him, the longing to punish being in proportion to the high expectations of bliss from which he had fallen. Very likely, as Nancy

Steffen-Fluhr suggests, what Wells really wanted from Isabel was the passionate recognition of himself in his own right, which he felt he had never obtained from his mother.[10]

The chance for revenge soon came. Isabel had decided to stop commuting to Regent Street and to retouch photographs at home, supplementing her income by training pupils. Ethel Kingsmill was one of the first. She had then been taken on as a helper and had worked at the house before Wells moved in. He describes her as 'cheerfully a-moral and already an experienced young woman'.[11] She certainly showed no great feelings of loyalty to her employer, and Wells was positively eager to betray his bride.

Wells suspected that Isabel had dropped a hint about his unreasonable lust to Ethel. At any rate he sensed some awakening of curiosity on her part. One day, when Isabel was taking some of her retouched negatives up to London, Aunt Mary out shopping and Wells marking college work, Ethel came downstairs to his study and began to flirt. One thing led to another:

> The sound of my returning aunt's latch-key separated us in a state of flushed and happy accomplishment. I sat down with a quickened vitality to my blottesque red corrections again and Ethel, upstairs, very content with herself, resumed her niggling at her negative.[12]

The fact that they were both violating a close relationship with Isabel seems to have made the act all the more shocking and thrilling for them. Significantly, Wells chooses to emphasize the moment when they might have been caught. A pleasure in risk-taking and defiance of propriety were emerging as important elements of his sexual behaviour.

But is his account the full story? The initiative is so regularly taken by the woman in Wells's confessions that it should put our suspicions on guard. Was it Ethel who made the first move that day, entirely out of the blue? Did he get together with her only the once and, if so, could she have been as 'content' with the experience as he claims? What was their relationship afterwards? When and how did Ethel stop working for Isabel?

The apparent frankness of Wells's reminiscences, especially concerning his love life after 1905, should never make us forget that we are reading what he wanted posterity to know. Just as with any other person boasting of their sexual conquests, the reality is likely to have been significantly different from the anecdote. With Wells, who felt keenly his lack of physical resemblance to an alpha male and longed to build self-esteem through his relationships with women, an element of self-deception is particularly likely.

Just as it seemed probable that Wells would settle into the ready-made work role of college teacher, so he now seemed likely to reproduce the family role inherited from his father: married to a woman with whom he was more and more out of sympathy, consoling himself with his paying hobby (in this case writing, rather than cricket), outbursts of cynicism and perhaps an occasional furtive affair. Late in 1892, however – after Wells had been married to Isabel for nearly a year – he encountered an educated and talented young woman, six years his junior, who became a serious rival to his wife and seemed to offer a chance of salvation.

Her name was Amy Robbins, though she preferred to be known by her middle name of Catherine. She was studying for a science degree through the correspondence college. Her father had recently been killed by a train, and she had decided to support herself and her mother as a high-school teacher. She appeared for the start of term in Wells's afternoon class still dressed in mourning. She sat with another bright female student named Adeline Roberts, and Wells was soon pulling up a stool between them to deal with questions in comparative anatomy that developed into freewheeling discussions of evolution, religion and society. Adeline was a Christian, but Catherine was very much in sympathy with Wells's secularist, reforming ideas.

When college was over the threesome would sometimes continue talking in a tea shop, Adeline's presence turning what might have looked suspiciously like an affectionate couple into an innocuous trio of friends. Since Catherine lived in Putney, the chats inevitably ended with Wells and Catherine taking the same train home.

> I thought her then a very sweet and valiant little figure indeed, with her schoolgirl satchel of books and a very old-fashioned unwieldy microscope someone had lent her, and I soon came to think her the most wonderful thing in my life.[13]

Wells didn't feel for Catherine the deep sexual obsession that he continued to feel for Isabel. She was physically attractive, none the less, and offered something Isabel did not, being not only more enthusiastic about his ideas but readier to look up to him as a teacher and to give him her unreserved support. It seems quite likely that she was seeking a father figure to replace the one she had just lost – another point raised by Nancy Steffen-Fluhr, who notes that Wells would in time manage to turn the tables and remake her into a kind of substitute mother figure. As the relationship developed, the two lent each other books and aspired to be platonic friends, but deep down Wells knew that was not really where he wanted to take the relationship or his life.

In the winter of 1892–3 that life consisted largely of teaching, preparing lessons, marking, contributing to the *Educational Times*, writing the *University Correspondent* and working on his *Text-Book of Biology*. This, Wells's first book, would appear in two volumes in 1893. The illustrations were by Wells himself, using his experience of drawing diagrams for Jennings. The introduction was by G.B. Howes, Huxley's former demonstrator. If this workload and the stress of marital unhappiness were not enough to be coping with, Wells now found himself confronted by two family crises.

In late November 1892 Sarah was told that her time at Uppark was coming to an end. The seventy-year-old gamely issued advertisements for similar employment, but no one replied. In January she was given a month's notice and on 16 February she finally left the place that had been her source of happiness and self-esteem. Wells and Isabel put her up for a few days at Haldon Road before she resigned herself to the inevitable and set off for Nyewood to resume family life with Joe and Frank. Wells sent his parents some college worksheets to copy out, hoping they would at least make a little money that way. Whether intended or not, this was another piece of revenge. Sarah and Joe had assigned him to unsuitable jobs for many years; now the situation was reversed.

In May 1893, when Wells was about to start preparing a Geology course, there came more bad news. Fred was being sacked from his drapery job in order to make way for his employer's son. Wells travelled to Wokingham to assess the situation and see if there was any way that his two brothers could be set up in business together, but it didn't look feasible. Rather desperately, he suggested an art scholarship at South Kensington. Eventually he would resort to Joe's old idea of emigration to the colonies.

In the meantime, on 17 May, all the stress became too much for Wells's health. He had been showing some fossils to a prospective student of the new Geology course. Around 9 or 10 p.m. he was lugging the bag of rocks along his usual route home down Villiers Street to the Underground station when he began to haemorrhage. Within a few minutes he was alone in a train compartment, sitting very still indeed, trying not to cough and clutching a handkerchief that had become bright red.

The attack seemed to pass. When he finally made it to Haldon Road he opted for defiance, hiding away the blood-stained handkerchief and eating a substantial supper. He was not going to go to bed early and he was not going to lose his teaching income. Defiance did not work. By three in the morning he was again struggling desperately not to cough:

> But this time the blood came and came and seemed resolved to choke me for good and all. This was no skirmish; this was a grand attack.
>
> I remember the candle-lit room, the dawn breaking through presently, my wife and my aunt in nightgowns and dressing-gowns, the doctor hastily summoned and attention focussed about a basin in which there was blood and blood and more blood. Sponge-bags of ice were presently adjusted to my chest but I kept on disarranging them to sit up for a further bout of coughing.[14]

Wells felt himself spluttering out of existence and wondering what the final reckoning of his life would be. He had let emotion and conventionality get the better of him and married the wrong woman. In order to achieve that marriage, he had, for the past five years, virtually given up his creative writing and his socialist commitments. If he had died that night, his memory would certainly not have troubled posterity. But, as it happened, he survived the attack, and, having done so, he began to redirect his life towards the dreams he had neglected.

6
AUTHOR
1893–1895

For a while, the course of Wells's life seemed unchanged. Recuperating, he enjoyed visits from several friends, including Elizabeth Healey and Catherine and played draughts with his brother Fred who had moved in to the Haldon Road house. For a man in the shadow of death Wells seems to have kept in good spirits.

Illness had finally freed him from the classroom. His old college friend Davies, still slowly working towards his own B.Sc. (he would ultimately attain a South Kensington professorship), agreed to take over the day-to-day teaching duties, while Wells remained the named specialist in the prospectus and continued the correspondence work. Though he assumed that he was in the process of dying young, Wells was determined to live out the rest of his life in a way that was true to himself. When Adeline Roberts tried to console him by sending him an evangelical book claiming traditional Christianity was unscathed by the findings of science, he sent her a stinging reply, though he soon regretted his blunt response to a well-meant gesture.

Wells was determined not to lapse into fear-inspired religious belief or into self-pity, preferring Carlyle's gospel of finding work that needed doing and applying oneself to it. In any case he had bills to pay and a reduced income. He arranged with Richard Gregory to write another textbook, *Honours Physiography*, for a one-off payment of £20, split between the two authors. Conception to publication took a brisk five months; the book appeared towards the end of 1893. The publisher was Joseph Hughes, an education specialist for whom Simmons and Gregory regularly worked. Like Wells and Bowkett in their schooldays, Wells and his college friends went in for reciprocal altruism, knowing that for men of their social and educational backgrounds the challenge of making a career would be greatly eased by mutual assistance.

Wells had pretty much dispatched his half of the textbook-writing by June 1893 when he went to Eastbourne with Isabel and Aunt Mary for a change of scene and some sea air. Even then, needing to keep up his income, he took along examination papers to mark and worked on articles commissioned by various educational journals. The family stayed at 6 New Cottages, Meads Road. Aunt Mary, who had become seriously ill, needed the break at least as much as he did. Fred did not accompany them, having in the interim been thrust on to a boat for Cape Town to seek his fortune, the British community there having grown increasingly prosperous since the recent discovery of gold.

Most days Wells spent several hours on the stony beach, soaking up the sun and conscientiously breathing the sea air before getting down to work in the evenings. Visiting a twopenny circulating library one day in search of an undemanding read, he happened upon a novel named *When a Man's Single* by J.M. Barrie, an up-and-coming writer still a decade away from the immortality of *Peter Pan*. It is easy enough to see why the title of Barrie's book caught Wells's eye, but it was what he found inside the covers that was to change his life. One of Barrie's characters, a writer named Simms, has a knack of turning trivial everyday objects such as a piece of straw or a flowerpot into subjects for light journalism, knowing that this kind of topic will have far more appeal to readers than heavy articles on politics, art or philosophy.

Intrigued by Simms's less-is-more formula, Wells at once produced an equivalent piece called 'On the Art of Staying at the Seaside' and mailed it for typing to his cousin Bertha Williams. He then submitted the article to the *Pall Mall Gazette*. The inconsequential but deftly written article was just the kind of agreeable filler the magazine needed. Wells was delighted when almost immediately he received a proof in the post.

He began to send in further articles that were also accepted, including the old 'Past and Future of the Human Race' paper for the Debating Society, rewritten as 'The Man of the Year Million'. A particularly successful piece, it first appeared in the *Pall Mall Gazette*, then with an illustration in the *Pall Mall Budget*, a weekly reprint of *Gazette* items, then was quoted in *Punch* with another illustration. Wells would eventually cap its success by building it into *The War of the Worlds.* Though he was not yet the creative author he had dreamed of being, he was soon making a living from writing, earning more after two months than he had done previously as a teacher. He was able to help support his parents as well as his immediate family at Haldon Road. His priority was to build on what he had achieved and not let the opportunity slip from him, as it had done after 'The Rediscovery of the Unique'.

Circumstances were on his side. The same expansion of education that had enabled him to escape from retail work and made possible his teaching jobs and science degree had also fostered a new level of mass literacy. By the middle of the 1890s more than two thousand magazines were in circulation in Britain and more than one thousand novels were being published every year, their readership multiplied many times over by library borrowing. The demand for print from an audience that did not yet have the alternatives of radio, television or the internet was making wealthy and eminent men of press barons such as ex-Henley House schoolboy Alfred Harmsworth, now publisher of the *Evening News* and *Comic Cuts*, with the *Daily Mail* poised on the drawing board. Wells, too, was in a position to profit. In 1893 he contributed sixteen pieces to the *Pall Mall Gazette*, but in 1894 a prodigious 111 to the *Gazette* and *Budget*.

Unlike many old-school authors, Wells knew the idiom and mentality of the lower middle classes from the inside. What he later called the 'pompous . . . patronizing and prosy' writing of the Oxbridge elite, respectful of orthodoxy, 'timid and indistinct in statement', was on its way out.[1] Once Wells had dropped his sights from philosophical issues to the everyday, he had an intuitive knowledge of what would appeal. In his writing as much as in his teaching for the correspondence college, Wells was not slotting into an existing type of job; he embodied the shift to a more democratic, middle-class culture.

With no further need to commute to Red Lion Square, the family decided to relocate to the cleaner air and sweeter prospects of Surrey. Isabel found a new home for them at 4 Cumnor Place (now 25 Langley Park Road) in Sutton, a prosperous commuter town about the same distance from London as Bromley. Isabel had suspicions about her husband's relationship with Catherine and may have hoped that a shift seven miles south would help curtail the friendship. Wells managed to dispose of his old house to Davies. For Wells, the move in August 1893 was a symbolic step towards health and success. He was certainly right about the latter, as commissions from editors kept on coming, though he may have overrated the benefits of country air; by October he was suffering from bronchitis.

In November Briggs asked Wells to revise Vol. 1 of the *Text-Book of Biology*. Its author's illustrations had not been nearly as well received as his text, so Wells enlisted Catherine to redo them, giving a convenient excuse for renewed contact with her. The book would be largely rewritten by Davies in 1898, to the fury of Wells who regarded the revision as a botched job, and lived on for several decades as a *Text-Book of Zoology*, with Wells, by then a best-selling author, prominently credited as its originator.

Alongside the growth of Wells's career as a writer, however, ran the deterioration of his marriage. In December Wells and Isabel paid a weekend visit to Catherine and her mother. Such an overnight stay was unusual for people who did not live particularly far apart and, as Lovat Dickson suggests, may have been a contrivance for Wells and Catherine to spend some time together.[2] On their return Isabel was not happy. Even in Wells's student days she had noticed a tendency for him to neglect her in favour of his more intellectual friends. It was plain to her that the relationship with Catherine had begun the same way and was going further. She put it to her husband that he had to choose between ending the friendship or the marriage.

Wells explained the situation in a letter to Davies, himself about to get married. He gives the impression that he had been enjoying the favours of both women and had initiated the break-up because of his own conscience, rather than because Isabel had put her foot down.[3] This may have been a piece of face-saving or he may have been preparing the ground for divorce, which at that time could be obtained only if one partner in the marriage had committed adultery. If the husband was the guilty party, the adultery had to be aggravated, at the very least by desertion. A divorce would not be granted if separation was by mutual consent.

Wells also confided the news to Gregory, asking him over, then explaining what had happened on a walk towards Banstead. He left Isabel the next day. Divorce being a taboo subject at that time, Sarah seems not to have received any kind of explanation until early February 1894 and even then she seems not to have discussed the matter with her husband, as Joe required a separate letter of elucidation as late as August. Wells indicated to his male friends that they might have to repudiate him and made it very clear to Elizabeth Healey that in his view she could not continue to associate with someone who had given his wife full grounds for divorce proceedings. Healey must have replied that she was resolved to carry on regardless, as their correspondence seems to have been unbroken.

It is not likely that Wells and Isabel would have gone ahead with the divorce if they had had children, but they had almost certainly been using contraception because of Wells's uncertain health. Though this would have been comparatively unusual at that time, Wells certainly followed this course in his second marriage. He had been a reader of the *Malthusian* in his teens and as a biology teacher was better placed than most people to find a supplier of contraceptives.

Wells moved out of Cumnor Place in January 1894, though he had to keep paying rent until June, and joined Catherine in ground-floor lodgings at 7 Mornington Place in North London. A return to the area of Wells's student days, though to a seedier part of it, this was a visible step down in the world. Publicly the couple pretended to be married to each other; privately they professed a disdain for marriage and a Romantic belief in free love. Catherine evidently saw herself as one of the liberated 'new women' of the period; her relatives, on the other hand, saw her as an innocent seduced by her teacher. Agitated visits from Mrs Robbins and intimidating ones from male relatives soon tipped off their landlady, Mme Reinach. Far from disapproving of their unmarried state, Mme Reinach was so pressing in her sympathy, her eagerness to know their secrets and to contribute her own confessions that Catherine, after returning to Putney for a few days to placate her mother, ended up arranging a move to premises in the next street.

Isabel, meanwhile, had found accommodation at 52 Broadhurst Gardens in Hampstead, where she lived at Wells's expense. Aunt Mary and Sarah both blamed her for the rift, presumably on the grounds that a husband whose wife was pleasing him wouldn't look elsewhere and that a wife fortunate enough to have a husband who was rising in the world ought to deal patiently with him. Isabel would later wonder if she had indeed been too hasty, and Wells, who was demonstrably polygamous by temperament, would certainly continue to yearn for her. In the immediate aftermath of the break-up he even tried to head her away from divorce.

Wells was no closer to realizing his sexual ambitions with Catherine than he had been with Isabel; he enjoyed only 'limited caresses and restricted intimacies'.[4] However, Catherine went much further than Isabel in subordinating her career to his, taking over some of his business affairs and acting as a sub-editor who offered constructive criticism of his drafts and deleted the unintended verbal repetitions to which he was prone. All of Wells's success in the coming decades was achieved with Catherine's active support. However, her duties meant that, though she had been a promising student, she never completed her degree.

It is tempting to interpret her subsequent life as the suppression of an independent woman by a domineering man, particularly since Wells deprived her even of her preferred name, replacing 'Catherine' with the plain monosyllable 'Jane' by which most of their mutual acquaintances would eventually come to know her. In fairness, there was not only a calculation on the part of 'Jane' that to be the mainstay of a successful man was her best chance to get what she wanted from life but also a genuine belief that her partner was a remarkably gifted individual who, with the correct support, could achieve great things and that she could achieve more by assisting him than she could do on her own.

By March the adulterous couple, whose extensive nicknames for one another also included 'Mr Binder' and 'Bits', were settled into a two-room apartment in 12 Mornington Road (now Mornington Terrace) with a more congenial landlady, Mrs Lewis. Wells's *Experiment in Autobiography* gives a glowing account of what must have been one of the most fulfilling periods of his life, reproducing many of the comic poems and 'picshuas' that poured from him in celebration of their life together. In the morning he and Jane would rise, wash, dress and read the post, hoping for cheques or some commissions, then breakfast on the coffee, eggs and bacon that Mrs Lewis had prepared.

> How vividly I remember the cheerfulness of that front room; Jane in her wrapper on the hearthrug toasting a slice of bread; the grey London day a little misty perhaps outside and the bright animation of the coal-fire reflected on the fire-irons and the fender![5]

After breakfast Wells would delve into the green, four-drawer cardboard box in which he kept all his notes and manuscripts, then set to work at his writing. Jane would make fair copies of his drafts, write, study or go out shopping. Later in the morning, when Wells had fulfilled his production quota for the day, they would stroll round Regent's Park or window-shop until dinner at one. In the afternoon they would go looking for material for future articles, investigating locations from London Zoo to Epping Forest. When it rained or after supper when they had had enough of work, they played chess or bezique and very occasionally entertained visitors such as Davies or a distant cousin of Wells, Owen Thomas, who was arranging the divorce. From time to time they went out for tea at Walter Low's.

Wells's fiction-writing career began to take off in the spring of 1894 after he paid a visit to the offices of the *Pall Mall Gazette* in Charing Cross Road. Finding himself in a magnificent drawing-room, he assumed that he was alone until he detected the sound of sobbing from behind a sofa, which proved to be the editor, Harry Cust, dealing with the emotional fall-out of his complicated love-life. At a discreet cough from Wells, Cust popped up, put away his handkerchief and, recovering his self-possession, told Wells how much he liked his work and asked how he had developed his writing skills and knowledge. Having done his best to provide an answer, Wells asked whether there was any chance of doing some book-reviewing to help build a regular income. Cust replied that he would bear it in mind, though there were no vacancies at present.

Cust then rang a bell to summon Lewis Hind, editor of the *Pall Mall Budget*. It had been decided that the *Budget* would cease to be a digest of the *Gazette* and become an independent weekly using original material. Perhaps Wells could be a contributor? Hind took Wells off to his much smaller office and made him a proposition. Wells's knowledge of science gave him some potentially very interesting subject matter that other authors did not possess. What if he were to produce some short stories – 'single sitting' stories, they would call them – that made use of this knowledge for, say, five guineas a time?

Cust's proposal was astute. Scientific progress had changed the world enormously during the lifetime of his readers. In the forty or so years since the Great Exhibition, railways, steamships and the telegraph had spread across the globe and been joined by new forms of transport such as bicycles, electric trams and trains and, more recently, prototype motor cycles and motor cars. Domestic developments, many still at a comparably early stage of development, included electric light, the telephone, the phonograph and the typewriter. Medicine was being revolutionized by anaesthetics, antiseptic surgery and vaccination, somewhat counterbalanced by the transformation of warfare by the machine gun. Significantly, the names behind the new technologies – Daimler, Pasteur, Edison, Bell – were less frequently British, as the initiative in research and development was passing to other nations, but every thinking person knew that their achievements would transform British life.

The public were more than ready to buy into fantastic tales that had an apparent basis in up-to-date science, rather than in old-fashioned magic and the supernatural. Hind was hardly the first to spot this artistic opportunity. Mary Shelley had begun the trend back in 1818 with *Frankenstein*, and since then many Victorian authors had tried their hand at the 'scientific romance'. But, in Wells, Hind had found someone who could bring unrivalled inside knowledge and personal conviction to the genre.

Wells agreed that the proposal was worth a try and went home to see what he could do. In June the *Budget* ran Wells's first paid venture in science fiction, 'The Stolen Bacillus', a comical story about a suicide terrorist who, in order to turn himself into a one-man plague, swallows what he erroneously believes to be cholera bacillus.

Once he got started, Wells found the challenge roused something deep in his imagination:

> I found that, taking almost anything as a starting-point and letting my thoughts play about it, there would presently come out of the darkness, in a manner quite inexplicable, some absurd or vivid little incident more or less relevant to that initial nucleus. Little men in canoes upon sunlit oceans would come floating out of nothingness, incubating the eggs of prehistoric monsters unawares; violent conflicts would break out amidst the flower-beds of suburban gardens; I would discover I was peering into remote and mysterious worlds ruled by an order logical indeed but other than our common sanity.[6]

Around thirty-five of Wells's short stories were published during 1894–5. Some read like practice exercises because that is what they are, but others are skilful pieces of light entertainment and a handful arguably cross the boundary into literature, which I shall define simply as writing that retains interest over the long term and compels and rewards rereading. For the most part Wells was not a practitioner of the modern short story as exemplified by Maupassant and Chekhov but of the traditional tall tale of Poe and Hoffmann, though refreshed with a contemporary tone and world view. His strongest stories are generally variations on a simple formula: something unexpected and exotic from a region as yet unconquered by science erupts into the everyday world and threatens to transform it.

'The Lord of the Dynamos', published in the *Pall Mall Budget* in September 1894, is a good example. Though it is set in an electricity-generating station for the London Underground railway, the unexpected factor does not come from the science of electromagnetics but from anthropology. The engineer who supervises the generators has a helper from the mysterious East whom he bullies and beats, metaphorically sacrificing him to the great dynamo they tend, only to be literally sacrificed to it in return. The dynamo-worshipper eventually kills himself as well, and Wells, the veteran freethinker, pronounces the verdict:

> So ended prematurely the worship of the Dynamo Deity, perhaps the most short-lived of all religions. Yet withal it could at least boast a Martyrdom and a Human Sacrifice.

'Withal' recalls those parodies of biblical language that Wells included in his letters from the Southsea drapery, but here the deviation of register is concentrated into a single word and dropped with pin-point precision into the final sentence, producing a surgical blast of satire at the expense of religion.

In contrast, 'The Remarkable Case of Davidson's Eyes', from the *Pall Mall Budget* of March 1895, is powerful because the narrator does not offer us any interpretation of the strange events. Davidson is a science teacher working in a college laboratory who, owing to a power surge from a thunderstorm, finds his field of vision transferred to an island on the other side of the globe. As he is led around or pushed in a wheelchair, his vision moves correspondingly around the island, at times passing through rocks, rising into the air or plunging into the sea. At the end of the story Davidson's sight gradually returns to normal, though, knowing that his unique vision will soon be lost, he becomes fascinated and obsessed by what had once horrified him until, in the end, after he marries the narrator's sister, the vision departs altogether.

It would be easy enough to turn this story into an allegory of some kind, but Wells declines to do so, leaving the piece open in its significance and disorientating in its effect, a mysterious experience for the reader as much as for the characters and, in this respect, a precursor to the riddling fantasies of Kafka. Wells was to develop this approach still further during the 1890s, becoming, as Bernard Bergonzi has argued, a symbolic and mythopoeic writer whose stories are closer to poetry than to normal realistic fiction.[7]

At the instigation of Cust, Wells made contact with another literary commissioner, William Ernest Henley: no mere magazine editor but a poet, critic, playwright and, perhaps his chief source of fame today, the model for Long John Silver in Stevenson's *Treasure Island*. Like the buccaneer, Henley was a powerful personality who liked to cultivate a swaggering, aggressive image as compensation for the amputation of his left leg below the knee. The gatherings of his protégés – known, inevitably, as the 'Henley Regatta' – included W.B. Yeats, who 'disagreed with him about everything, but . . . admired him beyond words'.[8] Yeats was dismayed when he found that Henley rewrote his poems before publishing them but consoled himself with the thought that he had probably done the same to Kipling a few years earlier. To be invited to Henley's riverside home near Putney was to have 'arrived' as an author.

Henley had, for six years, been editor of a magazine initially known as the *Scots Observer* and later, in a vain effort to broaden its appeal, the *National Observer*. Its low sales were in part due to its self-defeating combination of serious literature and jingoistic politics, repelling Conservatives and aesthetes in equal but opposite directions, but may also have been due to Henley's anti-Victorian readiness to deal openly with sex. When, for example, the *Graphic* serialized Thomas Hardy's *Tess of the D'Urbervilles* in an abridged version for family reading, the *Observer* happily published some of the 'adult' material that had been omitted. Henley conceded that his editorial policies meant he had had almost as many writers as readers, but he could certainly take pride in the class of writers that he attracted. Archer, Barrie, Gosse, Kipling, Mallarmé, Shaw and Swinburne were among them.

Henley, in his usual ebullient form, punctuating his speech by beating violently on the table with a paperweight, offered Wells a chance to become one of that visionary company. Wells in response went home and dug out his secret weapon, the *Chronic Argonauts.* In the years since it had first appeared in the *Science Schools Journal,* he had produced another draft in which Nebogipfel travelled into the future to find a world of idle aristocrats and underground labourers, a world that exploded into violent revolution. Dissatisfied, Wells had junked the character of Nebogipfel altogether and revised the dystopian future so that the oppression of the masses was achieved by hypnotism, though, in Davies's opinion, this was no improvement at all. Now, bearing in mind the success of his articles, Wells recast the story as a series of semi-fictional essays and mailed a sample to Henley for assessment.

Henley having found it agreeable, the first episode appeared on 17 March 1894. Disappointingly for Wells, it was an anonymous series without even a general title, though the second part carried the heading 'The Time Machine'. The new version bore little resemblance to the old *Chronic Argonauts.* For one thing, the Gothic trappings had been entirely shed, Wells having, possibly at the suggestion of Henley, undertaken 'a cleansing course of Swift and Sterne' in his efforts to improve his writing.[9] For another, it was no longer a narrative but a series of dialogues between an anonymous expositor – first known as the philosophical investigator, then as the time traveller – and an audience of stereotypes who gather at his house (an argumentative man with red hair, a German officer who exclaims 'Gott in Himmel!' and so on).

The series resembles Wells's science articles in so far as the time traveller uses Socratic discussion to convey mind-broadening ideas. However, there is also the outline of a story. The time traveller enters a world more than ten thousand years in the future, when the human race has evolved into two separate species, child-like creatures on the surface of the earth and ape-like 'Morlocks' below ground. When the Morlocks take an interest in his time machine, the Traveller fights them off and returns to the present. The story continually gives way to discussion, but there are enough dramatic moments and descriptions to suggest its potential if it were reworked as a full-blooded piece of fiction.

Seven instalments of the series were published at irregular intervals. Unfortunately, during April 1894 the *National Observer* was taken over by a new proprietor who disposed of Henley, then set about weeding out the less commercial material from the magazine. With the 23 June 1894 instalment Wells's contributions were terminated. The series has a reasonably satisfactory conclusion, however, suggesting that Wells had been forewarned.

Ironically, the time-travel series is very much a document of its age, not one for all time. This is typical of Wells's early writing, which is generally impressive for industry and facility rather than for lasting literary merit. While Wells's articles on education and science are informative and witty, they never quite escape the stiff tone of Victorian journalism. The 'filler' articles are livelier but have correspondingly little content and rarely do more than agreeably take us out of ourselves for a few moments. The time-travel series was apparently an attempt to produce a more substantial and sustained kind of writing by fusing the science articles with the lighter approach, but it did not quite come off and, with hindsight, is chiefly of interest in relation to Wells's early short stories.

Geoffrey West notes that in the short stories Wells is cannily synthesizing the styles and subjects of a number of successful contemporaries, from the exotic realism of Kipling to the Cockney humour of Pett Ridge.[10] More significant in retrospect is the recurrent conflict between, on the one hand, naturalism, a variation on realism in which life is portrayed as squalid and meaningless, with human beings little more than the victims of heredity and environment (the kind of fiction one might expect a convinced Darwinian to write) and, on the other, a militant fantasy supposedly endorsed by science but with its roots in Wells's religious upbringing and his own experience of self-transformation.

The limited, dispiriting world is the closed universe of late-Victorian Britain from which Wells wished to escape, while the fantastic symbolizes the alternative vision he found in science, politics and literature and which offered him a sense of hope. The conflict is summed up by an image used in 'Davidson's Eyes' and elsewhere in Wells's writing, of a 'dissolving views' slide show, where, as one picture merges into the next, the two overlap for a moment, neither taking precedence. Two incompatible views of life are experienced – the cynical and the ideal – and only time can show which kind will prevail.

John Huntington has suggested that one of Wells's early comic stories can be read as a kind of artistic and political manifesto.[11] In 'The Hammerpond Park Burglary', published in the *Pall Mall Budget* in July 1894, a burglar disguises himself as a landscape painter in order to steal jewels from a country house. Wells the writer and Watkins the burglar are both lower-class tricksters who take on the role of artist in order to break into the world of affluence, naturally epitomized for Wells by a country house like Uppark. Watkins's anger at the painters who query his artistic technique perhaps reflects Wells's exasperation with the judgements passed on him by magazine editors and prefigures his later touchiness at criticism from self-consciously artistic authors.

But Huntington has another, more subtle point to make. As Wells veers between

Cockney and upper-class speech, and plain and literary diction, he is also drawing upon conflicting aspects of his own identity, particularly the tensions between his respectable, upwardly mobile self and the concealed revolutionary who defies the marriage contract and dreams of a socialist utopia.

The story includes passages of brazen 'fine writing' that are a marker of art in the Establishment sense – an art that Wells notes in his opening paragraph would be spoiled by any 'mercenary element' – yet the story itself exists to obtain a much-needed payment of five guineas from Hind. Its concluding paragraph leaves us with the image of Watkins's easel standing in the park and the observation that 'One brief uncivil word in brilliant green sullied the purity of its canvas.' Huntington suggests that the unspoken profanity constitutes Wells's defiance of the literary Establishment and its narrow-minded, patronizing expectation that art equates only with pure and disinterested composition.

Seven years previously, in 'The Devotee of Art', Wells had set up a conflict between commitment to art and to love of a wife called Isabel. He now reworked the piece as 'The Temptation of Harringay' (*St James's Gazette*, February 1895), omitting the wife and concentrating exclusively on the artist. The picture with which the inept portrait painter Harringay is struggling gradually metamorphoses into that of a devil who offers him the chance to produce masterpieces in return for his soul. After a slapstick battle, Harringay succeeds in painting over the face, retaining his soul but losing his only chance to produce great art – leaving him in fact with a piece of pale green canvas which might have passed for a masterpiece in the era of Rothko. The story is a skilful and original piece of humour, but, from the biographical point of view, it leaves us wondering whether Wells is laughing derisively at the idea of art being sinful or laughing disdainfully because he has now turned away from the woman he loved and chosen the compromising career of the artist, embracing the destiny that Harringay was too weak to follow.

If Wells had entered into a Faustian pact, it was certainly not rewarding him with a primrose path. He was experiencing gland problems in his jaw, Jane was diagnosed as possibly tubercular and her mother was severely ill. In a renewed search for cleaner air than was available in the polluted atmosphere of London, all three decamped in July to lodgings at Tusculum Villa, 23 Eardley Road, Sevenoaks, a commuter town twenty-two miles south-east of London. The aim seems to have been to rent for the short term, while scouting the area for an affordable home. Jane's mother tried to rent out her old house in Putney, but, the first tenant having flitted, she eventually sold it and invested the money.

Life at Tusculum Villa proved considerably less jolly than that at Mornington Road. Relations between Wells and his supposed mother-in-law remained strained. She would sometimes have to eat in her room because she could not bear the company of the man who had led her daughter into disgrace. A similarly negative view was taken by the landlady when she found a writ from the divorce court in a drawer. She had already complained about the number of wild flowers brought into the house and the amount of lamp-oil used by Wells in his writing and had tried to add an extra sixpence to the bill for each meal Mrs Robbins took in her room. Now she lapsed into uniformly poor service and peppered her speech with scathing comments, even if she could not actually tax Wells and Jane with living in sin without admitting that she had read their mail.

There was worse to come, however, for Wells's writing career took a sudden downturn. In a letter to Joe that August Wells still sounds bullish. He refers to the *Pall Mall Gazette* as his staple source of income and announces that, with so many other journals now taking his writings, he is dropping his remaining college work. Placing short stories is still comparatively difficult, but he has hopes that the series in the *Budget* will change that. An agent is already working on getting some of the *Gazette* articles reprinted as a book, while Wells is working on a 'longer thing on spec'.[12]

We shall come to the 'longer thing' shortly. The agent was A.P. Watt, the first literary agent in Britain. Wells placed some work through him but did not hand over all his negotiations as he thought Watt overly preoccupied with more established and profitable authors such as Conan Doyle.

Soon after Wells wrote to Joe, problems developed. The new editor of the *National Observer* showed little interest in further contributions. The *Pall Mall Gazette* started to send his work back. The *Pall Mall Budget*, which had offered a secure market and prompt pay for the 'single sitting' stories, began to wind down towards closure in March 1895. Suddenly the Wells family income fell significantly below its expenditure.

Since magazines were holding unpublished work in proof, there seemed no point in writing further articles or stories for them. Instead, Wells gave a couple of weeks' undivided attention, plus subsequent tinkering, to the 'longer thing' that he had mentioned to Joe. This was the conversion of the *National Observer* time-travel series into a proper book-length story. Henley had told Wells that if he succeeded in starting up a new magazine he would be interested in serializing a fictionalized version of the time-travel idea.

Harassed from one side by Mrs Robbins, from the other by the landlady, with his career prospects fading and Jane visibly wilting under the pressure, Wells escaped into the expanding universe of his imagination. The time-travel story was not a piece of hack work; it was a project that meant a great deal to him. He had cultivated it for six years and judged that he had now developed the skills to realize the potential he sensed in it. Without having to worry too urgently about how an editor would react, he also had the time to listen to his intuitions and give free rein to his imagination.

Henley read the draft in September. He had had a terrible year, not just because of the loss of the *National Observer*. On 11 February 1894 his only daughter Margaret had died of cerebral meningitis, aged five. Her death plunged Henley into misery and erratic behaviour during his last years, but he did his best to live up to the creed of his famous poem 'Invictus', aspiring to be master of his fate, captain of his soul.

Despite his mental state, Henley could tell a good thing when he saw it and he declared Wells's draft to be enormously exciting. He advocated getting in touch with Heinemann, the publisher through whom he hoped to set up the new monthly magazine. By November 1899 the magazine was looking like a done deal, and by December Henley was requesting an urgent rewrite of the opening chapter ready for serialization. By September, too, the *Pall Mall Gazette* had regained its appetite for Wells's work. It turned out that its literary editor, novelist H.B. Marriott Watson, had been on holiday and the temporary blockage had been caused by a substitute who took a less enthusiastic view of Wells's efforts.

Jane had failed to find another landlady in Sevenoaks who was willing to take in the family, so in September Wells and Jane retreated to London, where, fortunately, their former rooms at 12 Mornington Road were still free. Poor Mrs Robbins, whom fate had robbed in succession of husband, daughter and house, could only billet herself on some friends in north London and await developments.

Her daughter's seducer, in contrast, found his fortunes were well and truly on the up. In the autumn Frank Harris left the *Fortnightly Review* and bought a controlling interest in the *Saturday Review*, which he briskly proceeded to turn into the leading weekly of its day. Measured, anonymous articles were replaced with lively, opinionated ones and the contributors included named crowd-pullers such as Kipling, Hardy, Shaw, Beerbohm, Cunninghame Graham and Arthur Symons. Harris was keen to enlist up-and-coming talent, even the perpetrator of 'The Universe Rigid'. He summoned Wells and Walter Low to the paper's office in Southampton Street. By the time Harris got round to seeing them it was lunchtime, so he spirited them off to the Café Royal, where they dined in high style while he held forth about how his new publication would sweep away the stuffy, genteel traditions of the Victorian era. Between November 1894 and April 1897, Harris gave Wells a prestigious new home for his science articles, reviews of scientific books and more.

Wells's career was now back in an upward spiral, each success leading to another. By December he had become a sufficiently well-known figure to speak on science teaching to the College of Preceptors, with his speech printed the following month in the *Educational Times*. In January 1895, the month that his divorce from Isabel came through, he became the drama critic of the *Pall Mall Gazette*, and from March he added to his jobs for the *Saturday Review* the role of principal fiction reviewer.

The job of drama critic at the *Gazette* was an unexpected and not entirely welcome one. Following Wells's requests for some regular income, Cust had sent him occasional books to review and had promised that Wells could have whatever vacancy next occurred. On 2 January 1895 Cust presented him with tickets for Wilde's *An Ideal Husband* the following evening. Wells, taken aback, felt obliged to confess that, apart from the Crystal Palace pantomime and some Gilbert and Sullivan operas, he had only twice been to a theatre. Cust replied that the fresh view of an outsider was exactly what he wanted. Leaving the office, Wells hurried to Charles Street in the theatre district (now Charles II Street), where an obliging tailor agreed to make him evening clothes in twenty-four hours. Respectably kitted out, Wells made it to the Haymarket Theatre in time for the first night and posted his copy into the Mornington Road pillar box before the 2 a.m. deadline. Cust was pleased enough with what he received for Wells to continue with the job.

On 5 January an assignment at the St James's Theatre brought him into contact with an American expatriate and an Irish one, both of whom would in due course become his intellectual sparring partners, Henry James and Bernard Shaw. James, having composed classic works of fiction for two decades, was now trying his hand at commercial drama with a play called *Guy Domville.* The play was comparatively well received by the more cultured part of the audience in the stalls but made a poor impression on the majority, as the hapless playwright discovered when the actor-manager George Alexander led him out to make his opening-night speech.

Wells recalled the occasion in his autobiography:

> I have never heard any sound more devastating than the crescendo of booing that ensued. The gentle applause of the stalls was altogether overwhelmed. For a moment or so James faced the storm, his round face white, his mouth opening and shutting, and then Alexander, I hope in a contrite mood, snatched him back into the wings.[13]

Witnessing James's humiliation no doubt helped Wells resist the power of the older man's gravity and reputation when he pressed artistic advice on him in later years.

Shaw had recently become the *Saturday Review*'s drama critic. In the decades since Wells had seen him speak at Fabian meetings, Shaw had remained a prominent socialist but had also made a name for himself as an outstanding music critic and a growing force in the theatre, co-author with William Archer of the *Quintessence of Ibsenism* and sole author of two highly controversial Marxist plays, *Widowers' Houses* and *Mrs Warren's Profession*, plus his recent commercial breakthrough, the comedy *Arms and the Man.* Wells had reservations about Shaw's intellectual indiscipline, referring to him in a letter of 1894 as a 'giddy creature', but happily seized the chance to make his acquaintance, perhaps remembering that when he was an invalid six years previously he had dreamed of working for him.[14] The two walked homewards together, Shaw lecturing his younger colleague about the theatre.

Wells continued to review plays, including in February 1895 the first performance of Wilde's *The Importance of Being Earnest*, but by May he was growing weary of the time-consuming nature of the work and, finding streaks of blood in his handkerchief, took the opportunity to resign on health grounds. His theatrical stint is commemorated in 'The Sad Story of a Dramatic Critic', a comic piece published in the *New Budget* that August. The critic of the title, Egbert Cummins, shares Wells's distaste for melodramatic acting but finds that the more plays he sees, the more his own behaviour becomes contaminated by it. Finally reduced to little more than a preposterous set of affectations, he is dumped by his fiancée and has no choice but to embrace the ultimate indignity and become an actor himself.

Wells was determined not to fall victim to the conformity he caricatured in Cummins and be passively absorbed into the literary scene, yet he was aware that, as he took on new roles in life he would need to construct a revised persona for himself. As the Invisible Man and Kipps would later find, suitable clothes and behaviour are necessary for such an enterprise. Discarding the silk hat of the drapery apprentice and purchasing suitable evening dress for the theatre were only part of the process needed to fit into the role of successful man of letters, soft-peddling, for the time being at least, his lower-class origins and his radical agenda for the future.

In 1894, after attending a formal dinner party at Verrey's in Regent Street to mark the closure of the *National Observer*, Wells felt he had been in danger of making a fool of himself over the unfamiliar cuisine. He and Jane therefore made a point of trying out different types of drink and ordering a range of food in affordable Soho restaurants. It was of course an excuse to enjoy themselves, but that, too, was a change of mentality, away from lower-middle-class prudence towards a more fulfilling way of life.

Wells was able to resign from drama criticism because, thanks to Harris, he had realized his ambition of a steady source of income through book reviewing. Now he could scoop up armfuls of likely volumes from the *Saturday Review* office and carry them back in a hansom cab to Mornington Road, where he and Jane would draft reviews to be written up in his fallow periods between stories and articles. The first batch of books consisted of fourteen titles. Over the next two and a half years Wells would review nearly three hundred, affording him an ideal opportunity to reflect on what constituted good fiction. One of his favourite titles was Hardy's *Jude the Obscure*, reviled by critics, lending libraries and the Church but hailed by Wells as 'a book that alone will make 1895 a memorable year in the history of literature'.[15] He insisted that Gregory and Simmons read it, knowing they, too, would appreciate its honest depiction of sex and identify with the lower-class Jude's struggles to achieve a university education.

One consequence of Wells's constant engagement with the writings of his contemporaries, and his conscientious reading of classics, is that his own fiction is informed by a strong sense of kinship to and dissent from other authors. His work is highly 'intertextual', imitating and parodying other books, as well as making explicit references to them. Despite its brevity, *The Island of Doctor Moreau*, for example, refers to Hugo, Huxley and Milton, and alludes to a range of sources including Swift, Kipling, Shakespeare, Mary Shelley, Darwin and the Bible, while *The Wheels of Chance*, a breezy comic novel of a similar length, packs in more than twenty explicit references to writers, including contemporaries such as Besant, Braddon, Corelli, Conan Doyle, Egerton, Gissing, Rider Haggard, Ibsen, Kipling, Ouida, Schreiner and Shaw.

While Wells was taking his place alongside these notables in the republic of letters, he was horrified to learn that his friend Walter Low was dying of pneumonia. Aware that he could perish just as suddenly and swiftly, Wells had decided to make his mark as quickly as possible by publishing several books during 1895, each from a different publisher, each distinct in its appeal. This scattergun approach maximized the chance that at least one book would catch on with the public.

His likeliest offering, 'The Time Traveller's Story', ran as the opening serial of Henley's *New Review* from January to May 1895. Henley was paying £100 for it, and Heinemann, which had a policy of attracting up-and-coming authors with generous terms, had promised an advance of £50 plus a 15 per cent royalty for 10,000 copies of the book version, which would appear under the title *The Time Machine*. Wells confided to Elizabeth Healey, 'It's my trump card and if it does not come off very much I shall know my place for the rest of my career.'[16] He had also been corresponding with John Lane, publisher of the fashionable literary and art periodical the *Yellow Book*, about putting together a collection of his magazine pieces, either humorous or scientific.

By Christmas 1894 he had drafted a second scientific romance, initially called, rather unpromisingly, *Mourget* – later improved to *Doctor Moreau*. By January Watt had Methuen interested in this project as well as in a collection of short stories, though Methuen eventually passed on *Moreau*, which Wells himself admitted was 'a trifle gruesome',[17] and opted for the short stories, which had already proved their appeal in magazines, leaving Lane to pick up the humorous pieces. Wells completely rewrote *Moreau* during 1895 and by the summer had placed it with Heinemann as their follow-up to *The Time Machine*.

Despite his workload of stories, reviews and articles, by the end of April 1895 Wells had also produced a 10,000-word sample of another book, *The Wonderful Visit* and was promising to have a finished version for the publisher, Dent, by the end of May.

Wells was keen to maximize his income because, in addition to supporting his parents and Jane, he was now paying £100 a year alimony to Isabel. He felt guilty about her situation, not unreasonably blaming himself for what had happened, and worrying that she lacked friends to support her after Aunt Mary's recent death. However, even with a few days off in Sidmouth during March, he had little time to meditate on past errors. There were books and articles to write and yet another house move to organize.

The return to London had always been intended as a temporary expedient, and with money raised from Mrs Robbins's old home the family now attempted a fresh move away from the smoke, this time twenty-five miles south-west of London, to a semi-detached house named 'Lynton' in Maybury Road, Woking. It was sited beside the railway line to London but also near a canal for canoeing and a heath for walking and cycling. Wells, Jane and Jane's mother moved in May 1895 and were settled in by the time the two books that marked Wells's establishment as a creative writer appeared on consecutive days. The two volumes could scarcely have been more different.

The first, which came out on 28 May, was *Select Conversations with an Uncle (Now Extinct) and Two Other Reminiscences*, published in a limited edition in London by John Lane in a series called 'The Mayfair Set' and in New York by Merriam. It was dedicated to 'My Dearest and Best Friend, R.A.C.', either a misprint for the initials of R.A. Gregory or, more likely, of Jane (Amy Catherine Robbins). The book contains twelve conversations between George, a figure based on Wells, and a fictitious uncle, plus two comic stories that also take the form of conversations. The *Athenaeum*'s description of it as 'a dreary and foolish assemblage of commonplace ideas expressed in stilted phraseology' is harsh but not entirely unjust.[18]

The Time Machine: An Invention, published the following day by Heinemann and dedicated to Henley, is a very different proposition. While the pieces in *Select Conversations* are designed to slot smoothly into magazines, *The Time Machine* stands out as unique, even visionary. 'H.G. Wells, who is writing the serial in the *New Review*, is a man of genius', the *Review of Reviews* had declared. The *Daily Chronicle* called the book a 'new thing under the sun . . . a strikingly original performance'.[19] In its confident leading of the reader into stranger and stranger worlds of the imagination, moving through mystery and violence to a hard-won sublimity, there had surely never been anything like it.

Carlyle had complained that the modern age substituted machinery and mechanical processes of thinking for intuitive awareness of the spiritual or, as he called it, the invisible. Embracing the accusation, Wells envisions a machine that can take us where previously only the speculative mind has gone, backwards and forwards through the invisible dimension of time, hunting for an authoritative perspective. With its saddle and controls, the time machine resembles one of the most liberating of Victorian inventions, the bicycle – or, more accurately, the tricycle, which was a much more stable vehicle than the nineteenth-century bicycle. Wells had been riding one since his teens and in 1892 had joined the Cyclist Touring Club. He knew from personal experience how cycling had allowed people of limited means, especially the young, to pursue freedom and adventure.

Used to machines working apparent miracles, readers are quickly drawn into the view of life to which the time machine transports them, sensing that it represents more than just an extremely tall story. The time traveller himself disarmingly sweeps aside the whole issue of representation, inviting the reader to consider his tale a dream in the workshop and judge it on its merits as fiction.

One reason that *The Time Machine* strikes us as more than a conventional story – one which, whatever its status, has something important to convey – is that in a condensed, ironic fashion it has many of the features of the epic. As a scientist and an explorer, the time traveller embodies the ascendant forces of his era. His journey dramatizes the assumptions and implications of his civilization, while affording opportunities for heroic battle against other-worldly foes. The setting is correspondingly grand in scale, ranging across the millennia to the last days, with allusions to the Triassic age, the Battle of Hastings, modern Africa, even Homer. The opening of the book announces the arguments and issues before plunging straight into the middle of the action – the time machine, having already been built, is now ready to be trialled – and in due course there is a revelatory journey into the underworld, where the traveller descends from the land of the gentle surface-dwellers, the Eloi, to confront the subterranean Morlocks.

The Time Machine departs most obviously from the conventions of the epic by a conspicuous absence of gods. The name 'Eloi' echoes the words of Jesus dying on the cross: 'Eloi, Eloi, lama sabachthani?' – 'My God, My God, why hast thou forsaken me?'[20] The Morlocks' name recalls the biblical Moloch, often taken to be a god to whom children were sacrificed, in effect a name for ritualized infanticide. By definition the traveller's godless quest cannot deliver a supernatural insight into the meaning of existence.

Instead, the traveller tries to understand the world of the Eloi scientifically, through a series of hypotheses, refined as new facts come to light. His original utopian interpretation proves to be literally superficial, for beneath the charming surface of the Eloi's world is that of the Morlocks. At first he takes the subterraneans to be servants, the surface dwellers having evolved from the upper classes and the underlings from manual workers, but eventually he realizes that, even if this were once the case, the relationship must have reversed over time and the Morlocks have now become the dominant species, breeding the Eloi for their meat.

The vicious fight scenes between the traveller and these supposed descendants of nineteenth-century labourers surely echo Wells's childhood feelings about the battles fought on Martin's Hill against the National School Water Rats but with a new, adult perspective. Picking up the concluding image from his 'Rediscovery of the Unique' article, Wells sends his scientific explorer down into the 'lower stratum' to cast light from his matches and lay bare the secret we would rather not see, that in the struggle for existence all human life entails exploitation of other living creatures, animal or human, for meat or labour.

The locations of this unwelcome discovery are beacons of respectability – Richmond, Wimbledon, Banstead – ironically rendered more beautiful and tranquil by the power of Wells's imagination. The deceptive pastoral landscape into which he transforms them owes something to Kew Gardens and something to William Morris's *News from Nowhere*, an eco-friendly Marxist Utopia that Wells rejected as naïve. The Palace of Green Porcelain stands out as a 'latter-day South Kensington', now fallen into neglect and decay.[21] However, the chief model for the corrupt world of the future, a lovely estate enjoyed by unearned privilege while unused potential festers in underground passages, is plainly Uppark.

The Time Machine satirizes class division, depicting a world that has decayed because it failed to evolve a progressive middle class with a constructive socialist agenda. It also mocks glib faith in future perfection, particularly the beliefs of Christianity and Marxism that humanity will one day resolve itself into two neatly differentiated groups, the saved and the damned, the proletariat and the bourgeoisie. However, Wells does not spell out his 'messages'. Leaving us to evaluate the nightmare world of 802,701 as best we can, the traveller presses on more than thirty million years into the future to find out how the story of the human race concludes.

The outcome is inevitable. Human beings have become extinct and only a few lower forms of life are left, slowly devolving back into sea creatures. Because the traveller could not survive the actual end of the world, Wells gives us a symbolic eclipse, described in ominous, atmospheric detail:

> The darkness grew apace; a cold wind began to blow in freshening gusts from the east, and the showering white flakes in the air increased in number. From the edge of the sea came a ripple and whisper. Beyond these lifeless sounds the world was silent. Silent? It would be hard to convey the stillness of it. All the sounds of man, the bleating of sheep, the cries of birds, the hum of insects, the stir that makes the background of our lives – all that was over. As the darkness thickened, the eddying flakes grew more abundant, dancing before my eyes; and the cold of the air more intense. At last, one by one, swiftly, one after the other, the white peaks of the distant hills vanished into blackness. The breeze rose to a moaning wind. I saw the black central shadow of the eclipse sweeping towards me.[22]

The irreligious implications of the silence and darkness were not lost on R.H. Hutton, reviewing the book in the *Spectator*, who noted disapprovingly the absence of divine purpose.[23] Closer inspection might have shown that the book was even more subversive than he appreciated. In a blasphemous parody of religion, the time traveller is a prophet with no message of salvation and a messiah who is incapable of rescuing the Eloi from the hell being prepared below them; like Jesus, the traveller concludes his mission by returning into the invisible world and failing to reappear, leaving his story to be passed on to those prepared to believe it.

It is highly characteristic of Wells that, even as he parodies religious mythology, he depends on it to give shape to his ideas. None the less, *The Time Machine* amounts to a forceful repudiation of Sarah Wells's Christian beliefs, and the positive recognition that it received was an apparent vindication. Wells had rejected Christianity, thrown up one job after another, even broken his marriage vows, yet he had still made a career and a name for himself. After years of rebellion, he had now made his point decisively.

Wells had not, however, shed the influence of his parents. The time traveller, with his curiosity about life, his propensity to gaze up at the stars for inspiration and his bursts of aggression, sounds like a distant relative of Joe. His tale is reported by an anonymous, self-effacing narrator, committed to getting through life from day to day and dealing with whatever it brings, who is more similar in temperament to Sarah. If, at a rhetorical level, the double narration is a way of framing the story to make it more believable and distance us from its horrors, at a personal level it is a way to give a hearing to both sides of its author, the reckless dreamer and the hard-working, practical man, just as it had been eighteen years earlier in *The Desert Daisy*.

The Time Machine sums up Wells's view of the cosmos. Having flung himself against an apparently rigid universe, the individual may find he is miraculously able to free himself from his immediate destiny, as Wells himself had done, but that freedom will inevitably prove to be limited. It is possible to vault over one's own death by looking into the distant future and transferring some of one's personal concern to the human species, as Wells again had done, but eventually the human race will die out and the earth come to an end.[24] Perhaps this view should leave the reader feeling despondent, but that is not the effect of the book. Instead, we are elated by the power of Wells's imagination and absorbed in the time traveller's quest.

The tension between immediate possibility and ultimate failure strongly echoes the thinking of T.H. Huxley in 'Evolution and Ethics', which he delivered as a lecture in 1893 and expanded for publication in 1894. Huxley rejects the crude Social Darwinist idea that civilization is simply a struggle for survival. On the contrary, human beings are engaged in an unending battle to contain that demeaning struggle and replace it with a more caring world that answers to their needs and ethical sense. However, this 'State of Art' can never be more than partially realized and is always destined to be destroyed by the 'State of Nature' surrounding it.

Wells did not share Huxley's views in every respect but would have broadly agreed with this perspective. He would have added that the state of nature lies within us, too. Human nature is a mix of competition and cooperation that evolved to suit Stone Age conditions and is often wrong-footed by the circumstances of modern living. Much of his fiction of the 1890s explores the darker implications of humanity's precarious position, under threat from without and from within. Wells acknowledged Huxley's influence by sending him a complimentary copy of *The Time Machine* as soon as it was in print. Huxley did not reply. He was busy losing his own personal battle with nature, dying exactly a month after the book was published.

The narrator of *The Time Machine* tries to end on a positive note by endorsing the obvious alternative to religious or political salvation – that is, finding meaning in life through personal relationships. However, the only example of the 'mutual tenderness' championed in the Epilogue is the traveller's 'queer friendship' with one of the Eloi called Weena, who we are twice told is 'exactly like a child'.[25] This dubious liaison across age and species boundaries is one of the less persuasive aspects of the book, and many readers have suspected it to be a symptom of something amiss in the Wellsian psyche, perhaps a fear of long-term relationships between equal adults.

It is marginal to the success of the book, however, which depicts a universe where relationships are little more than an irrelevance. More than a century after its publication *The Time Machine* remains a many-sided achievement: a gripping adventure story, a penetrating statement of what it means to live in a godless universe and an accessible equivalent to a symbolist poem, where all readers can find something in the dreamlike flow of events that corresponds to their own intuitions. If Wells had died in 1895 this one volume would have ensured him a place in literature.

However, he was not going to die just yet, and his head was teeming with ideas for more such stories. He must have been enormously buoyed up by his new-found success and fame – except perhaps when he saw the first American edition of *The Time Machine*, published in New York by Holt, with his name printed throughout as 'H.S. Wells'.

7
THE SCIENTIFIC ROMANCES 1895–1899

A cyclist swerves across a Surrey heath and, wobbling out of control, topples to the ground. He lies for a moment where he has fallen, rubbing the likely location of his next bruise, then clambers to his feet and remounts, determined to progress from tricycle to bicycle no matter how many painful setbacks it entails. The rider is H.G. Wells, displaying the determination that had helped transform him, only two years after becoming a full-time journalist, into one of the most notable new authors of the decade. During the five years from 1895 to 1899 he would publish twelve books, among them five works of science fiction and three volumes of short stories, destined to enthral readers for generations to come. Along the way he would also do a great deal of cycling.

The period in which Wells produced his most striking fiction – it comes as no surprise – was the period when he was most focused on being a creative writer, with the iconoclast of the South Kensington Debating Society held in check. True, the early fiction repeatedly implies that society is a deeply irrational and self-damaging tangle of customs and beliefs; from time to time it even mentions socialism. However, it rarely endorses the idea that the world might be changed for the better. Those characters who try to revolutionize it are portrayed as well-meaning fools or megalomaniacs. There is a powerful sense of liberation in Wells's stories, but it does not stem from political ideas; it comes from the realization that the world is capable of dramatic change and transformation. Habit and routine are ripped aside to reveal a stranger, more exciting universe than we had been led to expect.

Breaking through to a new reality is no guarantee of finding something better. Robert Weeks argues that the basic story behind all Wells's writing, one firmly established with the early fiction, is an escape that is initially exhilarating but ultimately followed by disillusionment or death. Anthony West goes further and claims that the early fiction is Wells's best writing because it acknowledges his core pessimism. Wells's later decision to try to reform the world, doing violence to his own deepest convictions, inevitably leads to work that is inauthentic and incoherent.[1]

Wells was certainly aware of his propensity to try to set the world right and knew that it had to be kept in check if he was to establish himself as a successful storyteller. He made his position clear in December 1895 in a review of Grant Allen's *The British Barbarians* for the *Saturday Review*:

> the sooner Mr Allen realizes that he cannot adopt an art-form and make it subservient to the purposes of the pamphleteer, the better for humanity and for his own reputation as a thinker and a man of letters . . . the philosopher who masquerades as a novelist, violating the conditions of art that his gospel may win notoriety, discredits both himself and his message, and the result is neither philosophy nor fiction.[2]

Wells gave a demonstration of how to provoke thought without lapsing into superficial preaching in his third book of 1895, *The Wonderful Visit,* published in September and dedicated to 'the memory of my dear friend, Walter Low'. *The Wonderful Visit* recounts a story so similar to Allen's *The British Barbarians* that it is hard to believe the two writers, who were on friendly terms, had not played around with the idea together before developing it separately. Both books tell of a naïve alien who explores late-nineteenth-century England and is baffled by its customs. He falls in love with a young woman, seems to be killed, yet in a burst of fire makes a final escape to his own world. Allen, reversing the basic plot device of *The Time Machine,* posits a visitor from the distant future. Wells, more whimsically, employs an angel mistakenly shot down by a vicar. The most important distinction between the stories, however, lies in the way that they are told. Allen relies on heavy-handed expository dialogue, Wells on a succession of comic incidents and characters.

Though Wells's angel is repelled by the class system, private ownership and the general enslavement of people to custom and propriety, he is also angered by the natural struggle for existence. We sympathize with his honest indignation but, recognizing the impractical nature of his idealism, we never feel that his outbursts make him our spokesman. Wells's satire faces both ways, then, mocking the existing order of things, on the one hand, and idealistic rebellion, on the other. While it is clear that Wells himself is anti-Establishment, it is not at all clear what alternative he might endorse. The nearest thing in the book to a privileged view is not that of a socialist or a scientist but of a 'Philosophical Tramp' who is scathing about the damage being done by the mindless conformity all around him but, like Joe and Frank Wells, rather than attempt to remedy it, withdraws to the margins of the society he despises.

The playfully fantastic *Wonderful Visit* takes a less powerful hold on the reader than the grippingly realistic *Time Machine,* yet the approach has its own rewards, inviting us to collude in a debunking of social and literary convention that at times presages the humour of Kurt Vonnegut. When a yokel hums a sarcastic tune at the Angel, for example, Wells gives us the notes on a stave so we can hum right along. Despite some signs of hasty composition, *The Wonderful Visit* is a highly original comedy. Wells reported its success to Sarah with some delight, proclaiming that four publishers now wanted his next book.[3]

In November, in the last stage of Wells's assault on the world of letters for that year, came *The Stolen Bacillus and Other Incidents*, giving wider circulation to fifteen previously published stories including 'The Temptation of Harringay', 'The Remarkable Case of Davidson's Eyes', 'The Lord of the Dynamos' and 'The Hammerpond Park Burglary'. The book was dedicated to the man who commissioned them, H.B. Marriott Watson. Wells continued to pour out short stories over the next few years, growing in skill until he could hold his own against any writer in the form.

Having established his presence as a creative artist, Wells's priorities now were to keep writing prolifically, network with fellow authors and develop a lifestyle that would help sustain his health and career. Conscious of his poor physical condition and hooked on the sense of escape and freedom, he made his new home in Woking a base for frequent cycling expeditions. He later noted that

> the bicycle was the swiftest thing upon the roads in those days, there were as yet no automobiles and the cyclist had a lordliness, a sense of masterful adventure, that has gone from him altogether now.[4]

Wells was the proud owner not only of conventional bicycles but a tandem made to his own specifications by the Humber company. Photographs of Wells and Jane with the bike suggest a covertly patriarchal form of transport – the woman borne at the front like a trophy, with the man in control – but in fact Jane was frail from ill health and the aim seems to have been to let her travel in relative ease while Wells did the hard work at the back.

By the end of 1895, after much painful application, Wells was confident in his mastery of the two-wheeler, but the effects on his health cannot have been entirely positive. Just bouncing along on the primitive suspension must have strained his body, while the brakes of the period were not always effective enough to prevent the cyclist hurtling past his intended stopping point and alighting with unexpected violence. Early in his attempts Wells rounded a corner and ran into a milk cart, ending up clinging to the head of an aggrieved pony.[5]

One day Wells wrote a description of the injuries that his legs had sustained in such incidents and found it growing into a comic novel about a cyclist, *The Wheels of Chance.* Wells used his travels to scout locations not only for this novel but for another, which would become one of his most celebrated books. During a visit from Frank, the brothers had discussed whether there might be life on other worlds. Just suppose beings from space were to descend here, Frank had suggested, indicating the peaceful Surrey countryside through which they were walking, and were to lay about them with futuristic weapons. Soon Wells was cycling through the Home Counties, marking down sites for destruction in *The War of the Worlds.*

While he incorporated his present environs into his fiction, Wells's mind could not help returning to South Kensington – and with some bitterness. While working on *The War of the Worlds* he informed Elizabeth Healey that he planned to

> completely wreck and destroy Woking – killing my neighbours in painful and eccentric ways – then proceed via Kingston and Richmond to London, selecting South Kensington for feats of peculiar atrocity.[6]

This sounds like a passing joke, but in December 1895 Wells had published a short story called 'The Argonauts of the Air' that is little more than an excuse to crash an experimental aircraft into his old college with as much force as possible. 'A Slip Under the Microscope', another piece written during 1895, depicts an idealist from a lower-class background who is expelled from South Kensington when he admits to having accidentally gained an advantage during an examination. From under a façade of artistic detachment the story radiates anger against the teachers and wealthy students who patronize and conspire against this young outsider.

Class resentment is also present in *The Wheels of Chance* but is held firmly in check by insulating the feelings of the lower-class hero from those of the middle-class narrator with a wedge of comical stereotyping. Having practically finished the book by October 1895, and done some basic work on *The War of the Worlds*, Wells offered both unsuccessfully to the American publisher Harper for serialization.

October was also the month Wells and Jane returned to Mornington Road for three weeks in order to get married, which they did on the 27th at St Pancras Registry Office, Richard Gregory attending as witness. The couple had found that once their unmarried status came to light servants became impertinent and neighbours curt or insulting, and they did not wish this pointless friction to continue.

Their apparent surrender to convention did not necessarily mean that they had changed their minds about free love. Wells, at least, still yearned for extramarital relationships, and it seems likely that from time to time he did have some recourse to 'loose women'. There are two exhibits in evidence.[7] A drawing of 1896 shows a disgruntled Jane watching as Wells struts down Folkestone Leas with a couple of floozies. The caption, 'Eh? Don't you believe it' is unlikely to have offered her total reassurance.

Then there is a poem called 'Episode', published anonymously in the 7 May 1894 *Pall Mall Gazette*:

> A meeting under the greenwood tree,
> In a soft, leaf-filtered light;
> A meeting or so, and a passion to know
> If I read your eyes aright.

A parting under the greenwood tree,
A delicate passion of pain
(And soberly I return to my
Mature and elegant Jane.)

The poem is likely to be by Wells, because he had clipped it out of the magazine and made the kind of minor revisions only an author would do. The date implies he was at least imagining being unfaithful within weeks of running off from Isabel.

Whatever his reservations about the sanctity of marriage, Wells took his other responsibilities as a family man seriously. Early in 1896 he moved Sarah, Joe and Frank from Rogate to a better house at Liss, Hampshire, about six miles north of Uppark. He also continued to correspond with, and worry about, his brother Fred, who had settled into the drapery trade in Johannesburg and would have been contemplating a promising future there if only South Africa had not become the site of an ominous clash between Britain and Germany. The international rivalry in science education that had fuelled Wells's escape from shop work was turning out to be part of a larger, more alarming story that would come to overshadow his life as it would the lives of millions of others.

Germany aspired to possess a global empire like the one that had made Britain so powerful, and one of the areas where it saw an opportunity for imperial acquisition was southern Africa, then a staging post on the British sea route to India. While Britain hoped to conciliate the Dutch and French settlers and draw their Boer Republic into the British Empire, Germany encouraged the Boers to proclaim their independence as soon as possible so that they could be groomed as a German satellite.

Impatient to extend British power and get his hands on the local gold, Cecil Rhodes, the Prime Minister of Britain's Cape Colony, sent a private army into the Boer territory at the end of 1895 to spur immigrants like Fred to rebellion. His force numbered only five hundred, however, and was over-reliant on whisky to stoke its patriotic fervour. Even though the immigrants outnumbered the Boers, they declined to rise up, and the so-called Jameson Raid was defeated in January 1896, triggering Rhodes's resignation. Fred dismissed the episode as no more than 'a Capitalistic enterprise', but, though he accepted the motive of British greed and later came to see the raid as entirely discreditable, Wells was sufficiently caught up in the imperialist mood of the time to lay much of the blame on German provocation. Cycling around the Home Counties, envisioning the battles between Martians and Earthlings, was a return to Wells's childhood fantasies of warfare and seems to have reawakened some of his youthful enthusiasm for military action.

Frustratingly, the rumours of war consequent upon the Jameson Raid had caused the publication of *Doctor Moreau* to be put back, but Wells's fears that his initial success would be quickly forgotten proved unfounded. One reader who had been particularly taken with *The Time Machine* was the cinema pioneer Robert Paul. He invited Wells to his office at 44 Hatton Gardens to discuss the possibility of a *Time Machine* fairground ride, a device similar to those found in theme parks today. Members of the public would stand on a platform that rocked to give them the feeling of travel, while noise and wind effects bombarded them and encircling screens, lit up by Paul's projectors, moved through a sequence of scenes from past, present and future.

Sadly, this pioneering franchise was never put into practice, but Wells's endorsement of the plan shows his go-ahead attitude towards the commercial exploitation of his literary property. Further evidence of this came in April 1896 when a copyright reading of dialogue from *The Wonderful Visit* took place at the Gaiety Theatre, Hastings, apparently to establish Wells's legal title to any future dramatization of the book. Wells blew hot and cold about the idea of turning his stories into plays and at this stage of his career was generally sceptical, presumably recalling the fate of Henry James on the opening night of *Guy Domville.*

On 13 January 1896 Wells was approached by J.B. Pinker, who had decided to set himself up as a literary agent to rival Watt. For all his socialist theory about common provision, Wells had respect for the practical benefits of competition. He had already made use of a second agent, Morris Colles, and begun a strategy of switching between publishers, looking for the best short-tem deal. Perhaps recognizing a kindred spirit in Pinker, who had risen from working-class origins through clerical work and journalism, Wells agreed to become one of his first clients. Wells would later employ a range of agents and sometimes handle negotiations himself.

Meanwhile he gave Colles disposal both of *The War of the Worlds* and of the American rights to *The Wheels of Chance.* Colles soon had *Pearson's Magazine* interested in serializing the former, but Pearson refused to commit for some months, demanding cuts for the magazine version and insisting on seeing how the story ended. Between May and June Wells cooked up a new project, and on 12 June he sent Pinker a 20,000-word version of it called 'The Man at the Coach and Horses'. It would soon develop into *The Invisible Man.*

The Island of Doctor Moreau finally appeared in April 1896, with an American edition following in August. There could be no serial publication owing to the gruesome and controversial nature of the story, which is presumably also the reason why Wells did not dedicate the book to anyone among his friends or family. Though *Doctor Moreau* shares some of the themes of *The Time Machine,* it is a much darker tale. Its narrator, Edward Prendick, is shipwrecked on a tropical island where Moreau, a notorious vivisectionist, is attempting to improve on evolution by surgically converting animals into people. Prendick is a former student of Huxley, and his adventures illustrate Huxley's point that, ultimately, nature will always defeat human endeavour, but they do so in a more alarming way even than in *The Time Machine*. The victims of Moreau's experiments, the Beast People, degenerate horribly from within, their bestial instincts gradually overriding their judgement.

Inspired by Swift's depiction of the Houyhnhnms in Book IV of *Gulliver's Travels,* Wells offers us a shocking model of human nature – we are not, as Christianity claims, heavenly spirits trapped in material bodies but animals whose evolution has left us tormented by regressive desires and impossible ideals. The Beast People worship their torturer Dr Moreau and build a religion around him in a vain attempt to understand their plight and curb their instincts. We, too, Prendick comes to realize, worship fictitious gods and follow irrational codes, with a comparable lack of success.

Wells argues the point in a spin-off article 'Human Evolution, An Artificial Process', explaining that the human organism does not seem to have changed appreciably since the Stone Age except in generating a complex culture that brings it both benefits and stress:

> what we call Morality becomes the padding of suggested emotional habits necessary to keep the round Palaeolithic savage in the square hole of the civilized state. And Sin is the conflict of the two factors – as I have tried to convey in my Island of Dr Moreau.[8]

In writing off religion *Dr Moreau* is more openly blasphemous than *The Time Machine*. Moreau spends six days creating an ape man, for example, then rests on the seventh day. Yet while the book mocks Christianity as a misunderstanding of how the world works, it seems to harbour equally negative implications for atheism and democracy, which, it seems, can only lead to chaos, as they do for the Beast People once they realize that their god is dead. Eventually Wells would be forced to follow the implicit logic of the story and seek some kind of religious authority to bind the savage individual into society. But his aim here is to entertain, not to reform.

In this he is certainly successful. *Moreau* is a more intense narrative than *The Time Machine,* its mood more consistent, its island setting ensuring unity of action. On the other hand, it is less original, with obvious debts to *Frankenstein, Comus* and *The Tempest,* and it is far more repulsive. Out to shock and offend, Wells succeeded admirably. Wells always defended the necessity for vivisection, but there is evidence here and elsewhere that the sufferings of animals under the knife upset a part of him.

The Times declared, 'The book should be kept out of the way of young people and avoided by all who have good taste, good feeling, or feeble nerves.' The *Review of Reviews* announced it 'ought never to have been written' and suggested that Wells withdraw it from circulation. Even Wells's colleague at the *Saturday Review*, Peter Chalmers Mitchell, thought the author had 'sought out revolting detail with the zeal of a sanitary inspector probing a crowded graveyard'. Wells considered that the only review to understand his intentions was the one published in the Anglican *Guardian*. Though the anonymous critic called *Moreau* 'exceedingly ghastly . . . unpleasant and painful', he admired the skill with which the story was told and speculated that Wells's aims were, on the one hand, 'to satirize and rebuke the presumption of science' and, on the other, to 'cast contempt upon the dealings of God with His creatures'.[9]

It was as well for Wells's reputation that his next book was the comic *The Wheels of Chance*, published six months later in October 1896, reassuringly dedicated to his mother. As previously noted, in this story about a drapery assistant who hates his job and fantasizes about being an author, Wells bypasses the potential pain of confronting his own experiences by dividing himself into two disconnected personas, appearing both as Mr Hoopdriver, the naïve, blue-eyed, skimpy-moustached hero, and as the anonymous narrator, a knowledgeable, confident commentator who sympathizes with his protagonist from a safe distance.

The story avoids the dull routine of life behind the counter and instead lets Hoopdriver take advantage of his summer holiday to embark on a series of improbable adventures, the most important being the rescue of an innocent upper-class girl from a would-be seducer. Hoopdriver eludes the social system by wearing the classless garb of the cyclist and, when pressed, by passing himself off as a colonial from South Africa like Fred. The result is an entertaining read that might be valued more highly by posterity had Wells not eclipsed it with *Kipps* and *Mr Polly*.

Genial where *Moreau* is gruesome, *The Wheels of Chance* is none the less its secret twin, tormented by the same obsessions. When Hoopdriver's passions are roused, 'The Man beneath prevailed for a moment over the civilized superstructure, the Draper', and the man disclosed to us is a 'Palaeolithic' savage tamed by society into inhibited behaviour and clichéd speech.[10] Defeated in his attempts to better himself, Hoopdriver has to return to the drapery in Putney High Street, while the narrator walks free, almost as Prendick leaves behind the deformed animals on Moreau's island. Socialism is mentioned as a more rational and inclusive replacement for the current social system, which might have helped save Hoopdriver, but also as an idea unlikely to make headway against social inertia.

The only way forward that Wells even begins to endorse is the imaginative revolution in Hoopdriver's head:

> his real life was absolutely uninteresting, and if he had faced it as realistically as such people do in Mr Gissing's novels, he would probably have come by way of drink to suicide in the course of a year. But that was just what he had the natural wisdom

> not to do. On the contrary, he was always decorating his existence with imaginative tags, hopes and poses, deliberate and yet quite effectual self-deceptions.[1]

We shall come back to Mr Gissing shortly. Wells deems Hoopdriver's fantasizing to be healthy because it expresses the knowledge that there is more to him than meets the eye. That the human mind is never wholly integrated and that we must struggle to reconcile its inconsistencies is a recurrent theme in Wells's writings. Wells knew from his own experience that compensatory fantasies were not always the lamentable lapse from seriousness that James Thurber would depict in his short story 'The Secret Life of Walter Mitty' but that they could be a vital weapon in the struggle for survival, keeping up self-esteem, articulating thwarted desires and stoking ambition. Unfortunately, Hoopdriver's fantasies remain separate from his workaday personality and are not connected, as those of Bertie Wells had become, to a vision that might coordinate his personal struggle with wider social changes.

In 'Human Evolution, an Artificial Process', the article in which Wells explains the place of *Doctor Moreau* in his thinking, he suggests where such an inspiring vision might be found. The development of culture does not lie in the hands of the nominal leaders of society but, rather, in a range of creative writers, journalists, preachers and political commentators, who are gradually articulating a vision of Utopia, based on 'a sounder science, both of matter and psychology'. One day 'the life of every human being, and, indeed, through man, of every sentient creature on earth, may be generally happy'.[12]

The idea of humanity being at odds with the rest of the universe is straight from Huxley; the rest not. While Wells the Artist was exploring the tragic implications of Huxley's philosophy by conducting radical thought experiments about time travel and vivisection, Wells the Social Reformer was heading boldly down the opposite path. The idea that artists and scientists will one day put their heads together and produce Utopia sounds like the vision from the biblical Book of Isaiah, secularized by way of Comte.

This apparent contradiction in Wells's thinking clearly has roots in his father's cynicism, on the one hand, and his mother's religious belief, on the other, but cannot simply be reduced to these. Joe and Sarah provided the mental template that Wells used to structure his ideas into opposites for purposes of dramatization and argument, but the issues themselves were substantial ones with which he would have to struggle all his life, not only through his thinking but in his writing, career and relationships – all of which continued to develop rapidly.

Between *Doctor Moreau* and *The Wheels of Chance* Wells's personal progress led him to yet another house move, the sixth in the two and a half years since he had left

Isabel. Part of the motive was to give more space to the ailing Mrs Robbins. Since he had made an honest mother-in-law of her, he had a much better relationship with 'Pinnie' and was keen to see her in comfort. He also had enough money to live in the style appropriate to a well-known author, having made almost £1,000 during 1896 – more than twice the earnings of the average doctor in general practice – and with an expectation of a steady rise to come.

The family's new residence, Heatherlea, was a spacious house in Worcester Park, a suburb to the south-west of London. When he was interviewed for a magazine called *The Young Man* he proudly showed off his first study.[13] The interviewer was struck by the modernity of its fittings, the sketches of contemporaries that covered two of the walls and the bookcases bearing a distinctive mix of fiction and science titles. Taking down a copy of Robert Burton's genre-straddling *Anatomy of Melancholy*, Wells declared it to be his favourite book. Decades later he would take it as a model for his own *Anatomy of Frustration*.

Asked about his work routine, Wells stated that he used the morning for chores such as letter-writing and proofreading and after lunch would take a walk, a bike ride or a jaunt on the tandem with Jane. After a tea break around 3.30 p.m. he would settle down to creative writing until dinner at 8 p.m. and sometimes, if sufficiently inspired, resume writing from 9 p.m. until midnight. (In a note for *Pearson's Magazine* of around the same time, Wells added that, to maintain quality, he burned at least half of what he produced.) Truth be told, this was Wells's default routine, from which in practice he quite often departed.

The interviewer noted the protective presence of Jane, 'the mainspring of her husband's success', who not only double-checked all his proofs but dealt with much of his correspondence. Wells explained that her handwriting was indistinguishable from his own. This was true, though Jane's writing tended to be somewhat larger. Since Jane wrote stories, too (first appearing in print in May 1897 with a story for *Black and White* with the unpromising title 'My Grandfather's Shirt-Studs'), the latter comment raises the question of whether Wells's prolific output, particularly of short stories, might be accounted for by an element of collaboration. Could Jane have done the first drafts of pieces that Wells finished off or tidied up penultimate drafts? There is no conclusive evidence, but there are hints in a couple of Wells's 'picshuas'. A sketch of November 1895, done in a copy of *The Time Machine*, shows Jane furiously writing above the caption, 'Got to write his old stories for 'm now'. Another of 1902 depicts future scholars concluding that Wells's writings are really the work of 'a woman's hand'.[14]

While discussing family matters, Wells mentioned that his parents took a keen interest in his work and reported also that his best friend from school, Sidney Bowkett, had recently reappeared as 'a successful actor and rising playwright' – a rather flattering description as it turned out. Wells had come across Bowkett's name in a newspaper report while he was living at Woking. His old friend was touring the provinces with a dramatization of George Du Maurier's hit novel *Trilby*. Unfortunately the script had been pirated from the official adaptation at the Haymarket and the producer was taking legal action.

Wells got in touch with Bowkett, who soon appeared and reported his adventures since their parting. He had gone to the USA with a small company led by W.E. Henley's brother Ted and had returned with considerable theatrical experience, a glamorous wife, a cocaine habit and a flair for extravagant boasting about his acting ability and sex life that Wells found entertaining, at least for a while. In time Bowkett became the original of Chitterlow in *Kipps*, a minor playwright whose bohemian love of intoxication and promiscuity make him a dangerous role model. Under his influence, Wells found himself 'disposed to covet Bowkett's wife', which is presumably not quite the effect Bowkett intended his locker-room bragging to have.[15]

Once settled into Heatherlea, Wells and Jane set aside Saturday afternoons for a regular 'open house' at which friends could drop by for tea, croquet and talk. The couple were not minded to build their social life around the local church, as middle-class people often did, nor the pub, as was common among the working classes. Instead they favoured weekend get-togethers with some guests stopping over, which as the years passed increasingly came to resemble the aristocratic country-house weekends with which Wells was familiar from Uppark.

The Bowketts were frequent visitors on Saturdays, as were such literary acquaintances as W. Pett Ridge, H.B. Marriott Watson, W.E. Henley, Frank Harris, Grant Allen, Israel Zangwill, Jerome K. Jerome and W.W. Jacobs. One particularly significant visitor was an old schoolfriend of Jane's called Dorothy Richardson. She was a dental clerk at the time but with the encouragement of Wells would become the author of a series of autobiographical novels in which her mentor appeared as 'Hypo G. Wilson'. Wells declared that the fifth of her 'Pilgrimage' series, *The Tunnel*, described life at Worcester Park with 'astonishing accuracy', though it has been suggested that Richardson is depicting Wells not so much as he was in 1896–7 as four or five years later.[16]

The party to which Richardson's *alter ego* Miriam has been invited is made up of literary intellectuals. She suspects that Hypo and his wife Alma, for all the enthusiasm with which they greet their guests, are too preoccupied with culture and ideas to really care for any of them as individuals. Alma seems to be working hard at playing the great man's wife, constantly stoking the conversation as if afraid what might be revealed if it expired. Hypo himself is snobbishly described as 'looking like a grocer's assistant' and having a voice with a 'cockney twang'.[17] On meeting Miriam Hypo establishes his dominance over her by turning all the questions he should be asking into statements: 'You caught the elusive three-fifteen. This is your bag.' Another trick is to make 'little subdued snortings at the back of his nose in the pauses between his sentences as if he were afraid of being answered or interrupted before he developed the next thing'.

Yet she is intrigued by the inner conflict between shyness and determination she detects in his voice and charmed by his clever way of putting things, which – despite what she considers his weak voice and mouth – finally makes him attractive to her. Wells himself summed up their relationship at this time as that of two people who took a grave interest in each other with a potential for adventure not yet explored.[18] As with Ethel Kingsmill four years earlier, Wells found himself being excited by someone close enough to his wife to offer the chance of reckless betrayal.

The Saturday get-togethers marked Wells's arrival as a literary figure. With *The Time Machine* and *The Island of Doctor Moreau* already published, and *The Invisible Man* and *The War of the Worlds* in the pipeline, he had made a distinctive niche for himself in the marketplace. He could have continued to produce science fiction, with occasional ventures into comic fiction, for the rest of his career, and many people since have wished he had done just that. Wells himself took a different view. He wanted to extend his reputation with fiction that was more carefully executed than his first books and which engaged more directly with social reality. Perhaps, as David Lodge has suggested, Wells felt guilty that he was making so much money from a career that was not advancing the cause of socialism or science, leaving the real-life Hoopdrivers trapped in the life of servitude he himself had escaped.[19]

Wells's new career direction was implicit in a verbal sketch published in 1896 in the Chicago magazine *Chap-Book,* evidently based on an interview with the subject and carefully worded to promote his image in the USA. The author 'Picaroon' observes,

> In himself Mr Wells is very much like his books – flashing in and out of many moods, and all of them delightful. In casual conversation you note the oddly humorous twist of his ideas, the faculty of standing apart from the ordinary line of observation and looking at everything, at himself even, from a new point of view. That, I take it, is what he aims at in literature – to establish a new proportion, to show the world under a new aspect. The peculiar union in him of the scientific and literary temperaments gives him a rare advantage . . . His ambition is to become the novelist of the lower middle class in England, to be a George Gissing with humour.[20]

Wells knew that it would not be an easy ambition to achieve. Once his finances began to stabilize, he made a conscious decision to cut back on the speed at which he wrote, reducing his output from a high of 7,000 words a day in the winter and spring of 1894–5 to a maximum of 1,000 from August 1896 – perhaps 2,000, allowing for the shedding of around half of what he wrote. In 1898 Wells acknowledged to a correspondent that he was tormented by the inadequacy of what he had produced in his rush to establish his career. *The Wheels of Chance* and *The War of the Worlds* were, he realized, full of amateurish workmanship.[21]

This did not stop Wells driving a hard bargain with his publishers. He wanted what he had written, whatever its defects, to reach the maximum number of people in well-produced form and to give him back a good income. He repeatedly berated his publishers for poor packaging, insufficient advertising, inadequate print runs and dubious accounting. A short story of 1899, 'A Vision of Judgment', eagerly anticipates God's doomsday verdict, not so much on the notorious figures of history as on publishers who deduct charges for additional printing costs.

J.M. Dent, publisher of *The Wonderful Visit* and *The Wheels of Chance*, was driven to call Wells's attitude to negotiation 'sordid'.[22] Two months after this clash, still dissatisfied with Dent's performance, Wells contemptuously offered to buy the unsold copies of his books so he could dispose of them himself. A similar offer was made the following year in a letter to William Heinemann, with an additional proposal that Wells would throw in the repayment of all his past earnings.[23] These letters seem to be expressions of anger rather than serious suggestions. Unlike Shaw, Wells never opted for self-publishing, though if he had lived a hundred years later, in the era of word processing and the internet he might conceivably have given it a try.

And what sort of book was the would-be novelist of the lower middle class going to offer his readers, now he had granted himself more time to write? If he intended to move beyond his existing niche as a scientific romancer, he would ultimately have to find some way of reconciling the pessimistic Huxleyite view of the cosmos that had informed his work so far with the utopian approach to society he wished to promote. The most obvious way forward would be to write a new kind of scientific romance, with the focus shifted from cosmic to social matters. This is precisely what Wells would attempt in *When the Sleeper Wakes*. He began this book in May 1897, telling Pinker that he hoped it would be the culmination of his career.[24] First, however, in September 1896, he set about a very different project, a realistic novel based on his student days which, as finally developed, would suggest that a socialist Utopia is little better than a fantasy and that the only sure source of meaning in life comes from personal relationships.

It is easy to assume that Wells was always working his way towards becoming a champion of 'progress', but it is not clear that in the last years of the nineteenth century Wells himself was sure of this. After all, many people who hold radical views in their student days change their perspective once they have to earn a living, and the socialist cause was now flagging. Recession had undermined the New Unionism, while the big craft unions were proving to be far more interested in free collective bargaining than in changing the world. The public mood had swung towards traditional patriotism and imperialism. As Wells puts it in *Love and Mr Lewisham*:

> eminent reformers have been now for more than seven years going about the walls of the Social Jericho, blowing their own trumpets and shouting – with such small result beyond incidental displays of ill temper within, that it is hard to recover the fine hopefulness of those departed days.[25]

In theory, Wells retained a positive view of socialist ideas, but his fiction of the 1890s never portrays socialism as a practicable design for the future, and on the strength of this evidence it would not have been surprising to see him drift further from the radicalism of his youth. In this context it is surely significant that it was while working on *Love and Mr Lewisham,* his least committed novel, that Wells befriended the unofficial laureate of disillusionment, George Gissing.

Wells had reviewed two of Gissing's novels for the *Saturday Review,* one under the heading 'The Depressed School'. He admired Gissing's artistry and seriousness but felt the unhappiness and pessimism of his work was excessive – a view echoed in the comment in *The Wheels of Chance* about Gissing's characters typically progressing by way of drink to suicide.

The two men met at a literary dinner held by the Omar Khayyam Club at Frascati's restaurant in Oxford Street on 20 November 1896. Wells had been struck by his own resemblance to a character in Gissing's *New Grub Street* and was keen to tell the author of the coincidence. Six days later Gissing received an invitation to Heatherlea, and a series of meetings followed that resulted in the two authors becoming close friends.

At first glance they make a decidedly odd couple. Where Wells poured out books that were exuberantly imaginative, filled with a sense of radical change and appealing to a wide range of readers, Gissing was a slow producer of naturalistic fiction that was gloomy, defeatist and lacking in popular appeal. Where Wells wrote in the tradition of Defoe, Swift, Sterne and Dickens, with a nod across the Atlantic to Poe and Hawthorne, Gissing drew on French and Russian models. Where Wells looked to the future, Gissing was a classical scholar who idealized the ancient world of Greece and Rome. Beneath these obvious dissimilarities, however, the two men had much in common.

Gissing, too, had started life in a shopkeeping family. An outstanding scholar, he had begun to rise in society through education, only to fail and fall into a period of poverty and uncertainty – his experiences in this regard being more severe than Wells's. At the age of eighteen Gissing had fallen in love with an alcoholic prostitute. Desperate to obtain cash for her, he stole it repeatedly from the cloakroom of

Owens College (later Manchester University), where he was a student, and was expelled, then sentenced to a month's hard labour at Bellvue Prison. On release he spent a year doing short-term jobs in the USA, before returning to Britain, seeking out the inspiration of his misfortune and marrying her. They lived unhappily for some time before the relationship broke up, partly because Gissing had spent their savings on publishing his first novel.

Before becoming a full-time writer in 1885 Gissing worked as a private tutor. He taught the sons of Frederic Harrison, the positivist leader whom Wells had envisaged as a possible employer when lying ill at Uppark. Gissing himself became a positivist and a socialist for a time, studying the thought of Huxley and identifying with the lower orders as fellow victims of society. The titles of many of his novels show his continued interest in radicalism: *Workers in the Dawn, The Unclassed, Demos: A Story of English Socialism, The Nether World* and, a story about feminists, *The Odd Women*. Though Gissing turned against social reform, he retained his hostility to conventional society and its Christian beliefs. His final point of resemblance to Wells was serious lung problems.

Wells was now a happily married and successful author; Gissing, nine years his senior, still attracted a limited numbers of readers (though his earnings had improved since he took the Wellsian decision to hook up with Watt, Pinker and Colles and to go in for short stories), and he was trapped in a disastrous second marriage. Believing no respectable woman would have him, he had decided, after his first wife died, to marry another working-class girl and train her up Pygmalion-fashion, starting with her elocution. This was hubris on stilts, and the consequences were aptly tragic. His new wife turned out to be a violently disturbed woman who would make both of their lives a misery and ultimately die in a lunatic asylum. The main reason for Gissing's sociability at this period seems to have been his fear of what would happen if he went home. After meeting Jane, he noted wistfully in his diary that she was 'a delightful little creature, a real companion'.[26]

On 10 December 1896, when the New Vagabonds Club made Wells guest of honour at one of its dinners, he invited Gissing along. On 16 February 1897 the two men met up for a meal at the Hotel Previtali, together with Gissing's doctor and old schoolfriend Henry Hick. In April, having completed *The Invisible Man,* Wells set out on the tandem for a cycling holiday with Jane, visiting Budleigh Salterton, where Gissing was then staying for his health. They remained with him for three weeks, hearing about his domestic problems and considering the idea of a joint holiday on the Continent, before resuming the journey round Devon by a mixture of cycling, walking, steamboat and train, arriving home towards the end of May.

In August 1897 Wells contributed an article to the *Contemporary Review* on 'The Novels of Mr George Gissing', an attempt both to raise his friend's critical standing and to encourage him to develop in a direction Wells favoured. While conceding that Gissing's novels lack entertainment value, Wells argues that they are, none the less, valuable contributions to literature. Gissing eschews the familiar commercial devices of a strong central character or a gratuitously complex plot and instead pursues an approach more familiar from continental fiction,

> displaying a group of typical individuals at the point of action of some great social force, the social force in question and not the 'hero' and 'heroine' being the real operative interest of the story.[27]

Wells cites Hugo, Balzac, Zola, Tolstoy and Turgenev as Gissing's predecessors.

He concedes that most of the novels do not actually fit his account of them but explains that this is because Gissing has only gradually been growing into maturity. He is now discarding his reliance on 'most favoured' characters as a crude way of inserting his views and beginning to realize that life is not about refinement but struggle and survival. Gissing, though grateful for the critical attention, did not recognize himself in Wells's description, and indeed the article is most significant for what it shows us about Wells's ideas for his own future career as he approached his thirty-first birthday:

> Very few novels indeed, of any literary value, have been written by men below thirty. Work essentially imaginative or essentially superficial a man of three and twenty may do as well as a man of forty; romance of all of sorts, the fantastic story, the idealistic novel, even the novel of manners; these are work for the young, perhaps even more than the old. But to see life clearly and whole, to see and represent it with absolute self-detachment, with absolute justice, above all with evenly balanced sympathy, is an ambition permitted only to a man fully grown. It is the consequence of, it is the compensation for, the final strippings of disillusionment.

This is in effect Wells's manifesto for *Love and Mr Lewisham* and his announcement of an artistic direction he might be following in the twentieth century. For the time being, however, Wells had plenty of unfinished business to attend to in his established guise as a purveyor of fantastic romances.

There was a second collection of short fiction in May 1897, *The Plattner Story and Others,* dedicated to his father. The seventeen stories included 'The Sad Story of a Dramatic Critic' and 'A Slip Under the Microscope', plus two remarkable pieces apparently inspired by their author's health problems, 'The Story of the Late Mr Elvesham' and 'Under the Knife'. 'Elvesham' contains a chilling description of what it feels like to be a young man trapped in a failing body – the narrator, a medical student named Eden, having been duped by the ageing Elvesham into a chemically induced body swap. The story ends on a note of unexpected irony. Elvesham disposes of Eden by leaving a poisoned drink for him, temptingly labelled 'Release', but by the time Eden has drunk it and perished Elvesham himself is already dead, having made careless use of his new body and been run down by a cab. The rigid universe wins again.

'Under the Knife' is narrated by a depressive man undergoing surgery. When the surgeon accidentally severs the portal vein, the same one Wells had clumsily cut in his first dissection, the patient's spirit is released from the material world and, free of physical inertia, he observes his body and house carried away along the orbit of the earth, leaving him floating in space, cut off from humanity. He watches in despair as the universe recedes. Building on biblical imagery planted earlier in the tale, this dreadful vision modulates into a series of apparitions, a voice declares 'There will be no more pain', echoing the Book of Revelation, and all the miraculous signs resolve into objects in the patient's room. He awakes with his sense of meaning and well-being restored.

This remarkably vivid story draws upon widespread contemporary speculation about the relationship between mind and matter. Were such phenomena as out-of-body experiences, premonitions of the future, telepathy and ghosts beyond the scope of science indicating that there might, after all, be a spiritual dimension separate from the material one, or did they constitute a new kind of physical challenge, the investigation of which could lead science into more sophisticated forms of material understanding? The recent discovery of radio waves, X-rays and radioactivity was already making obsolete the kind of physics Wells had been taught at South Kensington. If the universe was not, after all, made out of atomic particles knocking each other around like billiard balls, what was going on? The Society for Psychical Research, founded in 1882, attracted large numbers of scientists, philosophers, politicians and authors who wanted intelligent answers. Eventually Wells, too, would sign up, though all he would discover was 'much deception and still more self-deception'.[28]

In this context, 'Under the Knife' plays skilfully with a compelling topic without coming down explicitly on either side (though Wells drops broad hints that he is a sceptic about the supernatural). The story stands alongside Kipling's short story 'Wireless' and James's novella *The Turn of the Screw* as a response to contemporary spiritualism.

Neither *The Stolen Bacillus* nor *The Plattner Story* appeared in the USA. Instead, the publisher, Edward Arnold, supplied American readers with *Thirty Strange Stories*, a volume containing all the *Plattner* pieces and ten from *The Stolen Bacillus*, plus three not collected in Britain. Americans did get *The War of the Worlds* at the same time as British readers, however, as it ran simultaneously as a monthly serial in the British *Pearson's Magazine* and the US *Cosmopolitan* from April to December 1897.

Overlapping with it in Britain, *The Invisible Man* ran from June to August in

Pearson's Weekly, appearing as a book from Pearson in September and from Arnold in New York in November. Most of the writing had been done during July and August 1896 and January and February 1897. However, three weeks before *The Invisible Man* began serialization, Wells decided its narration was so clumsy that he had 'to take it all to pieces & reconstruct it. Since when', as he confessed in a letter in October, 'I have funked reading it.'[29] Like *The War of the Worlds, The Invisible Man* was heavily cut for serialization, with five chapters removed, many passages reduced and potentially offensive words such as 'God' and 'curse' replaced.

Conceived later than *The War of the Worlds* but published in book form before it, *The Invisible Man* interrupts Wells's sequence of Huxleyite thought experiments with an attempt to combine the two genres he had so far developed separately, the scientific romance and the comic novel. Like *The Wonderful Visit,* the story begins in a Sussex village where small-minded locals are confronted by a mysterious stranger, not a naïve angel this time but, unfortunately for them, an embittered and ruthless scientist who has made himself invisible and now cannot restore himself to normality. The slapstick violence he inflicts on the village is both entertaining and horrifying, just as the village itself is both a charming old-world spot and a coven of tiresome yokels, seemingly reflecting Wells's own mixed feelings as a young man in a hurry living in small towns like Midhurst and Holt.

Ambivalence and reversal dominate the book. Griffin, the invisible man, is by turns a homicidal monster and a heroic outsider driven to breakdown by rejection. Wells, who knew from his unemployed period what it was like to wander London as an invisible man, rejoices imaginatively at the revenge Griffin takes on an unappreciative world yet still makes it clear that his *alter ego* is a dangerous psychopath whose abuse of strychnine, 'the Palaeolithic in a bottle', leaves him with the primitive motivation of the savage natural man.[30] Griffin is defeated by a wealthy gentleman-scientist named Kemp, who occupies the place in the book where a hero should be yet is too smug and unsympathetic for that role, clearly inferior in knowledge and imagination to the man he betrays.

The nearest thing to a positive character in the book is neither of the scientists but, as in *The Wonderful Visit,* a comical tramp, Mr Marvel, a vagrant Griffin bullies into assisting him. In an epilogue missing from the first British edition, Marvel opens a pub called the Invisible Man and, like Wells, trades on a tale that challenges our ideas of human nature while himself contriving to retain everyday sympathy.

Even though Wells does not fully develop the thematic potential of *The Invisible Man* and settles for an uneasy mixture of comedy and creepiness, there is no denying that the book is intensely memorable. It is something of a shock to turn from it to *Certain Personal Matters,* a belated selection of Wells's early comic essays published in 1897 and realize how far Wells had travelled artistically in the course of just four years. Wells naturally retained affection for the writings that had launched his career, so much so that he became embroiled in a furious dispute about the contents and title page with the publisher, who eventually had to call in Gissing to act as a mediator and persuade Wells to climb down.

Gissing was not, incidentally, the only significant writer with whom Wells began a friendship during this period. In September 1897 he received a fan letter from Arnold Bennett, editor of the magazine *Woman*. Bennett had noticed references to his native Pottery district in 'The Cone' and *The Time Machine* and wondered if Wells had ever lived there. Wells replied with a brief account of his stay in 1888 and urged the aspiring novelist to read Joseph Conrad.

Wells had encountered the Polish expatriate as part of his work for the *Saturday Review*, which he kept up until April 1897, after which writing the *Sleeper* and *Lewisham* left little time for literary journalism. On 15 June 1895 he had contributed a favourable notice of Conrad's first novel, *Almayer's Folly*, and on 16 May 1896 he was even more complimentary about *An Outcast of the Islands*. True, 'Mr Conrad is wordy', and Wells spends most of the review humorously describing and analysing this prolixity. None the less, the novel may be the finest of the year because the characters and events are so vividly imagined.[31] Conrad's biographer, Frederick R. Karl, has praised Wells's notice for the positive guidance it gave. Sensing that Conrad was about to develop a more mature style, Wells had given him the right advice at the right time.[32]

Delighted by the comments he had received, Conrad obediently cut fifty-six words from a passage Wells had ridiculed. He was still more delighted when he discovered who it was that had written the anonymous notices and wrote to express his enthusiasm for Wells's work. Another letter followed publication of *The Invisible Man*, hailing Wells as a 'Realist of the Fantastic' who, amidst the most outlandish events, always kept his focus on human nature.[33] Wells maintained his enthusiasm for Conrad, telling the *Academy* in January 1898 that *The Nigger of the Narcissus* was the most striking piece of imaginative prose that year, exceeded as a contribution to the world of letters only by Henley's edition of Robert Burns and Henry James's *What Maisie Knew*.[34]

In truth, the most striking piece of imaginative work of the year was probably the serial version of Wells's own *War of the Worlds*. Begun early in 1895, completed in the first half of 1896 and revised in November 1897 for book publication, it appeared in Britain in January 1898, then in New York in March, dedicated to 'my brother Frank Wells, this rendering of his idea'. The serial made such an impact that two pirate versions were already appearing in magazines by the time the book came out, one in the New York *Evening Journal*, one in the Boston *Post*, both relocating the story in the USA to increase its appeal to American readers. Imitated and travestied from the moment it appeared, the book brought into being a whole new sub-genre, the space invasion story.

With Defoe's fake documentary *A Journal of the Plague Year* as his model, Wells offers a detailed, eyewitness account of interplanetary invasion. The vividness, and therefore the credibility, of the events is remarkable. Every location was scouted by Wells on his bicycle, then transformed with an extraordinary mixture of logic and imagination. Step by step we follow the escalation of events from a puzzled crowd around a space capsule on Horsell Common, through the horrific emergence of the Martians, the construction of their fighting machines, the one-sided battles by which they overthrow the imperial heartland and the remodelling of the capital's landscape into an alien wasteland of ruins and extraterrestrial Red Weed.

Wells describes the fantastic so clearly and confidently that we almost see it with our own eyes:

> How can I describe it? A monstrous tripod, higher than many houses, striding over the young pine-trees, and smashing them aside in its career; a walking engine of glittering metal, striding now across the heather; articulate ropes of steel dangling from it, and the clattering tumult of its passage mingling with the riot of the thunder. A flash, and it came out vividly, heeling over one way with two feet in the air, to vanish and reappear almost instantly so it seemed, with the next flash, a hundred yards nearer. Can you imagine a milking-stool tilted and bowled violently along the ground? That was the impression those instant flashes gave. But instead of a milking-stool imagine it a great body of machinery on a tripod stand.[35]

The thunderstorm is a standard Gothic device to create atmosphere and drama, but the tripod itself, as it emerges through the strobe-like lightning flashes, is as solid and convincing as the machines that had been displayed in the Great Exhibition.

There had been several bestsellers over the previous twenty years depicting German or French invasions of Britain, demonstrating a strong public demand for this kind of story. By replacing foreign soldiers with Martians, Wells raises the terror level to the top of the scale and at the same time removes distracting issues of defence spending and international relations, to create a timeless anxiety fantasy.

As a work of imagination alone the book is a colossal achievement, but Wells characteristically uses the scenario to explore disturbing issues, in particular Huxley's concept of 'sympathy' as a basis for human behaviour. Huxley wanted to explain how notions of right and wrong could have come about without divine intervention, how benevolence and self-sacrifice could evolve from competition for survival. His answer was that morality is a development of the 'sympathy' some creatures feel for others of their kind, a trait reinforced by evolution because it promotes the survival of the group. Modern Darwinians, knowing that natural selection operates at the level of genes, reject group selection in favour of more elaborate explanations. Either way, from a Darwinian perspective our sense of good and evil is not underwritten by divine authority, but is merely an accidental by-product of other developments, and therefore, though Huxley himself does not press the point, it is inconsistent, is at war with our other instincts and is variable from culture to culture.

In *Evolution and Ethics* Huxley had given some pertinent examples of the necessary limitations of sympathy. One is the construction and maintenance of a garden:

> What would become of the garden if the gardener treated all the weeds and slugs and birds and trespassers as he would like to be treated, if he were in their place?

Another is imperial conquest:

> Suppose a shipload of English colonists sent to form a settlement, in such a country as Tasmania was in the middle of the last century . . . They clear away the native vegetation, extirpate or drive out the animal population, so far as may be necessary . . . In their place, they introduce English grain and fruit trees; English dogs, sheep, cattle, horses; and English men . . .[36]

When the Martians descend to colonize our planet, they become the gardeners, we the pests to be disposed of; they the imperialists, we the backward natives. Wells echoes Huxley's second example when his narrator reflects on the Martians in the opening chapter of the book. Since Europeans exterminated the Tasmanians in fifty years, how can we complain if we receive similar treatment?

Naturally it is hard for humans to appreciate the Martians' fitness to take control of the earth, and Wells does not wish to undermine their dramatic power as monsters, but they are still allowed their point of view. When by a trick of fate they are eventually destroyed by earthly bacteria to which they have no immunity, we are unlikely to be impressed by the narrator's pompous talk about God's will and mankind's birthright. We may, however, feel some emotion at the desolate 'Ulla, ulla' emitted by the last Martian fighting machine, as the dying creature inside sends out a futile call across the city to its fallen comrades.

Identification of humans and Martians is strengthened by a plausibly argued theory that they are creatures like ourselves further along the path of evolution. In support, the narrator cites a forecast about human evolution made in 1893 by 'a certain speculative writer of quasi-scientific repute'[37] – that is to say, Wells himself in 'The Man of the Year Million' (recently collected in *Certain Personal Matters* as 'Of a Book Unwritten'). There is a hidden kinship between the aliens' 'intellects vast and cool and unsympathetic' and a human child who watches a man being crushed to death in a stampede of refugees 'with all a child's want of sympathetic imagination'.[38] 'What are these Martians?' wails a curate, his beliefs and wits overturned by events. 'What are we?' retorts the narrator, later clubbing his clerical companion over the head and leaving him to have his blood sucked out.[39] The narrator is able to escape death because he, too, is a ruthless combatant in the struggle for survival.

In Book II, Chapter 7, 'The Man on Putney Hill', a chapter not included in the serial versions of the story, Wells even introduces an Artilleryman who welcomes the Martian invasion because it puts people back in touch with their true Palaeolithic nature. He hails the extermination of the genteel, the conventional and the superficial and proposes the formation of an underground group who will achieve fulfilment as they die fighting the Martians. The Artilleryman's harangue is a device copied from Gissing's *The Whirlpool*, in which a character named Rolfe loudly proclaims his approval for the way people are turning against civilization, ready to embrace destruction in the coming war between empires. Yet Wells had condemned Gissing's use of such expository characters as artistically second-rate. In drafting *The War of the Worlds* he had already reduced the insurgent from the head of a provisional government to a lone fighter, and in the published version he soon dissociates himself from the Artilleryman's fanatical views. In an ironic twist, the would-be superman turns out to be a modern version of the 'braggart soldier', a stock character of comedy since Aristophanes, a fantasist whose project of burrowing into the sewers aptly sums up his mentality.

Such ready-made characters as the Artilleryman and the curate are the book's chief limitation. It is hard to feel much sorrow when the protagonist is separated from his wife, and their joyful reunion, apparently meant to provide an emotional conclusion to the book, has justly been described by Robert Crossley as so banal a 'made-for-TV movie could have done no worse'.[40]

There may be a reason for this. John Huntington has suggested that the basic 'emotional subtext of the novel' is, improbable though it may seem, Wells's frustration over his marriage.[41] Wells recorded that while he was cycling to research the novel he was also longing to encounter exciting women along the way. In a copy of *The War of the Worlds* he drew a comical picshua of Jane as a Martian, striding threateningly towards him on a tripod.[42] Several verbal clues suggest that the narrator of the story feels subconsciously hostile towards his wife. The Artilleryman's rant expresses contempt for the conformist majority who sleep with their spouses every night instead of pursuing their dreams. In this context the episode where the narrator is forced to share a house with the curate, squabbling over their living arrangements until he clubs him as his only means of escape, looks suspiciously like a displacement of marital feelings.

In his autobiography, Wells acknowledges his 'Domestic claustrophobia, the fear of being caught in a household' operating 'below the threshold of my consciousness',[43] a trait derived from his childhood in Bromley with parents who longed to escape from their home and each other. Peter Kemp has noted that, having spent much of his childhood there, trapped in a basement kitchen and scullery, Wells habitually uses images of underground enclosures to depict life at its worst: for example, the subterranean chambers of the Morlocks.[44] The kitchen and scullery of the house in Sheen in which the narrator and curate are trapped is another example. When a Martian space cylinder crashes next to them it flattens most of the house and piles up soil around their hiding place, effectively converting their refuge into a basement. It is unlikely that Wells recognized this element of the book, but the global destruction of *The War of the Worlds* does seem to have had its origins in his suppressed domestic frustrations.

None of this could be apparent or relevant to readers, who have rightly responded to the book's literary qualities, concurring with John St Loe Strachey in the *Spectator* that there is 'not a dull page in it . . . One reads and reads with an interest so unflagging that it is positively exhausting.'[45]

If a haemorrhage had carried Wells off in 1898, how would we see him now? His reputation would have been very different, probably much higher, and it would rest squarely on the scientific romances. The term itself, like the later 'science fiction', is a revealing oxymoron. 'Romance' is rightly the head word – since these stories of being spirited into other worlds, cursed with invisibility and menaced by monsters are deeply rooted in the fantastic tales of folklore, the Bible and the *Arabian Nights*, as well as in their author's subconscious. Writers such as Rider Haggard and Andrew Lang employed such material for stories that, in Wells's view, were conservative and escapist. He, in contrast, made his romances 'scientific' – the adjective identifies their distinctive quality – by using them to engage with contemporary issues and to promote and critique the world-view he had learned from Huxley.

Redeploying the prose techniques of realism built up during the eighteenth and nineteenth centuries, Wells skilfully renders impossible events convincing. In so doing, he explores social, scientific and philosophical themes, not through bolted-on discussions but by embedding them in the events. These events have a dreamlike aspect while at the same time offering accessible entertainment in the form of action-packed adventures. The heady mix of symbolist poem and tall tale had been pioneered by Poe, but Wells carries it off with greater skill, making his scientific romances, as T.S. Eliot observed, a treat for readers in 'the first class as well as the third class compartment'.[46]

Jorge Luis Borges has made the greatest claim of all for Wells's 'atrocious miracles', saying that their mythic quality will cause them to be remembered when their author and even the English language itself are forgotten.[47] This sounds like hyperbole but is not. In the world today there are millions of people who have never heard of Wells and cannot read English but who are familiar with stories of time travel and space invasion. Ironically, it would be in the 1940s and 1950s, the period when Wells's literary reputation was at its lowest point, that his literary influence would be at its height, with authors from Orwell to Golding zealously reworking his ideas to create a mythology for new times.

How was Wells to move on from what he had achieved? Inevitably, with great difficulty. Throughout the opening months of 1898 he continued to labour at two divergent, perhaps incompatible, ways forward, the socially engaged science fiction of *When the Sleeper Wakes* and the disillusioned comic realism of *Love and Mr Lewisham.* A letter to Gissing at the start of the year expresses pleasure at the progress made on the *Sleeper,* even though parts had had to be rewritten and four whole chapters of *Lewisham* had been cut as irrelevant. Three weeks later, while judging that the *Sleeper* contained some worthwhile conceptions, Wells was having doubts, fearing that he had taken on a task that was beyond him. He was still tearing out chapters, inserting new ones, rewriting others.[48]

Wells did not succeed in making the *Sleeper* the culmination of his career, as in his initial enthusiasm he had declared. Instead, early in March he threw in the towel and scamped the finish in order to maintain his cashflow while he embarked on his long-planned first holiday abroad. Gissing, now separated from his second wife, had removed himself to Italy in September 1897, urging Wells and Jane to join him when they could. By January 1898 the couple were planning their itinerary and Gissing was starting to arrange their accommodation.

On the morning of Monday 7 March 1898, the day after Wells stopped work on the *Sleeper,* he and Jane left Charing Cross station, seen off by Sidney Bowkett and the novelist Edwin Pugh. Pugh noted that Wells was 'dancing with excitement; he kept shaking hands with his friends and talking, talking, talking'.[49] His excitement is easy to understand. Ten years before he had been an invalid for whom exciting new horizons meant a visit to Stoke-on-Trent; five years before he had been an unhappily married college lecturer, working himself into a life-threatening haemorrhage. Now he was a celebrated author who received fan letters from as far afield as China, and he was off to see the world that he had begun to conquer.

After crossing at Dover, the Wellses took the Calais–Rome express, arriving in Rome on the evening of Tuesday 8 March and taking the shuttle carriage to the Hotel Alibert which Gissing had booked for them. They spent the rest of March, often with Gissing as their guide, seeing the sights – 'a time of wonderful sensations for me', Wells declared.[50] Things were less wonderful for Gissing who was receiving a series of painful letters about the activities of his wife. Receipt of these would leave him pale and trembling for most of the day, prompting Wells to take him for long walks, ply him with red wine and distract him with wide-ranging conversations.

One day, walking through some fields near Tivoli, Wells dreamed up a story that he tried out on Gissing and later wrote up as 'Miss Winchelsea's Heart'. A stereotypical schoolmarm, Miss Winchelsea sets off from Charing Cross for Rome with two college friends. During the course of their holiday she falls for a young man but throws him over in horror when she discovers his vulgar name, Snooks. One of her friends then moves in on him, persuades him to respell his name as Senoks, then Se'noks and finally Sevenoaks. The couple marry happily, leaving Miss Winchelsea to an embittered spinsterhood. No doubt Gissing laughed heartily and overlooked any personal application there might be in this satire on intellectual snobbery and irrational attitudes to choosing a spouse.

During April the Wellses took excursions outside Rome and on the 8th dined with two other literary men also on their travels, E.W. Hornung and Arthur Conan Doyle. A photograph taken that day shows three upright British gentlemen and a spindly, slouching little man who comes up only to Doyle's shoulder. In his autobiography Wells remarks, 'until I was over forty the sense of physical inferiority was a constant acute distress to me', and, as he peers defensively out of this picture, we get a real sense of Wells as a stunted invalid, the original owner of Mr Hoopdriver's weedy body and narrow shoulders.[51] At least, unlike Hoopdriver, Wells had been able to make his fantasies of becoming a famous writer stick, as was proved by his presence here in sunny Italy, alongside the creator of Sherlock Holmes.

On 12 April the Wellses left Rome and set off for Naples where they found riots taking place. People were angry over the rising cost of bread, compounded by the government's botched attempt two years previously to join the imperialist scramble, the outcome of which was seven thousand Italians dead in Ethiopia. The government would finally be forced from office during May. From Naples the Wellses took excursions to Capri, Pompeii, Vesuvius and Paestum. They also spent an enjoyable day at Isola de Gailo, at the home of Conan Doyle's sister.

On 4 May they went on to Florence, where they spent three days against a background of further riots. A planned visit to a café on the third night had to be called off, as Jane explained in a letter to Gissing:

> all cafés were closed and every window closely shuttered. Bands of carabinieri were parading the streets encouraged by a nervous little officer with a drawn sword! And the streets were all crowded with silent people. We saw what we could of it – there was some stone throwing but the smallest offender was instantly chased and seized and marched off with four revolvers at his head.
>
> Later there was some shooting – the police seem to have lost their heads.[52]

On 8 May they set out for Milan, but, after reading in a paper in Bologna that there was rioting there, too, they changed course and travelled to Chiasso and

Lugano, whence they returned home via Lucerne and Brussels. In Brussels they encountered yet more violence: an alarming demonstration outside their hotel with the 'Marseillaise' being sung and occasional revolver shots. French-speakers were angry because Dutch language and law were being given parity with their own. The Wellses travelled via Ostend to Dover on 11 May, reaching Worcester Park around 7 p.m., having had a glimpse of the militant nationalism which in the coming century would fuel two world wars and which Wells would spend much of his later life fighting.

And what had Wells gained from his baby-grand tour, other than a well-earned break in wonderful locations? With hindsight Wells considered that his experience of Rome had challenged his Protestant view of the Roman Catholic Church. Reflecting on the rise and fall of empires and cultures, he began to see that in its heyday the Church had represented a serious attempt to achieve a progressive global order, even if its thinking had now ossified.[53] Patrick Parrinder has pointed out that Wells would have already been familiar with a comparable historical perspective of civilizations falling and rising from Henry George's *Progress and Poverty*, in passages that probably shaped the vision of *The Time Machine*.[54] To read is one thing, however; to walk the streets of Rome another. Wells returned to England with an intimate sense of the historical process that he had not felt before.

Once home he continued to work on *Lewisham* and kept up with Gissing who was soon back, too. During July Wells helped Gissing learn to cycle and also allowed him to use Heatherlea to liaise with his French translator, Gabrielle Fleury. The relationship soon developed beyond the literary sphere, and by the following year Gissing was living with her in France. Wells's marital situation was also under strain.

Some time around this period he experienced a fierce resurgence of his desire for Isabel, with whom he had remained amicably in touch since the divorce. She had started up a poultry farm in Twyford, supported by Aunt Arabella. Wells paid her a visit, apparently to discuss investing in an extension to the farm, some time in 1898 or 1899, though the latter date seems an unlikely one as by then he was living further away and suffering ill health.

Filled with sudden yearning, Wells wanted to 'recover' her and 'implored' her. Isabel did not reciprocate. 'But how can things like that be, now?' she asked on discovering him in the early hours, distraught and preparing to flee:

> I wept in her arms like a disappointed child, and then suddenly pulled myself together and went out into the summer dawn and mounted my bicycle and wandered off southward into a sunlit intensity of perplexity and frustration, unable to understand the peculiar keenness of my unhappiness. I felt like an automaton. I felt as though all purpose had been drained out of me and nothing remained worth while.[55]

By the end of July the thwarted polygamist felt in urgent need of another change of scene to revive his flagging spirits. He and Jane cycled to Lewes, then Seaford, where he intended to spend three weeks working at *Lewisham* at the coast, hoping this would help him throw off his blues. By the time he arrived he had developed a bad cold, a high temperature and kidney pains. The couple had been planning to call in on Gissing's doctor, Henry Hick, a little later, but now it became their priority.

On 9 August Jane got Wells on a train to New Romney, where Hick diagnosed an abscess on the left kidney – a long-term effect of the rugby injury from Holt, exacerbated by cycling – and thought he might have to operate. As a patient facing dangerous surgery, Wells must have recalled the opening of 'Under the Knife': 'What if I die under it?' He wrote to Richard Gregory to ask whether the new X-rays might be worth a try, but was told that in the present state of science they were of no diagnostic value.[56] Fortunately, the specialist whom Hick called in declared that with bed rest the abscess would probably heal of its own accord.

Since Wells's cycling days seemed to be over, he gave Hick his bicycle along with the fees. To while away the time he wrote an illustrated children's story, 'The Adventures of Tommy', for Hick's daughter Marjorie (belatedly published in 1929 to help fund the medical career of a younger sibling).

Hick suggested that Wells should move permanently to the coast for the sea air, to somewhere sheltered, on sand or gravel. Heatherlea was duly let and later sold. After short-term lodgings at the Swan, Hythe, and the Homestead, Sandgate, the couple opted to rent a furnished house from 29 September: 2 Beach Cottages, Granville Road, Sandgate (now known as Granville Cottage). 'Beach Cottage' was no misnomer: waves broke over the roof. Wells complained to Elizabeth Healey that the back door was so close to the sea 'The shrimps will come in and whack about on the dining room oil-cloth'.[57]

While at Hick's house Wells had been visited by Henry James and Edmund Gosse. At Beach Cottages they were succeeded by J.M. Barrie. All had come to check discreetly whether he needed any financial support from the Royal Literary Fund, but his finances were healthy enough.

As Wells's physical health slowly recovered, he resumed work on *Lewisham.* Unable to rush on to his next project, he did the job properly but was disappointed that it was a more limited novel than he had first envisaged. Despite his own theories, his imagination could not do without a most favoured character rooted in autobiography. The large-scale vision of a Hardy or a Tolstoy was not his. On 5 October, the day he sent off the first draft to the publisher, a similar character appeared in the form of Kipps and was duly commemorated in a picshua. Wells seems already to have planned the work in which this comical draper's assistant would appear: a Dickensian novel in three volumes following the successive recipients of a legacy. The first volume, *The Wealth of Mr Waddy*, would deal with the cantankerous invalid who had originated the legacy. Even this central character was based on Wells himself, who in early October was still so weak that Jane had to push him along the seafront in a bath chair.

During November Wells made further revisions to the *Sleeper*. By mid-January he had produced a second draft of *Lewisham* and a first draft of *Waddy*, the latter a mix of developed chapters and outlines that he wanted Pinker to use as a basis for negotiation with magazines and publishers.

While at Beach Cottages Wells had been trying to buy a house. When the deal fell through, he decided to get one built to his own specifications, a particularly appealing strategy, as he feared he might have to spend much of his remaining life in a wheelchair and it would enable him to incorporate the facilities he would need. Where the 1898 edition of *Who's Who* listed Wells's recreation as cycling, the 1899 edition claimed it was 'detailed description of his various illnesses, and architecture'.[58] Since the break-up with Isabel Wells had set up home some seven times, only to be dissatisfied with the results. Now he intended to design himself a domestic Utopia, settle down and start a family.

8
A NEW PROSPECTUS
1899–1901

As the new century approached and his health began to mend, Wells drew up plans, first for himself, then for the world. By March he had received some promising house designs from Hick's brother-in-law, the notable artist and architect Charles Voysey. At the end of the month, requiring somewhere more sheltered than Beach Cottage to await the construction of their new home, Wells and Jane leased a semi-detached villa on the Sandgate coast named Arnold House (now 20 Castle Road).

Next door lived Arthur and Florence Popham, both from drapery-owning dynasties. A former architect, Arthur now worked in the bookbinding trade. Wells bought a new bicycle, and, as his health improved, he resumed cycling in the company of Arthur and of Sidney Bowkett. With the Pophams and their children he learned to swim to and from a raft moored off shore. He also took to organizing them and other friends and neighbours in shadow shows and in a type of rhyming charade known as 'Dumb Crambo'.[1]

From April to July he worked further on *Love and Mr Lewisham*, rewriting the last five chapters and reading them aloud to Jane. To enhance her secretarial role Jane bought a typewriter, a high-tech development that Wells approached with caution, declaring, 'I could no more bring myself to write on one of these infernal implements than I could wear tin underclothing.'[2]

All his life Wells wrote by hand with considerable fluency, adding extra words in marginal balloons and, when the flow of inspiration failed, leaving blanks to be filled in later. The draft was typed up in two or three copies, then further drafts produced. Wells rarely tinkered with individual words, instead discarding whole sections and chapters if they failed to deliver the desired effect. His latest production was two linked stories about an eccentric scientist named Cavor, which he sent Pinker in March as a sample for a magazine serial. As his hero would be visiting the Moon, Wells wrote to Richard Gregory for information on lunar craters and gravity.

Wells had already experimented with linked short stories in 'A Story of the Stone Age' (1897) and 'A Story of the Days to Come' (1899), collected in *Tales of Space and Time*, his most ambitious book of shorter fiction, published towards the end of 1899. The book comprised these two long pieces and three of his best short stories. 'The Crystal Egg' is a more accomplished variation on 'Davidson's Eyes', reconstructing the life of an unhappily married shopkeeper whose only solace is peering at the landscape of Mars through an alien crystal. 'The Star', one of Wells's most impressive short pieces, recounts the gravitational effects of a planet passing close to the earth, using a montage of viewpoints to build up a global experience of catastrophe. 'The Man Who Could Work Miracles' is a comic parable in which the gift of total power brings with it total destruction until a last-minute twist saves the world and neatly restores us to the start of the story.

The two longer pieces concern young couples who overcome others' disapproval and, after much tribulation, find their place in life. Though the concept may be autobiographical, the development is decidedly not. 'A Story of the Stone Age' tries to imagine the feelings of people and even animals in the far distant past. 'A Story of the Days to Come' mixes the speculative essay with genre pastiche, ridiculing many late-Victorian cultural targets. Neither piece represents Wells at his best, being fragmented in narration and stereotypical in characterization, but they are certainly testimonies to his ambition and resourcefulness.

When the Sleeper Wakes, published back in May, picks up many of the ideas of 'A Story of the Days to Come' but in a more earnest spirit. The story seems to derive from the abandoned draft of *The Time Machine* in which underground labourers of the future revolted against their masters. Washington Irving's 'Rip van Winkle' is an obvious influence, so is Edward Bellamy's bestselling Utopia, *Looking Backward* – both credited in the text. The sleeper of the title is Graham, a Victorian radical who falls into a coma for two hundred years and awakens to find that, thanks to canny investment on his behalf, he now owns half the world. As a legendary messianic figure, he has been revived by a politician called Ostrog in order to arouse the oppressed masses and bring about a coup. Graham realizes that Ostrog intends to carry on exploiting the ordinary people using him as a cover. Encouraged by an adoring young woman named Helen who calls him 'Master', Graham confronts the forces of reaction in an aerial battle, plunging to his death at the end of the story with the outcome of the fight still uncertain.

Critics and readers were disappointed. The story was 'dull' and 'commonplace', a slender Ruritanian plot weighed down by endless explanations.[3] 'There's good stuff in it,' Wells assured Bennett, 'but it's a big confused disintegrating thing.' Eventually he decided that the book was just 'a lurid exaggeration of present social conditions'.[4] While this may be true, it is not the source of his artistic failure. Rather, Wells had thought hard about content but settled for reach-me-down plot devices that weren't fit for purpose. Graham's struggles to gain a perspective on, and find a place in, the nightmare world of the future might have made him a sympathetic, even tragic, figure. Instead, Wells thrusts on him the ready-made, over-demanding role of unironic messiah he had withheld from the time traveller and the Angel.

Since Graham has no redeeming vision to offer his followers, he has to fall back on unconvincing invocations of Victorian values and God. Ostrog is a dull villain; Graham's supporters look suspiciously like the ignorant rabble Ostrog says they are; the portrayal of Ostrog's black troops is cheaply racist. As for the writing, like Egbert Cummins in 'The Sad Story of a Dramatic Critic', Wells seems to be in thrall to the Victorian theatre:

> 'Curse this complex world!' he cried, 'and all the inventions of men! That a man must die like a rat in a snare and never see his foe! Oh, for one blow! . . .'[5]

Despite its limitations the book proved highly influential. George Orwell, on whom it made a great impression, adapted several ideas for *Nineteen Eighty-Four.* Jack London, Yevgeny Zamyatin, Fritz Lang, Aldous Huxley and Ray Bradbury are among many others who found the story worth quarrying. None the less, in Wells's first venture into social science fiction he had plainly overreached himself. He rewrote much of the book in 1910 as *The Sleeper Awakes* but failed to improve it.

Conscious that he needed more sophisticated political ideas if he were to tackle such themes again, Wells was delighted to discover that Florence Popham had as a brother-in-law Graham Wallas, the socialist intellectual whom he had seen speaking in his student days. Wallas was now a highly respected figure in left-wing politics, one of the founders of the London School of Economics and Chairman of London's School Management Committee. Wallas's ideas were quite similar to Wells's, partly because Wells learned from him and partly because both were ex-Christians who retained an evangelical belief that salvation could be achieved by struggling to change the world for the better. Rejecting Marxism as naïve and socially divisive, Wallas supported the Liberal Party in Parliament while pursuing more radical, collectivist reform through the Fabian Society and other organizations. Wells found it refreshing to deal with such a rational, disinterested thinker, willing to take his ideas seriously and swap manuscripts for discussion.

By early 1900 Wells was working on a project provisionally entitled 'The New Prospectus'. He had given an interview the previous year to the *Puritan* magazine in which he put forward the idea that democracy had gone as far as was practicable and that henceforth power must inevitably flow toward skilled managers and engineers. The danger was that, under a façade of accountability, this social class would become self-serving (a fear sketched in *When the Sleeper Wakes,* echoed in *Brave New World, Nineteen Eighty-Four* and countless other dystopias and, arguably, confirmed by later developments such as the 'New Class' of the Soviet bloc). A key development in preventing this outcome was education, encouraging the public to think critically about the future.

If this priming of civil society was intended to form a new prospectus for Western civilization, it was also one for Wells's career. He would try to parlay his unorthodox class and educational background into credentials for what would later be called 'futurology', using the turn of the century as a psychologically opportune moment. If his *Sleeper* had failed to convince the public, maybe Wells could do a better job in his own person. If so, it would be an exciting complement to his established role as a fiction writer.

Wallas was not Wells's only cultural contact during the Sandgate years. The south coast was home to several authors who did not fit naturally into the British Establishment and who found it agreeable to position themselves some distance from London and enjoy each other's other mutual support, perhaps even reciprocal altruism. Ford Madox Heuffer later claimed that all the literary artists in England lived in a three- to five-mile radius of Wells's house, looking up to him because of his 'immense sales, and the gift of leadership'.[6]

Henry James had moved to Rye in 1897, and, after his visit to Wells's sickbed, he continued to take a close interest in the young author's development. The two men approached fiction with markedly different assumptions and would eventually fall out in spectacular fashion, but for fifteen years they met and corresponded with evident respect and muted reservations. In a review of 1895 Wells lamented of James:

> He has a positive distaste for the simple sentence, and he cannot avoid tangling his dependent clauses. His paragraphs remind one of a skein of wool after a kitten has played with it.[7]

However, Wells praised James's knowledge of human nature and, once he had made his acquaintance, became something of a devotee, vigorously defending a collection of his stories against a reviewer in the *Morning Post* and praising *The Wings of the Dove* to Arnold Bennett.[8] In turn James found Wells's work impressive in concept and content, if by his own standards unrefined in execution.

Joseph Conrad and his family had moved to Pent Farm, near Hythe, in September 1898. Wells exchanged visits, letters and reading matter with Conrad. He later recalled:

> Joseph Conrad and I used to shoot at breakable floating targets, bottles chiefly, at Sandgate, and as I have got a steady finger on a trigger while he was a jumping bundle of nerves I got most of the bottles. As he had a great pride in being a wild, wild man while I was a meek stay-at-home, this annoyed him.[9]

Between target practices they talked about Conrad's early adventures at sea and about the art of fiction. Arguably, both men were working in the romance tradition of Robert Louis Stevenson, so had something significant in common, though the increasing divergence of their approach was soon evident. On one occasion Conrad wanted to know precisely which words Wells would use to describe a boat passing them on the Solent. Wells replied that, since he did not share Conrad's impressionistic desire to do justice to each object, he would deal with the ship purely in relation to his story.[10] The reply must have frustrated Conrad who, to judge from a letter of January 1900, relished Wells's scientific romances precisely for their symbolist qualities, singling out his 'capacity to give shape, colour, *aspect* to the invisible' as well as to convey 'the *depth* of things common and visible'.[11]

By now Wells was moving away from the poetic and mysterious towards more direct social engagement, but he still found much to admire in Conrad's novella *Heart of Darkness*, serialized in *Blackwood's Magazine* during 1899. He paid tribute to it in *When the Sleeper Wakes*, along with stories by other local residents, 'The Madonna of the Future' by James and 'The Man Who Would Be King' by Kipling. Shortly after his reanimation Graham encounters all three of these tales in video adaptations, evidently still popular after two hundred years.

Hueffer, Conrad and James were not the only literary men now in Wells's orbit. There were others, less familiar to posterity, whose company Wells perhaps valued more. Professor York Powell, groundbreaking historian and man of letters, often visited Sandgate and cheered Wells with his humour. After suffering a stroke, Bob 'Spring-Heeled Jack' Stevenson, Robert Louis Stevenson's art-critic cousin, lodged in the town until his death in 1900. Wells missed his encouragement and the sustained absurdity of his talk and would later use him as a model for Ewart in *Tono-Bungay*. There were also visits from acquaintances such as Shaw and Bennett – recorded on camera as Wells took up photography at this time. ('What will you give us if we don't send you your photograph?' he asked Bennett. 'We haven't printed it yet but the negative looks good for a fiver to me.')[12]

An especially memorable acquaintance was the American author Stephen Crane, best known for his American Civil War novel *The Red Badge of Courage*. Crane had come to England in 1897 with his partner Cora Taylor, partly to escape scandal because Cora was a former brothel madam married to a murderer, partly to escape accusations that he himself was an alcohol and morphine addict, partly to flee harassment by the New York police for testifying against them on behalf of a prostitute, but mostly because he was as nomadic in temperament as Wells. In 1899 the Cranes set themselves up in Brede Place, a dilapidated fourteenth-century manor house where Crane entertained extravagantly while trying to keep up with his bills through writing.

The Cranes held an end-of-century Christmas celebration, culminating on 28 December 1899 in a play called 'The Ghost'. Crane was the chief writer, but part of the fun was to get other well-known authors to contribute snippets in order to create the most fabulous writing credit possible. In the end the programme named Crane, James, Wells, Gissing, Conrad, Marriot-Watson, Pugh and Haggard, plus

A.E.W. Mason (who played the Ghost) and the comparatively little-known Canadian journalist and author Robert Barr. Several of the scriptwriters, including Wells, took parts, while Jane provided piano accompaniment, largely filched from Gilbert and Sullivan.

During the night of 29 December, knowing of Wells's experience in such matters, Cora came to him and confided that Crane, who was tubercular, had just had a lung haemorrhage but was trying to conceal the fact. Wells immediately agreed to set out for Rye on a borrowed bicycle and rode 'into a drizzling dawn along a wet road to call up a doctor'.[13] The treatment helped Crane through this episode, but five months later he perished in a German sanatorium, aged twenty-nine.

Wells had previously written appreciatively of Crane in the *Saturday Review*. Now he composed an eloquent tribute, 'Stephen Crane, from an English Standpoint', which was published in the *North American Review* of August 1900. Wells praised Crane's 'freshness of method . . . vigour of imagination . . . and . . . essential freedom from many traditions that dominate this side of the Atlantic'.[14] American authors, he suggested, were readier than British ones to trust to their own originality and risk experiment. Crane stripped out many of the expected ingredients of fiction and was willing to be influenced by the impressionism of modern painters such as Whistler as much as by the narrative methods of Tolstoy.

While Wells was scornful of received wisdom and was working on his own ideas for experimental narrative, he did not plan to embrace Crane's artistic austerity. His preference was for the English tradition in which a narrator openly compères the story, generating 'satire, irony, laughter and tears', and indeed he questioned whether fiction could find a popular audience without the mediation of such a personality. As a spellbinding talker since his youth, and as a writer who had first achieved literary success with conversational pieces, Wells was confident that he could do this kind of thing well. He had already made a promising start with *The Wheels of Chance* and fared even better with *Love and Mr Lewisham*, serialized from November 1899 to February 1900 and published the following June. As in the earlier novel, the central character suffers many of Wells's youthful frustrations, while the guiding narrator is the successful Wells of today, their common identity suppressed so that he can keep psychological distance from his younger self.

George Lewisham is a gauche schoolteacher who is admitted to the Normal School of Science, becomes a socialist, speaks on politics in the debating society and dreams of a future as a political leader. Unfortunately for his career, he falls in love with and marries Ethel, the stepdaughter of a confidence trickster called Chaffery. When Chaffery absconds, leaving his son-in-law to support the pregnant Ethel and her mother, Lewisham has to abandon his dream of changing the world and console himself with the thought that the most important job in the struggle for existence is parenthood.

After the disappointment of *Sleeper*, many reviewers considered *Love and Mr Lewisham* Wells's best book so far and something of a breakthrough in creating engaging characters and depicting the workaday world. The *Athenaeum*, *Manchester Guardian*, *Academy*, *Bookman* and *Atlantic Monthly* were all enthusiastic. The *Daily Telegraph* suspected that many would regard it 'as by far the most fascinating piece of work he has given us'. The *Daily Chronicle* thought the novel was 'Mr Wells at his very best' and noted that his deft balance of sorrow and humour conveyed life at the poorer end of the middle class far more effectively than did Gissing's insistence on 'the gray-tragic view'.[15]

Wells's old college friends testified to the authenticity of Lewisham's experiences. Both Simmons and Healey thought the downbeat ending a little contrived but judged that *Lewisham* represented Wells's way forward, the latter urging, 'Write more books like this one.' Even Edmund Gosse, a privately educated literary scholar, found he could relate to the story, declaring to Wells that he read the book 'with great emotion' and 'a full heart' because he had once been poor and almost made the same mistake in marriage. He judged that the book was written 'with rare skill and firmness of vision'.[16]

Henry James was more cautious in his enthusiasm, indicating reservations about the composition but assuring Wells that he admired his humour, pathos, truth and fancy. The book was 'a bloody little chunk of life'.[17] Gissing naturally relished the pathos but admitted that Wells's 'humorous method' gave it an original and effective twist.[18] While Bennett admired the book, he shared the *Speaker* magazine's view that Wells's greatest talent was for science fiction. Wells retorted that books like *The Time Machine* came to him intuitively, whereas more realistic works like *Lewisham* were the product of serious, long-term commitment:

> I want to write novels and before God I *will* write novels. They are the proper stuff for my everyday work, a methodical careful distillation of one's thoughts and sentiments and experiences and impressions.[19]

In fairness to Wells, for all the autobiographical element, the novel was not a slice of life hacked off the carcass of reality with the literary equivalent of a butcher's cleaver, as James had insinuated, but a work of careful workmanship and invention. The main characters are not copies; in particular the weak and rather untrustworthy Ethel is no Isabel. Nor is Lewisham Wells. Or, rather, as he had done before, Wells represents himself through two contrasting characters, one of them bent on transforming himself and the world, the other sharply sceptical. Earlier doubles such as Moreau and Prendick or Graham and Ostrog had not engaged with each other's views quite so explicitly as do the idealistic Lewisham and the cynical Chaffery, making this the first of Wells's novels to show clear dialogic tendencies.

Initially it seems that the opposition between Lewisham's science and Chaffery's phoney seances is a contrast between truth and deception, but Chaffery argues that science is only approximately true and that much of its truth can be demonstrated only under special laboratory conditions. The rest of culture is an outright fiction, designed to reconcile us to a world that is fundamentally irrational and unjust: 'Lies are the mortar that bind the savage individual man into the social masonry.'[20] Lewisham's socialism is an exemplary delusion. The only way forward for an intelligent person who seeks integrity is to 'engage in some straightforward comparatively harmless cheating' rather than succumb to 'self-deception and self-righteousness'. Even this limited integrity is an uncertain accomplishment, however, because every human being is a bundle of inconsistent impulses.

The story appears to endorse Lewisham and reject Chaffery, yet Chaffery's arguments go unanswered and Lewisham's love rests in part on sentimental clichés. The final chapters, which were repeatedly rewritten, bring the book to a reasonably satisfyingly dramatic conclusion, since we are more interested in Lewisham's fate and the attitudes he displays towards it than the arguments he uses to get there. The unresolved issues are left open, however, to resurface in later books.

The biographer of Wells is left with a puzzle. If the *Sleeper*, Wells's first attempt to make social themes central to his fiction, fared comparatively badly with the public, while *Lewisham*, where he put forward love as the main source of fulfilment in life, was hailed by critics and personal acquaintances as a breakthrough in his career, why did Wells not follow the obvious course and write more books like *Lewisham*?

One obvious reason is that Wells was a romantic artist whose work was rooted in his own experience and inspired by a longing for transcendence. He could write successfully about being an unhappily married teacher because he had been one. Despite requests from friends, he could not write a sequel to *The Wheels of Chance* or *Love and Mr Lewisham* because he did not have that subsequent experience to draw on; his temperament did not 'do' resignation and his whole life and career was a defiance of realistic expectations.

Clues to a further reason are inscribed in several of the novels, beginning with *Lewisham* itself. What happens to someone who shares Wells's belief that culture is a set of empty conventions but who does not adopt a counterbalancing belief that a utopian organization of human affairs may be possible in the future? Answer: he turns into a confidence trickster whose life's work is telling lies in order to get money from fools. Chaffery's duplicity is analogous to being a novelist whose books do not transmit a redeeming vision. Unless Wells had an ideal future to authenticate his fiction, he, too, would be a dealer in lies, his writing a mere game of skill like his father's cricket. And he himself would be left a thwarted victim of conflicting impulses and motives.

While he clearly felt the inadequacy of the *Sleeper* and the attractions of *Lewisham*, Wells simply could not give up the quest to direct himself in a more evangelical direction. He did the best he could with the *Lewisham* approach meanwhile, attempting a comic novel that would at least balance 'message' and artistic merit. He had decided that his plan for a three-decker *Wealth of Mr Waddy* was not going to come off, and from December 1899 to April 1900 he tried rewriting the project as *Kipps*. Wells had realized that three-volume novels were no longer economically viable, but it may also be that, as his health improved, he simply lost interest in the invalid Waddy. In the abandoned draft, only six chapters focus on him, after which Kipps begins to move centre stage, rendering the first volume of the trilogy rather pointless.

By August Wells was confessing to Pinker that he did not yet have a decent draft of *Kipps* to show publishers.[21] The urgent job now was to work up his Professor Cavor stories into a scientific romance that would maintain his reputation with his core readership. *The First Men in the Moon* proved to be a more compelling book than *When the Sleeper Wakes* and stands up reasonably well against the previous scientific romances but has a more elaborate genre identity than any of the earlier works and is less successful in unifying the components, making it a more episodic reading experience.

It starts as a comic novel: a scientist is befriended by a cynical rogue called Bedford who wants to exploit his discoveries and inventions for profit. The book turns into a science-fiction adventure when the two use a gravity-repelling substance to fly to the Moon. They are taken prisoner by the insect-like Selenites who live inside the Moon, but Bedford manages to escape and return. By this point Wells has already introduced an element of satire by making Bedford an embodiment of Rhodes-style imperialism, massacring Selenites in order to annex the Moon and obtain their gold while babbling Kiplingesque cant about the White Man's Burden. Wells developed the satire further during serialization by adding five chapters in which Cavor, trapped inside the Moon, sends back an analysis of Selenite society by radio.

For contemporary readers this was cutting-edge stuff, since it was only in 1898 that Marconi had transmitted the first signals across the Channel. The important point, however, is what Wells does with his transmissions, turning the final section of the book into a double-edged satire derived from *Gulliver's Travels*, in which Selenite society is portrayed as superior to ours in some respects yet a ridiculous exaggeration of ours in others. For example, the Selenites deform their offspring to suit the labour market, producing big-headed administrators, musclebound police and hands who are little more than hands. The description mocks the specialized education system and constricting social roles of our world, yet the Selenites' extreme methods have at least achieved a cohesive and efficient society, which is more than we can claim.

Some people have been puzzled about exactly what Wells is trying to say (is he advocating socialism or suggesting its pitfalls?), but this is to misread the book. Neither Bedford, who tells most of the story, nor Cavor, who supplies the final section, is meant to be a reliable narrator. Both are subject to frequent irony and their joint production is not an instructive fable but a playful adventure. Tellingly, in most versions of *The First Men in the Moon* Bedford adopts the name 'Wells' at the end of the story in order to gather untidy truths behind a single respectable persona.

Versions of the story were serialized in Britain and America from late 1900 to summer 1901. The book was published in November 1901 to a positive reception from readers and critics. Unfortunately, the US edition accidentally omitted a whole page, including some of the descriptions of the lunar dawn that T.S. Eliot would later call 'quite unforgettable', and these have remained absent in most subsequent American editions.[22] Henry James was sufficiently impressed by the book to suggest collaborating with Wells on his next scientific romance or on *Kipps*.[23] This was one radical possibility for the future that Wells did not take up.

Despite the enormous amount of research and writing that went into *The First Men in the Moon* and 'The New Prospectus', Wells found time for a holiday during the spring. His first trip abroad having been so agreeable, European jaunts became a common feature of the Wellsian lifestyle. During May 1900 Wells, Jane and Frank cycled in the north of France, visiting both the Paris Exposition and George Gissing. From late January to March 1901 Wells and Jane went to Italy and Switzerland, again calling in on Gissing on the way back. Horrified to find their friend ill and emaciated, they took him in as a visitor during the spring of 1901, feeding him up until he had gained seven pounds. This hospitality was possible because by then their dream house had been constructed.

Keen as always to get a new project under way, Wells had found the creation of his home a trial. To begin with, there were the negotiations with Voysey, who designed every aspect of his houses down to the smallest detail. Wells wanted the door handles in a low position so children would be able to reach them. He also objected to the heart-shaped letter-plate for the front door, which he thought kitsch. Eventually Voysey agreed to turn the heart upside down to make a spade and called the building Spade House. The operators of the cliff lift which ran past the front door quickly incorporated the name into their patter, assuring tourists that the owner was none other than the famous gambler and con man Charles Wells who had won several fortunes in the Monte Carlo casino, presumably via the ace of spades. As a result, Wells claimed, he 'went about Sandgate and Folkestone like a Wagnerian hero with a motif', errand boys greeting him by whistling 'The Man Who Broke the Bank at Monte Carlo'.[24] The Monte Carlo casino soon became an ironic location for weekend charades.

After lengthy negotiations with the landowner and builders, actual building work began on Spade House in February 1900 and went on until November. Wells visited the site in Radnor Cliff Crescent most days, fuming with impatience not only at the pace but at the methods of construction, which, in the case of wall-building, appeared to him to have progressed little since the days of the pyramids.[25] On Saturday 8 December Wells and Jane finally moved in. 'Got there at last!' Wells exclaimed on a postcard to Bennett. 'No carpets no dining room table or chairs, little food but still – *there!*'[26]

The house was sited near the sea, on the upper road between Sandgate and Folkestone. It had a long, sloping red roof, roughcast walls and iron lattice windows. The rear faced south, ninety feet up the cliff, with an impressive sea view and garden. The latter, Jane's pride and joy, featured several lawns, summerhouses, a rockery and a covered walk. It was a handy spot to play tennis and badminton, familiarity with the coastal wind that blew across the court giving Wells a pleasingly unfair advantage over more experienced players. The rooms were large, the bedrooms and living-rooms placed together on the ground floor in case Wells became a permanent wheelchair-user.

Even while the house was being built, however, Wells's improving health, increasing savings and the discovery of an insurance company willing to cover him had caused a change of plan, and an upstairs nursery was included. By the time of the move Jane was two months pregnant, though it was not until June 1901 that Wells felt confident enough to break the news to Bennett, telling him,

> Mrs Wells and I have been collaborating (and publication is expected early in July) in the invention of a human being.[27]

Wells had arrived in Sandgate at a low ebb; but now, with further bestselling books in the shops, a custom-made house built and a child on the way, he must have been elated. His mood seems to be caught in a story, published in the *Strand* magazine in December 1901, called 'The New Accelerator'. A research chemist living in the Upper Sandgate Road concocts a drug that enables human beings to live at thousands of times their normal speed. Having dosed up himself and the narrator, he bursts exuberantly on to the Folkestone Leas and hurtles around the seemingly frozen people, inspecting and commenting on them. The drug wears off just as the two men are about to ignite from friction. The madcap raid surely reflects Wells's renewed energy and desire to pursue his own agenda, regardless of dangers.

His continuing yearning for sexual adventures, for example, had taken a worrying turn during 1900. The previous year J.F. Nisbet, a writer on science and literature, known to Wells as *The Times* drama critic, had died. With a generosity that would prove typical, Wells offered to pay the school fees for Nisbet's illegitimate daughter, May, and later funded a year of study at the School of Dramatic Art before she became a music teacher.

He had never met May, but it seemed a nice idea to invite her to Sandgate for her holidays. One day he looked up and found the teenager coming towards him in a tight bathing suit. The sight made such an impression on him that it was still on his mind twenty-two years later in *The Secret Places of the Heart*, where the protagonist becomes so fixated by a similar vision that he spends the rest of his life seeking a 'goddess' who can live up to it.[28]

Fortunately, Wells's attempts to flirt with May came to nothing and he decided to sublimate his feelings into a book, *The Sea Lady*. Begun in the summer of 1900, *The Sea Lady* tells of a mermaid who comes ashore at Sandgate and, having adopted the name 'Doris Thalassia Waters', seduces a rising Liberal politician called Chatteris. Chatteris has to choose between, on the one hand, his political responsibilities and engagement to a respectable young woman and, on the other, his desire to pursue imagination and sexual fulfilment. Eventually he succumbs and is hauled beneath the sea. Wells read some of the *Sea Lady* to Jane and Pinnie, who were so amused 'it gave 'em fits', the implications for Wells's future sexual fidelity having clearly eluded them.[29]

Jane gave birth to a boy, George Philip Wells, on 17 July 1901. For the first twenty-four hours there was doubt that either of them would survive. Wells recalled that his wife 'seemed a very little fragile thing in that battle'.[30] Once the worst was over, however, Wells did not respond to fatherhood with the commitment of a Mr Lewisham. He would later assure Bennett that

> Having one's first child is a very amazing & wonderful experience . . . I think there is nothing quite like one's first encounter with the wet little exquisite thing.[31]

This has the ring of sincerity, yet there is little doubt that he had counterbalancing feelings, too.

In a particularly heartfelt passage in the *Outline of History* he would describe Gautama's reaction to the birth of his son. He receives the news while reflecting on how he might seek 'some deeper reality' and responds, 'This is another tie to break.'[32] After an agony of decision-making, he decides to leave his family for ever. He looks longingly at his wife and child, then steals away.

Less than a month after the birth of 'Gip' Wells stole away on a cycling tour to Petersfield and back, looking for a location at a substantial distance from his family where he could write. He opted for a farmhouse at Hill Farm, Aldington, which, in the event, he used for only a few months. During September he was off again, calling in on his parents at Liss and fetching up in Ramsgate.

Anthony West has suggested that Wells invested in the solid structure of Spade House precisely because he knew the strength of his own restlessness. He was trying to create a home from which he could not escape.[33] For now it seemed to work. After a lengthy absence, during which his whereabouts were sometimes a mystery, Wells returned, but it was with a determination to tear up traditional assumptions and behaviour, particularly those connected with the family, and establish himself as an independent agent.

The death of Queen Victoria in January 1901 felt like the end of an era, and many people, Henry James included, were fearful of what would come next. Wells, long provoked by his mother's identification with the Queen, had entirely the opposite reaction. He later compared Victoria to a 'compact and dignified paper-weight' whose removal symbolized the blowing away of old ideas and the end of 'an epoch of tremendous stabilities'.[34] Wells sensed that the new century would be a contrasting age of instability, and he was eager to plunge into the flux.

Anticipations, the finished version of 'The New Prospectus', made a suitable splash. It ran in the *Fortnightly Review* from April to December 1901 with the subtitle *An Experiment in Prophecy*. For the book version, published in November (an American edition appeared the following year), it acquired the rather more imposing title *Anticipations of the Reaction of Mechanical and Scientific Progress Upon Human Life and Thought*. In a letter to Elizabeth Healey Wells admitted that his agenda was not as objective as this march-past of abstract nouns suggests. The book was

> designed to undermine and destroy the monarch, monogamy, faith in God & respectability – & the British Empire, all under the guise of a speculation about motor cars & electrical heating. One has to go gently in the earlier pages but D.V. the last will be a buster.[35]

(D.V., or *Deo volente*, meaning 'God willing', was a favourite ironic flourish in Wells's letters.)

Anticipations contains a good deal of informed speculation, arguing, for example, that motorized transport will cause cities to spread much further outwards, that the next major war will be a mechanized one involving whole populations and that in a hundred years' time there will be an acceptance of many types of relationships beyond traditional marriage. Wells even foresees by the beginning of the twenty-first century the growth of a European federal community centred on the Rhine, though if this development is retarded by German imperialism a series of wars may have to occur before German integration is achieved. Britain, he notes, will not fit readily into the New Europe but will see itself instead as part of the English-speaking community led by the USA. However, Wells would later blame himself for being timid in his forecasts of powered flight, especially as the pioneer aviator J.W. Dunne had given him advice on the subject, demonstrating with paper aircraft in the Spade House garden before going off to meet his commitments as an army officer.

Having established his intellectual authority with informed speculation, Wells unleashes the eyebrow-raising notion that globalization, technological progress and warfare will ultimately foster a movement for a new order, the 'New Republic', a consensus of technical specialists that will supersede capitalist democracy and establish a global Utopia based on state education and selective redistribution of wealth. This suggestion, based on the proposition that Wells's own outlook might resemble that of 'a respectable mechanic of the year 2000'[36] – a view that closely recalls how the mad scientist Nebogipfel in *The Chronic Argonauts* conceived of the future – was the most controversial part of the enterprise and, as we shall see, continues to provoke fierce reactions to this day.

The book was widely hailed as a triumph, in part because systematic thinking about the future was rare at that time and Wells was a gifted pioneer in the field and also because he had launched his project at an opportune moment. Not only was it the start of the twentieth century, when every thinking person knew that great changes were on their way; it was also the time of Dunne's destination, the Boer War.

After the Jameson fiasco of 1896 the British government had tried to negotiate with the Boers about the status of 'uitlanders' like Fred Wells, but, since what it was demanding was effectively control over southern Africa no agreement could be reached. In 1899 the British gave up negotiations and engineered a war that they expected would enable them quickly to seize the gold fields. By 1902, however, the fighting was still going on. The war could be won only by tactics such as herding the enemies' families into camps, where they died from malnutrition and disease. A quarter of all Boer women and children perished in the conflict; no one bothered to count the dead Africans.

While most Britons supported the war, they were shocked by the effort required by the greatest empire in history to subdue so small an enemy and were left asking why. The answer generally reached was lack of 'national efficiency'. How could the Empire prevail when almost one-third of army recruits had to be turned down because they could not meet the low physical standards? Was the British Empire now about to go the way of the Roman one, into decadence and destruction? Over the next few years many groups, from the eugenics movement to the Boy Scouts, wheeled out plans to reform the British outlook and breeding stock.

Wells's many references to the war made it clear that he, too, was contributing to the efficiency debate. Tommy Simmons (whose name had appeared as an in-joke in *The First Men in the Moon*) wrote to Wells praising his effort and condemning the 'vested interests', 'mutual admiration' and 'present muddles' that needed to be tackled by the New Republican technocrats – heroic successors to South Kensington graduates such as themselves. Despite his normal good nature Simmons was especially inspired by the chapters on war and 'the extinction of the unfit'.[37]

Nothing has done more damage to Wells's reputation than the concluding chapter of *Anticipations*. Much of it sounds like an ill-advised collaboration between the Artilleryman from *The War of the Worlds* and Mr Kurtz from Conrad's *Heart of Darkness*. The 'new class of modern efficients', Wells assures us, are likely to be idealists inspired by a new notion of God as unlike the Christian God as possible.[38] In the name of this vague belief they will set up a programme of sex education to get rid of the physically and mentally diseased and the lower classes in general. The death penalty, carried out mercifully with an opiate, will be used much less than now but will still have to be retained for the incorrigibly anti-social, since the New Republicans will 'have an ideal that will make killing worth the while'.[39] Life-wasting prison sentences, which achieve nothing, will be replaced by the brief application of 'good scientifically caused pain' – one should perhaps think of the electric cattle prods employed by the Selenites. Race relations will be strictly impartial but with a presumption that the majority of 'those swarms of black, and brown, and dirty-white, and yellow people' will not be up to the required standard and 'will have to go'.

This is not a rational extrapolation from existing knowledge. It is not even the speculation of a fearless thinker. It is the fantasy of a sickly, squeaky-voiced individual who would have been rejected if he had tried to enlist, a Victorian schoolboy who had read adventure stories which made him afraid of savage natives and who felt threatened by the rough lads from the National School – though, to be fair to Wells, these seem to have been attitudes widely held among the educated classes, many readers greeting his concluding chapter with particular enthusiasm. To their credit, others such as Conan Doyle and Chesterton denounced his ideas, a reaction that seems to have quickly set him rethinking his position.

Perhaps the key criticism to be made of the New Republic is that Wells founds it on a bogus appeal to Darwinism, claiming that the movement is part of 'the mighty scheme' of natural selection in which 'the tiger calls for[th] wisdom and courage out of man'. Wells was evidently short of a tiger or two when he adopted this perspective, as the basis of biological evolution is adaptation to existing conditions, not hypothetical future ones. Global, revolutionary change may be advisable and can be linked to evolution by arguing that our ability to think ahead is part of our biological inheritance, but no utopian vision can be justified by Darwinism, which, by its nature, is explanatory of the past, not predictive of the future. Wells had lapsed, not for the last time, into a naïve secularization of religious ideas – a widespread practice among late Victorian and Edwardian thinkers but an invalid one.

Evolution is driven by environmental pressures on the gene pool, not by individual or collective willpower; evolution with a conscious purpose is the unscientific concept that Wallace and Darwin replaced by the mechanism of natural selection. Since purposeful evolution requires some kind of cosmic will, a pseudo-deity inevitably pops up at key moments in both the *Sleeper* and *Anticipations*. Gissing wrote to Wells praising *Anticipations*, particularly the last chapter, but as an atheist he baulked at the way the word 'God' was used. Wells had recently assured John Galsworthy he was 'an extensive skeptic, no God, no king, no nationality', but his own foresight saga failed to maintain that scepticism.[40]

Lovat Dickson's observation that the New Republic carries a suggestion of 'strong-armed fascism' is fair comment.[41] In recent times, however, several books and websites have gone much further, blanking out Wells's impressive work against racism and totalitarianism throughout the first half of the twentieth century and focusing exclusively on the handful of pages sketching the New Republic as though these represented a lifelong mission statement and an unguarded disclosure of what socialists, liberals and Darwinians secretly believe. It is difficult to mount a scrupulous defence against such claims without seeming to endorse the 'New Republic'. We shall try, however, concentrating on the claim that Wells was an anti-Semite, which does at least contain some substance, though not as much as has been claimed.

Michael Coren, in particular, ramps up the charge with a compromising quotation from *Anticipations* that Jews possess an 'incurable tendency to social parasitism'.[42] Here is what Wells wrote:

> If the Jew has a certain incurable tendency to social parasitism, and we make social parasitism impossible, we shall abolish the Jew, and if he has not, there is no need to abolish the Jew. We are much more likely to find we have abolished the Caucasian solicitor. I really do not understand the exceptional attitude people take up against the Jews.[43]

Taken in its entirety, the passage is plainly a defence of Jews against anti-Semitism, suggesting that profiteers and usurers should be tackled in their own right, not by scapegoating an ethnic group.

This is exactly what we would expect, given that Wells's closest friends in his early years, Sidney Bowkett and Walter Low, were both Jewish. Since Coren confidently assures us that Wells had few Jewish friends, we had better add that he was not only friendly with Israel Zangwill, the best known Zionist in Britain, but that his agent, Pinker, was Jewish, as were many later acquaintances such as Philip Guedalla, David Lubin and the Korda brothers. Even if we discount the half-Jewish (all-Zionist) Martha Gellhorn, Wells scarcely exhibits the networking profile of a rabid anti-Semite.

This is not to deny that Wells sometimes dropped into the casually disparaging attitude towards Jews that was common in British speech at least until the 1960s, nor that he used Jewish stereotypes in his fiction alongside many other stereotypes, nor that he mocked Judaism alongside other religions. (If Wells baited anyone in his work it was Roman Catholics and then only in his last years.) In the 1920s Wells would draw a distinction between 'broad Jews' tolerant of other cultures and 'narrow' Jews, reserving his criticisms for the fanatics, just the same distinction he made between broad and narrow Christians or socialists.[44] Bryan Cheyette, a Jewish scholar who has made a serious study of Wells's views, reaches the conclusion that Wells was not a racist, since he saw 'Jewishness' as a cultural, not a biological, category and positively admired the 'Hebraic moral tradition' for its pursuit of justice and learning. However, those he perceived as 'unassimilated' Jews often riled him and triggered the stereotype of anti-public-spirited acquisitiveness.[45]

We may add a couple of supplementary reasons why Wells would sometimes show limited sympathy for persecuted Jews and partially blame them for their own plight. First, as one who had little sympathy for any form of nationalism, Wells was exasperated by Zionism. Its adherents did not at that time have a territory to be territorial about. If even they could not be brought to identify with a larger community, what hope was there of established nationalisms withering away in favour of human unity? Second, Wells came to see that one of the consequences of globalization would be multiculturalism. In theory he approved, but as a Victorian Englishman he could not help feeling uneasy about the consequences for social cohesion. The only ethnic minority group he had encountered was the Jewish one, and this naturally became the focus of his anxieties.

Read in the shadow of the Holocaust, Wells's references to Jews may cause some discomfort, but he was writing before the Holocaust, and his alternating praise and criticism of Jews, however dated the terms in which it is expressed, does not condemn him to the category of anti-Semites occupied by Belloc, Pound and Eliot. In a context where Wells is often reputed to be a proponent of forced sterilization, lethal chambers and genocide, we had better be clear about what he does and does not say in *Anticipations*.[46] Far from being a white supremacist, he writes admiringly of Hindus, the Japanese and Chinese. He does employ extreme stereotypes of lower-class white people, mixed-race people and people of African origin but does not propose they should be harmed. Indeed, he does not propose much at all but speculates what an imaginary twenty-first-century elite might do.

He suggests that this hypothetical state will not treat the 'inferior races . . . as races at all' but as individuals, and, while there is an assumption that most of them will prove to be failures, there is an equal assumption that, if this is not the case, they will be accepted as New Republicans. People such as congenital alcoholics and gamblers, who do prove inferior, regardless of race, will not be killed but discouraged from having children by removing state subsidies and offering contraception. Once science has progressed sufficiently to allow diagnosis, people who are carrying serious transmissible diseases will, however, be forbidden to have children on pain of death.

Anticipations is both the starting point and the lowest point in Wells's career as a social thinker, an attempt to catch the public attention with some fashionably radical views. Did Wells actually believe his rhetoric, or was he just using the language of Social Darwinism and imperialism because he knew that they had popular appeal at the time? Certainly Wells was out to connect with a wide readership, and he never wrote anything else in this vein. Equally, he had floated some pretty extreme notions through characters such as the Artilleryman and Chaffery. The problem was that, in attempting to reduce the natural polyphony of his imagination to a single point of view, he had subtracted the irony that had previously contextualized his wilder imaginings.

As ever, he was a quick learner. Within two years Wells would be arguing against negative eugenics; within three defending black people against race prejudice; within four advocating the desirability of a multiracial society. Wells was not the sort to make a public confession of his errors, but he would ultimately, despite having dismissed the idea in *Anticipations*, become a leading advocate of universal human rights. Those who wish to examine Wells's ideas on race should not, therefore, confine themselves to his initial groping with the subject in the last few pages of *Anticipations* but look at more typical chapters such as 'Race in Utopia' (*A Modern Utopia*), 'The Tragedy of Colour' (*The Future in America*) and 'The Rights of Man in South Africa' (*'42 to '44*), all curiously absent from his detractors' reading lists.

At the turn of the century what struck the public was not so much Wells's premature conclusions as the exciting way he articulated them and the vista of future-thinking he was opening up at a time when the leaders of society were evidently floundering. A *Westminster Gazette* reviewer commented that, while he did not agree with everything Wells had to say, the book 'applies a useful explosive to the conventional, acquiescent, complacent frame of mind'.[47]

With eight editions printed in its first year, *Anticipations* was a bestseller, and Wells had found a new calling. The established author of science-fiction and comic novels was now also a fashionable social commentator, whose opinions everyone wanted to hear. The book, perhaps even because of its controversial conclusion, had given him the career boost he had desired and opened up a whole new adventure. He confided to Richard Gregory, 'The amount of treason I am discovering is amazing . . . I am going to write, talk & preach revolution for the next five years.'[48]

9
ANNEXING THE FUTURE
1902–1905

Wells has left us an inimitable summary of his standing in the early twentieth century:

> Mr H.G. Wells has a considerable vogue on the continent, all his books are to be found in the Tauchnitz edition, and he has been translated into French, German, Norwegian, Danish, Italian, Spanish and Czech. His work is popular for serialization in the English magazines; but in the circulating library and in the hearts and homes of England and America, his position is one of extreme insignificance . . . Every author writes for an imaginary reading public of his own, and the public of Mr Wells' dreams would include the bulk of the medical, legal and engineering professions, most schoolmasters, some schoolmistresses, and every English-speaking student between the ages of seventeen and twenty-five. Instead of which – he probably gets the public he deserves.[1]

By the time he penned this wry summary, however, Wells was developing a role that would make him more than a source of casual entertainment, giving him the high status, distinctive identity and loyal readership base he sought.

In 1899 he had given Pinker the marketing advice, 'For this year I'm the futurity man.'[2] With that claim firmly established in *Anticipations* his position grew more commanding as time passed. Even in the four years covered by the present chapter the Victorian era was falling away and a new one taking its place: motor vehicles beginning to appear in urban areas; the Wright Brothers flying; Caruso recording; cinema gaining the narrative techniques of *The Great Train Robbery* and the special effects of *A Trip to the Moon*; aspirin and radio valves being invented; even Einstein baffling his fellow scientists with relativity theory.

People needed new guides for a new era. George Orwell recalled that

> Back in the nineteen-hundreds it was a wonderful experience for a boy to discover H.G. Wells . . . here was this wonderful man who could tell you about the inhabitants of the planets and the bottom of the sea, and who knew that the future was not going to be what respectable people imagined.[3]

That reputation would still retain its force half a century later when Wells appeared on the cover of the Beatles' *Sgt Pepper* album, aptly located between Marx and the *Mona Lisa*.

He gave a high-profile lecture at the Royal Institution on 24 January 1902 – originally planned for 1899 but postponed owing to his poor health. He was never a strong public speaker and, according to Wallas, who was in the audience, he delivered *The Discovery of the Future* too rapidly.[4] None the less, his reflections made a positive impression. They found a wider public in *Nature* on 6 February, appeared in book form later in the month and reached the USA the following year as part of the *Annual Report* of the Smithsonian.

Wells asserts that humankind is moving from a way of thinking based on passively submitting to social norms and religious commandments to critically evaluating them, freeing us from the dead past. The breadth of our roads, the design of our houses, our clothing, speech, spelling, weights and measures, coinage and religious and political theories are all relics that require re-evaluation.

Wells distinguishes his own ideas from those of Comte and the positivists. They assume the past and future to be stable and the present to be a temporary period of turmoil; he sees change as continuous. Or so he claims. In practice he does have a single reference point, a hypothetical world state, if not static then remarkably consistent over time; he ignores whatever may come after his secular heaven and dismisses the ultimate extinction of humankind by simple disbelief. As with *Anticipations*, Wells starts off with rational enquiry, then shifts to a form of religious mythology, concealing the join by his Chaffery-style patter.

For the public, the philosophical coherence of Wells's lecture was a minor consideration. The thought-provoking discussion made its author a man to watch. At an emotional level Wells's words recalled the wonder he had felt when peering through the telescope at Uppark – a key moment of his life invoked in the rather strained concluding passage, presumably written shortly after the birth of Gip:

> beings who are now latent in our thoughts and hidden in our loins, shall stand upon this earth as one stands upon a footstool, and shall laugh and reach out their hands amidst the stars.

Little Bertie – the ill-nourished, poorly educated boy from Bromley, rejected by society and, quite possibly, damned by God – had managed to reinvent himself not just as a man of learning but a prophet, ready to pass judgement on the world and give it a sound kick in a more satisfactory direction. Prestigious London clubs welcomed him. In January he dined with Sidney and Beatrice Webb and in March with Winston Churchill. The administrators and the politician were alike in thinking that the author of *Anticipations* was a brilliant journalist who, once they had clarified the importance of administrators and politicians, might help promote their own views. They were wrong.

Wells's readiness to defy authority and keep rethinking his own ideas were both evident in a Sociology Society debate on eugenics at the London School of Economics in May 1904, when he ridiculed Francis Galton's suggestion that bishops' sons were fittest for mating and that criminals should not be allowed to breed. Such views, he had come to realize, confused nature with nurture. Many criminals were probably above average in their courage and enterprise, just operating under adverse conditions.[5]

If Wells's fixation with the future had not helped him to anticipate his own changing ideas neither did it make it clear where to take his writing career. He continued to toy with the idea of becoming a dramatist, under the impression that theatrical success would be a quick way to make money and subsidize his less commercial writings, despite warnings to the contrary from Shaw. In his attempt to be a playwright, however, Wells showed his usual industry, planning a collaboration with Bennett to be called *The Crime* and considering the dramatization of *The Sea Lady*, the novel version of which was published in July 1902, with a US edition later in the year.

Through the tale of a mermaid who seduces and destroys an aspiring politician, Wells was sending himself the coded message that, if he had to choose between extramarital sex and respectability, it would be respectability he would sacrifice, whatever the damage to his career. There is, however, nothing passionate and shocking about the novel itself, which is essentially a dull reworking of *The Wonderful Visit*, relocated to the Pophams' house, with characters and situations loosely parodying Mrs Humphrey Ward's now forgotten bestseller *Marcella*. Despite one or two satirical flickers, the enterprise suffers from fundamental self-indulgence, and, aptly enough for a story about a man drowned by a mermaid, it has since sunk into oblivion.

In a French edition of the book Wells drew a picture of Jane as the mermaid, indicating that his present desire for other women was a continuation of his original feelings when he ran off with her.[6] There is reason to believe, as we have seen, that Wells continued to be promiscuous at least occasionally in the early years of his second marriage, but all he has to tell us on the subject is that he developed a 'compromise' with Jane 'after 1900' and that 'the first wanderings of my desire are very hard to trace'.[7]

A passage from *Anticipations* on the strains of monogamy has the tone of confession.

> For the man it commonly involves considerable restraint; he must ride his imagination on the curb, or exceed the code in an extremely dishonoring, furtive, and unsatisfactory manner while publicly professing an impossible virtue; for the woman it commonly implies many uncongenial submissions. There are probably few married couples who have escaped distressful phases of bitterness and tears.[8]

We may posit several such episodes of bitterness and tears. Presumably Wells's 'don't you believe it' picshua of 1896 marks one of them. Eventually he must have renounced his furtive escapades in favour of openness, reminding Jane that they were believers in free love who had married as a convenience, that they were also students of biology who should take a dispassionate view of the powerful drive to reproduce one's kind. Did Jane want a divorce with all the consequences for her and the rest of the family, or was she prepared to accept Wells as he was, as indeed she knew him to be when she took him from Isabel?

This is mostly guesswork. As Wells burned his early correspondence with Jane it is impossible to recover the truth. Such letters from her as we have suggest that she had a huge emotional dependence on her husband and a deep insecurity about him, probably compounded by guilt at having taken him from Isabel, and would have put up with almost any treatment as long as she could remain his wife.[9] By the early 1900s Jane seems to have known and accepted that her husband was engaged in occasional extramarital activities; they probably did not take the form of sustained affairs until the middle of the decade.

A letter to Wallas of 1902 does at least gives us a clear picture of Wells's attitude towards sex at this time.

> A man or woman ought to have sexual intercourse. Few people are mentally, or morally or physically in health without it. For everyone there is a minimum and maximum between which lies complete efficiency. Find out your equation, say I, and then keep efficient.[10]

Wells admits that venereal disease is a complicating factor, as is emotional attachment with all its attendant jealousies, but he is optimistic that the latter at least may be curbed.

Moving in radical intellectual circles, Wells was becoming familiar with several husbands other than Bowkett, whose enthusiasm for promiscuity matched or even surpassed his own, giving his illicit behaviour a suggestion of normality. Bertrand Russell was one, Hubert Bland another. Bland, a leading Fabian, and his wife Edith (who paid the family's bills as the children's writer E. Nesbit) had a house in Eltham and a summer residence in Dymchurch, just a cycle ride from Sandgate. Visiting them proved an eye-opener. The children were all Bland's, but were they his wife's? And what was the relationship between Bland and the housekeeper and, for that matter, with that intense young woman playing badminton? Beyond the private lives of the Blands, Wells must also have heard gossip about such public figures as Herbert Asquith, David Lloyd George and the King himself, sarcastically dubbed 'Edward the Caresser' by Henry James.

Wells resisted the idea that he belonged to a set of philanderers, preferring to see himself as someone who had become averse to marriage because of the experience of his parents and who now wished to pioneer more open forms of contract. He later admitted that he might have been unhappy if Jane had adopted the same policy, and he was furious when he found out that Isabel had remarried, to a man named Ted Fowler-Smith. He claimed that she had kept the marriage secret in order to retain his alimony payments.[11] In his autobiography, however, Wells concedes that, whatever right may have been on his side, he had succumbed to the irrational jealousy that he had been blithely hoping to eradicate through free love. He destroyed all Isabel's letters and photographs and ceased to correspond with her for five years. It was a regression to the Palaeolithic:

> If we had lived ten thousand years ago I suppose I should have taken my axe of stone and set out to find and kill her.[12]

Such surges of passion did not, however, distract Wells from family responsibilities. Late in March 1902 he took Jane to Belgium. In May Fred came over for a holiday visit, hoping to catch Edward VII's coronation. In June Wells and Jane headed for Switzerland precisely in order to miss the coronation, though in the event it was postponed and they were back in time for the celebrations. They were off again during August and September, probably with Fred this time, to Paris and Locarno.

The presence of Fred in Wells's life at this period is more significant than it may at first appear. Wells's drastic change in attitude towards black people seems to have come from greater knowledge gained through reading and discussion, and he particularly mentions a conversation with an unnamed man from a dry goods store in Johannesburg whose attitude to native Africans he found shocking.[13] The extreme opinions Fred had picked up in South Africa were apparently a factor in encouraging his younger brother to question the rationality of his own views on race. (Despite falling dangerously ill with typhoid at the end of 1907 Fred kept up his successful business career in South Africa and in 1909 opened Wells' Drapery Store at the corner of Hay and Turf Club Streets at Turffontein in Johannesburg.)

Another member of Wells's family made a guest appearance in his writing in a 1903 short story called 'The Magic Shop', which describes a visit by Gip and his daddy to an agreeably haunted London toy store. With Gip now walking and talking, Wells was inspired to follow *Anticipations* with *Mankind in the Making*, a discussion of New Republican reforms in child-rearing and education. Wells himself was not, it must be said, a hands-on parent during the infant years. Though he was an affectionate father and Jane seems to have breast-fed, the couple followed the fashionable practice of handing over their children (Frank Richard, named after Uncle Frank, was born on 31 October 1903) to a nurse, Jessie, only seeing the children for about one hour a day – very unlike the personal attention Sarah had lavished on baby Bertie. As the children grew, however, contact increased more and more.

Mankind in the Making was published in September 1903. British copies were exported and rebranded for a US edition in 1904. Shedding the confident bluster of *Anticipations*, Wells adopts what would become his standard line on prophecy, that his aim is not to impose his views on others but to open up new perspectives for readers to use as they please; toleration of different opinions and values is not an option but a condition under which we live, as knowledge grows and the limited nature of human understanding becomes clearer. His renouncement of authority does not, however, prevent Wells from demolishing the monarchy with relish or pulverizing the eugenics movement for its simplistic assumptions in a critique informed by Mendel's rediscovered laws of inheritance.

Wells is up to date with his research and succeeds in ventilating important issues, albeit with a few moments of backward-looking prejudice, but inevitably the book has dated and today's readers will probably find it naïve in its eagerness to interfere in other people's private lives. We may sympathize with Sidney Bowkett's reaction, reported by Florence Popham:

> He was enthusiastic about the book – but the life of the New Republican appears too strenuous for him – where does *pleasure* come in? that's what he would like to know – real pleasure – not the sickly sort of pleasure you may derive from doing your duty to the coming race.[14]

Wells himself was troubled by the way reviewers missed the dialogic nature of his work, seeing a 'glib finality' in what he had intended to be exploratory.[15] The problem of combining hypothetical ideas and strong presentation was one with which he continued to struggle.

Posterity has found rather more to its liking in *Twelve Stories and a Dream*, a collection of shorter fiction published in October 1903. Though the book does not contain any of Wells's very best stories, there are impressive highlights – not only 'The Magic Shop', 'The New Accelerator' and 'Miss Winchelsea's Heart' but also 'The Truth about Pyecraft', 'The Inexperienced Ghost' and 'Jimmy Goggles the God'.

While his ability to spin a yarn was clearly undiminished, it was not his priority at this time. Advising Bennett on how he wished to be presented to the American public in an article for *Cosmopolitan*, he was particularly keen to escape the title 'English Jules Verne':

> There is something other than either story writing or artistic merit which has emerged through the series of my books, something one might regard as a new system of ideas – 'thought'.[16]

Bennett complied but was careful to balance his praise of Wells the 'moralist' with that of Wells the 'artist', the two united in their 'gift of seeing things afresh'.[17]

In September Bennett sent Wells his *Anna of the Five Towns*, a book that admirably fitted the recipient's criteria for the grown-up, disillusioned novel, but by now Wells had moved away from the sober literary aims he had set down five years earlier.

His new vocation as a fashionable thinker was, after all, taking him into elite circles in a way that would have been inconceivable when he left school at the age of thirteen. In November 1902 the Webbs invited him to dinner with John Burns, Herbert Asquith, Lady Elcho and the Shaws. Unsurprisingly, he alternated between being tongue-tied and assertively clever, but he made enough of an impression that the following month he was one of a select few invited to form the 'Co-efficients', a talking and dining club with which he remained associated until 1908.

Those websites that claim Wells to have been a lifelong advocate of eugenics and genocide will also tell you that the Co-efficients were ruling-class conspirators who precipitated the First World War in order to protect the British Empire. (If so, it was a policy that backfired pretty badly.) Actually they emerged from the hubbub about 'national efficiency' at the close of the Boer War: the aim was to bring together people with a range of views and expertise who were prepared to exchange ideas about the way forward for Britain and its empire. The original members included Liberal politicians R.B. Haldane and Edward Grey, Conservatives Leo Amery and Alfred Milner, Fabians Sidney Webb and William Pember Reeves and the philosopher Bertrand Russell. The group did not reach much agreement except about where to dine – at the Ship Tavern, Whitehall, and St Ermin's Hotel, Westminster, each member taking it in turns to present a topic.

From December Wells took a year's lease on a London flat, 6 Clement's Inn, positioning himself for easy access to the centres of political debate. In February 1903 Wallas and Shaw sponsored his membership of the Fabian Society. Of all the socialist groups, it had the most appeal to him because it consisted of middle-class professionals who wanted to instigate rational, collectivist reforms for the common good. The Fabians were keen that the working classes should have decent conditions and justice, but, unlike other socialist groups, they did not want to see the country run solely in their interests. On the other hand, as would soon become apparent, Wells had many reservations about the Fabians' stealthy approach to socialism, which he judged inadequate to the challenge they faced.

Within a month of signing up, on Friday 13 March, Wells was reading them a paper on 'Administrative Areas', a topic dear to him since the building of his house. Improved transport and communication were changing the scale of life, he pointed out – through commuting, for example – rendering many existing administrative systems obsolete. More comprehensive, expert bodies were needed to run things efficiently. This sounds uncontroversial enough, but, as John Partington has observed, the lecture implicitly rebuked the Fabians' tactic of permeating key institutions by suggesting that the institutions might then become obsolete.[18] Wells printed the talk as an appendix to *Mankind in the Making*, then for the time being left the Fabians to their own devices.

In June 1903 he and Jane returned to Italy, where he was apprehensive to find himself in the same hotel as Mrs Humphrey Ward. Fortunately the resemblance between *The Sea Lady* and *Marcella* seemed to have escaped her attention. Despite a recurrence of his kidney trouble in August, he spent the first half of September on a walking tour in the Swiss Alps with Graham Wallas. He was fascinated by the latter's views on mass psychology but found him tiresome as a companion, not least because he was unsupportive of Wells's attempts to pick up passing women. Wells confided in a letter to Jane that Wallas was constantly boring him with details of his marriage. He would 'use W freely in the next novel'.[19] This was no idle threat.

The book guying Wallas had, however, to join the end of a growing queue. *Kipps* was still in progress, a scientific romance called *The Food of the Gods* was speeding along, and Wells also undertook a lecture for the Oxford Philosophical Society, 'Scepticism of the Instrument', which was delivered on 8 November 1903 and printed in *Mind* in July 1904.

Anticipations had been based on the assumption that the future, though hard to foresee, is predestined, giving the impression that the New Republic was almost a scientific theory. *Mankind in the Making* had placed more emphasis on our lack of knowledge. 'Scepticism of the Instrument' strikes a balance, acknowledging the possibility of a predetermined universe but accepting our practical experience of the future as open. Wells explains how his early training (boldly re-evaluated into three years of solid scientific work) made him into what today would be called a sociobiologist. The human mind, he argues, is as much a product of adaptive evolution as a lung and has therefore no access to absolute truth. The world mediated through our senses does not show, for example, the subatomic level of reality, and the language we use to reason about existence is a mere human system of representation.

If these ideas seem highly up to date, the conclusion Wells draws from them has worn less well: 'One's political proceedings, one's moral acts are, I hold, just as much self-expression as one's poetry or painting or music.' His actions over the next few years would show that he wasn't fooling. However, typically of Wells, this argument is instantly destabilized by a counter-argument, that individuals may find their decisions are compatible with others' and so build up new, empirically grounded communities of belief. While the reader is trying to reconcile these two views, Wells follows them up with the proposal that, just as the reality we experience emerges from the subatomic world, so a form of god may emerge from our world.

There are any number of objections that could be made to these notions, singly and in combination, but they are the ideas Wells would try to live by for the rest of his life. His main way of resolving them would not be philosophical discussion but creative writing. That point is forcibly made at the end of the lecture, where he singles out 'insight' as a quality of mind to be cherished:

> insight which when it faces towards the contradictions that arise out of the imperfections of the mental instrument is called humour. In these innate, unteachable qualities I hold – in humour and the sense of beauty – lies such hope of intellectual salvation from the original sin of our intellectual instrument as we may entertain in this uncertain and fluctuating world of unique appearances . . .

The closing ellipsis is Wells's signature punctuation device, indicating that he could elaborate his ideas for ever but must stop somewhere.

Wells was called back from his abstract speculations in December 1903 by a summons from the Continent. A few weeks before he had been worrying about how Gissing's children were going to cope with their father ill and hoping to get them a pension from the Royal Literary Fund. On Christmas Eve a telegram arrived from Gabrielle: 'Gissing is dying. Entreat you to come. In greatest haste.' Gissing had gone down with double pneumonia complicated by a heart infection. Wells took a horsedrawn fly to Folkestone Pier, set sail on the afternoon boat, still wearing his garden clothes, and, after Christmas dinner in Bayonne, reached Gissing late the same day.

Wells was shocked to find Gissing gaunt and delirious, research for a historical novel venting from his brain as Latin babbling, fragments of Gregorian chant and strange exclamations. Assisted by an Anglican parson, he hired a 'religieuse' to nurse the sick man and spent all the time he could rubbing his chest with a handkerchief dipped in pure alcohol, then, when that ran out, methylated spirits, perhaps recalling the ice packs that had formerly saved his own life.

He had taken a room at an inn at the other end of the village and returned there, drained, in the early hours.

> St-Jean-Pied-de-Port is a lonely frontier town and at night its deserted streets abound in howling great dogs to whom the belated wayfarer is an occasion for the fiercest demonstrations. I felt like a flitting soul hurrying past Anubis and hesitating at strange misleading turnings on the lonely Pathway of the Dead.[20]

The two days during which Wells attempted to nurse Gissing turned into a kind of tragic farce because Wells believed the dying man needed nourishment, while the doctor and Gabrielle held that he ought to fast. Perhaps Wells had not changed so very much from the untrained assistant who dispensed his own choice of treatment in Midhurst. When Gabrielle was out of the room Wells attempted to sneak food to Gissing, prompting the accusation from her and some subsequent commentators that he killed the patient, though the consensus is that Gissing's time had come regardless of treatment. Under the impression that Gissing's friend Morley Roberts would shortly be arriving to take over the vigil, Wells eventually left on 27 December. Roberts was delayed, and Gissing perished in the early hours of the 28th.

From the point of view of Wells's life story, there is something unavoidably symbolic in the death of George Gissing, whose pessimistic outlook Wells had cautiously embraced in *Lewisham* but from which he had now turned away. Wells seems to have sensed that something of himself was dying with Gissing. Before long he would incorporate a version of the deathbed scene into his most ambitious novel, *Tono-Bungay*.

For now there were urgent practical matters to attend to. Wells wrote to Gosse and Frederic Harrison in a renewed attempt to secure funds for Gissing's sons and through the latter succeed in securing a Civil List pension. (This was typical of Wells's wish to support people who were less fortunate than himself. He had recently sent Conrad £25, knowing that his bank had gone bust taking his savings with it.)

Wells also composed a preface to Gissing's unfinished novel *Veranilda*, hoping his introduction would secure its publication and so help make some money for the bereaved family. His honest estimate of Gissing's limitations as a novelist and a human being were not, however, well received by the other executors, who commissioned a tribute by Harrison as a replacement. Wells retitled his rejected piece 'George Gissing: An Impression' and sent it to the *Monthly Review*, which published it in August 1904. Wells resigned as an executor over the clash but remained a trustee of the children's pension. Twenty years later he was still angry that Gissing's sister had never arranged for them to thank him.[21]

Having been drawn into the exposure of Gissing's private life in his confidential letters for the pension bid and having realized with horror what would emerge when he himself died, Wells burned all his early correspondence from Isabel and Jane and asked his friends to return letters so he could vet them and destroy the more revealing ones. A couple of years later he even bought up back issues of the *Science Schools Journal* to obliterate *The Chronic Argonauts*. Wells later came to regret his zeal in covering his tracks, a view heartily endorsed by his biographers – present company included.

By the spring of 1904, perhaps as a consequence of this caution, Wells seems to have been having second thoughts about seeking the limelight in the company of politicians. Wallas had recently resigned from the Fabians over a number of issues, particularly their support for the import tariffs the Tories were proposing in order to protect the British Empire from global competition. Wells followed suit in March 1904, citing the same cause.[22] Unwilling to lose their new star, the Fabian leaders cajoled him into withdrawing his resignation. It was a response they would later have cause to regret.

The on-off Fabian resignation is a significant context for one of Wells's most famous short stories, 'The Country of the Blind', published in the *Strand Magazine* during April 1904. It tells of a South American mountaineer, Nunez, who – having fallen into a valley inhabited by a blind tribe – assumes he will be able to use his superior understanding to rule over them. Instead, they treat him as mentally disabled and force him to live by their restrictive conventions. He falls in love with a conformist blind woman – a kind of Isabel of the Andes – who tries to persuade him to have his eyes removed. He finally flees back into the mountains, where he apparently dies a welcome death. The detached, ironic narrative – which, in scrupulously acknowledging Nunez's own limitations, never quite allows him to achieve the role of hero – turns what could have been a self-regarding allegory of Wells's life into a haunting parable with many possible applications.

In May, having finally completed *Kipps*, Wells fell ill for two months. He recuperated with a holiday in Switzerland during June, followed by a walking holiday in the Italian Alps during October, both in the company of Jane who had developed a passion for the mountains. By now he was also working hard on *A Modern Utopia*, and by the time he finished it during August, he was grappling with a play based on *The Wheels of Chance* called *Hoopdriver's Holiday*. Though completed, it was never staged and was not published in his lifetime.

The Food of the Gods and How It Came to Earth appeared in late September, having been serialized between December and June. This tall tale of what happens when a growth-inducing drug gets out of the laboratory proved to be a step down even from the *Sleeper*. The first part of the book, in which giant creatures menace unsuspecting humans, produces some genuinely frightening moments. The story takes a very different turn once the drug is fed to children, who grow into outsized adolescents tormented by their inability to fit into present-day society.

Presumably inspired by watching his own children grow and reflecting on their destinies, Wells construes the giants as beings symbols of human progress and concludes by repeating the 'child on a footstool' image from the *Discovery of the Future*. His intention was a burlesque recalling Rabelais and Blake; the actuality is an ill-conceived fantasia on his talk for the Fabians in which realistic presentation undermines the symbolism. The notion that the giant children represent an improvement on normal people has no basis except in the self-interested opinion of the giants and the irresponsible scientists who have caused their deformity.

The book was rubbished, genially but devastatingly, by G.K. Chesterton in his critique of modern thinkers, *Heretics*. Chesterton attacks Wells's recourse to binary oppositions – the unique and the general, the past and the future, freedom and order – because, looked at closely, they are not true opposites. Future progress, for example, cannot mean a total departure from past values, as Wells seemed to be suggesting, because the whole notion of progress is meaningless unless a criterion of goodness persists unchanged through time. Wells's choice of giants as symbols of his ideal, Chesterton argues, is a symptom of power worship and impatience with people's weaknesses and self-divisions. If we wish to deal with our limits, we have to come to terms with them, not turn away from them into fantasy.

Chesterton also criticizes Wells's next book, *A Modern Utopia*, on the ground that all Utopias avoid major issues about human nature while confidently pontificating about how the world might be organized if human nature could be changed. Actually Wells's Utopia makes considerable allowance for this criticism, since an admission of the problem is built into its very structure. *A Modern Utopia* was serialized in the *Fortnightly Review* from October 1904 to April 1905, then published as a book during April.

An opening 'Note to the Reader' points out the piece's indebtedness to the dialogic fiction of Peacock and Mallock. A section called 'The Owner of the Voice' tries to dissociate Wells from the sometimes strident tone his narrator adopts. This narrator is initially a lecturer, giving a talk with the aid of a slide projector. As he speaks, he takes on the hypothetical role of someone on a walking holiday in Switzerland who is suddenly and mysteriously transported with his botanist companion to another planet identical to ours except for its utopian culture. To some extent, the text then becomes a conventional narrative in which they struggle to understand the world about them, while simultaneously it remains a discussion of Utopias in which the narrator decides what will happen next. This curious mixture of passive and active is compounded by the narrator's failure to get the botanist to comply with his vision.

Resolved to escape the monolithic outlook of *Anticipations*, Wells calls for a 'world-wide culture of toleration'[23] to replace the petty local orders now breaking up and insists that an ideal world must, by definition, be a multiracial one in which mixed marriages are commonplace. Pointedly, the elite who run the Utopia, though primarily modelled on Plato's Guardians, take their name from the Japanese samurai caste.

The botanist and the narrator, having travelled from Switzerland to London in their explorations, argue so fiercely that the utopian vision disintegrates and they find themselves in Trafalgar Square in the 1900s. The narrator is left reflecting on the discrepancy between vision and dispiriting reality and on the conflicting impossibilities of formulating his ideal persuasively or of letting it go. 'Scepticism of the Instrument' is appended as a final comment on the philosophical issues raised. The book's elaborate structure, requiring constant shifts in the reader's imaginative and intellectual engagement, makes it not so much a modern as a post-modern Utopia, flaunting its workings like the Beaubourg Centre in Paris.

A Modern Utopia received widespread praise, yet despite Wells's Herculean efforts many readers insisted on taking it literally. The poet Harold Munro, for example, drew up a rule of conduct for a samurai order, while his friend Maurice Browne published proposals for a voluntary nobility based on Nitobe Inazô's *Bushido*, Wells's apparent source for the samurai idea. The fact that *A Modern Utopia* was published around the time of the first Russian Revolution and the imprisonment of the early suffragist militants certainly gave it an aura of being in tune with changing times.

Keen to stoke his reputation as a cutting-edge thinker, in January 1905 Wells delivered a spin-off paper to the Co-efficients discussing the part the 'coloured races' might play in the future of civilization and in June outlined 'A Woman's Day in Utopia' for the *Daily Mail*. Around the same time he boldly requested the Prime Minister, Balfour, to subsidize him at the rate of £1,000 a year, perhaps in the form of an academic post, so he would not have to rely so heavily on the marketplace to fund his sociological work.[24] The request was politely turned down.

Though recognized in the field of utopian studies, *A Modern Utopia* has not won a place in the mainstream literary canon. Churchill identified the chief problem as lack of story.[25] The comment is a just one, though we need to recognize that the book is not a novel but what the critical theorist Northrop Frye terms an 'anatomy': a playfully discursive work that downplays narrative in favour of an exuberant, obsessive delight in arguments, lists and learning, and bizarre juxtapositions of the small and the great. Having begun his career by fusing the novel and fantasy, Wells's next target was to fuse the novel and the anatomy. In this he would never be entirely successful, being too much in earnest to achieve an entertaining perspective.

Beyond the lack of narrative interest, *A Modern Utopia* has a major political defect. While Wells tries to convince us that we are being shown a credible social order he cannot quite bring into focus, what we actually get is a myth that cannot resolve the issues to which it is being applied. The foregrounding of sceptical liberal attitudes in the presentation does not alter the substance behind it: an undemocratic one-party state in which truth is established not by critical discussion but by shared faith. E.M. Forster would skewer the book's unhealthy conformism in his 1909 science-fiction story 'The Machine Stops'.

A Modern Utopia embodies a persistent flaw in Wells's social thought. While he can critique the present in the spirit of the New Liberalism, and envisage an ideal future in the spirit of Comtean socialism, he struggles for a credible way to get from the one to the other. Worse, he has little idea of the importance to this process of democratic accountability or the need for checks and balances to prevent the abuse of power. Though Wells is a thinker with roots in the Enlightenment, his notion of the ideal comes from the otherworldly visions of Plato and the Bible. Wells's Utopia purports to be built on the rock of reason but is as much an act of faith as Chesterton's Christianity.

Put another way, where Wells's best work productively balances his 'Sarah' and 'Joe' sides, *A Modern Utopia* is 99 per cent evangelical, not only in its mission to save the world but in its reliance on faith and its hostility to alternative opinions and lesser activities. A contemptuous dismissal of cricket as puerile and those who excel in it as fools, outranting anything in Sarah's diary entries on Joe, must have raised some eyebrows in Liss.[26] It is clear – particularly in the inhibited, underwritten meeting with Wells's utopian self, the man he could have been under better circumstances – that, much as he is moved by a desire to save the world in general, he is tormented by a more specific longing to replace himself with someone worthier. It was only once he had got this evangelical self-criticism out of his system that the Sandgate sinner could let the world have the subversive comedy of *Kipps*, a return to the human scale and democratic outlook of *Lewisham*.

Seven years after he had first conceived of his eponymous hero *Kipps* was serialized from January to December 1905, with the book version published in October. The novel returns to the premise of *The Wheels of Chance*: a young drapery apprentice is dissatisfied by his job and seeks escape. This time, however, the portrait is on a more generous scale, following Artie Kipps from his childhood play with his friends Sid and Ann Pornick, through his dismal apprenticeship at Shalford's Drapery Emporium, trapped in his employer's inhumane time-and-motion system, to his unexpected release. Escape is supplied by Harry Chitterlow, an actor-dramatist modelled on Sidney Bowkett, who first causes Kipps to behave outside the rules by plying him with whisky then discovers that he is no ordinary apprentice but the lost heir to Mr Waddy's fortune.

Sudden wealth precipitates Kipps into a new world that is more accommodating than the drapery but no more ready to let him be himself. The upper-class Helen Walsingham, who had been teaching him wood-carving at an adult education class, rapidly transmutes into his fiancée, and the snobbish Chester Coote (who surely bears some resemblance to Henry James) trains him in upper-class propriety to fit him for her world. Exiled from his background, especially after he is forced to give 'the Cut' to a couple of old friends, yet ill at ease with the customs of the upper classes, Kipps is as alienated from society as the Invisible Man had been and finds himself similarly forced to go hungry in London because he dare not disclose his transformed state. Where Griffin could not show his erased face, Kipps has the less monstrous but equally embarrassing problem of what course to order and which cutlery to use.

Eventually Kipps finds true love with his childhood sweetheart Ann, but even then he cannot find his place in life. His attempts to build a home are spoiled by the pretensions of his architect and by a self-conceit that makes him angry with his wife's failure to live up to their social position. It is only after his legacy has been squandered by Helen's brother, a vulgar Nietzschean solicitor, and he has put his remaining wealth into a bookshop, cushioned by his investment in Chitterlow's hit play, that he attains a viable place in life.

Much autobiographical material lurks in the novel, not least the struggle to construct an identity to fit a changing social position and the personal tensions that threaten the protagonist's marriage. Able to draw on first-hand knowledge, Wells had produced a novel which was confident in its pace and sense of direction, lively, observant and supported by an almost unbroken flow of comic invention. It was far and away his most accomplished piece of fiction to date.

Judging that he had a potential bestseller on his hands, Wells urged Frederick Macmillan to mount a major publicity campaign with posters at Portsmouth station proclaiming 'KIPPS WORKED HERE', advertisements in theatre programmes and sandwich-board men strategically working the City of London in the run-up to Christmas. Despite Macmillan's starchy refusal to adopt such down-market tactics, the book sold 12,000 copies by the year's end, Wells's best sales figure so far, and by the 1920s this had risen to over a quarter of a million.

Henry James called the novel 'not so much a masterpiece as a mere born gem', praising Wells's sustained use of irony, the comparative lack of condescension with which he depicted lower-middle-class characters and his vividness of characterization. He declared, 'you are, for me, more than ever, the most interesting "literary man" of your generation'.[27] Note, however, the inverted commas around 'literary man' and the loaded phrase, 'mere born gem'. James continued to take much the same view of Wells as Ben Jonson had of Shakespeare: his colleague was a natural who broke effortlessly through obsolete conventions yet lacked the artistic self-consciousness that raised his own work to a higher level.

Bennett, too, was impressed but noted how far Wells had moved from his old ideal of even-handedness, portraying the higher classes with a satirical gusto very different from the god-like compassion that remained his own aim.[28] A similar point was made by Tommy Simmons, who objected to the negative depiction of middle-class women and noted that Kipps seemed more passive and patronized than Hoopdriver had been.[29] His implication was that, as Wells grew away from his source material, he was falling back on stereotypes. It was a fair point. While most readers at the time were won over by the love of Kipps and Ann, today they seem like two sets of quaint mannerisms performing comic business, not two people sharing an experience.

The most pleasing response to the book from Wells's point of view was that of an unnamed Australian visitor, who sent him a fan letter inviting him to call on her and repaid his literary efforts with something more than words of praise. He was so pleased, in fact, he returned several times: 'I remember her still for her ruddy sunburnt skin and straw-coloured hair.'[30] Wells is characteristically vague about when all this practical criticism took place, but it may stand as an example of how his life was changing. Having lost his old undernourished look, he entered his forties feeling more confident about his physical appearance and with the happy discovery that fame was an aphrodisiac.

The episode also casts a revealing light on *Kipps* itself, where the draper's temporary leaning towards promiscuity is ridiculed as immature. As Simmons saw, the book did not fully represent Wells's own world-view. No doubt to champion sexual permissiveness would have damaged the texture of the novel and alienated potential publishers and readers, but there were also problems in communicating the author's political radicalism.

To give Kipps talent and ambition like those of his creator would have brought an unwelcome complexity to the character, for a more savvy Kipps might have seemed guilty of betraying his class and behaving irresponsibly towards others. It is Kipps's naïvety that enables him to remain uncompromised by the situations in which he finds himself. His role is to be, as the book's subtitle asserts, 'a Simple Soul'. The obvious alternative method of introducing sociopolitical perspective into the story would have been through the omniscient narrator, who is a much less simple soul, but this would have risked interspersing the story with finger-pointing lectures. Wells is therefore sparing in his comments, though most critics have still judged them to be intrusive.

Another method would be to introduce the kind of spokespeople Wells had formerly condemned in Gissing. He does this, too, but carefully limits their appearances and confines them to raising issues rather than putting forward solutions. The main input comes from a journalist friend of Sid's called Masterman. His physical appearance seems to commemorate W.E. Henley, who had died in a railway accident in 1903, but the views of this former science student at South Kensington, who spits blood between speeches, also represent Wells as he might have been if he had not escaped his illness and become a successful author. He takes exactly the political line we have seen in the early fiction, sympathetic to socialism but doubtful whether it can be put into practice. This is another example of Wells's dialogic approach, voicing his own residual scepticism through Masterman's assertion that society is doomed to war and destruction, while the narrator, representing the new, more positive Fabian Wells, queries whether such pessimism might be rooted in self-pity.

Revealingly, Wells concludes the book by giving Kipps the words 'I don't suppose there ever was a chap quite like me before', acknowledging that the story's focus has been on the unique rather than the general.[31] In *Kipps* Wells is dealing with particulars on which it is difficult to erect convincing generalizations, just as in *A Modern Utopia* he had discussed generalizations that were difficult to translate into particulars, though in both cases the effort to bridge the gap is an important part of the final effect. Both books were remarkable achievements, and *Kipps* remains a living presence in English literature, but they still left Wells with the challenge of fully integrating the particular and the general into one artistic frame.

In 1906 a Liberal government was elected in Britain with a huge majority, the voters having demonstrated the same hostility to the Tories' imperial preference policies as Wallas and Wells. During this Parliament the chancellor, Lloyd George, would introduce old-age pensions and start to redistribute wealth through his celebrated 'People's Budget'. It was to be a time of reform and social change. In literature it would be the age of Wells, Shaw and Galsworthy, citizen-authors who engaged with the issues of the day in their writings and political activities alike. Wells, however, would take his commitments somewhat further than the other two. In the midst of social comment, philosophizing and attempting to redirect the Fabian Society, he would also try to push back the boundaries of sexual behaviour, then report his experiences in novels that scandalized a generation.

10
FABIANISM AND FREE LOVE 1905–1909

Sarah Wells died, aged eighty-two, on 12 June 1905, after six months of mild dementia. Going to bed on Easter Monday, she fell downstairs and broke her ankle. At first she seemed to be recovering but passed into a sudden decline, apparently due to an undiagnosed spinal injury. Wells reports that she 'died a little child again', discarding her adult cares and returning in her mind to her girlhood in Midhurst, laying the table for her father and learning to crochet.[1]

Though Wells seemed to take her death calmly, the fact that he photographed his mother's laid-out corpse from several angles in close-up suggests the deep significance of the bereavement for him. Surely having children of his own must have helped him sympathize over the loss of Fanny, but, if so, it came too late to undo the damage. He had already made it a tenet of his writing that, far from being a substitute for someone else, everybody was unique – not least Herbert George Wells. Now that Sarah would no longer be monitoring his exploits he would become much more openly militant as a champion of socialism and a rebel against sexual propriety – defying the traditional values that, according to his mother, his sister had incarnated.

From this point Wells ceased to behave as though his sexual escapades were a private matter and embarked on a series of outrageous love affairs that almost amounted to a kind of performance art. In his autobiography he tells us bluntly, 'I suspect the sexual system should be at least the second theme, when it is not the first, in every autobiography, honestly and fully told.'[2] His own 'sexual system' had long been an essential element in his self-conception, and he now acted to make it public knowledge – not in the newspapers of his day, which would have ruined his career – but in the talk of eminent contemporaries and ultimately in the records of posterity. The affairs disclosed are a kind of parallel project to his books: a mixture of entertainment and politics that set out to challenge accepted norms and start each time with a surge of conviction but come to questionable ends.

In May, as Sarah lay dying, Wells at last consummated his relationship with his wife's friend Dorothy Richardson. The long-deliberated romance would last just two years; in retrospect both parties realized that they had been looking for incompatible pleasures. Wells was after 'a sensuous affair' but found the pleasures of the flesh came with a heavy admixture of Dorothy's philosophical reflections:

> she seemed to promise the jolliest intimate friendship; she had an adorable dimple in her smile; she was most interestingly hairy on her body, with fine golden hairs, and then – she would begin intoning the dull clever things that filled that shapely, rather large, flaxen head of hers; she would lecture me on philology and the lingering vestiges of my Cockney accent, while there was not a stitch between us. The adventurous student who cares to turn up her Dawn's Left Hand may confirm these statements.[3]

They may indeed, but will not be surprised to learn that her lover was equally prone to lectures, though of a more socio-political variety.

Not content with supplementing Jane with Dorothy, Wells industriously supplemented Dorothy, too. His evasiveness over dates makes the order of events murky, but a letter of May 1906 confirms that among those with whom he had been involved by that point were Ella d'Arcy and Violet Hunt.[4]

D'Arcy, an author of experimental short stories about sexual relationships and marital failure – known as 'Goblin Ella' to her friends owing to her small physical stature – was in her late forties around this time, almost ten years older than Wells. A self-effacing figure on the literary scene, but described by Frederick Rolfe as 'a mouse-mannered piece of sex',[5] she had previously had affairs with the publisher John Lane and the science-fiction and adventure writer M.P. Shiel, who would later caricature Wells as the dastardly womanizer E.P. Crooks in his story 'The Primate of the Rose'. Wells seems to have had a fairly brief fling with D'Arcy, possibly even before the Richardson affair.

Violet Hunt was a feminist author and practitioner of free love with whom he had a casual but sustained relationship starting late in 1906. Hunt, a friend of Arnold Bennett and a former lover of Somerset Maugham, was older than Wells, too, though only by four years. Among the things the couple had in common was that they had both reviewed the opening night of James's *Guy Domville*, Hunt's notice observing that the derided author left the stage 'sadly and patiently, rather like an elephant who has had a stone put into his trunk instead of a bun'.[6]

Wells was pleased to be taken up by an experienced woman who knew the ways of the world. He records that she taught him

> the mysteries of Soho and Pimlico. We explored the world of convenient little restaurants with private rooms upstairs, and the struggling lodging-houses which are only too happy to let rooms permanently to intermittent occupants. So without any great disturbance of our literary work and our ostensible social lives, we lunched and dined together and found great satisfaction in each other's embraces.[7]

There is an element of understatement here, as Hunt was hardly averse to causing 'disturbance'. At one point in 1907 she raised eyebrows among the guests at Spade House by playing tennis in bare feet and flirting outrageously with Wells in front of Dorothy Richardson and Jane. She also refused to be intimate with Wells except outdoors, apparently hoping Richardson would catch sight of them rustling around in the bushes.

Wells allowed his readers a very limited glimpse into his feelings about free love and the death of his mother in a fantasy novel called *In the Days of the Comet,* published in book form in the summer of 1906. The first part is a vivid first-person account of conflict between individuals, social classes and nations, the second a romance in which all of these are dispelled when the earth passes through a comet's tail. With jealousy eliminated, the protagonist, perhaps aptly named Willie, finds himself in a four-way relationship, involving not only the woman he has long loved but also his rival for her affections and the woman he has married. Willie's mother dies shortly before the foursome swings into action, but before she does she speaks to Willie about his late sister, whom she lost not aged eight as Sarah had lost Fanny but three, after which Willie goes out and cries aloud in his 'rage at all the irrecoverable sorrows of the past'.[8]

In the Days of the Comet is much more effective than *The Food of the Gods* in conveying Wells's passion to break out of the prison of what has been, yet it has the same obvious flaw as the earlier book: a commanding metaphor incapable of doing the job required of it. The transfiguration brought about by the comet is a spiritual change not an institutional one (many characters respond to it as the Second Advent), and Wells's repeated attempts to make the comet stand for science and political reform serve merely to discredit his ideas. Reviewers in the *Times Literary Supplement* and the *Daily Express* were only too pleased to discover that free love was one of the goals of socialism. Wells backtracked indignantly, claiming that there was 'no relation whatever' between socialism as he understood it and the ideal depicted in his book.[9] He had none the less handed his enemies a convenient weapon at the very moment when he had decided it was again time to prioritize his political activities.

Though Wells had been a Fabian for more than two years, he had not been an active one. On 5 June 1905, however, a few days before Sarah's death, he suggested an enquiry into the organization's effectiveness. The mischievous star of the South Kensington Debating Society was about to be reborn. In fairness, Wells would not have got far with the campaign if he had not been a figurehead for widespread frustration among those (Dorothy Richardson for one) who had joined the Fabians hoping to change the world, only to find they had signed up to a cliquey institution controlled by Shaw, the Webbs and other members of the 'Old Gang'. Wells's neighbours the Pophams even adopted 'Webb-head' as a term of abuse.[10] Among Wells's most enthusiastic supporters, they were denied a chance to enjoy the coming fracas: Florence died of heart failure following an operation in November, aged forty-seven, and Arthur, perhaps as a consequence, died the next year.

Wells decided, literally, to read the Fabians a lecture. Persuaded that the talk he had scheduled for 12 January 1906 was too controversial in the run-up to a general election, he instead substituted a performance of his article 'This Misery of Boots', which had appeared the previous month in G.M. Trevelyan's Liberal journal, the *Independent Review.* The article takes poor footwear as emblematic of how capitalism failed ordinary people. Wells recalls his childhood at Atlas House watching ill-shod feet passing the kitchen grating, recaps a discussion with George Gissing and builds up to a passionate affirmation of socialism. The talk was the opposite of the detached, analytical approach associated with the Webbs but was greeted with enthusiasm and reprinted as a Fabian pamphlet in 1907.

On 9 February 1906 Wells was allowed to deliver 'The Faults of the Fabian' at a strictly members-only meeting at Essex Hall. The thrust of his argument was that, while labour organizations were winning over manual workers to socialism, not enough was being done to recruit doctors, teachers and other professionals to the cause. Such proselytizing seemed to him to be the Fabians' natural mission, but at present they were wilfully underfunded, under-resourced and unbusinesslike. The 'Basis' to which members pledged their allegiance was narrow and off-putting. The Fabians lacked purposefulness, preferring indirect methods and the exchange of in-jokes to getting on with the work.

It was an excellent speech, well argued and witty, as when Wells compares the Fabians' attack on capitalism to that of a mouse that decides to assail its oppressor in polite, circuitous ways: 'It is believed that in the end the mouse did succeed in permeating the cat, but the cat is still living – and the mouse can't be found.' Permeation was at best only part of the solution. To create socialism, it was first necessary to create a socialist public. Faced with such an eloquent expression of discontent, the Old Gang conceded the merit of a review. The review committee balanced members of the existing executive against reformers, including Wells himself, with Jane, as ever adopting a supporting role, as secretary.

The Liberals' massive election victory the previous month gave force to Wells's contention that now was the time to aim for a shift in public consciousness. Was the Fabian Society going to remain in its niche as a think tank, chipping away gradually at elite opinion, or was it going to take advantage of its reputation to give a lead to the whole progressive movement, steering it away from class warfare towards a more constructive agenda? There were an unprecedented twenty-nine Labour MPs in the new Parliament, who might represent a popular movement capable of sweeping aside the middle-class socialists.

Later in his campaign Wells made a point of contacting key Labour figures to test their sympathy for his approach. Ramsay MacDonald, who had quit the Fabians over their support for imperialism and the Boer War, told Wells that he was wasting his time on the Old Gang. Keir Hardie concurred, suggesting that Wells leave the Fabians for the equally non-Marxist and gradualist Independent Labour Party as a parliamentary candidate, an offer Wells declined, though he does seem to have joined both the ILP and Social Democratic Federation as part of his socialist research.[11] While he admired MacDonald and Hardie, he had no faith in most of the ILP leaders and would hardly have relished pitting his shrill voice against hecklers.

John Galsworthy, anticipating the view of posterity, advised Wells that commitment to any kind of political organization was a mistake. As a writer, what he should be doing was expressing his vision on paper.[12] For Wells, however, writing and doing were not alternatives. He thought of his books as actions as much as texts and indeed did not think of literature merely as the three major forms – fiction, drama and poetry – but as any kind of writing animated by verbal intelligence and creativity. If at the critic Walter Pater's end of the spectrum literature aspired to the condition of music, at Wells's end it aspired to several more worldly conditions, including sociology.

The historian Eric Hobsbawm has noted the emergence of sociology as an important discipline in this period, prompted by the great question of how societies could cohere when traditional customs and beliefs were losing their power to justify social structures – a question Wells puts explicitly in such books as *A Modern Utopia* and *Tono-Bungay*.[13] Hobsbawm notes that the status of sociology itself was, and is, controversial, leaving it a 'field' rather than a scientific discipline with an agreed content and methodology. Wells, a founding member of the Sociological Society in 1903, naturally had his own take on this issue.

In an article of October 1905 he asked the readers of the *Fortnightly Review*, 'Is Sociology a Science?' and supplied them with a clear answer: 'No'. On 26 February 1906, less than three weeks after exposing 'The Faults of the Fabian', he tackled the Sociological Society itself on the subject of 'The So-Called Science of Sociology', his text published the following May in the *Independent Review*. He gave the talk at the London School of Economics' new premises in Clare Market, an area that had just been demolished and rebuilt in the interests of modernization; ironically, the LSE had in part been set up with money diverted from a Fabian bequest – and this was a key reason for the lack of funds about which Wells had been complaining. Fortunately for the Old Gang, he did not spot the significance of the venue.[14]

The basis of Wells's argument about sociology is his familiar insistence on the importance of the unique. In the 'hard' sciences it may be possible to aggregate data into sound generalizations, but in the study of people firm laws are harder to achieve. Despite the claims of Comte and Spencer there will never come a day when the sociologist will wield the seemingly value-free authority enjoyed by, for example, 'a sanitary engineer'. Sociological discussion ought to acknowledge this by openly positioning the perceiving subject, becoming 'knowledge rendered imaginatively, and with an element of personality; that is to say, in the highest sense of the term, literature'.

From this perspective, Wells champions both large-scale readings of history such as his old favourite, Carlyle's *French Revolution*, and explications of social values in the form of Utopias such as those of Plato and More. His approach to sociology is an unorthodox one, open to criticism for excessive subjectivity, but it has none the less been defended in recent years by Krishan Kumar, who suggests that much sociological thought is damaged by a failure to pass from the accumulation of data to an imaginative interest in its consequences.[15]

Approaching politics and sociology from a literary point of view was helping Wells develop a reciprocal perspective for his fiction. Though he was so involved in public affairs that in 1907 he had no books to publish – the single year of dearth in a prolific half-century – he was busily secreting the experiences and ideas for a set of new novels. By early 1906 he was already working at what would prove the most important of these, *Tono-Bungay*. To express his impatience with the triviality of much of what currently passed for literature and social thought Wells had also been working on and off on a satire called *The Mind of the Race*. Begun in July 1905, it would surface ten years later as *Boon*. A sample target of his scorn is 'Shoners' like Herbert Spencer. Shoners? 'You know – evolution, differentiation, concatenation – chaps who think in terms of –tion.'[16]

The impatient, mischievous side of his character visible here was also evident in his Fabian dealings. With a committee now set up to review the society's progress, Wells tried to push through publication of a draft report, giving the impression that it had been endorsed by the Old Gang. Beatrice Webb was distinctly unimpressed by this tactic, condemning in her diary Wells's 'odd mixture of underhand manoeuvres and insolent bluster' and blaming his lack of training in civilized cooperation. 'It is a case of "Kipps" in matters more important than table manners.'[17] The element of snobbery in her attitude would not pass undetected by Wells, and this perception would only fuel his defiance of her and the other members of the Old Gang.

Wells was particularly impatient to resolve the Fabian issue as he was about to leave the country for two months. His writings had made him a figure on the world stage with few destinations outside his scope – the most prominent of them Bromley. Asked to lecture there in September, he declined, citing pressure of engagements.[18] He evidently had no wish to return to his home town and the memories it held of an earlier, less purposeful version of himself.

At this time he seems to have been especially highly regarded in the Francophone world, where the Belgian Maeterlink declared his imagination was 'the most surprising, most inexhaustible, most complete and most logical of his era'.[19] The place he was keenest to go, however, was the USA. He had long wanted more contact with 'that marvellous disorderly continent',[20] and, having secured a deal to record his findings for *Tribune* in Britain and *Harper's Weekly* there, he set sail from Liverpool on 27 March 1906. Wells was amused to discover that one of the questions the US authorities required him to answer before his departure was 'Are you a polygamist?'

Equipped with introductions from many friends, including Henry James, who was himself writing a book on *The American Scene*, Wells enjoyed a busy and stimulating schedule. Initially he based himself in New York, investigating the city and the surrounding region from Columbia University and Ellis Island up to Niagara Falls. He heard at second hand about the horrors of the recent San Francisco earthquake and at first hand about two cases of injustice that gave him a disturbing view of public attitudes in the 'land of the free'.

One of these concerned Billy MacQueen, a British anarchist serving five years in Trenton Prison, New Jersey, on a charge of inciting a riot during an industrial dispute. Wells sympathized with the workers and saw no evidence that MacQueen had done any wrong in his address to them. Having visited MacQueen in gaol, Wells tried to lobby on his behalf but found the authorities unmoved. His efforts as a high-profile foreign visitor may have done more good than he realized, however, since, contrary to his expectation, the prisoner was later released after serving only three years. Nevertheless, MacQueen's health had been weakened by his imprisonment, and he died of tuberculosis in 1908.

The second dose of injustice was meted out to the Russian author Maxim Gorky, who was visiting the USA to raise funds for the Bolshevik party in the aftermath of the failed 1905 uprising. Wells met him at a party held in Gorky's honour and was stunned when, virtually overnight, the American press, having discovered that he was not married to his companion, Madame Andreieva, ceased to treat him as a liberator and instead vilified him as a libertine. The scandal seemed to eclipse concern over the repressive nature of Tsarist Russia. Given his own record as an unfaithful husband, this reaction induced a sense of dismay in Wells, and he took care to seek Gorky out and offer him further support when the Russian visited London in 1907.

Wells later wrote that, when he thought of all the wonder and promise of the USA, he would also remember the other side of the story, embodied in MacQueen, Gorky and Booker T. Washington.[21] He interviewed the black leader in Boston and recorded the conversation as part of 'The Tragedy of Colour', a chapter in his account of his US experiences that vigorously condemns both American and British racism and has therefore been passed over in silence by his detractors.

Wells was taken aback by Washington's strategic willingness to accept many aspects of segregation and, while conceding that his subject knew the feasibilities of change better than he did, found himself in the rather incongruous position of urging greater black militancy. This view reflected his reading of W.E.B. Du Bois's *The Souls of Black Folks*, a classic of African-American literature that also happens to be an excellent example of the sociology/literature synthesis he had recently been advocating.

Wells did not forget the plight of black Americans after he returned to Britain. In February 1907, having praised the mixed-race teacher and writer Mary Church Terrell in a piece in the *Independent Review*, he received a letter of thanks from her. He read her article on chain gangs in the *Nineteenth Century* later that year and suggested that she should collect several of her pieces into a book, a possibility she had not considered as she did not think the public was ready to face such ugly facts.[22] She was probably right. It would be more than thirty years before a book from her appeared, though when it finally did so it would be due to Wells's continuing encouragement and endorsement.

Around the beginning of May Wells moved from the East Coast to Chicago, where – as he records in a letter to Jane – he spent a memorable Saturday night with Doc Green, a Republican vote organizer, visiting numerous saloons and brothels, a Buddhist temple, an opium den and an African-American play at a theatre in the Chinese Quarter.[23]

While her husband was living it up, Jane was missing him and almost masochistically questioning her fitness to be the partner of so eminent a man. In a rare surviving letter, mailed to Chicago, she confesses:

> If I set out to make a comfortable home for you to do work in, I merely succeed in contriving a place where you are bored to death. I make love to you & have you for my friend to the exclusion of plenty of people who would be infinitely more satisfying to you. Well, dear, I don't think I ought to send you such a letter. It's only a mood you know, but theres [*sic*] no time to write another & I have been letting myself go in a foolish fashion. It's all right, you know, really, only you see I've had so much of my own society now, & I am very naturally getting sick of such a person as I am. How you can ever stand it! *Well.*[24]

Though, at the risk of distressing his wife, Wells was prepared to investigate Chicago's nightlife, he turned down a chance to visit its stockyards, made notorious that year by Upton Sinclair's fictional exposé *The Jungle*, declaring he was repelled by the killing of helpless animals.[25] The sentiment is a surprising one from a defender of vivisection, perhaps attributable to his childhood next door to a butcher's. He did visit the University of Chicago and also Hull House, a 'settlement' modelled on London's Toynbee Hall where volunteers from privileged backgrounds were able to help out in an area of deprivation.

From Chicago Wells travelled by express to Washington, arriving a mere five minutes late because the train ran over a man on the way – 'One of these Eyetalians', in the words of a bystander.[26] This was all the more of a shock to Wells as he had construed the train as an 'Image of Material Progress'. Could the story of someone coming to America to seek a new life only to be destroyed be equally symbolic?

From his base at the Cosmos Club Wells dined with Oliver Wendell Holmes and other notables and went to see the Library of Congress, the Smithsonian and the Senate. Thanks to the intervention of the investigative journalist Lincoln Steffens, he had also managed to secure an interview with the President. In the event, the intended climax of his journey was a disappointment. Theodore Roosevelt, though progressive in his willingness to use government power in the interests of social justice and environmental conservation, was very much a capitalist and an imperialist. Wells did not bother to take notes of Roosevelt's remarks. His sole quotation from the President is a mangled allusion to *The Time Machine* that marginalizes him and puts Wells back centre stage.

The English investigator had arrived in Washington promising himself 'arduous intercourse with a teeming intellectual life' but had found no one whose ideas were compatible with his own.[27] Leaving the White House that afternoon, wanting to take his thoughts off the unproductive meeting, he decided to try intercourse of another kind and asked a cab driver to take him to what was then known as a 'gay house'. 'White or coon?' asked the driver. Wells replied firmly, 'Coon'.

The part of Washington today known as the Federal Triangle was then an extensive red-light district, and it was to an upmarket establishment in this area that the horse-drawn cab would have taken Wells, the kind of place that catered for visiting dignitaries and for politicians collecting their reward for voting as corporate lobbyists had instructed them. Having been welcomed into the house, Wells was introduced to a number of scantily clad women for whom he was required to buy no doubt expensive drinks. After passing some time in conversation with them, Wells selected a partner and followed her to her room.

> She was a mixture of white and Indian and negro, dark-haired and with a skin the colour of smooth sea sands, and, I thought, much more intelligent than most of the women one meets at dinner-parties. She was a reader of books, and she showed me some verse she had attempted; she had been learning Italian, because she wanted to go to Europe, see Europe, and come back 'White' as pseudo-Italian.[28]

Naturally she was keen to cultivate her European client, and Wells had a momentary temptation to propose some kind of long-term liaison. When he concluded their tryst by paying her above the rate, however, she realized it was a sign that they would never meet again. Even so, Wells remained taken with her, and, when he thought back on his first visit to America, it was not Roosevelt who came most forcefully to mind but a mixed-race prostitute. It would be easy enough to portray Wells as a hypocrite here, exploiting an oppressed black woman while sentimentalizing about her situation, and there might be some truth to that view. He could, after all, have asked the cab driver to take him to the African-American Howard University. Equally, it could be said that, having felt the limits of talking to politicians and reading journalists' views, Wells wanted to engage with America at a more intimate level, especially with someone at the other end of the social scale and, though politically incorrect in the extreme, this might be true, too.

Wells returned to Britain at the end of May. His thoughts about the journey, *The Future in America,* were serialized from July to October and published in the latter month. The book celebrated America's energy but questioned the limits of its doctrinaire individualism when applied to key issues from racism to child labour. Wells saw little sign that socialism was emerging as a counterbalance, yet in its very newness the USA at least promised surprises to come, as Wells neatly suggests in a closing image of the New York skyscrapers on his departure looking like 'piled-up packing cases outside a warehouse'.[29]

The Future in America was Wells's first book for eight years to carry a dedication. It recorded his friendship with 'D.M.R.' The relationship with Richardson continued into 1907. The standard account is that by the spring she had decided to break off the affair but found she had become pregnant, that she then suffered a miscarriage followed by a nervous breakdown and that they broke up either before or after this, though they remained in touch and Wells helped Richardson out later by paying her to proofread some of his books. This version of events raises puzzling questions, however.

Most of all, why the pregnancy? Violet Hunt never became pregnant by Wells, nor for that matter did she give him the syphilis with which she was apparently infected at the time of their affair, two facts which indicate that he was still a habitual user of condoms. Was the pregnancy then deliberate or a result of using the riskier withdrawal method? And did Wells abandon Richardson after she had the breakdown, or had she already made it clear by then that they were through? Richardson's novelized version of the events, *Clear Horizon,* skirts around these issues and seems to suggest a false pregnancy.

Anthony West, apparently drawing on spoken comments from Wells, proposes that the pregnancy and miscarriage were a fiction made up by Richardson as an excuse to break off the unsatisfactory relationship and contrive a six-month leave of absence from her job.[30] This account seems to fit the facts, but, given the lack of evidence, it remains extremely hypothetical.

*

The Webbs, paying a visit to Spade House on 15 July 1906, found Wells as unresponsive to their political ideas as he had been to Roosevelt's. Shaw took the Old Gang's argument back to him in a letter in September, saying the worst danger facing him was that they might walk away, leaving him to run the Society without any experience in the frustrating art of collaboration.[31]

The day before the Webbs' visit the *Daily Chronicle* published one of Wells's best short stories, 'The Door in the Wall', which suggests that his political commitment was indeed far from wholehearted. It tells of a cabinet minister named Lionel Wallace who is haunted by a vision from his childhood in which he passed through a door into a magical garden. Among the remarkable things he witnessed there was a beautiful woman who showed him a book containing his life, not in pictures but 'realities'. At crucial moments of his life Wallace again glimpses the wonderful door, but passes it by in the name of responsibility or personal ambition. Now he tells the narrator that he has made up his mind to enter it if it reappears, whatever the cost. Several weeks later Wallace is found dead, having opened the doorway of a building site and fallen down a railway excavation shaft.

The power of the story rests on the narrator's refusal to class Wallace's behaviour as deluded, even though the politician literally lost his hold on reality, and instead to entertain the possibility that Wallace had achieved some kind of revelation. The story is a superior variation on the theme of *The Sea Lady*, repeating the polarization between the objective world of public affairs and the subjective world of the imagination. In the eyes of worldly people, public life is the place to pursue status and self-esteem, the inner life an immature distraction, but the story speculates that the imaginative realm – by implication encompassing art, sexual relations and religion – may after all be the deeper source of meaning and motivation.

Conrad's dedication of his 1907 terrorism novel *The Secret Agent* to Wells as the 'chronicler of Mr Lewisham's love, the biographer of Kipps and the historian of the ages to come' suggests by omission that, like many of Wells's admirers from the 1890s, he was unhappy at the time and energy Wells was now using up on political activity. Despite such doubts and his own reservations, Wells was determined to get a result from the Fabians if he could.

The report he drafted for his review committee, which essentially recommended replacing the Fabian Society with an entirely different body called the British Socialist Society, was controversial to say the least. As relations between Wells and the Old Gang grew worse through the autumn, Wells began elaborating his ideas about socialism in a series of lectures and articles aimed both at his sympathizers and the general public, a set of position statements with obvious potential to be gathered into a book. By late October–early November, when he and Jane were on holiday in Italy, he was negotiating the US serial rights with the McClure Syndicate.

In late November a revised version of the Wells committee report was circulated to Fabian members, along with a reply from the Executive questioning the practicality of the more radical proposals but cautiously welcoming some others, plus an invitation to debate the issues at a meeting on 7 December at Essex Hall. Before radio and television, the fame of authors was far greater than today, and over one-third of the membership turned up for the confrontation between two stars at the height of their reputations: Wells, the author of *Kipps* and *A Modern Utopia*, versus Shaw, the author of *Major Barbara* and *Man and Superman.* Wells spoke for over an hour – unwisely, given his limitations as an orator – with the result that the meeting had to be adjourned before a vote could be taken. Worse, his speech strayed from issues to personal attacks and amounted to a confrontational demand for a no-confidence vote in the current executive.

Shaw, a world-class public speaker, took advantage of this tactical error when an even bigger audience gathered for the rematch on 14 December. His entertaining speech shifted the listeners' sympathy to the executive, and, faced with an ultimatum that the Old Gang would all stand down if Wells's proposal was carried, even keen reformers realized that their champion had led the Society to potential meltdown. Wells was obliged to concede defeat and withdraw his amendment.

He was not yet ready to climb down completely. He campaigned during January and February 1907 to get his supporters elected to the executive, and in March several of them won through, including Jane and Wells himself (a creditable fourth in the poll), but they did so alongside a majority opposed to radical reform. Wells gritted his teeth and set to work with Webb and Shaw to draft a new 'basis' acceptable to all of them.

During this period he took up another form of public service as a Justice of the Peace for the Borough of Folkestone, improbably swearing an oath in February 1907 to 'be faithful and bear allegiance to His Majesty King Edward the Seventh . . . So help me God'.[32] Sessions papers record that between April and July 1908, along with other justices, Wells sat on eight cases. A charge of theft of soda siphons was dismissed. Obstruction with a barrow earned a fine of two shillings and sixpence, cruelty to a horse thirteen guineas, soliciting fourteen days' imprisonment, theft of shoes one month and begging between fourteen and twenty-one days' hard labour.[33]

There must have been other sessions of which there is no record. Wells continued to be officially listed as a JP until at least 1913 but seems to have been uncomfortable in the role and desisted from it quite soon. During 1908 he reflected that, as he passed judgement on those brought before him, he could not help wondering whether the condemned were not living at the cutting edge of life while he and his fellow magistrates evaded it.[34] Conscious that his public-spirited activities might be damaging the momentum of his literary career, he was also switching more energy into his writings, not only developing *Tono-Bungay* and the socialist book, but, after taking advice from J. W. Dunne, proposing a new scientific romance based on aerial warfare.

His sexual energies were also flowing strongly, though in a direction that calls into question the seriousness of his continuing attempts to reform the Fabians, since he now began to seduce his colleagues' daughters. As a tactic this might have impressed Sir Harry Fetherstonhaugh and his Regency pals, but it was hardly likely to increase Wells's effectiveness as a campaigner and carried a very serious danger of triggering a career-destroying scandal. It seems that in middle age he was trying to recreate the inspiring excitement of running off from Isabel with Jane twelve years before. There may also have been an element of revenge: demolishing the fathers by deflowering the daughters. In April 1906 the Fabians had set up a 'Nursery', a group of junior members composed mostly of their own older children, admirers of Wells's free-spirited, forward-thinking attitudes. The secretary of the group, upon whom Wells now set his sights, was none other than Rosamund Bland, whose father was the most belligerent member of the Old Gang.

Hubert Bland's Catholicism and imperialism would have infuriated Wells, quite apart from Bland's opposition to Fabian reform, but Wells also considered his enemy to be a liar and hypocrite, opposing the extension of the vote to women while living comfortably on the royalties of his long-suffering wife and piously championing the traditional family unit in public while pursuing a life of promiscuity and oafishly boasting to Wells about the details when they were alone together. Rosamund herself was an embodiment of her father's sins, being the daughter of one of his mistresses, Alice Hoatson. Bland had persuaded Edith to take on the fallen woman as their housekeeper and raise her child as their own, only later revealing to her that he was actually the father.

The Blands and the Wellses had spent a lot of time at one another's homes over the previous two or three years. By March 1907 Wells was confiding to Violet Hunt, 'I have a Pure Flame for Rosamund who is the Most – Quite!'[35] His later claim that Mrs Bland turned a blind eye to the affair is not as implausible as it may seem, as Edith passionately resented Rosamund as a cuckoo in the nest. After the Blands' youngest son Fabian died during a tonsil operation when Rosamund was thirteen she heard Edith, whom she believed to be her real mother, screaming, 'Why couldn't it have been Rosamund?' If Wells feared deep down that his mother had not fully loved him, Rosamund must have felt certain about hers, with a correspondingly urgent need to find a parental figure whom she could respect and who was willing to offer her love.

Wells characteristically blamed everyone but himself for their affair. Not only had Edith practically colluded but Hubert was so highly sexed that he might have committed incest with his daughter had not Wells pre-empted him. This seems a rather desperate excuse, but it has been given some credit by the biographer and social historian Ruth Brandon, based on the emotional subtext of Bland's 1906 book, *Letter to a Daughter*.[36] Wells's ultimate, if dubious, defence was that he had been corrupted by the sexually charged atmosphere of the Blands' home and that he was virtually assigned to Rosamund by the family. Certainly he used the example of her parents as a precedent in his attempts to persuade her that what they were doing was acceptable.

What happened next is largely a matter of unsubstantiated gossip. The affair was presumably consummated at some point during 1907 but brought to a swift conclusion when Wells tried to carry out a romantic flit to the Continent. Bland caught up with the lovers on Paddington Station, snatched back his daughter and gave Wells the punch that many people by now must have been longing to administer. Since Bland was built like a bouncer, it is surprising that we have no sightings of Wells with visible damage, and we may wonder whether the Paddington story, if not apocryphal, is somewhat exaggerated. On the other hand, Wells was on holiday in Switzerland during September so could have been nursing his bruises there.

Whereas most of Wells's lovers were the kind of strong, independent women he had yearned for in his youth, Rosamund seems to have been something of a victim of those around her. In 1909 she was reluctantly married to the Fabian Nursery's treasurer, Clifford Sharp, who later become the first editor of the *New Statesman*, only to lose the job owing to alcoholism. She wrote to Wells twenty years later confirming that he had been right to warn her against the marriage.[37] By now she was the family breadwinner. Beset by creditors, she had found a job with an advertising agency and needed Wells's permission to let his picture appear on a cigarette card, which he granted.

Back in the 1900s Wells soon found another paramour from the Nursery, though one this time who would prove every bit as strong-willed as he was. His love life was being brought uncomfortably to light meanwhile through *In the Days of the Comet*. The book had gained a notoriety out of proportion to its modest sales, as readers who had reacted indifferently to the crude racial hostility of *Anticipations* threw up their hands in shock at the hint of sexual freedom at the end of *Comet*. During the Altrincham by-election of October 1907 the Conservative candidate William Joynson-Hicks cited Wells's book as proof that socialists wanted wives to be held in common. The allegation was taken up by the corrupt journalist and politician Horatio Bottomley, then working as a Tory election agent, who manufactured a convenient quotation from Wells: 'in future it will not be my wife or your wife, but our wife'.

Wells became embroiled in a lengthy press campaign trying to dissociate himself from the idea of sex outside marriage while industriously practising it, albeit in a rather different version from that attacked by the Tories. Some of his critics, such as his former admirer St Loe Strachey in the *Spectator*, seem to have been quite aware of what he was up to. Looking back, Wells felt that he should have been forthright in stating his true view, that traditional marriage was no longer necessary and would be replaced by a range of options, state-funded where children were concerned, but to have done this would have certainly damaged not only his own career but the electoral chances of the many socialists who did not share his views. Instead, he sent an 'open letter' to numerous newspapers, clarifying his conception of socialism and distinguishing it from the dream vision of the *Comet*. (The *Daily Mail* published it as 'Mr Wells's Pathetic Confession'.) Many further letters were targeted at papers and individuals, assuring them that he really did support marriage and fidelity and also that he really knew how to sue for libel.

The *Comet* dispute encouraged Wells's participation in the campaign then running against censorship in the theatre, a medium in which sexual behaviour was even less susceptible to serious discussion than it was in the novel, since every play had to be licensed in advance by a former bank manager named George Redford. While farces about adultery flourished on the West End stage, Shaw's *Mrs Warren's Profession*, a determinedly non-pornographic discussion of prostitution as a rational response to gender roles in capitalist society, had been banned (and remained excluded from the public stage for thirty-two years).

Wells was one of seventy-two authors who signed a letter to *The Times* in October 1907 calling for the abolition of the censorship system. When a license was refused to *Waste*, a play by Harley Granville Barker, one of the most important directors and actors in the history of English drama and a Fabian to boot, Wells and Jane joined the Shaws and the Webbs in a celebrity copyright reading at the Savoy Theatre in January 1908. By 1909 the government felt sufficiently pressured to set up a committee to consider the issue. It reported in favour of the status quo. While the censorship system gradually became more open-minded, theatre-goers had to wait until 1968 for its final abolition.

Having tackled marriage and censorship, Wells turned to the economic and political basis of conventional society in *New Worlds for Old*, his collection of socialist articles published in March 1908. Foreseeing that the Liberal Party's divisions might ultimately prove fatal to its electoral prospects and that the Labour Party might, after all, do more than represent the sectional interest of manual workers, he began to incline towards Labour as the vehicle for what he termed 'constructive socialism'. His book offers critiques of the alternatives, suggesting that a just society would try to preserve some of the ideals of anarchism but as a matter of practicality would have to be collectivist, though it would not achieve its aims by Marxist faith in working-class consciousness or by the back-door tactics of the Fabians. Change would have to be the step-by-step work of educated, participating citizens of all backgrounds, including Christians, since socialist ideals were clearly compatible with religion.

New Worlds for Old sold well. It was reprinted five times over the next six years and later went through two revisions. Such was its currency that Leopold Bloom can be found citing it enthusiastically in the 'Night Town' section of James Joyce's *Ulysses.* From today's perspective, however, Wells's rejection of market mechanisms looks wrong-headed, his faith in the supreme competence of the state naïve. All attempts to create socialist states based on collectivization of property have notoriously ended in unproductive, repressive dictatorships, though Wells might retort that the societies in question were backward ones committed to the defective Marxist model and hardly a fair test of his ideas. *New Worlds* insists on the importance of socialists carrying over liberal principles such as freedom of speech and information, warning that a Marxist revolution might produce an intrusive bureaucracy. Devolution of power from the centre and elements of competition must be built into the system; loss of private property needs to be balanced by rights and entitlements. Despite the claims of his critics, Wells's ideal was not Stalin's but Gorbachev's.

Most advanced nations have, however, gone down the Theodore Roosevelt route, opting for a competitive capitalist economy regulated by a democratically accountable government, with supplementary welfare services provided by the state. Capitalism has, however, become infinitely more socialistic than Wells could have foreseen, supplying many of the reforms he advocated and which others at the time regarded as utopian, including full democratic rights for women and ethnic minorities, educational opportunities for all and state welfare provisions.

An Edwardian transported to our time, undistracted by the Leninist tradition of the years between, might well consider our world to be a highly socialistic one, especially since one-fifth of the world's population lives in Communist China and the 2008 'credit crunch' showed the corporate global financial system to be effectively underwritten by state subsidy. Faced with the twenty-first century, Wells might conclude that he did not have to abandon his political ideas so much as update them for interesting new conditions.

In February 1908 he was defending himself in the *Labour Leader* against accusations of hypocrisy, on the grounds that being a well-off author and a socialist were not compatible. He replied that, since he was against poverty, he had no intention of surrendering himself and his family to it, in so doing destroying his ability to contribute to the cause. Socialism was, he claimed, the chief luxury his wealth had brought him, costing him £2,000 over the previous four years in time, energy and lost sales.

Wells probably put a lot more thought and care into *New Worlds for Old* than his scientific romance *The War in the Air*, published in October 1908, which he knocked out in four months and regarded as a potboiler. The book owes something to the science fiction of George Griffiths, acknowledged in the text by a reference to his *Outlaws of the Air.* Wells was exasperated when Beatrice Webb told him she preferred *The War in the Air* to *Tono-Bungay*, but her judgement is defensible. The scientific romances were Wells's most distinctive contribution to literature, and this was the best one since *The First Men in the Moon*, if not *The War of the Worlds*. It also succeeded in incorporating comedy, political concerns and foresight, making it one of the most quintessentially Wellsian of his books.

Its protagonist is a cycle dealer and sometime beach entertainer named Bert Smallways, who is accidentally carried from Britain to Germany in a hot-air balloon. Mistaken for an aviation pioneer whose flying machine constitutes a leap forward in the arms race, he is taken to the USA by an invading German airship fleet. Wells manages to give a much more spirited and humorous account of America here than he had done in *The Future in America*. When the Chinese and Japanese intervene in the conflict, industrial civilization is incinerated by world war. Hardened by his experiences, Bert takes his revenge on militarism by shooting the German leader at Niagara Falls, then makes his way back to his sweetheart in Britain and lives as a vigilante leader in the ruins where, decades after the Great Exhibition marked the triumph of globalization, its collapse is symbolized by the splintered pinnacles of the Crystal Palace.

The combination of omniscient narrator and globally mobile hero enables Wells to connect the general and the particular exceptionally effectively, with the movement between overview and involvement synchronized with Bert's ascents and descents. Argument and adventure are neatly dovetailed, showing that the persistence of rival nation states in an era of advanced technology is likely to lead to mass destruction, world war and even the breakdown of civilization. In contrast to *New Worlds for Old*, *The War in the Air* has probably gained in power in the hundred years since it was written, many of Wells's prophecies having proved remarkably accurate.

Back in April 1908 Wells had come up with a new way to buzzwhack his Tory enemy Joynson-Hicks, who was now standing for election in North-West Manchester. He penned an open letter to the electors, via the *Daily Mail*, offering them advice on which way to vote – certainly not for Joynson-Hicks who was distinguished only by use of dubious quotations.[38] Wells had, if anything, an even lower opinion of the socialist candidate, whom he wrote off as an extremist. Instead, he recommended a vote for the current MP, his friend Winston Churchill, who had switched from the Conservative to the Liberal Party over the issue of imperial preference. The electors ignored his advice and opted for Joynson-Hicks; Churchill was soon able to re-enter Parliament through another constituency.

The main result of Wells's intervention was to outrage many socialists, who saw it as disloyalty to the cause. Wells in return despised the narrowness of their allegiance. He did not believe in political parties for their own sake, and he would soon begin to endorse the Proportional Representation Society's campaigns for a fairer electoral system in the hope that it would diminish divisive party influence. When Wells's intervention was criticized at the Fabians' annual meeting he walked off the platform and offered his resignation from the executive in the *Fabian News*. No one bothered to reply.

It was now clear that his days in the Society were numbered. His attempt to produce a revised basis, incorporating what had become his favourite reform proposal, a children's allowance paid to the mother, was not well received. Shaw complained that his proposed basis contained little socialism, no democracy and no women's suffrage.[39] A less tactful comrade might have questioned whether the cherished allowance was not designed to benefit the men who impregnated the mothers, leaving the state to take responsibility for the children's support.

On 16 September 1908 Wells finally resigned from the Fabian Executive. Jane remained until 1910. His plans for revolutionizing the Fabians had not been without merit, but his methods had been preposterously confrontational and self-indulgent. It was not his enemies who had forced him off track; he had followed the script set out in fables such as *The Sea Lady*, 'The Door in the Wall', 'The Country of the Blind' and 'A Dream of Armageddon': a rebel tries to change the world but his real commitment is to an inner world of imaginative desire that makes his behaviour irrational and self-destructive. With his recent experiences fresh in his mind, Wells would be able to tell the story once more – this time in a detailed, realistic fashion – as *The New Machiavelli*.

Deep down Wells had always known he was the wrong man for the job. He had summed up his flaws as a politician clearly enough in a letter of March 1907:

> I'm a thoroughly immoral person – not 'non-moral' or anything like that – but just discursive, experimental & fluctuating & I have no organizing energy & very little organizing capacity. I am interested in discipline, I try out all sorts of things, I have presented this idea of the Samurai & I shall probably return to it & kindred problems again. But I couldn't create any 'order'. I think an 'order' could be created by a man or group of men of the right sort now upon the lines of my Samurai, but I am the last man to do it.[40]

In 1910 Wells's place in Fabian history was commemorated in a stained-glass window commissioned by Shaw from the artist Caroline Townshend. This mock-Tudor piece depicts Shaw and Sidney Webb purposefully attacking the world with hammers, admired by a row of kneeling dignitaries, while Wells starts up from among them derisively thumbing his nose. Mysteriously unclaimed, the window remained in the artist's studio until 1947, after which it seems to have taken on an existence of its own, refracting its times like a prop in a magic realist novel.

To mark the 1945 Labour victory, the window was installed at the Webbs' former home near Dorking, where it was unveiled by the Prime Minister, Clement Attlee. There it remained, converting the passing light into a confident proclamation of the socialist future, until 1978, when the post-war welfare consensus was breaking down, at which point, appropriately enough, thieves broke in and made off with it. While Margaret Thatcher was trying to remodel Britain's economic culture into a crude imitation of American practice, the window was reborn in Phoenix, Arizona. It came back to Britain as Labour prepared to return to power and was installed in its current home at the London School of Economics, unveiled in 1996 by Tony Blair, a leader with a laudable, if ill-conceived, ambition to synthesize the heritage of Attlee and Thatcher.

This historical digression is worth making because Wells's resignation from the Fabians is a point in his life at which many have concluded that he was merely playing at politics while the Webbs were laying the foundations for the welfare state. The judgement is a persuasive one, but we should note that the Webbs' proposals for reform of the Poor Law were not actually implemented and arguably were misconceived and that in any case the scope and affordability of welfare provision have become problematic over the long term. Perhaps there would have been more public support in Britain for a high-tax/high-welfare regime along continental lines if socialism had been seen as benefiting the whole community and had not become identified with the sectionalism of working-class militants – just as Wells warned when he urged the Fabians to seize the political agenda.

Even so, it is undeniable that he had achieved little as a Fabian. There were just three positives for him to salvage. First, he had established himself in the public eye as a socialist spokesman and found a constituency of progressive intellectuals who looked up to him if not as a leader then as an inspiring maverick. Second, he had been able to draw on advice and debate with like-minded people to formulate the world-view that he felt necessary to his mental development. This took the successive forms of a credo circulated to friends late in 1907, a Fabian lecture of December 1907 entitled 'The Faith I Hold', three lectures for the Fabian Nursery during 1908 and finally a whole book called *First and Last Things*.

Parts of this were printed in the *Independent Magazine* during July and August 1908; the book itself was published in November. Deploying arguments familiar from 'The Rediscovery of the Unique' and 'Scepticism of the Instrument', Wells puts the case that all beliefs must be provisional. Since we need beliefs of some sort, he adopts the pragmatic view that where they cannot be established scientifically they must be justified by personal effectiveness. Here Wells is taking his cue from Henry James's brother, the psychologist and philosopher William James, whom he had recently come to know personally and whose work he admired. Like James, his next move is to reinstate as part of his working beliefs a religious perspective.

Drawing from his evangelical background, Wells assumes the universe has coherence, significance, even an underlying personal identity that might be called a god, though not the Christian creator with His promise of a happy ending imposed from above. Wells instead looks to the human species struggling to bring order into a recalcitrant world, every individual achieving salvation in so far as they contribute to the process. At the political level this struggle takes the form of socialism, though one day it may be subsumed into a religious quest within the framework of the Catholic Church.

From his hedonistic side, Wells draws a firm line between his own views and traditional religion. He rejects the figure of Jesus, whom he finds too pure to be a credible role model, blasphemously claiming that in his youth he preferred the author Oliver Goldsmith, someone blundering and repeatedly humiliated yet persisting in his quest for self-realization. Nor is Wells willing to accept a Christian definition of sin that classes acts as good and bad by reference to simple commandments, regardless of contexts, intentions and consequences. Human beings should be prepared to explore all their potential, including pride and physical desire, and, while monogamy is likely to suit most people, there may be exceptional types suited to, say, a 'triangular mutuality'.[41]

First and Last Things contains a clue as to exactly whom Wells had in mind when he cites 'an able paper read this spring to the Cambridge Moral Science Club by my friend Miss Amber Reeves'.[42] Wells's third important achievement as a Fabian was the discovery of this young woman whose sexual attractiveness rivalled Isabel's and whose ability to be his soul mate and work partner challenged Jane's. It was a winning combination that Wells would have found difficult to resist – even if he had been willing to try.

Amber Reeves was the daughter of leading Fabians William Pember Reeves, High Commissioner for New Zealand, and his suffragist wife Maud Pember Reeves. Amber met Wells through her parents when she was seventeen or eighteen. Wells records that she had a 'sharp, bright' face, 'a shock of very fine abundant black hair, a slender nimble body very much alive, and a quick greedy mind'.[43] It may be significant that Willie's wife in *In the Day of the Comet* bears the name 'Anna Reeves'. As John Hammond has pointed out, if this was a daring hint regarding Wells's feelings for young Amber, it would have been an easy one for her to register and a correspondingly hard one for anyone else to challenge.[44]

In 1905 Amber entered Newnham College, Cambridge, to study Politics, Philosophy and Economics, known then as Moral Sciences. A brilliant student, she would emerge at the other end with the equivalent of a double first but would not be awarded an actual degree since, unlike the University of London, Cambridge did not deem women fit for academic status until 1947. Amber quickly helped to found a branch of the Fabian Society at the university and, inspired by *A Modern Utopia*, began working on a Samurai Society, too.

She seems to have initiated her personal relationship with Wells by an invitation early in 1906 to come and talk to the Cambridge Fabians. He declined owing to his forthcoming visit to the USA, but she persisted, assuming a tone of confident familiarity and displaying a sure sense of how her hero's mind worked, declaring, 'If you do not come, you will gain the reputation of a Fickle, Shifty and Undecided Person, and please to remember that we have in our midst several (future) famous historians.'[45]

Amber became a familiar guest at Spade House. Jane seems to have been as keen on the girl wonder as her husband was, sending her a photo of Gip and Frank and receiving an invitation to a debate on socialism against Girton College at which Amber was chief speaker. Fiercely intelligent and a tireless admirer who shared Wells's opinions and read his books with enthusiasm, Amber was Wells's ideal come to life. He must have wished that he had known someone like her in his student days. Whatever feelings he may have been experiencing about his young fan, however, he had his hands more than full until 1907 in dealing with Dorothy Richardson, Violet Hunt and Rosamund Bland.

While his loathing for Rosamund's father probably added spice to her seduction, his feelings of gratitude and respect towards Amber's parents ought to have been a barrier to intimacy. It is true there were some similarities between the Reeves and Bland families. The Reeveses had named a son Fabian, and William was somewhat old-fashioned in his attitude to his wife and daughter. On the other hand, William was a fellow Co-efficient who had taken Wells under his wing and arranged his membership of the Savile Club, and Maud was one of Wells's keenest supporters. When he came fourth place in the 1907 Fabian vote, she came sixth, remaining on the executive until 1919 and writing the classic study of poverty, *Round About a Pound a Week*. Wells in turn supported the liberal feminism to which she and Amber were devoted, attending a huge suffrage rally in May 1908 in Hyde Park as a celebrity guest alongside Shaw, Hardy and Zangwill.

Wells claims that for a long time the relationship with Amber remained above board. Nevertheless, their frequent close contact and enjoyment of one another's company developed step by step towards intimacy. Having read the *Sleeper*, she showed a willingness to call him 'Master'. He reciprocated with the nickname 'Dusa', short for 'Medusa', a tribute to her unruly hair.

Inevitably, Wells tells us that the shift in the relationship was Amber's doing. He offers a brisk summary of what happened after she expressed her feelings to him in the spring of 1908.

> One day she broke the thin ice over my suppressions by telling me she was in love, and when I asked 'with whom?' throwing herself into my by no means unwilling arms. The conception of group marriage and mutual solace, as I had embodied it

> in *A Modern Utopia*, provided all that was necessary for a swift mutual understanding, and we set about the business of making love with the greatest energy. We lay together naked in bed as a sort of betrothal that night; we contrived a meeting in Soho, when we became lovers in the fullest sense of the word, and before she went back to Cambridge for her examination for Part II of the Tripos, she went off, ostensibly to read by herself in an imaginary cottage of an imaginary friend in Epping Forest, but actually to join me in a lodging in Southend. There we had some days of insatiable mutual appreciation, which did not in the least impair her success with the Mental and Moral Science examiners. I remember lying on the beach with her and planning the thesis she was to write when she came to London. For her Cambridge career was to be prolonged as research student at the London School of Economics. And I remember also that, after our luggage had gone down to the waiting cab, we hesitated on the landing, lifted our eyebrows, and went back gleefully for a last cheerful encounter in the room we were leaving.[46]

The reason that they did not become lovers 'in the fullest sense of the word' at Clough Hall, Cambridge, seems to have been lack of a condom, a glimpse of Wells's sexual etiquette that perhaps reinforces doubts about Dorothy Richardson's pregnancy. Wells makes the affair sound romantically spontaneous – he was swept away by Amber's youthful enthusiasm – but cynics will note that, with the Richardson affair over and the Bland one forcibly closed down, Wells had been without a principal mistress for several months and was perfectly capable of sending Amber signals that now was the time to show her hand.

Once she had completed her degree Amber moved back to her parents' home in Kensington. Every eight or ten days, however, she would go off to a room which Wells had rented at 126 Warwick Street, Eccleston Square, behind Victoria Station, where they were known as 'Mr and Mrs Graham Wells', perhaps with reference to Graham and Helen in the *Sleeper*. The name 'Peter Wells' also appears in correspondence, apparently the name of Wells's cat – a piece of identity theft unlikely to fool a determined private investigator.

Using Warwick Street as their base, they would go for long walks, dine at restaurants or eat chicken salad in the room 'like two buff savages'. Sometimes they roved further afield, making love 'among bushes in a windy twilight near Hythe' and asking a sexton if they could inspect a belfry (Wells thinks this may have been at Paddlesworth) but instead enjoying sex inside the church, then again in the woods on the way home. Wells tells us they relished the sense of sin, and, looking back a quarter of a century later, he still felt 'unregretted exhilaration and happiness' at what they got up to in the summer of 1908.

And what of Jane? As usual, she seems to have accepted what was going on both as part of Wells's larger-than-life personality and a natural consequence of her own limitations. A previously unpublished exchange of letters between Jane and Amber gives a rare glimpse of the relationship between the wife and the outside woman, both courteous, honest and trying hard to be friendly, though under awkward circumstances. During August 1908 Jane had visited Amber at Bretforton House in Honeybourne, a holiday cottage in the Vale of Evesham. Amber's letter thanks Jane for sending her a copy of the *Sleeper.*

> And there is something else I want to thank you for, wanted to thank you for when you were here. Only I was clumsy and couldn't manage it. Sometimes you try so hard to find just the right way of saying a thing that you do not find any way at all. And ever since you went away I've been planning letters that did not get written. But I am grateful, not only for the wonderful thing you are letting me have, but because it is coming from your dear little white hands – you have got the most adorable hands Jane. If I am doing this horribly it is my own fault for being an idiot, but please don't mind the way it is said, and don't curl up because you think I am being sentimental. I'm only feeling like a well-intentioned elephant. But I am grateful and I also love you. Amber.[47]

The least possessive of wives, Jane replied:

> I wish we could have had more talks. It does take an awfully long time to get things said – get them really thought out and honest and right. One can express moods of course, and then be sorry, because one goes away and leaves the thing that was just a mere streak out of a whole complicated pattern, the permanent and only thing in the other person's mind.
>
> Love to you, my *dear*
>
> from your Jane.[48]

While Jane was evidently in the know, Amber's parents remained oblivious to what was going on. Yet gossip was already circulating at Cambridge, and Beatrice Webb regarded the couple with suspicion. In September her diary referred to

> the brilliant Amber Reeves, the double first Moral Science Tripos, an amazingly vital person and I suppose very clever, but a terrible little pagan – vain, egotistical, and careless of other people's happiness . . . A somewhat dangerous friendship is springing up between her and H.G. Wells. I think they are both too soundly self-interested to do more than cause poor Jane Wells some fearful feelings, but if Amber were my child I should be anxious.[49]

By the autumn the relationship was under attack from within as well as without.

Wells's plan for Amber to write a thesis at the London on 'Why and How are Men Citizens?' was foundering. She was proving to be less than wholehearted in her devotion to the project and even perhaps to Wells. It is easy to believe that she was in a state of some emotional turmoil, adoring him as a hero and companion yet sensing that a married man who wanted to co-opt her career into his plans for changing the world was not an ideal partner. For all her professions of love for him, she flirted with younger admirers, particularly a Fabian barrister called Rivers Blanco White who on Sundays accompanied her on long walks in the country and was horrified by what she told him of the illicit relationship.

In a letter postmarked 18 October 1908 Wells is anxious to reassure her of his love after a row with her.[50] Other letters, undated and therefore hard to place in the chronology of their affections, similarly suggest a turbulent relationship. A postcard from Wells to 'Dear Dusa mine' complains that she has been lying to him: 'Really I wanted to kill you. My world has smashed to pieces.' A letter written at 2 a.m. on a Saturday morning records that he has just torn up a 'perfectly vicious letter' written the previous night, provoked by her inconsistent behaviour. Now, having chided her for wasting the time she should be spending on her thesis, he wants to reassure her that she is the supreme thing in his life.[51]

A particularly vivid glimpse of their relationship is afforded by the following letter (again undated and previously unpublished) in which violent arguments in the bedroom are set against a conviction that they are paired for life, a conviction with potentially serious implications for Wells's marriage to Jane.

> We may hurt each other, all sorts of things may happen, we will do our outmost to get the good things and around the bad ones, but deep down eternally you and I lie in one another's arms for ever and ever. These are things of the surface. I may bully you like a churchwarden bullying a schoolgirl, you may lie and weep upon the bedroom floor, you may go off with your nose in the air to do a hundred silly extravagances. *Mind if you like but don't mind really.* Dear one I love you. There is no music in the world like your voice saying; 'Look here, old Thing.' I don't want to live unless I can feel your heart beating. Living doesn't matter anything or mean anything apart from you. There's no such thing as 'chucking' ever to be thought of between us. We can't. We will get all the life we can together and if we are sillies and make a mess of that, we will die together. This isn't Promises, this is how things are.[52]

It was inevitable that such an affair should become a public scandal. Wells blamed Amber for telling some of her lecturers at Newnham, her mother and her student friends; Beatrice Webb's diary points the finger at a lecturer's wife and the indiscretions of Wells himself. By whatever means, the news was soon circulating sufficiently widely that an anonymous Fabian letter-writer passed it on to Amber's mother.

Several of Amber's boyfriends, considering themselves a much better match than a 42-year-old man with a wife and children, offered to rescue her through marriage.

According to Wells, it was Blanco White who brought things to a head by disclosing the situation to Amber's father. William had limited time for his womenfolk's feminism and no time at all for unconventional behaviour. While Maud frantically tried to conceal any prior knowledge, William fiercely declared that Wells should be shot. Legend has it that he then took up a position in the window of the Savile Club in Piccadilly, a loaded pistol beside him, and waited for his man to appear, an embarrassing situation that caused the club to contact Wells and ask him if he wouldn't mind resigning his membership. The tale, circulated by Compton Mackenzie, may be an exaggeration, but, if so, it is a serviceable metaphor for the stressful situation in which Wells had placed himself by the end of 1908.[53] Things were no less stressful for Reeves, a governor of the London School of Economics and from 1909 its director. By the time he took up his appointment the scandal about his student daughter was widely known, and he suffered acutely at the gossip behind his back.

Amber, in contrast, seemed to thrive on the intensity of the situation. Virginia Stephen (later Virginia Woolf) was teaching literature at the Morley Memorial College, which offered evening classes to workers, when in 1909 Amber gave a talk there on women's suffrage. The two met at a dinner and, impressed, perhaps even slightly intimidated, by this remarkable young woman Miss Stephen wrote her up in her notebook:

> she always leans forward, as though to take flight; her whole figure and pose indicating an ardent interested spirit. When she is silent, she thinks – her eyes intent on one spot. But she talks almost incessantly, launching herself with the greatest ease – but says nothing commonplace. Her talk at once flies to social questions; is not dry exposition, but very lucid and vigorous explanation. 'We think . . .', 'we find' and so on; as though she spoke for the thinking part of the nation.[54]

Amber's decisive attitude produced a swift response to all the attempts by family and friends to part her from Wells. She phoned her lover and arranged a final meeting at Warwick Street. '"Give me a child," said Amber, "whatever happens."'[55] At this point Wells might reasonably have replied that he was a married man with two children who had a career as an author and intellectual journalist that he valued enormously. His marriage and career would very likely be destroyed if she became pregnant, along with her own chance to achieve such things for herself. That was not, however, Wells's response. He complied enthusiastically.

To fling away the condom and enjoy the full pleasures of the flesh may have held an overwhelming appeal to masculine instincts, but there were further implications to the act that even a tumescent Wells could hardly ignore. To make Amber pregnant would be close to a pledge to marry her. Though he was reluctant to admit it, even he, looking back after a quarter of a century, conceded 'I do not see how that idea could have been absent from her mind.'

Five months or so before conception, they were so confident they were going to have a daughter called Anna Jane that Wells had dedicated his novel after next to her. Inspired by embarking on a new phase of his life, he had two novels in progress on top of *Tono-Bungay*. It sounds as though Amber had requested he should dedicate one of them to her. Wells reported:

> The New Machiavelli is now lunging forward. I'm going to dedicate *Ann Veronica* to A.J. & I'm not going to dedicate *Tono* to anyone. Now don't let me hear any more about dedications ever.[56]

If, consciously or otherwise, Amber was trying to lure him into a divorce from Jane, what was in his own mind? Fundamentally he wanted to keep up the 'triangular mutuality' of man, wife and mistress, but this option was clearly coming to an end. One solution is sketched in an undated letter, possibly from this period.

> I've had things out with Jane. Item she is to have a baby. I know Spade House is to be over. Then you & I will live together. Jane will have a house in London & you will have a little flat for your alleged home. (You cannot be there much.) If that does not work – divorce.[57]

Wells was deluding himself that Jane would go along with any plan that could result in her ceasing to be Mrs Wells. Even she had some limits, and Wells's self-centred behaviour was at last bringing them out. He complained in a letter to Amber that his wife had had the temerity to object to him displaying a photograph of his mistress in their house. 'Jane & me talked for an hour about your photograph. It was going to hurt her – when I'm away she would want to smash it – you are getting all over her life and things like that.' Eventually Wells started 'crying like a baby' and put his head under the bedclothes, only to give himself a nosebleed which 'smothered myself & the bed & pillow with blood'.[58]

The red-blooded Romeo had to decide which way he was going to jump. All his life he had rejected confining roles, from draper to scientific romancer. In middle age this might be his last big chance to take a risk, to wade into the sea with the mermaid, to go through the door in the wall, to push the lever of the time machine, to plunge into a new world and, even at the risk of self-destruction, feel himself transformed.

One day in the spring of 1909 Wells and Amber made their move. They rendezvoused at Victoria Station, travelled to France, rented a furnished chalet at Le Touquet-Paris-Plage and awaited the consequences of their actions.

11
NOVELIST
1909–1911

Leaving Amber and Wells in Le Touquet for a time we must give some consideration to Wells the novelist, who – despite or perhaps even because of the furore elsewhere in his life – was reaching something of a peak in his career. Much as he enjoyed sexual and political intrigue, Wells knew th at his literary skills were what brought him all his other freedoms. 'The literary life is one of the modern forms of adventure,' he declared to Russian readers in a 1908 preface, later reprinted as 'Mr Wells Explains Himself', adding with what a century later has gained a wholly appropriate trace of *double entendre*, 'One is lifted out of one's narrow circumstances into familiar and unrestrained intercourse with a great variety of people.'

> I have friends and intimates now at almost every social level from that of a peer to that of a pauper, and I find my sympathies and curiosities stretching like a thin spider's web from top to bottom of the social tangle.

Friends did indeed note the unusual ease with which Wells socialized with anyone and everyone, from politicians to vagrants. By September 1909, for example, he was considering a collaboration with a socialist bathchairman called George Meek, a book that would report Wells's experiences at an upper-class Ascot party, intercut with his reflections on Meek's writing and conversation, delivering a complex critique of class society. He never did find time for this experiment, making do instead with a conventional preface to a book of Meek's writings. None the less, the proposed mix of reportage and debate indicates the trend of his literary career.

Wells explained that, having written a series of 'so-called sociological works' in order to gain perspective, he was now in a position to put both sociology and fantasy behind him and write nothing but novels for some years. The outcome would not be prophecy, just honest reflections that might offer some bearings to others.

In May 1911 Wells followed up these ideas in a lecture to *The Times* Book Club on 'The Scope of the Novel', later revised and published as 'The Contemporary Novel'. He begins by dismissing, on the one hand, the philistine view that literature should be undemanding entertainment and, on the other (without quite mentioning Henry James), the connoisseur's view that it should conform to set aesthetic standards. His choice of enemies was prescient. A look round any bookshop will show that today novels are published and marketed almost exclusively either as genre fiction or as art fiction, with social reportage and analysis stacked on the non-fiction shelves and Wells's books, when present at all, scattered haphazardly between the three.

Wells places himself in the inclusive tradition of Laurence Sterne and Henry Fielding. Staying comparatively close to the sources of the novel in biography, journalism, history and letters, this approach acknowledges the presence of the constructing author and the construing reader and embraces contingency, digression and self-reflection or, as Wells rather tentatively puts it, 'comment that seems to admit that, after all, fiction is fiction, a change in manner between part and part, burlesque, parody, invective, all such things are not necessarily wrong in the novel'.[1] The Wellsian novel, in other words, does not try for either a watertight unity or a consistent illusion of 'real life' but acknowledges itself to be a construct, a communicative vehicle that can cover a great deal of mental terrain thanks to its wide range of gears.

Knowing the intelligentsia's perennial belief that continental fiction is sophisticated and British pedestrian, Wells takes care to furnish French examples of what he is advocating: namely, *Jean-Cristophe* by Romain Rolland and *Bouvard et Pécuchet* by Gustave Flaubert. Dropping the name of Flaubert, customarily idolized as the ultimate in scrupulous artists, is a smart piece of one-upmanship, particularly as the book he mentions was as yet untranslated. Wells then sidesteps Jamesian assumptions a second time by taking as his example of an intrusive narrator not Dickens – such a vulgar genius – but the admirably pure artist Conrad, though Wells cannot resist also citing Elizabeth von Arnim, a better-selling but less prestigious author whom he presumably wished to promote because of her place in his love life at that time.

Wells had long since given up his ambition to attain self-detachment and disillusionment. Even so, he had no intention of lapsing into propaganda. He explains that he regards the novel as a valuable medium precisely because it can avoid religious and political dogma, move past the vague generalizations of sociology and explore social issues through individual psychology. While the novel has less documentary value than biography and autobiography, it has greater capacity to offer perspective and frankness.

By common consent, the book in which Wells comes closest to realizing his ambitions is *Tono-Bungay*, which was serialized in the opening numbers of the *English Review* from December 1908 to March 1909. The editor, Wells's old friend Hueffer, aimed to set a new literary standard for the era, mixing established names like Hardy and James with more recent stars such as Bennett, Conrad, Galsworthy and Yeats, plus newcomers like Pound and Wyndham Lewis. The book version of *Tono-Bungay* was published in Britain in February 1909, probably some weeks after the US edition.

Tono-Bungay is narrated by George Ponderevo, whose opening words echo Wells's Russian article. His career, too, has been an adventure – 'another kind of life', unorthodox in its perspective – which has given him insight into almost all levels of society and left him, as his name suggests, pondering its further evolution:

> Most people in this world seem to live 'in character'; they have a beginning, a middle and an end, and the three are congruous one with another and true to the rules of their type . . . But there is also another kind of life that is not so much living as a miscellaneous tasting of life. One gets hit by some unusual transverse force, one is jerked out of one's stratum and lives crosswise for the rest of the time, and, as it were, in a succession of samples. That has been my lot, and that is what has set me at last writing something in the nature of a novel.[2]

George claims he can pin down the typical because he is unique and can generalize because he is exceptional, but the paradox casts doubt on his conclusions. How much does his perspective reveal truth, how much distort it? 'It may be I see decay all about me,' he has to admit, 'because I am, in a sense, decay.'[3]

George's mother is housekeeper of a country house called Bladesover, its name suggesting the poised sickle of Father Time. Bladesover is a stagnant world that George comes to despise yet which also becomes his template for analysing more recent social developments. After a spell with some lower-class relatives, the Frapps (a typically Wellsian caricature of religious believers), George is apprenticed to his uncle Edward, an enterprising pharmacist whose aspirations are the antithesis of the Bladesover ideal. Edward is a vigorous comic character full of outlandish scams and inventions, such as 'the Ponderevo Patent Flat, a Machine you can Live in'.[4] (The phrase 'A house is a machine for living in' is universally attributed to the modernist architect Le Corbusier in 1923 but had previously circulated among Futurist artists and very likely originated with Wells here. As we shall see, it is a standard move in modernist cultural history to airbrush Wells out of the picture.[5])

After Edward becomes bankrupt, George continues with his scientific studies. Their paths cross again in London, where Edward persuades George to help him market his new patent medicine, Tono-Bungay. Friar Bungay was a legendary medieval charlatan, so the name suggests a tonic that is more symptom than cure. Its huge success rests on people's desire to escape from unstimulating, meaningless lives, while its potential for harm (the lozenge form contains strychnine) shows the failure of the state to protect its citizens from exploitation. Wells was probably inspired by the similar-sounding Coca-Cola which was originally marketed as a tonic and which contained traces of cocaine.[6]

Edward is almost as much a case of image over substance as his creation. Eventually his financial power turns him into an egotist with a failing sense of reality, again with a contemporary model in the bankrupt financier Whitaker Wright. George longs to break with his entertaining but irresponsible uncle – a personification of a society that has lost touch with reality – but he struggles to find an alternative way of life. His marriage is a failure, his affair with the drug-addicted aristocrat Beatrice Normandy only emphasizes how the ruling class has abandoned its traditional role and is busy selling itself to moneyed interlopers, his artistic friend Ewart is happy to fit himself into the system through the advertising industry, and his hopes for socialism are dashed when he makes the mistake of attending a Fabian meeting.

Science seems a better source of certainty. Piloting his experimental gliders and airships, George seems to be freed from the past and his own limitations, soaring above a world his dedication and courage have diminished into perspective. Yet the motif of ascent and descent does not separate him from Edward, whose personal imagery evokes riding up and down the treacherous waves of the business cycle. Just as the symbol of liberating flight persists from many earlier Wells stories, so the flux image recurs from *The Time Machine* ('the whole surface of the earth seemed changed – melting and flowing under my eyes'), *The War of the Worlds* (when the emergency services and railways are lost in a 'swift liquefaction of the social body') and *A Modern Utopia* ('everywhere societies deliquesce, everywhere men are afloat amidst the wreckage of their flooded conventions').[7]

Seen in a moment of crisis or deep reflection, human existence seems without ultimate shape or purpose. Edward surfs this void as successfully as Wells the author. George, like Wells the thinker, craves a more secure reality. He tells Edward,

> I want something to hold on to. I shall go amok if I don't get it. I'm a different sort of beast from you. You float in all this bunkum. *I* feel like a man floundering in a universe of soapsuds, up and down, east and west. I can't stand it.[8]

When Edward's financial empire crashes, his nephew helps him flee across the Channel in his latest airship but it, too, crashes into the sea. The name of the airship, *Lord Roberts* , supposedly a tribute to Britain's Boer War commander, ironically suggests the inevitable demise of nationalism and empires. When the Ponderevos finally attain France, Edward dies, lost in hallucinations.

George's unreliable aircraft are not the only indications that science cannot offer total certainty. In a bid to put Edward's business on a secure foundation, George attempts a fashionably imperialist solution and leads an expedition to a West African island in search of a rare resource, a radioactive mineral called 'quap', which proves to be the epitome of disintegration. 'It is in matter exactly what the decay of our old culture is in society, a loss of traditions and distinctions and assured reactions.'[9]

Wells's former fear that the world might be predestined – a machine made out of atoms, each knocking the next into its allotted place with no scope for free will – was being overthrown by scientists such as Rutherford and Soddy, but their replacement view was at least as alarming: a world in which atoms consisted of elusive components that were sometimes inexplicably spat out. The material world was beginning to look like the outcome of randomly churning, incomprehensible forces. 'So that while man still struggles and dreams his very substance will change and crumble from beneath him.'

Previously Wells had championed the unique against the general in order to discredit the rigidity of the existing order, but it seems to have occurred to him here that a proliferation of anomalies, atomic or social, must undermine any order. To combine stability and freedom the world must somehow be neither closed nor open. Traditional science and religion suggested total closure; now atomic physics was suggesting randomness and uncertainty. In such a universe what scope could there be for an enduring Utopia organized by a scientifically informed elite?

Under the influence of quap, George finds himself succumbing to primitive impulses of hatred and aggression and eventually he guns down a native in an almost random act of violence that he feels has no connection with anything else in his life. The cargo of quap rots the timbers of George's ship, which sinks – taking with it any chance of salvaging the Ponderevo project.

Wells had considered ending the novel, rather as he had the *Sleeper*, with the protagonist's death in a flying accident. This would have been in keeping with the structure and themes of the story but awkward to bring off in the first person. Instead, controversially, Wells has George build a destroyer and sail it down the Thames on a speed trial, dismissively interpreting what he sees along the banks and passing at last into the open sea, declaring that his warship is not intended for the British Empire or any European power. The writing off of England is emotionally powerful (it inspired the finale of Vaughan Williams's *London Symphony*) but unclear in its implications. It could suggest a transfer of loyalty to the coming superpower of the USA, but it was Edward who admired American capitalism, not George; the motif of riding the waves is also Edward's. Wells's attempt to write the uncle's mentality out of the book is not therefore entirely successful.

And George himself continues to be depicted with irony. Having struck his noble pose against a country ruined by an irresponsible alliance of upper-class tradition and capitalism, he has to turn around and return. The book none the less ends with George affirming a quasi-religious commitment to a vision of an alternative order:

> I do not know what it is, this something, except that it is supreme. It is something, a quality, an element, one may find now in colours, now in forms, now in sounds, now in thoughts. It emerges from life with each year one lives and feels, and

generation by generation and age by age, but the how and why of it are all beyond the compass of my mind . . .[10]

The positioning of this passage in the last couple of pages suggests a summing up, and the concept, though vague, is neither unappealing nor even eccentric. Compare the view of Gilbert Murray, writing to Bertrand Russell in 1902, that the meaning of life was to be found in 'a thing like Heaven or God, of which one can get glimpses in many different ways – music, poetry, mathematics, heroic conduct &c'.[11] In the end, though he is by his own account an unreliable observer and his views are not quite Wells's, George does seem to turn into a Wellsian prophet, throwing the book significantly off balance.

Tono-Bungay is animated by the interaction between the viewpoints of George and Edward, representing the evangelical and playful sides of Wells, and when the novelist ceases to maintain his inner dialogue it is the novel that crashes. Patrick Parrinder puts this well: '*Tono-Bungay* remains a rich and exhilarating novel as long as it has two contrasted heroes; at the end, when Edward has left for his heavenly mansion, it is overwhelmed by a single, garrulous performance.'[12]

Why did Wells find it impossible to sustain the balance? The clue lies in the way George's life parallels his own, Wells's move into a writing career being replaced by George's into quack medicine. This suggests that at one level Tono-Bungay must stand for art and Edward for the wayward imagination that produces it. Indeed, Edward is no sober businessman but a creative genius inspired by 'the Romance of Commerce'.[13] Like Chaffery in *Love and Mr Lewisham*, he is a displaced storyteller, a symbol of the artist as charlatan. His activities make people feel better about life but only by exploiting and deceiving them. He embodies Wells's fear that, unless the novelist can contrive some sort of prophetic message, he will be part of the problem, not of the solution.

It is fitting, therefore, that Edward's death is modelled on that of the lapsed socialist novelist George Gissing. Edward's deathbed scene at a foreign inn, the last of the many residences that are used to define him at different stages of his life, finally 'places' him for us as a phoney but leaves us in need of a true prophet. The first-person narrative confers more credibility on George than Wells may have initially intended, shifting him towards a prophetic role and allowing his tentative affirmation of a greater meaning in life to become awkwardly entangled with the ambiguous symbol of the destroyer.

If Wells had reneged on his promise to his Russian readers that his novels were not going to deal in prophecy, does this amount to a minor flaw in an otherwise powerful novel or a fatal flaw in a book that is pretentious and incoherent? The quality of the writing is undeniably inconsistent: superb at best but less impressive in the crude depiction of George's marriage and the distracting decision to make the quap episode a pastiche of *Heart of Darkness*, complete with a sea captain who speaks fractured English like Conrad. For those who conceive literary merit in terms of Jamesian composition, *Tono-Bungay* can be dismissed as incoherent fragments of artistry. Read on its own terms, the novel embodies an ongoing struggle to wrestle experience into meaning, holding together a number of conflicting forces, not least those within Wells's own personality, before the inevitable explosion.

Reviewers then and now were divided about what Wells had achieved. Predictably, Bland trashed and Bennett praised.[14] One young schoolteacher who would shortly become a contributor of stories and poems to the *English Review* was in no doubt about the book's quality, urging a friend to read *Tono-Bungay*, declaring it not only Wells's best novel but the best novel he had read for many years. He struggled with Wells's comic spirit, wishing that the characters were depicted with more dignity. A later letter disparages Wells's science fiction as 'theoryish', presumably because the cosmic perspectives that he could not appreciate marginalized the characterization, which he could, but he continues, 'read *Kipps*, *Love and Mr Lewisham*, and read, read *Tono-Bungay*, it is a great book'.[15]

D.H. Lawrence, the admirer in question – soon to be the major English novelist of the generation after Wells, Bennett and Conrad – had more in common with Wells than might be supposed. He, too, had risen from lower-class origins to be a schoolteacher and wanted to write books that would challenge artistic and social conventions, acknowledge the importance of sexual desire and prophesy a better way of life. He, too, had been indelibly marked by the apocalyptic thinking of evangelical religion and by conflict between his parents that he had internalized and sublimated into conflicting forces in his fiction. He even scorned the idea of the well-made novel and shared Wells's preference for redrafting a book from start to finish each time, deeming it complete when he had explored his conflicting feelings sufficiently, not when he had composed them into a conventionally acceptable form. Edward Mendelson has argued that Lawrence's *Women in Love* is in some respects a rejoinder to *Tono-Bungay*.[16]

It is evidence of *Tono-Bungay*'s strengths that it inspired a range of very different writers. The Liberal politician Charles Masterman repeatedly draws upon it in his 1909 study, *The Condition of England*. T.S. Eliot's early poetry parallels surprisingly closely some of Wells's phrases and ideas. As Scott Fitzgerald devoured Wells in his formative years, it is hardly surprising that there are similarities between *Tono-Bungay* and *The Great Gatsby*, from a compromised narrator reporting on an associate whose rise and fall epitomizes an era, both characters representing aspects of the author, down to an uncertainly ironic conclusion invoking the image of a boat failing to maintain its heading.[17]

Such continuities need to be stressed because the literary establishment has come to believe that some time around 1910 the naïve, sloppy writing of the 'Edwardians' was superseded by the painstaking artistry of a group of writers retrospectively dubbed the 'modernists', who plainly could have had no time for the likes of Wells. As Chris Baldick has shown in his literary history of the period, this is a foreshortened, simplistic account of what actually happened, which has resulted in misreading and undervaluation of those caught on the wrong side of the line. *Tono-Bungay* is a formidable anomaly in this scheme, a missing link occupying the supposedly empty space between two literary eras, evincing, on one hand, a typically Edwardian ambition to apply familiar ways of thinking to unfamiliar subject matter in the interests of a new synthesis and, on the other, a modernist submersion in dissonance, depicting a wasteland that can only acquire significant form through the compositional techniques of the artist. If *Tono-Bungay* looks like a failure against traditionalist and modernist criteria, it is in large measure because its greatness resides in its refusal to conform to either set of assumptions.[18]

By the time he had got *Tono-Bungay* ready for publication, Wells was already on the second draft of his next production, *Ann Veronica*, the tale of a young woman who rebels against convention. A lighter, more straightforward tale, it again explores social ideas through an entertaining and provocative account of individual experience – too provocative for its intended publisher, Frederick Macmillan. His letter of rejection praises the book as very well written and welcomes its even-handed satire on suburban life and the dissidents opposed to it but baulks at the last part of the book where Ann Veronica falls in love with her university teacher, despite his adulterous past, and makes herself his mistress. The book would offend Macmillan's public.[19]

Fortunately for Wells, another publisher, Fisher Unwin, had recently contacted him as part of a recruiting drive for well-known authors. Two days before Macmillan's final rejection, he was already negotiating with this rival and eventually succeeded in obtaining an advance of £1,500 while retaining the US and translation rights for separate disposal. The book appeared in October 1909, dedicated as promised to 'A.J.'

Most of the initial reviews, while noting the controversial nature of the heroine's behaviour, thought that Wells had produced an entertaining and thought-provoking novel, though *T.P.'s Weekly* worried about the effect on impressionable young women. The storm broke on 20 November with an anonymous review in the *Spectator* by the magazine's editor, Wells's old opponent John St Loe Strachey, now a prominent member of the National Social Purity Crusade. As in his earlier attack on *In the Days of the Comet*, distaste at Wells's private life seems to have added to Strachey's ferocity. He condemned the book as 'poisonous' because it treated female sexuality and sex outside marriage not as shockingly sinful but as natural behaviour. Wells's characters were not human beings capable of self-restraint, he declared, but 'scuffling stoats and ferrets'.[20]

Subsequent statistics on the decline of the nuclear family and the adverse effects on children, parents and the community endorse Strachey's concern about damage to the institution of marriage. On the other hand, Wells was surely right that the Victorian conceptions of sexual behaviour and the family were unduly rigid, sometimes hypocritical, and to close one's eyes to common behaviour in the name of purity was neither grown-up nor helpful. To drive his points home, during June Wells contributed several articles to the *Daily Mail* on family life, marriage and the endowment of motherhood.

Strachey's attack received support from such dignitaries as the headteacher of Westminster School and the president of the Young Men's Christian Association, and the novel was banned by many libraries, including those of Hull, where Canon Malet Lambert, a member of the Library Committee, declared, 'I would as soon send a daughter of mine to a house infected with diphtheria or typhoid fever as put that book into her hands.'[21]

The furore greatly boosted Wells's sales but was uncomfortable for him personally, especially as it coincided with many people he knew turning against him over the affair with Amber Reeves. Yet, though Ann Veronica's personality, tricks of speech and mannerisms were derived from those of Amber (as, for that matter, were those of the outrageous Hypatia Tarelton in Shaw's contemporary play *Misalliance*), it is not the case that the book is a crude justification of their liaison. Wells does not take the opportunity to satirize Amber's family or their mutual acquaintances, and the relationship between Ann Veronica and her tutor Capes owes at least as much to Wells's affair with Jane as it does to his affair with Amber.

To confirm the point, Wells inscribed a copy of the title page 'To Jane who also Ran away with her Biological Demonstrator', under a picshua of his wife speeding along with him tucked under her arm. Another picshua of 1909 is addressed 'To Jane Veronica'. Perhaps most revealingly, Wells decorated the title page of a 1912 French translation, *Anne Véronique*, with a picshua of himself apparently engaged in painting his wife but instead producing a self-portrait, suggesting the book was about his view of women rather than an account of any one woman.[22]

If Wells's contemporaries were unduly obsessed with the gossip element of the novel, recent critics have been almost as single-minded over the topic of female representation. Wells has been given qualified praise for depicting his heroine as an active woman in control of her own sexuality but reprimanded for other aspects of the book, especially the comic depiction of feminists and their raid on the House of Commons, based on an actual suffrage protest of October 1908. Oddly, feminist critics never comment on the fact that most of the male characters are also comic stereotypes.[23]

Among literary readers of the time, Lawrence found the novel a let-down after *Tono-Bungay*, and James had his usual reservations about composition, though he still declared:

> You must at moments make dear old Dickens turn – for envy of the eye and the ear and the nose and the mouth of you – in his grave . . . the total result lives and kicks and throbs and flushes and glares . . . you are a very swagger performer indeed.[24]

Gosse agreed the book was vivid, but was rightly appalled by the contrived ending, when Ann Veronica and Capes marry and the latter becomes a best-selling playwright, a development that abruptly shifts the novel from realism to romance and evades all the difficult practical issues. Wells himself came to think the book 'rather badly constructed' with 'an excessive use of soliloquy'.[25]

He had none the less made a better job of turning Amber into a fictional character than he had of pursuing his love affair with her. Several pages ago, we left the couple holed up in the French coastal resort of Le Touquet-Paris-Plage. Presumably Wells had been hoping for the kind of creative companionship he had experienced with Jane in 1894, but he was no longer a young man with an open future and limited responsibilities, which may be why he chose to abscond a mere forty miles from Sandgate. According to Amber's testimony, Wells returned to England whenever he got an invitation from a hostess such as Lady Desborough.[26] Wells in turn resented Amber's liking for the company of young men.

Wells's later summary of what happened is a little rose-tinted, but the outcome is plain enough. After three months of defiance they abandoned the elopement.

> We walked and talked about the silvery dunes, and sat and made love in the warm night darkness under the silent sweeping beams of the two lighthouses and discussed what lay before us . . . I found the idea of a divorce from Jane intolerable. Neither of us relished the prospect of wandering about the Continent, a pair of ambiguous outcasts – quite possibly hard up . . . Amber drooped. 'I shall go back and marry Rivers.'[27]

In fact Amber remained unenthusiastic about the marriage option, even though by this point she knew that she was pregnant and would need a husband very soon if she was to maintain any appearance of respectability. She later claimed that she considered drowning herself by going over the side of the Boulogne-to-Dover ferry. Finding the manoeuvre impossible to execute in a tight Edwardian skirt and having attracted the attentions of one of the crewmen, she had no choice but to continue homewards. She was not at all pleased when on her return her mother suggested the solution to all her problems would be an abortion.

However, neither she nor Wells seemed able to reach a firm alternative decision. Their most definite plan at this stage seems to have been to meet up again in France and go on a walking holiday in Belgium. Amber's interest in this project was probably cooled by a previously unpublished outburst from Wells in which he alternates between professing his love and threatening her. If she was going to prove untrue, he told her, she should say so now or flee him. 'Run for your life, skedaddle, go back to London, get your mother's help if needful, do anything rather than face a cruelly clear sighted, vindictive enemy.'

> Are you going to fail me again? Our Thesis was to be our intellectual child, a fine & noble thing to do, & you have wasted a year in snatched holidays, in vulgar & silly flirtations, in scuffles for kisses & the company of silly inferiors.[28]

When they are in Belgium, will she find a frightfully interesting medical man with a motor car and go off, leaving him to do the work? He is not going to adopt the role of 'the strong patient submissive loyal man supporting & protecting a wonderful feminine personality'. He believes they can achieve great things, but if she lets him down he will hand over her fare to London and set off for England without her, 'Anna Jane or no Anna Jane'.

In the face of this tirade, Amber turned for counsel to Sir Sydney Olivier, the Governor of Jamaica and one of the most experienced and accomplished Fabians, as well as a star turn at the Wells family's charades. (His acting fame would later be eclipsed by that of his nephew, Laurence Olivier.) Sir Sydney advised her to stick with the marriage and try the stabilizing experience of motherhood. On 7 May 1909 Amber married Rivers Blanco White at Kensington Register Office.

In later life Amber liked to claim she was strong-armed into the marriage by Wells and Blanco White acting together, but it is plain from the correspondence that Wells was taken aback, if not by the marriage itself then by its timing.

> I didn't think you'd get engaged to Rivers until after you'd been abroad but I suppose you found it difficult to wait & as things are perhaps it's the wisest thing you could do. So there won't be any Belgium & I suppose you won't come down on Thursday. But if you do the latter I'll see that things are all right & we'll have a last walk on the hills in honest open country – & no nonsense.[29]

Wells dwells on his disappointment about Belgium as though stunned but tries to adopt a resolute attitude to match hers, sending £25 to cover her debts and suggesting arrangements for clearing their flat.

Wells remained based in Le Touquet, working on his next novel. The family came over for a few days at the start of May, the opportunity to play with the children easing the reconnection with Jane. Wells found himself almost in awe of his wife's understanding, which was so different from the firm ultimatum he had received fifteen years previously from Isabel – with whom, incidentally, he made up during 1909, their relationship now 'free from all the glittering black magic of sex'.[30]

Jane viewed her husband's promiscuity as 'a sort of constitutional disease' and after a while they were virtually discussing the case in the third person.[31] They decided to sell Spade House and move to London, which they did during August. Jane wanted access to concerts and art galleries; Wells wanted to cheer himself up by mixing with those friends who were still on speaking terms with him. In any case, Spade House represented an ideal of settling down and domesticity that Wells had now decided was beyond his temperament. Jane could afford to be tolerant of her unruly spouse. She had won and would remain Mrs Wells.

In choosing their new home, a seventeenth-century house at 17 Church Row, West Hampstead, they failed to notice that, being located near a church and a crematorium, it was on a prime route for funeral processions. The family tried to adapt to the grim parade of black horses outside their windows but found the size of the house and garden constricting. Wells escaped much of the time to a small flat in Candover Street, off Great Portland Street, 'for purposes of work, and nervous relief', by which he meant encounters with 'various friendly women'.[32]

Despite their respective fresh starts, Wells and Amber were still reluctant to give up their affair completely. Wells rented a cottage for her from the feminist playwright Elizabeth Robins, located in Butler's Dean Road, Woldingham, near Blythe in Surrey. He often visited, and Blanco White came down at weekends. Sometimes both men seem to have been present at the same time in what must surely have been an uncomfortable *ménage à trois*. Jane remained supportive, and, while she was spending a few days in London, sent her sons to keep Amber company.

Others were less tolerant. Sidney and Beatrice Webb terminated their friendship with Wells during August, Beatrice's diary endorsing William Pember Reeves's description of Wells as a 'vile impudent blackguard'.[33] Beatrice then intervened to set things right, travelling to Woldingham to exercise her powers of rational persuasion over Amber. This was not successful. Amber proved contrary, insisting that she would continue to be Wells's companion and her father would simply have to fund her.

If Amber thought such an irregular partnership could be permanent, Wells had some bad news. Another previously unpublished letter, written while staying with Lady Elcho at Stanway Manor House, Winchcombe, offers her the prospect of marriage, but what it gives with one hand it snatches back with the other:

> Always among beautiful things I want you – & all this morning I have been walking on the hills longing to feel your shoulder touching mine. Always when I am unhappy I want you. And always when I am proud of success, or thinking out my work I want you. And when I perceive I am a silly fattish baldish little man, then I

> want you – to tell me it is not so. I do want to live with you, to be always in call of you, to sleep near you & eat with you & share our child together. I want this so much that if you are willing, you will send me the hand-clasp now, I will never (except for petulant & fatigued moments) depart from the work of so arranging things that we may live together as man and wife.
>
> But now Dusa here are the difficulties we have to face. You and I are both pampered people. I am accustomed to be waited on, to take no thought even of the brushing of my clothes, to have my work & my mind made the ruling facts in my life. It is clear that this cannot to the same extent be the case if we defy the world. I didn't expect that at Paris-Plage. My dear, I will gladly carry pails of water & clean your dear boots if needs be, to have you once again. You too will have to pay for me, in hardship, in a narrow life, in *battles*. Your fight with the Blythe servants was only a sample of the long personal battle you will have as my paramour. We have frankly to give up *comfort* for the love we bear each other. Do you think we can? We can't altogether – make no mistake. We shall sweat & what is more we shall both *shirk* (I know us). We shall quarrel over petty things of that sort sometimes quite wickedly. I am ready to trust our love to carry all that off like a flood washes away straws. Are you?[34]

For good measure, Wells notes the possible damage to his relationship with his sons and to his career, the huge stress, the need for both parties to abjure promiscuity, and the possibility that one or other of them will fail to secure a divorce. In effect, while claiming to offer marriage he is manoeuvring Amber into taking responsibility for saying no. Her reply is not recorded.

After Amber moved into a nursing home in Cambridge Terrace, near Regent's Park, Wells continued to visit her. Anna Jane was born on 31 December 1909. Wells sent several affectionate notes, one addressing the baby as 'Dear Pup' and assuring her, 'Your daddy adores you'.[35] Another refers to Blanco White as 'only a husband and protector on trial' who may have to be divorced if he isn't up to the job, but this was bluster.[36] According to Anthony West, Blanco White, tired of his role as fall guy, beard and cuckold, had threatened Wells with a libel action.[37] He had secured depositions from several witnesses that Ann Veronica was a recognizable depiction of his wife. There was no limit to the damages that could be awarded for an allegation of premarital unchastity, quite apart from the effect such a case would have on Wells's reputation. Defeated, Wells agreed to stay away from Amber for at least the next two years. It would be longer than that before either she or their daughter would reappear significantly in his life.

Wells compensated himself for defeat by producing a comic novel whose hero, in contrast to himself, succeeds wholeheartedly in defying his responsibilities. Wells started *The History of Mr Polly* in May 1909, and it was published in April 1910.

Though it was his greatest work of comedy, he wrote much of it 'weeping bitterly like a frustrated child'.[38]

Alfred Polly is a draper's assistant.[39] He rebels against life's dullness not by taking up science or politics but by daydreaming, by reading and by a habit of eccentric mispronunciation that conceals ignorance as affectation – thrusting competitors for jobs, for example, becoming the 'Shoveacious Cult'.[40] His carefree youth, cycling adventures and ill-advised marriage are presented in a series of hilarious flashbacks. By the time the story starts he has declined into an unhappy shopkeeper facing bankruptcy who decides he may as well set fire to the shop and slit his throat. The blaze will conceal his suicide, the insurance payout support his wife.

Once he has started the fire, Polly sensibly changes his mind and, after rescuing an elderly lady next door from the blaze, he is hailed as a hero. The conflagration proves a life-changing experience. In one of the key passages in the Wells canon, Polly concludes, 'If the world does not please you, *you can change it*.'[41] Before long he has left his wife and become a tramp, much like the Philosophical Tramp in *The Wonderful Visit* or Mr Marvel in *The Invisible Man*. Eventually, he finds work as an 'odd man' at the Potwell Inn, an idyllic riverside tavern recalling the heyday of Surly Hall. Confronted by the landlady's delinquent nephew, Jim, Polly realizes there are some responsibilities that should not be evaded, and, after due soul-searching, tackles his tormentor in a slapstick life and death battle. Jim later drowns and his corpse is mistaken for Polly's, allowing the hero to escape his past and be reborn into a pastoral world of contentment.

Wells does discuss the social implications of Polly's adventures but keeps them very much in the margin of the novel, attributing them to a dull but worthy intellectual resembling Sidney Webb. This prioritizing of the story in its own right has helped make *Mr Polly* one of Wells's best-loved novels. Walter Allen, author of the standard history of the English novel, has reservations about much of Wells's fiction but judges *Mr Polly* perfect of its type, equalling the work of Fielding and Dickens.[42] H.L. Mencken, too, thought the novel confirmed Wells's achievement as an Edwardian Dickens, less elaborate than the original but more in tune with the democratic sensibility of twentieth-century readers:

> I know very well that the author of *David Copperfield* was a better artist than the author of *Mr Polly*, just as I know that the Archbishop of Canterbury is a more virtuous man than my good friend, Fred the Bartender; but all the same, I prefer Wells and Fred to Dickens and the Archbishop.[43]

Wells suggested the novel was a tribute to his brother Frank, but it was probably even more of a tribute to their father.[44] Perhaps the attempted suicide was too close to home for Wells to name Joe, who, like Polly, had struggled with a small shop and unhappy marriage before escaping into genteel vagrancy. Six months after *Mr Polly* was published, at 11.30 a.m. on 14 October 1910, having enjoyed a good lie-in, Joe decided it was time to get up, swung himself out of bed and slumped to the floor like a puppet with its strings cut. He had died of heart failure. Whereas the death of Sarah had liberated Wells to deal with 'adult' topics and confront social conventions head on, the death of Joe neatly coincided with the end of his major period as a creative writer. The timing was appropriate, since Wells's decline was largely the result of suppressing the comic, subversive side of his literary personality that was his father's legacy. However, the change was probably not a case of cause and effect.

If we want a psychological explanation, the trigger is likelier to have been the failure of the elopement with Amber. Wells had been forced to admit to himself that he was anchored by wife, children and reputation, and in consequence the radical, exploratory nature of his work, based on his experience of successful self-transformation, would give way to presentations of his existing world-view, gradually diminishing in force. His novels would increasingly be dominated by the opinionated voice of George Ponderevo, not the comical inventiveness of Edward, reducing the interaction between prophecy and scepticism, earnestness and humour, which had formerly given his work its supple intelligence.

With hindsight, the problem is visible in Wells's next novel, *The New Machiavelli*. The narrator, Remington, is a version of Wells, as is Wilkins the novelist, who had previously made a cameo appearance in *Ann Veronica* and who would appear in several later novels. Among other recognizable figures, Isabel Rivers is based on Amber, Oscar and Altiora Baileys on the Webbs, Willesley on Wallas, Evesham on Balfour, Cossington on Harmsworth and the Cramptons on C.P. and G.M. Trevelyan. For contemporary readers, this was history hot from the press, enlivened by scathing pen portraits.

Wells offered the book to Macmillan in October 1909, assuring him that it was a political novel that contained nothing morally controversial. By June 1910, having read the final chapters in proof, Sir Frederick (knighted during 1909) knew he had been misled by the author, for Remington abandons his career and wife for Isabel of the 'amber-brown' eyes, who bears him a child.[45] Macmillan told Wells that there was twice as much reason to reject *The New Machiavelli* as there had been to reject *Ann Veronica*.[46] After threatening legal action, Wells became conciliatory and set about revising the book to emphasize that Remington paid for his sins with his career. Macmillan took a look at the modifications in July, was unimpressed and began looking for another publisher on whom he could offload the offending tome.

Wells meanwhile put in some time with his family. They set out for Germany via Rotterdam on 18 July, a day after Gip's ninth birthday, and returned on 21 August. In April Gip had suffered appendicitis, but, thanks to scientific progress, the condition that had destroyed Fanny could now be set right by an operation, carried out in the Church Row study, followed by a couple of weeks' recuperation at a Surrey farmhouse. (Brother Frank would get the same life-saving treatment in 1925.) The party stayed the best part of a month in Neunkirchen – enjoying a trip on the Rhine, walks in the Odenwald and visits to Heidelberg, Dusseldorf, Cologne and Mannheim. Jane returned to the Channel by train; Wells, Gip and Frank cycled back, acquiring along the way a pet red squirrel called Hans.[47]

In Wells's absence Macmillan had offered *The New Machiavelli* to Heinemann and to Chapman and Hall, but neither of them wanted anything to do with it. By September the novel had been seen by all the leading publishers' readers and was the talk of the London clubs, but this advance publicity was not getting it into shops and libraries. To reduce the potential for libel action from the Webbs, Wells rewrote some of the material about the Baileys, attributing their more malicious actions to a parallel couple called the Booles, perhaps a hit at the Blands. Years later he would quietly reverse these revisions and give the Webbs the drubbing he had originally intended.

Amber sent a helpful letter in September 1910, stating that she and Rivers saw no grounds for legal action, and confessed that she was very excited about the book. She had written ninety thousand words of a novel of her own, which would be completed by the end of October. (This novel never found a publisher, though her later ones would.) 'Anna Jane is very well and very beautiful. She has four teeth and she can say Ma-ma-ma and Nan-nan-nan and do other entrancing things. She hopes to make Gip's and Frank's acquaintance when she is older.'[48]

Eventually *The New Machiavelli* found its way to Wells's first publisher, John Lane, less prestigious and respectable than Macmillan, who brought it out under the Bodley Head imprint in January 1911. Each review copy was accompanied by an interview with Wells denying his identification with Remington and any intention to titillate. The book was still banned by a number of libraries, and the *Spectator* not only refused to review the book but also to carry any advertisements for it. On the whole, however, scandalous fiction from Wells had lost its novelty value, and there was less controversy than there had been over *Ann Veronica*, though enough remained to double the sales above any previous Wells title. Wells told Edwin Pugh around this time, 'My personal unpopularity is immense but amusing & people listen with blanched faces to the tale of my vices & go & buy my books.'[49]

In many respects *The New Machiavelli* was a considerable achievement. The creation of a believable character reflecting on his intimate and his public life, involving us in his efforts to find a way through to a redeeming perspective, points ahead to the similarly intense, loquacious novels of Saul Bellow (hence perhaps the tributes to Wells in Bellow's *Mister Sammler's Planet*). 'I know what master-work is when I see it,' Conrad told Wells. 'And this is it.' Upton Sinclair agreed: it was the author's masterpiece, 'one of the most powerful of English novels'. D.H. Lawrence found Wells's vision depressing but 'awfully interesting', admitting of the author 'I do like him and esteem him, and wish I knew half as much about things.' Even Beatrice Webb had to admit, 'The portraits are really very clever in a malicious way . . . Some of the descriptions of Society and of the political world, some of the criticisms of the existing order, are extraordinarily vivid; and the book, as a whole, to a large extent compels agreement with its descriptive side.'[50]

She had a very different view of the quality of Wells's political ideas, a reservation shared even by Arnold Bennett, who rated the novel highly in most respects but thought that Remington's eventual defection to the Conservative Party and the public success he achieved with vacuous slogans such as 'Love and fine thinking' were unconvincing.[51] In part the problem lay in having to create a character who shared many of Wells's views but, thanks to a more right-wing place in the political spectrum, was readily distinguishable from him. Trying to figure out where Wells ends and Remington begins is part of the fun, but there are awkward moments when it is unclear whether Remington's political and moral claims are meant to be read ironically or seriously. Either way, he is no Machiavelli. When James told Wells that his use of the first person had been a mistake, depriving him of artistic detachment, Wells had to agree.[52]

In truth, Wells had enough skill to finesse the first-person difficulty if he chose, but to do so would have meant subverting Remington's earnest monologues with comic irony and abandoning his own opportunity for a prolonged public sulk. We glimpse the potential for a much livelier book only towards the end, in an episode where Remington and his ruling-class cronies lament imperialist atrocities over dinner while the house catches fire around them and a drunken lecturer jeers at Remington's empty ideals. Bizarrely, the episode is based on a real dinner held by Harry Cust in 1902, when a fire broke out and the guests, including Wells, Balfour and Churchill, determinedly unflappable English gentlemen in the tradition of Raleigh and Nelson, continued to converse and dine despite the blaze.[53]

To consolidate his literary reputation, Wells now put together a compendium of his short stories. He had long since ceased to write these on a regular basis, leaving several still uncollected, including two of the best, 'The Country of the Blind' and 'The Door in the Wall'. *The Country of the Blind and Other Stories*, containing thirty-three pieces, was published in 1911, a reminder of a very different Wells, one who put not realism and discussion but fantasy and symbolism at the heart of his work. George Orwell would recall how as schoolboys he and fellow writer Cyril Connolly were so fascinated by the book that they constantly stole it from each other.[54]

US readers missed out on the *Country of the Blind* collection, presumably because it would have clashed with a compendium of a mere eight stories that Wells had agreed to issue on the other side of the Atlantic in a limited edition illustrated with ten photographs by Alvin Langdon Coburn. Some six hundred copies of *The Door in the Wall And Other Stories* were printed in November 1911. By January 1915 at least sixty leftover copies of the supposed collectors' item were imported to form an even more limited British edition.

Wells's restless journey from science fiction through the comic novel, utopianism and political comment to experiments in the social novel had made him, in the words of Frank Swinnerton, the 'champion surprise packet' of the literary world.[55] It was said that, despite Wells's republicanism, even Edward VII was a devoted reader.[56]

But Edward had died in May 1910, and under George V dreams of Utopia would carry less conviction. The Liberal government's plans for welfare spending had already been hit by an expensive arms race with Germany, and now it was locked in a dispute with the Conservative-controlled House of Lords in an attempt to implement the 'People's Budget'. Though the government would win that battle during 1911, permanently curbing the power of the unelected Lords, two General Elections failed to restore its majority, leaving it dependent on the Labour Party and the Irish nationalists. Inflation having pushed wages painfully below turn-of-the-century levels, the miners went out on strike in 1910, followed by the seamen, dockers and railwaymen in 1911. There were riots in Llanelli and Liverpool, requiring intervention by troops. Some suffragists adopted quasi-terrorist tactics of window-breaking, arson and bombing. Worst of all, a civil war seemed to be brewing over Home Rule, with many members of the armed forces ready to turn against their own elected government and fight to keep the northern Protestants outside a future Catholic Ireland.

Violently divided among themselves and challenged by Germany's growing industry and military might, the people of Britain had cause for anxiety. When the *Titanic* sank in 1912, one reason they responded so strongly to the disaster was that it seemed symbolic of the times. Looking around them, it must have been hard to see how things could get worse.

In 1914 they would find out.

12
JOURNALIST
1911–1916

Wells's fame had now reached the stage at which fictional characters were being based on him. (Hueffer was one of the first in print with his 1912 novel *The New Humpty Dumpty* in which Wells figures as a conceited journalist called Herbert Pett, a compliment that twenty years later he would repay with compound interest.) Acquaintances were also recording the Wellsian lifestyle for the benefit of posterity. One particularly well-placed observer was Mathilda Meyer, governess to Gip and Frank for five years from October 1908. Her reminiscences tactfully omit what a trusted employee should overlook but paint a clear picture of much else, as do the comments of novelist, publisher and critic Frank Swinnerton, who became one of the family's regular guests while he was writing a book about Gissing.[1]

Both report the continuation of the family's weekend dressing-up parties and charades, at which visitors found themselves taking part in parlour games, performing comic dances or even, equipped with a curtain toga and flowerpot helmet, improvising Roman speeches – unless, like Henry James, they backed into the hall and adopted the role of the speculative observer. Wells took an individual interest in all his guests – he was, says Swinnerton, a 'conversationalist' not a 'raconteur' – and kept everyone amused. When not partying, Wells sometimes put his eloquence to less constructive use, losing his temper as spectacularly as his father had done years before and berating victims out of proportion to any offence they had given, then assuming a disarming cheerfulness when he next met them. These outbursts would become more common and less discriminating as the years went by.

A keen music lover, as many references in his novels testify, he took breaks from his writing schedule to enjoy Beethoven, Schubert and others, peddling the music out of a pianola which had been recommended by Shaw. Until the gramophone and radio were perfected, this was the most effective way for a non-player to explore the classics. Jane was able to play the piano and spinet, though her main hobby was gardening.

Miss Meyer gave the Wells boys lessons in English, French and German. Other classes were covered, aptly enough, by a Mr Classey. Home schooling enabled Wells to control the curriculum, and the move back to London offered valuable places for educational outings: museums, parks, the zoo and even the Golders Green Crematorium, to which Wells took his sons after Gip asked what the curious white building with the large chimney was for. At bedtime the boys would sit either side of Daddy while he drew each in turn a comical picshua. When the occasion arose, however, he was ready to spank them as hard as justice demanded.

One aspect of Wells's home life that he himself publicized was the 'floor games' that he initially played with the children in the schoolroom but eventually extended into the garden and opened up to selected visitors. After Wells made them a feature of Remington's childhood in *The New Machiavelli*, he was asked by a publisher, Frank Palmer, if he could do a whole book on the subject. Typically, he managed two.

Floor Games, which was published in December 1911, advises parents about the purchase of toys, building blocks and other props and gives ingenious examples of their use. Topical and satirical asides for adult readers vary the texture. The author contributes photographs, and each page carries lively drawings by J.R. Sinclair. The book remains an enjoyable read, more so than many of Wells's adult novels of the period, even if the presence of a few 'negroid savages' and 'Red Indians' dates the proceedings. In recent years it has enjoyed a perhaps surprising vogue among child psychologists as a model for non-verbal psychotherapy.[2]

Its sequel, *Little Wars*, came out in July 1913, again featuring drawings by Sinclair. This time the photographs are by Jane, some of them showing Wells crawling round the garden in conscious imitation of Uncle Toby in *Tristram Shandy*. The book, which focuses entirely on battlefield games, lacks its predecessor's lightness of touch but compensates with detailed discussion of rules, which has kept it in print and given it a new life on the internet, this time as a source for war-gaming enthusiasts.

During February 1911 the family enjoyed full-sized winter sports in Wengen, Switzerland, skiing, skating and tobogganing, until Jane was taken ill and the rest of the party went down with flu. In June, having recuperated, they relocated themselves to Normandy for four months at a rented house in Pont de l'Arche, near Rouen, where Wells simultaneously avoided the coronation of George V and worked on his latest novel. Their many visitors included Arnold Bennett, who was the victim of a train crash on his way back to Paris, pitched into 'a storm of glass, flying doors, and hand-luggage'.[3] (Bearing in mind that Jane's father and W.E. Henley were killed by trains, it is plain how hazardous rail travel was in these years.) Bennett survived to proofread Wells's new novel, which was dedicated to him, and to perform the same service for several later ones.

After all the controversy over *Ann Veronica* and *The New Machiavelli*, *Marriage*, published in September 1912, was greeted with relief by publisher and reviewers alike. *T.P.'s Weekly* observed that 'it can be placed on a puritan family's bookshelf'; even the *Spectator* approved.[4] Followers of Wells the artist, however, were disappointed. The marriage in question is that of Marjorie Pope to Richard Trafford, a scientific researcher who dramatically enters her life when his plane crashes on a vicarage lawn. Marjorie's expensive tastes force Trafford to give up pure research the first book-length studies of Wells, qualified his enthusiasm with a 'best before' date. Since *The New Machiavelli* his ideas had become little more than a 'perfunctory repetition' and the experiences he depicted carried less conviction.[9]

Take *The Passionate Friends*, published in September 1913, in which an idealist called Stephen Stratton recounts his fraught love affair with Lady Mary Christian, which ends in her suicide. The book is of some note for introducing two of Wells's key ideas for political reform: the banding together of people of good will in 'open conspiracies' to create a world state and the publication of a new canon of world literature to foster a progressive world-view. As an exploration of sex and marriage, however, the novel fails badly, being compounded of romantic clichés and abstract discussions.

Wells's old college friend Tommy Simmons was less disturbed by the novel's relentless dullness than by its characters' self-absorption. He questioned how Wells could reconcile his utopianism with the notion of privileged people following their passions regardless of the consequences. Presumably thinking of Jane, he requested:

> some day if you can & will write us a book reversing the situation, and make the rather pathetic, much neglected, background people with their quiet uncomplaining self-sacrifice the central figures & interpret their thoughts for us.[10]

Wells had dedicated *The Passionate Friends* to a mysterious 'L.E.N.S.', most likely a reference to his principal lover in the period after Amber, Elizabeth von Arnim, whom he had nicknamed 'little e'. (She in turn called him 'Geak'.) Born Mary Beauchamp in Australia, raised in England, she had run off to the Continent at the age of twenty-five with a German aristocrat and, finding herself unhappy in the marriage, had taken up authorship and produced a bestseller, the autobiographical *Elizabeth and her German Garden*. She and Wells became lovers late in 1910, around the time her estranged husband died. Jane, as a gardener, was an admirer of the 'Elizabeth' books. She seems to have welcomed the new mistress as an experienced, mature woman who, valuing her own independence, had no intention of poaching someone else's spouse.

Since 'little e' had a neighbouring flat in St James' Court, she and Wells were able to make many an unobtrusive rendezvous. Building a large house at the ski resort of Montana in Switzerland, the Château Soleil, she equipped one of its visitors' rooms with a secret door behind a wardrobe so that when she had said goodnight to the other guests Wells could slip through and join her for a night of passion.

Before and after the building of the Château the couple spent many days in the Swiss Alps, writing in the mornings and in the afternoons strolling, occasionally making love on heaps of pine needles – which sounds uncomfortable for the person underneath, presumably 'little e' – and, as Wells reports, on any other convenient surface.

> One day we found in a copy of *The Times* we had brought with us, a letter from Mrs Humphrey Ward denouncing the moral tone of the younger generation, apropos of a rising young writer, Rebecca West, and, having read it aloud, we decided we had to do something about it. So we stripped ourselves under the trees as though there was no one in the world but ourselves, and made love all over Mrs Humphrey Ward. And when we had dressed again we lit a match and burnt her.[11]

On walking tours, the couple stopped at local inns, where their nocturnal activities twice broke the bed. Since 'little e' was as small as her name suggested, it took much ingenuity and charm on her part to explain how the fatal spring-pounding had occurred.

It was while staying at the Château Soleil in January 1913 with Gip and Frank that Wells began work on a new science-fiction story, *The World Set Free*. It would be published in 1914 and dedicated, unusually, to a book, Frederick Soddy's *Interpretation of Radium*, which had shown Wells that if an atom could be split it would release unprecedented amounts of energy. The consequences of doing so might be beneficial – he envisages an atomic motor invented by two Bengalis, characteristically defying imperialist notions about backward natives – but there might also be terrible dangers.

In the story a world war breaks out and the gory horrors of *The War in the Air* are repeated with atomic bombs. Wells conceives these as hand grenades that are lobbed out of aircraft and continue to explode for months on end. The war is so devastating that ultimately a world state is set up to prevent its repetition. The evil King of the Balkans resists but is killed off, and, with his death, nationalism quickly disappears and Utopia comes into being. The final chapter centres on a prophet of scientific progress who, almost like Moreau, looks ahead to the ultimate perfection of the human race through surgery.

On the positive side, Wells had not only spotted the military significance of atomic research, a remarkable achievement in 1913, but had written a perceptive outline of the two coming world wars. In literary terms, however, the book begins as an essay and never develops into a properly realized work of fiction, while its politics are wilfully naïve, assuming that an ideal state will be free of political parties or even what *A Modern Utopia* calls the 'courteous admission of differences'.[12] One part prescient to five parts puerile, the book represents a serious decline in his vision. 'Heaven defend us from his Utopias!' concluded one American reviewer. 'But we like his explosions.'[13]

After the visit to 'little e' during which the story was commenced, Wells and the known. Wells's lower-class origins, scientific training and liberal-socialist outlook made him seem the epitome of twentieth-century Britain, and his gift for story-telling had already led to three editions of his works appearing in Russian translation. Tolstoy himself had written to Wells in 1906 asking for copies of his books so that he could appreciate them in the original.[20] Now British author and Russian public would have a chance to meet.

Setting out on 20 January 1914 and travelling via Berlin, accompanied by the Russophile writer Maurice Baring, Wells visited St Petersburg where he made the obligatory tour of the Hermitage and attended a session of Russia's aspiring parliament, the Duma. Vladimir Nabokov, whose father was a liberal politician and journalist, recalled Wells coming to their house for dinner. The Englishman was young Vladimir's literary idol, so he was aghast when another guest, Wells's translator Zinaïda Vengerov, casually announced that her favourite book of his was *The Lost World*. Nabokov Senior hastily repaired the damage by explaining that she must mean the war of the worlds the Martians lost. (Twenty-three years later Wells would use confusion between himself and Conan Doyle as a joke in *Star-Begotten*.)[21]

Proceeding to Moscow, Wells visited the Kremlin, the Church of St Basil, a ballet and a literary cabaret and saw performances of *The Seagull* and *Hamlet* at the Moscow Arts Theatre. He came home via Warsaw and Berlin, reaching England on 9 February. He reported his findings in an article for the *Daily News*, contrasting the Russians' passionate commitment to their beliefs with the habitual irony of the British. For a more detailed account the public would have to wait until Wells's 1918 novel *Joan and Peter*.

In the meantime a sketch of the visit was incorporated into *The Research Magnificent*, which was published in September 1915. In this, the most interesting yet also the most maddening of the 'prig novels', Wells pushes aspects of his idealism to an extreme through the figure of William Benham, a believer in rule by natural aristocrats, who divides his time between philosophizing over the weakness of other people and challenging himself by impulsively putting his life in danger. When he intervenes in a violent mining strike in Johannesburg (researched by Freddy), he is gunned down by the troops sent to suppress the rioting.

In theory, Wells had found an effective way out of the rut into which he had recently slid. Benham's quest for authentic experience through reckless, even suicidal, behaviour opens up a fruitful path for the novel that would be followed by Hemingway, Mailer and others. But, despite some interesting narrative devices, Wells does not come up with a fresh language for his protagonist's inner life. Once Benham starts to speechify he is every bit as pompous and abstract as Trafford or Stratton, and the rise and fall of his marriage to Amanda Morris is told in a self-centred way that rarely comes alive. Wells claimed that Amanda owed something to Amber,[22] but seems to have drawn her at least as much from Rebecca, down to the nicknames the lovers have for each other, Amanda as 'Leopard', Benham 'Cheetah'. In real life the cat-loving Wells was 'Jaguar', Rebecca 'Panther'.

By February 1914 Rebecca had relocated to a semi-detached villa called Brig-y-don in Victoria Avenue, Hunstanton, a seaside town in north Norfolk. Wells could spend time with her here while building alterations were being carried out at Easton. According to Anthony West, Wells chose the comparatively obscure location of Hunstanton in order to achieve the secrecy he had singularly failed to pursue in his dealings with Amber. Wells's contentment with the arrangement is clear in a letter postmarked 14 April:

> I shall lay my paw upon you this Wednesday night and snuff under your chin and bite your breast and lick your flank and proceed to other familiarities. I shall roll you over and do what I like with you. I shall make you pant and bite back. Then I shall give you a shake to quiet you and go to sleep all over you and if I snore, I snore. Your Lord. The Jaguar.[23]

Rebecca was spending much of her time writing a study of Henry James for Nisbet's 'Writers of the Day' series. (During 1914 the series acquired a primer on Wells by J.D. Beresford, whose 1911 novel *The Hampdenshire Wonder* seems to be both homage to and critique of his subject.) Like Wells, Rebecca admired James but found his later writings exasperating, noting that the Jamesian sentence had become 'a delicate creature swathed in relative clauses as an invalid in shawls'.[24] While outspokenness was Rebecca's stock in trade, Wells kept his reservations about James to himself. However, this discretion would not last.

In March 1912 James and Gosse had invited Wells to join the Academic Committee of the Royal Society of Literature. Given Wells's then notoriety, it was a considerable gesture of solidarity and respect. Wells was disinclined to join anything that was royal, however, and distrusted the Society's potential as a source of 'controls and fixed standards'.[25] Encouraged by Bennett, he turned down the offer, yet professed his affection and respect for James. The next day Wells paid a call on James at the Reform Club to expand his views and, along the way, explained that his focus had now shifted away from literary matters. He had made it clear in *The Time Machine* that in the long run all human achievement is fleeting. Trying to create immortal works of art, he would come to believe, is futile, all writing being provisional and transient.[26] James reported to Gosse, 'he will still do a lot of writing probably – but it won't be *that*'.[27] The prig novels confirmed the truth of the forecast.

Convinced that Wells had opted out of literature for good, and possibly stung by a sense of rejection, James decided to make an example of him. Since many modern adherents of 'Queer Theory' are convinced that James was a repressed homosexual, it is surprising that no one has suggested James's tolerance of Wells's literary rule-breaking and his bitterness when Wells rejected his tutelage might have originated in sexual attraction to the younger man. (Since writing this I have come across a thoughtful article by Janet Gebler-Hover that also proposes this idea.)[28]

During March and April 1914 James undertook to assess 'The Younger Generation' of novelists in the *Times Literary Supplement* but spent most of the article warning would-be authors not to take Wells and Bennett as role models. Their novels, he warned, were lamentably heavy on content and light on form. Bennett's masterpiece *The Old Wives' Tale* was every bit as shapeless and pointless as *War and Peace.* As for Wells, he is 'a novelist very much as Lord Bacon was a philosopher':

> The more he knows and knows, or at any rate learns and learns – the more, in other words, he establishes his saturation – the greater is our impression of his holding it good enough for us, such as we are, that he shall but turn out his mind and its contents upon us by any free familiar gesture and as from a high window forever open (Mr Wells having as many windows as an agent who has bought up the lot of the most eligible to retail for a great procession).

No doubt James imagined the 'agent' crack to be a witty aside, though he delivers it with a pomposity that makes Dr Johnson sound like Dorothy Parker. Incensed, Wells dug out *Boon,* the literary satire he had been working on since 1905, and set about his revenge.

Not content with working simultaneously on *The Research Magnificent* and *Boon,* Wells had a third book in progress, *Bealby: A Holiday*. As its subtitle suggests, this novel is a diversion from the prig series, intended to give an overdue airing to his comic, subversive spirit. The main plot concerns Arthur Bealby, thirteen-year-old stepson of a gardener at a country house. Refusing to follow in his family's servile footsteps, Bealby goes on the run, causing unintended chaos wherever he goes. He falls in with a thieving tramp named Bridget, the reverse of Mr Polly, whose presence marks Wells's abandonment of the ideal of the romantic vagrant. A subplot opposes to the selfish, small-minded tramp the honourable figure of Captain Douglas, a military man with a keen interest in science, loosely modelled on Wells's aeronautical adviser J. W. Dunne (who had taken him for his second flight, over the Isle of Sheppey, in a tailless, V-winged biplane on 12 July 1913). Douglas's fascination with the application of science is matched only by his fascination with a young actress. Faced with a choice between love and his public commitments, he makes the opposite choice to Lewisham and embraces scientific progress. Bealby, meanwhile, is returned to the country house and takes his place in the system.

Bealby, Bridget and Douglas are clearly aspects of Wells, and their interaction

The young H.G. Wells, known as Bertie, (seated) and brother Frank, *c.* 1869

Bertie around the age of ten, 1876

Wells's mother, Sarah, as a young woman

Wells's father, Joe, aged eighty, July 1908

Wells, the rebellious student, mimics T.H. Huxley at the Normal School of Science, South Kensington.

Isabel, Wells's cousin and first wife, *c.* 1891, with the couple's visiting card (top)

Wells and his second-wife-to-be, Jane, in the garden of Tusculum Villa, Sevenoaks, Kent, summer 1894, during the writing of *The Time Machine*

Wells and Jane go boating, 1895

Wells and Jane go cycling, Woking, Surrey, 1895

The War
of the Worlds

ooer

Wells's 'picshua' of Jane as a Martian, *c.* 1898

'Waiting for the Verdik', a 'picshua' of Jane reading the second draft of *Love and Mr Lewisham,* January 1899

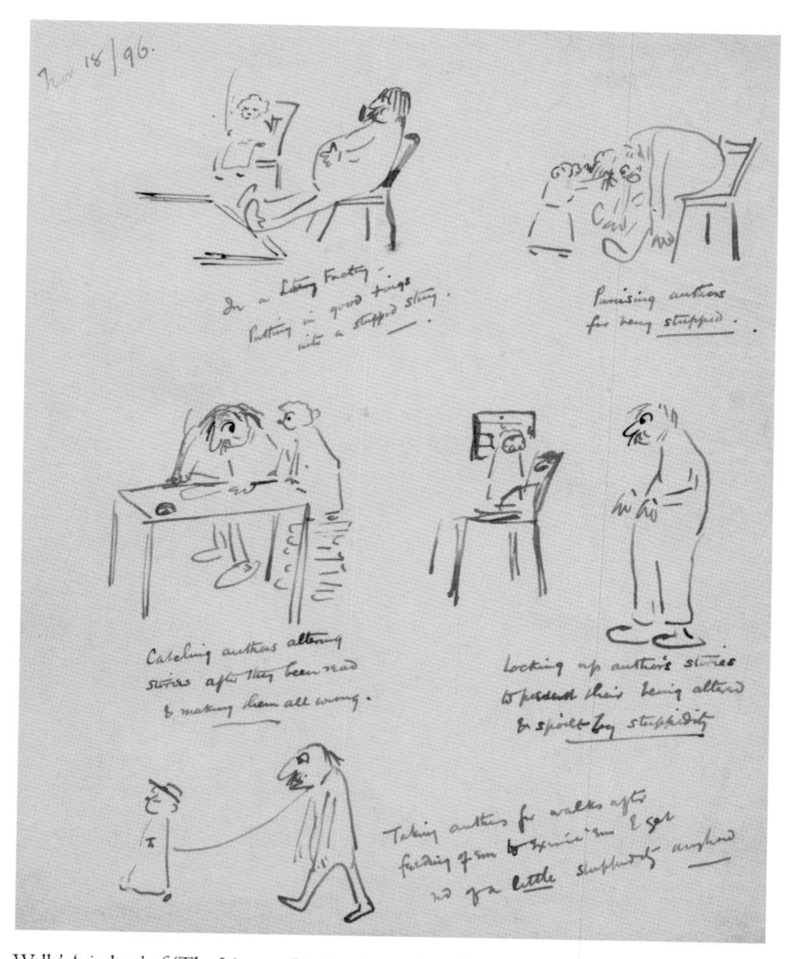

Wells's 'picshua' of 'The Literary Regimen', a series of interventions by Jane that save him from his own 'stuppidity', November 1896. From top left: 'In a Literary Factory – Putting in good things into a stuppid story.' 'Punishing authors for being stuppid.' 'Locking up author's stories to prevent their being altered & spoilt by stuppidity.' 'Taking authors for walks after feeding of 'em to exercise 'em & get rid of a *little* stuppidity anyhow.' 'Catching authors altering stories after they been read & making them all wrong.'

Jane with that 'infernal implement', the typewriter, *c.* 1899

Top: Wells, Jane and their sons Gip and Frank in the nursery at Spade House, Sandgate, Kent, *c.* 1907; train set by Uncle Frank, Wells's brother

Above: Wells and Sarah on the terrace at Spade House, *c.* 1904

Right: Gip and Frank in sailor suits, *c.* 1907

Gip and Frank, *c.* 1907

Amber Blanco White and baby Anna Jane. Amber was Wells's mistress from 1908 to 1909 and Anna Jane their daughter. By the time this picture was taken, *c.* 1910, Amber had married Rivers Blanco White, who raised Anna Jane as his own.

Rebecca West, *c.* 1912. A notable author in her own right, Rebecca was Wells's mistress from 1913 to 1924 and bore him a son, Anthony West.

Wells, Gorky and Moura Benckendorf in Petrograd, September 1920. Wells's official guide in the Soviet Union, Moura soon became his lover as well. From 1929, as Moura Budberg, she would become the last great love of his life while apparently continuing her work as a Soviet agent.

Wells and Lenin at the Kremlin, October 1920

Wells and 'little e', Elizabeth von Arnim, a popular author and Wells's lover from 1910 to 1913. This picture was kept in Elizabeth's 1922 journal but was presumably taken a decade earlier.

Odette Keun, hard-hitting travel writer and Wells's mistress from 1924 to 1932, pictured on the terrace at Lou Pidou, his house near Grasse, Provence

Wells in 1934, the year he published his autobiography; portrait by celebrity photographer Howard Coster

Wells on the set of *Things to Come* with Pearl Argyle and Raymond Massey, 1935

Anthony West, *c.* 1935, Wells's son by Rebecca West; he later became a novelist in his own right

Martha Gellhorn, travel writer and war correspondent, pictured in Spain in 1937. Wells claimed that she had been his lover in 1935, when he was sixty-nine and she twenty-seven, something she later denied vigorously.

Wells in his study at Hanover Terrace, London, 1940

In his final photoshoot, in March 1945, Wells curses his neighbour's sycamore tree for dropping its seeds into his garden, taking it as a symbol of the world's evils. He added in a letter that, for good measure, he was also cursing his enemies, 'all the smart Alecks of Reaction'.

expresses a desire to reject selfishness (Bridget) and sexual fixation (negative Douglas) in favour of higher purposes (positive Douglas), along with a mischievous defiance of the establishment that cannot help bursting out but must be regulated (Bealby). The coherence of the book depends on the assumption that Bealby and Douglas are complementary in their hostility to the existing order, but the intuitive play of the child and the purposive thinking of the soldier-scientist are never effectively linked. While Bealby's adventures make for a lively read, the Douglas subplot is pedestrian, and the book, though Wells's most exuberant since *Mr Polly*, fails to integrate the various sides of his literary personality into a fresh whole.

Still, *Bealby* showed that Wells had not lost the ability to spin a comic yarn if he chose. Published in 1915, the book carried a dedication to the Lord Chancellor, R.B. Haldane, whom Wells had repeatedly mocked in the text but with hindsight wished to honour for his constructive work when he was Secretary of State for War.

Wells had a further opportunity to re-engage with the comic muse in June 1914 when he spent a weekend making a slapstick home movie. Instigated by J.M. Barrie and directed by Granville Barker, the project enlisted a number of celebrated authors ready to give the Keystone Cops a run for their money. Since the days when Robert Paul approached Wells about a *Time Machine* ride, cinema had grown from a fairground attraction into a promising new medium that fascinated many intellectuals. Even the ultimate logophile, James Joyce, had been manager of Ireland's first silent cinema for a couple of months at the turn of 1909–10. In Granville Barker's scenario (the film itself appears to be lost) a crazy chase leads to a village inn where, characteristically, Wells and Chesterton try to broach a beer barrel while Shaw urges them to control themselves. The beer barrel contains cowboy clothes that all three put on; they then roll down a hill in the barrel before mounting a motorbike and hurtling towards a precipice, jumping off at the last possible moment, and so on.

Perhaps Wells's exuberance in the first half of 1914 was linked to the impending birth of his fourth child. When Anthony Panther West was born on 5 August, Wells wrote to Rebecca, 'I am radiant this morning. With difficulty I refrain from giving people large tips.'[29] Later in the day he called by to see how mother and baby were doing. Yet his joy was inevitably mixed with apprehension, for the previous day Britain had declared war on Germany.

Such a conflict had come close on several occasions but had been headed off by sensible compromises between the major powers. The latest danger erupted, as is well known, after a Serbian terrorist assassinated the Austrian heir, Franz Ferdinand. Though the Serb authorities did everything they could to placate the Austrians, there was no doubt they coveted parts of the Austro-Hungarian Empire, and Vienna was determined to take the opportunity for a pre-emptive strike. However, as the Serbs were allied with Russia, it was not possible to initiate hostilities without major power backing.

People have wondered ever since why the German government pledged their support. Possibly they thought any resulting war could not last long, Britain would be kept out by its internal problems and gains were likely to outweigh losses. Whatever the case, Berlin gave Vienna its licence to kill. Three weeks after the assassination Austria-Hungary declared war on Serbia; the next day Russia began to mobilize; in response Germany declared war on Russia and for good measure on Russia's ally, France, which was certain to intervene in any conflict in order to recover the territory lost in 1870.

Committed to fighting on two fronts, the Germans planned to knock out France while the Russians were still mobilizing, then deal with the Russians later. The obvious flaw in the plan was that, to get around the French defences, they would have to go through Belgium – and risk bringing into the war Belgium's ally, Britain. Even the mentally unstable Kaiser balked at the prospect, questioning whether the French attack might be postponed, but his generals explained that, as they were engaged in modern warfare, the troop movements were based on the railway timetable so could not be altered.

The first impact of the war on the Wells household was the calling up of the family's tutor, Kurt Bülow. Kurt had taken over from Miss Meyer in July 1913 and had developed a special closeness to the family's pet squirrel – not Hans, who perished in the winter of 1910, but a replacement known as Fritz. After a year at Easton, Kurt was summoned back to the Fatherland for military service as a mounted artilleryman. He sent the family a series of rueful letters recording his progress.

Like every other informed household in Europe, the Wells family scrutinized the newspapers for clues about what would happen next, and, like everyone else, they were shaken by the invasion of Belgium and the British declaration of war. Since the latter occurred on a sunny Bank Holiday Monday, Wells and Shaw were left to mull over the situation in the incongruous setting of the Easton Lodge annual fête and flower show. That night Wells sat down and wrote out his thoughts in an article.

Public support for the war at this stage was almost universal. The key division was between those who espoused total hatred of the Germans and those who distinguished between the German people and the forces temporarily controlling Germany. Wells was firmly in the second camp, proclaiming that the war should be about Germany's freedom as well as Britain's. What he wanted was regime change. When the militarists had been overthrown, there should be a peace settlement guaranteed by all the world powers, a first step towards the world state that Wells saw as the only effective form of government in an age of globalization. Wells gave his article the title 'The War That Will End War', a first-class slogan, though one that would later cause him embarrassment.

The article appeared in the *Daily News* on 14 August and became the title piece of a collection published in September. In the other pieces Wells calls for US involvement in the war and suggests that an eventual settlement should include the reunification of Poland and a rationalization of the Balkans into a federation of republics. This was the first of a small library of books and pamphlets that Wells would produce in response to the world crisis. In the post-war years he looked back on his initial reaction as embarrassingly naïve, but if so he was typical of his time.

In a letter written some days before Wells's article, for example, a contemporary enthused about his chance of becoming a soldier. 'For I like to think this is the last War of the World!' A later letter deplored the killing of educated men that war would bring but was sanguine about the effects on the working classes for whom 'the guns will effect a little useful weeding'.[30] These were the words of Wilfred Owen, later the greatest of the anti-war poets.

The outbreak of war prompted Wells to remake his will to ensure that Gip and Frank would be looked after if he and Jane were killed. Having passed their College of Preceptors examinations in January, the boys left home in September 1914 to become boarders at Oundle School in Northamptonshire, which Wells and Jane had chosen because of its Liberal headmaster, F.W. Sanderson, a product of one of the National Schools that had been judged beneath little Bertie. Sanderson had so modernized the Oundle curriculum and facilities that during the war the science laboratories supplied metal parts for munitions.

While Wells had made sound arrangements for Gip and Frank, and Anna Jane enjoyed the support of the Pember Reeves and Blanco White families, to give Anthony a good start in life was much more of a problem. The little boy was brought up to call his parents 'Wellsie' and 'Auntie Panther' and would be variously identified as a son, nephew and adopted child as he moved from house to house and school to school. During 1915 Rebecca even considered handing him over to foster-parents so she could get on with her writing. Realizing her situation, servants and neighbours grew hostile and made Rebecca's life 'disagreeable', just as they had Amber's in Blythe and Wells and Jane's long before in Sevenoaks and Woking. Wells, by his own account, disapproved of the 'idiotic lies and pretences' to which Anthony was subjected, which he claimed were the work of Rebecca's family, though of course he bore considerable responsibility for the difficult position in which mother and child had been placed.[31]

Rebecca and Anthony moved in September 1914 to a furnished farmhouse called Quinbury in Braughing, only about fifteen miles from Easton. Wells was able to spend a considerable amount of time with them there, thanks to his purchase of a motor car, one of 130,000 that had appeared on British roads by 1914. The car, Gladys, seems to have been a Willys Overland. As a veteran cyclist Wells found the pedals, steering wheel and pre-synchromesh gearbox perilously hard to master and would always remain to motoring what Sir Patrick Spens was to seamanship. None the less, the car enabled him to take Rebecca for jaunts to places like Monkey Island Inn, near Bray on Thames, not far from where Surly Hall had been. Rebecca would use the setting in her 1918 novel *The Return of the Soldier,* in which the psychiatrist Dr Anderson is modelled on Wells, and there is a passing reference to the tragic story of Tom Pennicott and his daughter Clara.

Rebecca was uncomfortable in Braughing, however, with its limited facilities and disapproving villagers, and, after a couple of months at the Riviera Hotel, Maidenhead, she moved in July 1915 to a house called Alderton in Royston Park Road, Hatch End, near Pinner. From this base in outer London, she could visit friends, attend Fabian summer schools and mix with the literati and glitterati, though as a result she saw much less of Wells. Eventually, in September 1916, Wells took rooms at a boarding-house, 51 Claverton Street, Pimlico, so they could spend more time together. Letters to the novelist Enid Bagnold suggest that at the same time he was at the least flirting with other potential mistresses.

Meanwhile the war, which most people had hoped would be over by Christmas, had become a production line of slaughter. The Germans' plan to knock out France failed. Neither side being able to gain the upper hand, the Western Front bogged down in 25,000 miles of squalid trenches, and the conflict began to be pursued ruthlessly elsewhere.

Within Britain conspiracy theories were widespread that victory was being held back by a secret organization undermining the war effort. Thanks to the efforts of professional troublemakers such as Horatio Bottomley and Emmeline and Christabel Pankhurst, foreigners were beaten up, friendly Germans expelled from the country and prominent people with German-sounding names driven from office. D.H. Lawrence, now married to a relative of the German air ace the 'Red Baron', quit the country. He never came back. The royal family changed their name from Saxe-Coburg-Gotha to Windsor. German Shepherd dogs prudently became Alsatians. Throughout the hysteria Wells consistently fought xenophobia, propounding the view that the war was not caused by the German character but by a range of factors, including the influence of the armaments industry, secret treaties, unaccountable monarchies and the nationalistic teaching of history.

Perhaps surprisingly, posterity has taken less interest in these important ideas than in the publication in July 1915 of *Boon.* Modelled on W.H. Mallock's anatomy *The New Republic,* it is a miscellany of stories, discussions and drawings by or about a fictitious author, the late George Boon, compiled by his executor Reginald Bliss with an 'Ambiguous Introduction by H.G. Wells'. Boon is supposed to have been a successful writer of orthodox novels for the marketplace who secretly longed to prophesy for a developing collective consciousness or Mind of the Race but died in despair, his faith undermined by the horrors of the Great War.

As in *The Desert Daisy* thirty-five years earlier, Wells splits himself into two main characters, with Bliss puzzling over the unresolved mixture of earnestness and irony in Boon's writings. These include two fables and a satirical literary symposium featuring many contemporary authors. In addition to these sketches, the book is noteworthy for its passing critique, contributed by a third *alter ego*, Wells's persona Wilkins, of the racism of Nietzsche and the proto-Nazi ideologue Houston Stewart Chamberlain. Just as *The Research Magnificent* anticipates the existentialist movement in fiction, so *Boon* looks ahead to the satirical discussion novels of Aldous Huxley but with insufficient plot or characterization to turn the book from an intellectual curiosity into a good read.

Only Chapter 4, 'Of Art, Of Literature, Of Mr Henry James' (one can almost see Wells rolling up his sleeves as he utters the words), retains a position in the margin of the literary canon, though its presence there has done little for its author's reputation. James is first glimpsed in a cross-purpose conversation with George Moore, subjecting his colleague to an interminable series of clauses, prepositional phrases and interjections, some taken directly from the offending 'Younger Generation' article, pausing only to trill 'Mm, Mm!' as he searches for the *mot juste*.[32] Boon declares that if literature is to embrace many kinds of writing, including philosophy and the literary canon, to offer a 'conscious direction of life', then the Jamesian aesthetic must first be dislodged.

As Boon formulates it, James's heresies are to treat art as an end, not a means to an end, and to aim for too tight a coherence in an art form that by its nature cannot be experienced as a whole like a picture and is instead incorrigibly plural and exploratory. To Wells, what James calls 'selection' is effectively 'omission'. Conventional, conservative values are accepted by default; characters are permitted to exist only in an etherealized form. They 'never make lusty love, never go to angry war, never shout at an election or perspire at poker'. Boon acknowledges the strength and abundance of James's mind but is exasperated by its disproportionate application, comparing him to a hippopotamus trying to pick up a pea.

After description, analysis and abuse Wells finally skewers his victim with a parodic scenario called 'The Spoils of Mr Blandish'. Blandish, who – as a mocking drawing makes clear – is based on James, resolves to settle in England and construct a decorous place there for himself. Yet there is a mysterious aspect to his new home, which he gradually comes to comprehend is a cellarful of brandy. Blandish tries to dispose of the intoxicating spirit for which he has no use by preposterously elaborate means, only to find his butler has already got rid of it by the Wellsian method of saturation, and now lies 'dead or at least helpless' on the cellar floor.[33]

Wells could hardly tell James face to face of the derision he had heaped upon him, but nor could he simply wait for James to hear the bad news from someone else. By way of a compromise, he went to James's club with a complimentary copy (to use a misleading phrase). On 5 July James opened the book and the following day he wrote to express his dismay that Wells had found him 'extraordinarily futile and void' and had published such an opinion to the world.[34] Some authors might have laughed off the attack, some been angry, some replied in kind; but James put an end to the friendship with quiet dignity.

Used to losing his temper, then making up without much interest in who had been right or wrong, Wells mishandled the situation, writing back to assure James that *Boon* was 'just a waste-paper basket' and that, if James's views were to define art, he 'had rather be called a journalist than an artist', two simplistic concessions that, when retailed to posterity, would largely undermine his position.[35] He signs off as 'your very keenly appreciative reader, your warm if rebellious and resentful admirer', sentiments that are perfectly sincere but sound dangerously like a man in the wrong trying to ingratiate himself. Now that Wells had put himself on the defensive James possessed all the advantages.

A magisterial final letter condemns Wells's bad manners, points out (unanswerably) that the whole point of a waste-paper basket is not to publish the contents, disclaims (absurdly) any prescriptiveness in his own views and ends with the ringing declaration, 'It is art that *makes* life, makes interest, makes importance, for our consideration and application of these things, and I know of no substitute whatever for the force and beauty of its process.'[36] This assertion has often been quoted as if an incontrovertible truth, but Wells is surely correct to point out that, as a piece of special pleading for art against all other disciplines, it is little more than a piece of Tono-Bungay. 'I can only read sense into it by assuming that you are using "art" for every conscious human activity.'[37]

Sensing that, as in the Fabian dispute and the Amber Reeves affair, his head-down self-assertion had left him in an exposed position, Wells followed his usual procedure of shrugging off the whole business. When James suffered a mortal stroke in December Wells showed he had no hard feelings by adding his signature to a letter urging the Prime Minister to award the dying man the Order of Merit. James died in February 1916 after taking British citizenship to show support for his adopted country in the Great War. With James departing the world as a committed artist and a supporter of freedom, while Wells lived on as a prolific commentator whose best books had been written at the start of his career, the quarrel between the two men was soon turned into a kind of critics' myth, epitomizing the clash between sham and great art.

In the most common version of the myth, the dispute was a spiteful, unprovoked attack by a best-selling writer who had no interest in issues of style or form on a great artist whose work was too serious to be appreciated by the general public. In the long run, James has been vindicated because his books have survived, while, in contrast, those of Wells, the mere journalist, have not. Or if fifteen or twenty or however many of Wells's books have somehow managed to survive, then it must be on the strength of their author's colourful life or their historical interest or something – anyhow they can't be literature and no doubt people will stop reading them soon.

If we set aside this widely syndicated piffle, we can see that it was actually James, after years of lauding Wells's work in private, who had launched an unprovoked public attack in his 'Younger Generation' article. Wells's iconoclastic response was unwise: mockery of an elder statesman of letters by a more prosperous and famous author was bound to look distasteful. None the less, Wells's counter-attack is an impressive bout of flyting – an exuberant mix of vituperation, argument and parody that demonstrates his command of style and form and reminds us why James admired Wells in the first place.

There was never likely to be a meeting of minds between someone who regarded his every endeavour as a unique improvisation and someone who chewed every mouthful of food forty times. Still, Wells's view of James was far from eccentric. Thomas Hardy, who also failed to conform to James's standards, lamented his 'ponderously warm manner of saying nothing in infinite sentences', while E.M. Forster, former tutor to Elizabeth von Arnim's children and himself a practitioner of invasive narration, sided with Wells and agreed that, if the competing forces of 'life' and artistic closure could not be balanced, then life should take priority.[38]

Far from defending serious art against mediocrity, James in his 'Younger Generation' article, while praising Conrad and Wharton, relegates Lawrence to the 'dusty rear' of contemporary fiction and detects greater potential in Compton Mackenzie. Wells, more far-sightedly, picks out James Joyce in *Boon* as a 'first-rater'. He would go on to boost Joyce's reputation further by reviewing *A Portrait of the Artist as a Young Man* as a piece of 'great writing' and for more than ten years subsidizing the composition of *Ulysses* and *Finnegans Wake*.[39]

To refute the assumption that James triumphed in the debate with Wells, one might point to a continuing 'Wellsian tradition' in fiction, of saturaters, discussers and genre-fusers from Zamyatin, Aldous Huxley, Orwell, Capek, Priestley, Steinbeck and Borges, on through Bellow, Lessing, Pynchon, most of the science-fiction school (Clarke, Pohl, Vonnegut, Lem, Aldiss, Ballard, Dick, Priest et al.), up to such contemporaries as Julian Barnes, with his foregrounded narration and his mixing of fiction and non-fiction forms, and Hanif Kureshi, a Bromley dissident with a mission to throw light on previously neglected parts of the community and startle readers with sex. (His *Black Album* pointedly features a drug dealers' pub called the Morlock.) One hesitates to include Nabokov in the list, even if he did maintain that Wells was a far greater artist than Conrad.[40]

If we attempt an objective scoring of the Wells–James dispute, the result is likely to be a fifty–fifty draw, with James correct to pull Wells up for burdening his stories with unassimilated ideas and for writing carelessly, especially in his later work, and Wells correct to question the narrowness of James's conception of literature, his affected prose style, especially in *his* later work, and his generally unadventurous subject matter. (James's clumsy and reactionary attempt to deal with class struggle and terrorism in *The Princess Casimassima* is the exception that proves the rule.)[41]

If we have dwelt on the clash between Wells and James here, it is only because it retains a disproportionate place in both Wells's reputation and the history of letters. Comparable flare-ups like that between William Empson and T.S. Eliot are virtually forgotten because it suits received wisdom that Empson and Eliot should be bracketed together as practitioners of Modernist Poetry and New Criticism, even though they had little in common, just as it is convenient that James and Wells shall be contrasted as the master and the mediocrity, even though both men had a long history of genuine enthusiasm for one another's work.

At the time Wells had more urgent things to think about than a literary quarrel. He continued to produce articles reflecting on the war, the more substantial published in book form in May 1916 as *What Is Coming?* With the benefit of hindsight, we know that Wells's main contention – that the centralization and rationalization required by the war would lead to a United States of Europe – was, if not wrong, then at least extremely premature. The most pertinent section in retrospect is 'The "White Man's Burden"', in which Wells firmly opposes the pacifist idea of buying off the Germans by giving them more colonies, recalling their genocidal treatment of the Hereros in Southern Africa. Wells rejects the whole concept of 'subject races', predicts that people in Africa and the Middle East will soon be taking their fate into their own hands and suggests that the outcome may be a renaissance of Islamic civilization. Meanwhile, the British should stop deluding themselves that Indians welcome the Raj and start to plan their departure from the subcontinent.

In May 1916, along with Lankester and Sanderson, Wells spoke at a meeting to launch a committee against the neglect of science. Here he befriended the explorer and enlighted imperialist Sir Harry Johnston, who would become one of his key advisers. Wells's thoughts on how lack of investment in science was holding back education, industry and the armed forces were published during July and August as a series of anonymous letters in *The Times*, over the initials D.P. They were then issued in book form as *The Elements of Reconstruction*, supposedly the work of 'two friends', with an introduction by Lord Milner. Half a century later, without realizing the author's true identity (though, as with *Boon*, Wells was credited in later editions), the historian Arthur Marwick would single out the book for its intelligent criticism of the Government's *laissez-faire* policies.[42]

The month before his fiftieth birthday, Wells reluctantly went on an official visit to the Front. He had resisted previous invitations, partly because he feared that what he saw might unbalance his attitude towards Germany, partly because he did not want to be seen as a government propagandist. It is true that Wells had been one of twenty-five prominent authors summoned by Charles Masterman in September 1914 to discuss how they could contribute to the war effort. However, Wells had shared Chesterton's view that no author worth his salt would suppress reservations about the war's aims and conduct.[43]

Wells sailed for France on 8 August, intending to make his way to Italy, but was delayed in Paris until the 18th, during which time André Citroën showed him around his former car plant, now a munitions factory; he made a brief trip to the French Front at Soissons; and he met Joffre, the Commander of the French army at his headquarters, where he was presented with a set of coloured postcards of the French generals. In a letter to Jane he characterized his experiences as 'silly shiftless mucking about . . . an imbecile expedition', though he seems to have been impressed by Joffre himself.[44] The following week he travelled via Venice to Udine, from where he travelled on to meet the Italian king and saw something of the Isonzo Front and the Trentino offensive. He later reported that several shells landed within a few yards of him in both France and Italy but luckily for him failed to explode. He returned to France via Verona and Milan, inspected the trenches at Arras, Dompierre and Fricourt and, wishing to learn more about aerial reconnaissance, visited the British Front beyond Albert.

Though Wells was sceptical about the value of the expedition, he wrote it up as the centrepiece of *War and the Future*. The book fairly seethes with opinions, but, with the benefit of hindsight, Wells's perspective seems a limited one, not only in his uncomprehending hostility towards conscientious objectors but in his belief in the 'untiring, victorious thrust' of the Somme offensive.[45] Despite this dutiful endorsement of Allied strategy, a government censor demanded the removal of criticisms that the military authorities were too often backward-looking. Instead, Wells burned the requested amendments and sent the text to the publishers with an assurance that it had been passed. When the puzzled censor later wrote requesting the return of his proofs, Wells coolly claimed they were lost.

Wells's visit to the Front resulted not only in an outspoken book but, remarkably, a piece of military hardware. Wells had been horrified to learn how painful it was for soldiers to carry supplies forwards and how contrastingly easy it was for them to slither into mud-filled trenches or craters where, weighed down by the packs that were strapped to them, they drowned. One sleepless night he envisaged a series of T-shaped poles supporting two transport wires that would be powered by a motor lorry. This system, easily erected by pulling a third wire, would carry rations and other supplies much better than individual soldiers could.

Wells sent his plans to his old friend Winston Churchill who, after losing his job as First Lord of the Admiralty over the failure of the Gallipoli expedition, had now returned as Minister of Munitions. Churchill was supportive, and Wells attended tests carried out on his 'telpherage system', but he reports in his autobiography that, thanks to the closed minds of the military, the device was never put into practice.[46] Some smart detective work by Rose Tilly has shown that he was wrong. The system was actually used very successfully in several locations. A War Office report concluded that, in transporting ammunition to the Front at night the system enabled fifteen men to do the work of between 1,500 and 2,000, but because it was a military secret no one ever informed Wells of its success.[47]

Paradoxically, Churchill did give Wells praise over the tank, though its initial introduction was far from a success and Wells's description of a similar weapon in his 1903 story 'The Land Ironclads' was not a particularly close fit to the reality. The army went so far as to give Wells a ride in a tank after his return from the Front. His consequent conviction that he had invented the tank would get him into trouble in 1940 when he libelled a rival claimant in a radio broadcast. In September 1916 he was making a fool of himself in a different way, by asserting that the war would be won by the following June. Coming after two years of similarly over-optimistic claims, the forecast did serious damage to his credibility.

In truth, history does not remember 1916 as a good year for the Allies. On the Western Front, it was the year of Verdun (where 315,000 Frenchmen died) and the Somme (where frontal attacks on the German lines killed 19,000 British soldiers on the first day, leaving 146,000 Allied troops dead or missing by the end). These actions were actually counted as victories, since the industrial carnage slaughtered even more Germans. In Iraq, in the worst humiliation suffered by the British army to date, a force that had set out to seize Baghdad was taken prisoner by the Turks, more than two-thirds of them dying under the brutal treatment they then received.[48] In Dublin an uprising against British rule was successfully put down, but the execution of many of the ringleaders cemented anti-British feeling and ensured Ireland would soon become ungovernable.

It was increasingly difficult to maintain belief in the war to end war. Perhaps the conflict was nothing more than it seemed: an unintelligent squabble between nation states, likely to lead to more of the same. Perhaps the effect of new scientific developments would not, after all, be greater civilization, only more efficient mass bloodshed.

If Wells's life constitutes a kind of modern epic, the Great War is his descent into the underworld. He began to experience a general breakdown in health, losing some of his hair from an attack of alopecia and encountering a condition he could surely never have anticipated in his worst nightmares: erectile dysfunction.[49] Just as he had previously distanced himself from his cynicism and pessimism by ventriloquizing them into the mouths of fictitious characters, so Wells had diverted his fears about the war into the pronouncements of Boon, but they remained his. Boon had realized the war could not be redeemed as a regrettable episode, hellish in the short term but with colossal benefits in the long run. Quite the contrary.

> War is just the killing of things and the smashing of things. And when it is all over, then literature and civilization will have to begin all over again. They will have to begin lower down and against a heavier load, and the days of our jesting are done.[50]

13
PROPHET
1916–1919

It had been five years since Wells produced a book of indisputable literary merit, so readers of the May 1916 issue of the *Grand Magazine* must have been agreeably surprised by the first episode of *Mr Britling Sees It Through* which, initially at least, combined the charm of *Mr Polly* with the reflectiveness of *The New Machiavelli*. Macmillan having refused Wells the pre-war-sized advance he wanted, the author offered the novel to Newman Flower, chief editor at Cassell, who was keen to have more Wells titles and who would become his main British publisher for the next ten years. Cassell published the book in September and sold 30,000 copies by November. It went through thirteen editions by Christmas, was quickly translated into several languages including German (a tactfully abridged edition distributed from Switzerland) and brought in a hefty £20,000-worth of royalty payments from the USA. Some of the translations may have been less than faithful, judging from titles like *M. Britling commence à voir clair* and *Mr Britling's Weg zur Erkenntnis*, which mistakenly celebrate the hero's perspicacity rather than his perseverance.

In ironic homage to James, the story begins with a third-person narrator recreating the consciousness of an American visitor to Europe. Mr Direck has come to offer a speaking engagement to Hugh Britling, a well-known British intellectual. Neither Britain nor Britling are quite what Direck expects, but he is charmed by the gently bohemian lifestyle of his host's home at Matching's Easy, a home matched very easily to Easton. Britling is unmistakably a version of Wells, his mistress Mrs Harrowdean recalls Elizabeth von Arnim, while Lady Homertyn stands in for Lady Warwick.

Wells sustains the Jamesian method for about forty pages, then, as he warms to his subject, demotes Direck to a symbol of US–British relations and refocuses on Britling's thoughts, with which we are thereafter saturated. The result is a demonstration of exactly what Wells meant when he described himself to James as a 'journalist', not a cliché-spouting sensation-monger but an author in the tradition of Defoe and Dickens, reimagining documentary subject matter into more compelling forms. His book is not a Jamesian composition, nor even a vehicle for a socialist message, so much as an account of a human process, involving us in the developing feelings and thoughts of Britling as he attempts to make sense of overwhelming personal and political crises. 'I see more than ever before how distinctly you differ from other writers,' Richard Gregory told Wells: 'it is in the free admission that you give to the workshop of your mind. We are not presented with puppets on a wooden stage but with the actual thoughts of a real man.'[1]

Like his creator, Britling responds to the coming of the war by writing a naïvely optimistic article, 'And Now War Ends'. He realizes that the conflict can produce a just world order only if public opinion is mobilized in favour of appropriate war aims, but the swift collapse of German imperialism he anticipates does not occur and the British ruling class prove neither so efficient nor so idealistic as he had hoped. Britling becomes increasingly disillusioned, especially after his eldest son, having lied about his age to go on active service, sends him letters reporting the horrors of the Front. The ultimate challenge comes when Britling learns of his son's death, an episode that Wells recounts with such conviction that many readers assumed he had been bereaved. Even Kurt Bülow, whose fictional counterpart Herr Heinrich is killed in the story, was alarmed by what he had read in a newspaper article and sent a request for reassurance.

Britling's response to the death of his son is contrasted with that of Letty, the wife of his secretary, who believes that her husband has been killed in battle. Until she learns that the news is false, she fantasizes the assassination of all those responsible for starting the war. Britling, seeking a more constructive reaction than her self-diminishing hatred, writes an article on 'The Better Government of the World', yet he remains aware that his ideas are over-ambitious and inadequately expressed. His grief at the loss of his son and his sense of his own insufficiency are superimposed on a long-term ambivalence about whether his liberal, informal way of life is something to be cherished for its playful creativity or discarded because frivolous and undisciplined, and in particular (something Wells would never have admitted in his own person) he feels a quiet guilt over his 'troublesome, undignified and futile' love affairs.[2]

Alarmed at his growing hatred of the Germans Britling struggles to discover the origin of human cruelty, tracking it back to a perverted sense of righteousness, which – having a residue of good in it – must be capable of redemption, coming at last to forgiveness and a religious perspective. In the final pages of the book he is possessed by belief in a finite god, the Captain of the World Republic, a living personification of the evolving Mind of the Race in which the dead such as Hugh and Herr Heinrich can be said to persist. Whether this idea is comparable to Letty's crazy fantasies or is their opposite is for the reader to decide, but, as with George's affirmation in *Tono-Bungay*, the positioning of the idea at the climax of the book tends to weight it with authority. Wisely, Wells ends on an ambiguous image of harvest – 'From away towards the church came the sound of some early worker whetting a scythe'[3] – fusing the death toll of the war with the inevitability of death for all, the clearing of dead thoughts from a living mind and possibilities of spiritual and social revolution.

Wells had certainly caught the mood of the moment. The religious shift at the close of the book came at a time when grief was driving many towards supernatural consolation. Classic examples are the angels who were supposed to have fought alongside the British at Mons, the decision of the eminent scientist Professor Oliver Lodge to drop physics and devote himself to communicating with his son in the afterlife, and the endorsement given to the hoax photographs of the 'Cottingley fairies' by Conan Doyle, who had also lost his son in the war, along with his brother and several other members of his family. Beatrice Webb noted how typical it was of the era that, after Amber's brother Fabian was killed while serving as an airman in France, Maud Pember Reeves came to believe her son accompanied her as an invisible presence.[4]

Wells was not cynically jumping on a bandwagon, however. He had moved away from hard-line secularism as long ago as the 1890s and, while keeping his distance from religious commitment, consistently made use of Christian imagery and ideas in his work, generally ironically but sometimes less so. Despite his repudiation of Christianity, Wells retained his mother's assumption that there was a single body of truth, belief in which could lead to something like salvation. While part of him believed no one had access to absolute truth and that progress could be achieved only through dialogue and experiment, another part still aspired to the prophet's role. When Charles Watts of the Rationalist Press Association told Wells he was uncertain about reprinting *Anticipations* because of its references to God, even though Wells had used the word figuratively, Wells answered him, 'Not so figuratively as all that'.[5] Among his recent works, *Boon* had vigorously defended the idea of a god, albeit not in the author's own voice.

An advertisement at the end of *War and the Future*, published shortly after *Britling*, announces that in his next work Wells 'will develop further the conception running through this book, of the Kingdom of God as the only possible ruling idea for the greatest, as for the most intimate of human affairs. Place an order with your Booksellers in good time.' Agreements for *God the Invisible King* and *Britling* had been mailed to Cassell on the same day. Characteristically, Wells did not want to leave his ideas within the category of fiction but to push them through the frame into the reader's world, where they could present a bigger, bolder challenge. 'I am a MALE,' he wrote to Rebecca in excited free verse. 'I have got Great Britain Pregnant . . . She is full of Theological Discussion'.[6]

Wells told a correspondent that he did not aim to found a new religion, only to add his voice to a trend in modern thought, and that he expected *God the Invisible King* to be forgotten within twenty years.[7] The estimate was generous. There was little to forget since Wells's faith was essentially a Protestantism so diluted that only the faintest trace of belief remained. His distinction between God the Creator (the mysterious source of nature) and God the Redeemer (the personification of humanity's struggle with nature), the second of whom claims our allegiance, had been far more memorably expressed by romantic poets like Blake and Shelley. Since Wells has no comparable mythology or poetry to offer, much of his text comes down to a prosaic review of the theological distinctions between other faiths and his own.

Wells's apparent 'conversion' none the less caused quite a stir at the time, comparable to those of W.H. Auden or Bob Dylan for later generations. In Wells's case, Christians soon realized that his god was not theirs and wrote him down as a lost soul still struggling towards the light, if by a wilfully devious route. Secularists were more angry at what they saw as betrayal. Watts commissioned William Archer to write *God and Mr Wells,* which questioned whether Wells's deity was anything more than a symbol of his own ideas and memorably compared him to a ventriloquist prostrating himself before his dummy. Tommy Simmons offered a slightly more sympathetic response, telling his old college friend that, while he was striving towards a similar vision, he was unpersuaded by Wells's conviction, which was 'too much like the old time evangelical conversion for my wants'.[8]

In due course Wells would come to agree with his critics and to apologize for what he felt had been an unhelpful detour in his thinking caused by the stress of war. Yet he could never quite repudiate the intention behind his words. Even if the traditional religious language was an error, the belief that the individual is part of a greater existence remained.

In Wells's support, one might say that all societies, however little else they have in common, feature religious beliefs of some kind. If human beings have evolved to produce religions just as they produce language, families and social structures, it would be irrational to propose a description of human nature or a sketch of an ideal society that assumes that religion can be eliminated from the picture. Even those keen to proclaim the Death of God are usually quick to substitute a 'transcendent signifier' (the Will to Power, the Aristocratic Ideal, History, Science), a source of meaning that will fulfil at least some of the same functions.

In many ways Wells was peculiarly well equipped to build a bridge between science and religion. From early on his writings show not only an engagement with scientific understanding but a recurrent sense of being part of a greater consciousness and an intuition that a perfect world is as latent in the structure of things as mathematics or music.[9] Philosophically, he accepted Immanuel Kant's distinction between 'phenomena' (things as our senses reveal them) and 'noumena' (things as they are), which might have led him to the view, often encountered today among religious apologists, that science and religion are complementary ways to transcend the limits of individual experience and attain a constructive overview, rooted in generations of reflection but open to continual modification. However, Wells had to contend with many religious believers who claimed their beliefs were unproblematically true and who formed one of the most reactionary groups in society. Since he needed the authority of science to challenge them, it is hardly surprising that his chief attempt to square the scientific and religious mentalities failed to stick, especially since he was formulating his ideas while teetering on the brink of a nervous breakdown.

The eccentric religious conclusion that helped to make *Britling* popular at the time may be one reason why it is now so little read. Nor does the book's account of an unfinished war, the significance of which is still open to negotiation, sit easily with the neatly retrospective versions of the Great War often taught in schools and universities. However, it cannot be denied that there are also artistic issues that impede the book's canonical status. With the prig novels Wells had begun a descent into solipsism – the action essentially takes place in the head of an autobiographical character, leaving the other characters underdeveloped and the action muted – and *Britling*, for all its merits, does not break out of this limitation, so that many readers have found their initial interest diminishing as the book goes on.

Whatever doubts he may have been harbouring about the Invisible King, Wells stuck to his guns, producing a revised version of his credo *First and Last Things* with enhanced holiness (it would be resecularized in 1929) and in September 1917 a second religious novel. Like *The Sea Lady*, it was a riposte to Mrs Humphrey Ward, this time reconceiving *Robert Elsmere*, her novel about a pastor undergoing a religious crisis. *The Soul of a Bishop, A Novel (with Just a Little Love in It) about Conscience and Religion and the Real Troubles of Life* is as dismissive of Christianity as its main title suggests – and as defensive about its positive agenda as is its subtitle.

The titular bishop, Scrope, having lost faith in the creed of his Church, is struggling to come to terms with contemporary political crises, not least those represented by the Great War. Suffering from stress, he falls into the hands of a radical therapist, Dr Dale, a forerunner of R.D. Laing and Timothy Leary who, scorning tranquillizers, prescribes a stimulant that will take the patient so far into his discomfort zone that he comes out the other side. With his mind whacked open by Dale's drug, Scrope has encounters with an angel who lectures him on Wells's doctrines. The reader may feel less convinced by these than Scrope, especially since they appear to depend so heavily upon chemical assistance. Whatever the merits of his theology, Scope is a typical Wellsian solipsist and the supporting characters are exceptionally thin and uninteresting.

Though Wells defended his god to Frederic Harrison, using arguments more often used to defend constitutional monarchy, the Invisible King was the sole monarch he was prepared to acknowledge.[10] He was delighted to hear of the February revolution in Russia, followed by the Tsar's abdication in March, and sent a message to the Provisional Government via the *New York Times* and *Daily Chronicle* hailing the new republican democracy. Three weeks later he dispatched a letter to *The Times* in

London calling for a republican society to be formed in Britain, though he was forced to backtrack on this proposal because of the hostility it provoked. ('There goes my earldom,' remarked the newspaper's proprietor, Lord Northcliffe – in a former life Henley House School pupil Alfred Harmsworth.[11])

Russia's liberal revolution would soon come to grief, presenting a challenge to foreign supporters such as Wells who had to decide whether they would condemn its more radical successor or continue to offer their support. The Germans had taken advantage of Russia's breakdown to send in the revolutionary leader Lenin, who favoured a separate peace. Their plan succeeded better than they could have hoped. Lenin's Bolsheviks staged a coup in October, and, when a subsequent election gave them a poor second place, they responded by destroying their country's fledgling democracy and murdering the royal family. By the end of the year Russia was riven by civil war and had effectively surrendered to Germany. In the subsequent peace treaty Germany collected its pay-off: one-third of Russia's farming land, one-third of its population, two-thirds of its coal mines and half its heavy industry. Though the recruitment of the USA to the Allied cause in April 1917 offered major compensation, the closure of the Eastern Front was one catastrophe among many, including mutinies in the French army, defeat for the Italians at Caporetto and 324,000 British casualties at Passchendaele.

Even Wells and Rebecca found themselves coming under fire after the latter moved to Leigh on Sea, Essex, in March 1917. From her new house, Southcliffe, on Marine Parade Rebecca had been hoping to enjoy life at the seaside with Anthony and access to London by train. Unfortunately, the house proved to be on the flight path for Gotha bombers heading for London, hitting other targets as they went. ('*Pretty* aeroplanes!' exclaimed Anthony at the sight of them. '*Lovely* guns!')[12]

Wells experienced several of the terrifying air raids. To test his nerve, just as his creation Benham would have done in the circumstances, he made a point of standing on the Southcliffe balcony during the bombing. He was infuriated by Rebecca's contrasting lack of stoicism and criticized her for her constant moans of 'Oh God!' To cheer his youngest son through a bout of mumps and tonsillitis, he further defied the enemy with an illustrated story, 'Master Anthony & the Zeppelin', in which the eponymous hero tames a dirigible, teaching it to build a nest and lay eggs. The story was later published in a book to raise funds for babies in the Flanders war zone.[13]

When Wells and Rebecca visited Southend and an incendiary bomb came down just seventy yards away, Rebecca decided it was high time to evacuate Anthony to a Montessori school run by one of her friends in London. Like Wells she was suffering a general breakdown in health and had also turned towards religion, in her case through the conventional method of attending church services. Insight into her relationship with Wells at this time is limited, because he seems to have burned most of her letters during the Second World War on discovering both of them were on the Nazi black list, presumably fearing that in the event of invasion the correspondence might be used to their mutual discredit. The existing evidence suggests that their relationship remained as stormy as Wells's other love affairs, with Rebecca struggling painfully to balance the roles of author, mother and mistress while Wells, by her testimony, swung between being kind and caring (the role he tended to adopt in person) and selfishly demanding (as he often became in his letters).[14]

While Wells was doing his best to provide for both Rebecca and Jane, he could take no direct responsibility for the other woman who had borne him a child. She has therefore tended to slip under biographers' radar. It is easy to assume that Amber, her career destroyed, had accepted the default roles of housewife and mother. In fact, in the eight years since she had split from Wells, as well as giving birth to two more children, she had published three novels and, by way of war work, become an administrator at the Admiralty, then, at Churchill's request, at the Ministry of Munitions, where she ran the Women's Wages Department. Under her regime women's pay more than doubled, so it might be argued that, despite her lower profile, Amber achieved more in practical terms during these years than did Wells.

None the less, he, too, had found more constructive war work than repackaging religion. His call for a new world order in *The War That Will End War* had been prophetic. Many people had begun campaigning for an international organization to enforce a fair conduct of world affairs, a body that by 1915 had come to be called a League of Nations. While writing his autobiography, Wells was reminded by the writer Philip Guedalla that he had sent a letter via the American diplomat Bainbridge Colby to President Woodrow Wilson in November 1917, two months before Wilson set out the key Fourteen Points for which the USA was fighting. Wells's letter put forward ideas similar to Wilson's, including the setting up of a League. Wells doubted whether Wilson had paid any attention to his views, but the possibility shows how much his globalizing idealism had moved into the mainstream of political thinking.

Early in 1917 Wells became a leading member of the League of Nations Society. Mistrustful of its pacifist members, he helped found a rival League of Free Nations Association in 1918. (Wells favoured the word 'free', which he took to imply that the nations who signed up would repudiate monarchy.) In the event the two groups soon merged as the League of Nations Union, with Wells on its executive and research committees.

During 1917 he wrote many articles advocating a League. The best known, 'A Reasonable Man's Peace', appeared in the *Daily News* on 14 August and was twice printed as a leaflet by League-promoting organizations. It was collected in Wells's book *In the Fourth Year*. Later in 1918 the League of Free Nations Association put out a shortened version of the book under its original subtitle, *Anticipations of a World Peace.* Dismissing monarchy and imperialism as a secure basis for the new order, but having little time for party politics either, Wells advocates a democratic peace settlement made by representatives elected by proportional representation, using the single transferable vote.

Early in 1918 Wells was given a golden opportunity to promote his ideas for reconstruction. The Prime Minister, Lloyd George, though he hated the newspaper owners whose campaigns had brought down the previous government, had decided in self-defence to bring them on to his team. Lord Beaverbrook, the proprietor of the *Daily Express,* became Minister of Information, and Lord Northcliffe became Director of Propaganda. Northcliffe at once sent for Wells as one of his top writers and put him in charge of propaganda to Germany.

During May 1918 Wells found himself presiding over activities such as designing leaflets to be dropped over enemy territory, faking demoralizing newspapers, drawing together research on the performance of the German economy and liaising with League campaigners around the world. What he really wanted to do, however, was take advantage of his new-found job to impose progressive war aims on the government. With encouragement from his colleagues, he sent a 'Memorandum of War Aims' to an Advisory Committee of the Foreign Office. His sales pitch was that if the Germans believed they would get fair treatment, they would be more inclined to surrender. To his disappointment, the outcome of his initiative was a meeting with the head of political intelligence, who subjected him to a lecture that, in his view, would have done credit to a patriotic schoolboy of eight.

Undeterred, Wells and his colleagues decided to produce their propaganda as if Britain's war aims were what they wished them to be. The historian A.J.P. Taylor judged this to be a successful ploy. Northcliffe's team at Crewe House, the Ministry of Propaganda's headquarters, committed Britain to the League of Nations, and the government followed for lack of anything better.[15] This was not how Wells saw it. To him, the British and other governments went along with their ideas only in outline and as a cover for short-term national self-interest.

Wells did not wait until the arrival of the peace settlement to get disillusioned. After only a few weeks in his propaganda job, he complained to Northcliffe that, while they were trying to win over the Germans with a just peace, the *Evening News* and *Daily Mail* were persecuting German-born Britons and calling for a vengeful settlement. Northcliffe cited editorial independence and the need to keep up the fighting spirit; what he really meant was that he made his money by giving the public what they wanted rather than showing leadership. On 9 July Wells resigned from the directorship in disgust and on 30 July resigned from the committee altogether.

His brief official service over, Wells resumed his familiar role of freelance author, but it was a role that was becoming increasingly problematic. In the 1890s he had been a rising star of literature; in the Edwardian period a creative writer with an interest in social thought; in the 1910s he had made a decisive shift towards being an intellectual journalist whose novels dramatized his ideas. To a considerable extent, his credibility as a thinker rested on his power as a novelist, and, despite the huge sales of *Britling*, this was less secure than it had once been.

The challenge he faced was clear in his latest work, *Joan and Peter: The Story of an Education*, written during 1917, published September 1918. The book was dedicated to 'P & J', presumably Panther and Jaguar, and is an account of the years 1893–1919, focused on the education of two orphans whose guardian, Oswald Sydenham, struggles to save them from the forces of reaction. In some respects it is a distinguished piece of work. Even Jane Austen might have been impressed by the waspish wit with which Wells dispatches Lady Charlotte at the opening of Chapter 5, but the author probably had more up-to-date models in mind, acknowledging the competition he faced from new quills on the block. The stream-of-consciousness account of Dolly's drowning at the end of Chapter 3 looks suspiciously like a response to the death of Tom Brangwen in Lawrence's *The Rainbow* and Peter's childhood feelings at the start of Chapter 4 to the opening of Joyce's *A Portrait of the Artist as a Young Man*, though neither comes close to matching their originals.

To a degree, the book also parallels Lawrence's story 'England, My England', which had been published in the *English Review* during 1915, its title alluding to a bad patriotic poem by Henley. Lawrence's story succeeds as an account of the English mentality in the period leading up to the Great War, however controversial the analysis, because he skilfully embodies his ideas in his characters. In Wells's story the ideas increasingly take over the proceedings. By Chapter 12 Oswald is racing preposterously around the world so that his creator can comment on the global scene, and, having begun with real artistic power, the book ends as little more than a clumsily fictionalized article.

Looking back, Wells would not only acknowledge this but own up to a fatal lack of coherence, since his attempt to produce a novel about education ran out of space, causing the secondary school and university sections to be violently abridged. He was unabashed by these failings, having lowered his literary expectations to local excellence and short-term impact. These were precisely the virtues Virginia Woolf found when she reviewed the novel. *Joan and Peter* has a 'continuity and vitality' that comes from Wells's 'fiery passion for the rights of youth' and from the way he visualizes his ideas until they constitute a 'whole world'.[16] His work is undeniably 'vivid', yet in the end the characters exist in order to embody the author's ideas and are not depicted with the care required for lasting art.

A convenient way to audit Wells's public standing as a fiction writer in the post-war years is to look at which of his books were adapted for the feature-length silent films that began to appear around this time. Though Wells's novels proved ill-suited to the stage – *Kipps* managed about seven weeks at the Vaudeville Theatre in 1912, *The Wonderful Visit* lasted less than a month at the St Martin's in 1921 – the big screen proved more accommodating.

Pathé had ventured into Wellsian territory back in 1909 with a slapstick special-effects short, *The Invisible Thief.* Wells signed a contract with them in 1914 in hope of credit and payment for future projects. The war rendered this void, however, and it was Gaumont that produced the earliest official Wells film, *The First Men in the Moon,* in 1919. To give the story mass appeal, the script adds a love interest between Cavor's niece and a telegraphist called Hannibal Higben, brought together in a happy ending when Cavor's radio messages expose Bedford as a dastardly villain. Geoffrey Wells reports that the film showed a few inadequate scenes inside the Moon, with a Grand Lunar who looked like a giant baby from *The Food of the Gods.*[17]

Gaumont having proved unequal to Wells, the Stoll Company took up the franchise in 1920. With their theatrical background, Stoll were probably uncomfortable with the special-effects requirements of the scientific romances. Their decision to opt for more conventional properties paid off with a hit version of *Kipps,* in which George K. Arthur played the hero in the style of megastar Charlie Chaplin. Arthur was back as Hoopdriver the following year in *The Wheels of Chance,* much of it shot on the original locations, but the second film did not do such good business, and it was with some reluctance that Stoll let Pinker talk them into parting with a third payment (around £1,000 per movie) to make an adaptation of *The Passionate Friends,* perhaps hoping the title would lure the punters. The *New York Times* dismissed the film as 'sedulously dull, with the iron hand of British breeding shackling its content'.[18]

Paramount put out advance publicity for an effects-laden *War of the Worlds* but did not actually deliver the goods for another thirty years. In 1927 Fox made a final attempt to adapt Wells for the silent screen with *Marriage.* Walter Winchell in the *New York Evening Graphic* delivered the inevitable verdict, 'Advice for those about to try *Marriage*; don't.' The filming of one scientific romance, two comic novels and two prig novels may suggest that the general public did not see Wells as a novelist in decline but might also reflect Pinker's efforts to promote the recent fiction. Wells certainly continued to move in literary circles and to behave as a respected artist who took an interest in up-and-coming authors.

As well as supporting the ground-breaking work of James Joyce, for example, he stood up for Hueffer's *The Good Soldier,* a sophisticated narrative along James/Conrad lines, complaining to Chesterton about the way it had been treated in his magazine the *New Witness.* Today *The Good Soldier* is not attributed to Ford Madox Hueffer but to Ford Madox Ford. This name change seems to have arisen because, between 1910 and 1918, Hueffer had paired up with Wells's former lover Violet Hunt but refused to marry her. She ingeniously changed her name to Hueffer and he then thwarted her by switching his name to Ford.

Wells admired Hueffer/Ford for having lied about his age to fight in the war. He felt a similar admiration for Siegfried Sassoon, whom he urged to downplay his campaign against the war leaders in favour of his creative work. Through Sassoon, he met Wilfred Owen in November 1917, a year before Owen's death in battle. Owen enjoyed his hour's worth of conversation with Wells, though he was embarrassed when Wells tried to inveigle him into making fun of the gaudy handkerchief Bennett was sporting. In January 1919 Wells and Rebecca, taking a holiday at Weymouth, called in on Thomas Hardy. According to Rebecca (rarely a reliable witness), Hardy was complaining that the *Daily News* had described his poems as pessimistic, only for Florence Hardy to comment, 'Well, dear, they aren't what you would call *hilarious*.'[19]

These literary contacts suggest that Wells remained secure in his reputation, yet he himself knew that he was adopting a more narrowly journalistic approach to his writing, and, with the arrival of Lawrence, Joyce and Woolf, the criteria for literary excellence were starting to shift away from him. The newcomers may have sold few copies while he remained a staple of the libraries and bookshops, but the prophet in him knew his reputation among discerning readers was becoming compromised. As early as 1917 he confided to Bennett, 'My boom is over. I've had my boom. I'm yesterday.'[20]

Wells's reputation was not much assisted by *The Undying Fire*, though he himself thought this meditation on suffering, published in May 1919, one of his best pieces of writing. The book is an ingenious update of the biblical story of Job, concerning Job Huss, a headmaster modelled on Sanderson, who suffers a succession of tragic misfortunes during the Great War. Huss is driven to repudiate the glib Victorian equation of evolution with progress. Having weighed the suffering of all living creatures, including king penguins slaughtered by humans to the verge of extinction for their oil, he arrives at what is effectively a green critique of mankind's arrogance towards nature. More would be heard of Wells the ecological campaigner.

Almost twenty pages are devoted to a vivid account of the evil done by, and done to, the crews of U-boats. Wells had originally researched this material for purposes of Crewe House propaganda, but, as developed in the book, the figure of the German submariner becomes a chilling symbol of humankind, trapped and condemned by aggressive power structures and technologies that have run out of control.

The Undying Fire is Wells's most open confrontation with the horror of existence since *Dr Moreau*, even reintroducing from the earlier book the image of a dead rabbit, torn and bleeding, that taps into Wells's ambivalence about dissection.

However, the comparison exposes the new book's limitations. In the 1890s Wells had worked his dread into a richly symbolic adventure story; twenty years on he converted it into a parade of ideas leading to a predetermined conclusion: that the one true god is the yearning for the ideal in the human heart, which can be successfully developed through education. Hence the book's dedication 'To All Schoolmasters and Schoolmistresses and every Teacher in the World'. It is a sane conclusion, but by the nature of the project it is delivered through a hasty and contrived resolution and received by thinly allegorical characters.

In September 1918, while Wells was taking a break with Rebecca and Anthony at the Sandringham Hotel, Hunstanton, the Germans' final offensive on the Western Front failed and the Allies found themselves sweeping to victory, compelling the Germans to sign an armistice on 11 November. The victory was a bitter one, however. Nearly a century later the best estimate is that more than eight million people had been killed, a considerable number of them non-Europeans who had been drawn into the conflict through imperialism. The death toll rises to more than thirteen million if consequences of the war are included, such as the Russian Revolution and the famines and epidemics that raged through Europe's weakened population.

Wells told a correspondent that he and Rebecca were victims of the flu pandemic and that he had nearly died early in 1919.[21] The illness led him to resign from his League of Nations committee work in January. Later in the year he fell out with his colleagues in his usual style and quit the League of Nations Union altogether, his final work for the cause being contributions to two Oxford University Press pamphlets published in 1919 as *The Idea of a League of Nations* and *The Way to a League of Nations*.

Meanwhile, the Kaiser had abdicated, the Austro-Hungarian and Ottoman empires collapsed and Imperial Russia imploded. Inspired by the Bolsheviks, there were revolutionary outbreaks across the Continent, including an armed uprising in Berlin. In China and Ireland civil wars were beginning. The peace settlement of June 1919, generally known as the Treaty of Versailles, tried to take control of the situation. As Wells had advocated, a League of Nations was set up, territorial boundaries were redrawn along ethnic-linguistic lines and imperial possessions were taken over by the victors, to be prepared for self-government. However, as he had feared, the settlement was a drastically punitive one that stripped Germany of much of its territory and demanded unrealistically large war guilt payments for years to come.

As Amber's old tutor John Maynard Keynes pointed out at the time, to damage the German economy in this way would inevitably rebound on the prosperity of the rest of Europe. Worse, when the Germans one day regained their economic and military strength, they would be united in their determination to overturn the order that had victimized them. In trying to draw a line under the Great War, the victors had instead created the conditions for a possible second world war.

In the meantime, the refusal of the US Senate to sign up to the League fatally weakened the the latter's capacity to deal with major power conflicts, the redrawing of the map of Europe created as many tensions as it resolved and the new 'mandates', supposedly being developed towards self-government, were treated by Britain and France as imperial acquisitions. The British government's ingenious idea of winning international support by offering displaced Jews a home in Palestine, where three-quarters of a million Muslims already lived, lit a fuse to future catastrophe.

It was soon clear that the Great War had achieved little except to set a chasm across history and bring into being a new world of manifest instability. Since the colossal suffering had not achieved the goals that the war leaders had proclaimed, the pacifist case, put forward by a minority during the war, became widely accepted. The war had been unjust, caused by greed and ruthlessness on all sides. Its ostensible causes were bogus. The real blame lay with a system led by lying politicians and incompetent generals and endorsed by well-meaning dupes such as Wells. A blanket suspicion of authority and established ideas became common among the educated young and has remained in place ever since.

Church attendance went into steep decline. Army service spread cigarette smoking and sexual profanities from the lowest classes to men of all stations. Many young women, not content with the introduction of the vote, demonstrated their equality with men by smoking and drinking in public, kitted out for the purpose in unprecedentedly short skirts. European light music was challenged by the exuberant syncopation of jazz and high-tempo dances like the Charleston. Einstein's theory of relativity, Freudian psychology and Surrealist art were embraced, often indiscriminately, as the latest word in modern thought, their validity underwritten by their apparent irrationality. To many disheartened by the war and its consequences, Russian Communism or Italian Fascism came to seem dynamic, purposeful alternatives to the ignoble and corrupt wheeling and dealing of the past.

Back in 1915 Henry James had foreseen that the war would have equally radical consequences for literature, as under the pressure of events words had 'deteriorated like motor car tires'.[22] Ernest Hemingway consciously echoed the master in his 1929 novel about the Italian campaign, *A Farewell to Arms*, singling out 'sacred', 'glorious' and 'sacrifice' as cant terms regularly used to dignify a slaughter no more noble than the business of the Chicago stockyards. Elsewhere in the novel, a character praises a book called *Mr Britling Sees Through It*. 'No he doesn't,' parries Hemingway's hero, implying that Wells's books were further verbiage to be discarded.[23]

The new generation turned away from the piety and abstraction that the war had promoted in favour of rendering more sharply the individual experience and feelings it had so often crushed. Some authors even wanted to throw off the shackles of a conventional storyline, point of view and chronology, which they felt to be outworn methods of linking events that distorted their inner significance. Discrediting of language was not the only factor behind the artistic revolution, which, after all, occurred in all the arts and had been in process some time before the war – realism and naturalism having been explored to the point when many felt a new approach was long overdue – but the war hugely encouraged the trend.

Just as the growth of photography had devalued realism in painting and encouraged new visual movements from Impressionism to Cubism, so the growth of sociology, popular journalism and light fiction that had been the making of Wells drove highbrow authors to follow the example of James, producing texts which, in their deviation from stylistic norms and cavalier way with exposition, raised the bar for readers. They were a luxury product, designed to identify the intelligentsia by excluding everyone else.[24]

These top-of-the-range novels aspired to the cohesion of scripture, with every detail brimming with meaning. Their ideal consumer was not a reader but a devout student, willing to work at unorthodox sentences and narrative structures and to notice a detail on page 4 and link it to another on page 404. For Wells, in contrast, the novel had the linear, improvised quality of speech or, to risk a slight anachronism, a jazz or blues performance, to be enjoyed by all comers for its exuberance, momentum and ability to achieve a satisfying coherence within a reasonably familiar form, despite digressions and stretches when inspiration plateaued. There was no need for an equal intensity of meaning throughout, no desire to impose intrusive dissonance and ambiguity on the reader, no exclusivity or idolatory.

By the 1920s, however, to consume the productions of Joyce and Woolf was to identify oneself as a highbrow of education and leisure, enthroned at the top of the brain chain, looking down on the benighted common reader who still thought Wells racy and controversial. Bennett sensed the shift from the old conventions as early as 1911 when, contemplating Cézanne and Gaugin, he reflected, 'supposing some writer were to come along and do in words what these men have done in paint, I might conceivably be disgusted with nearly the whole of modern fiction, and I might have to begin again'.[25] When Bennett approached Wells in February 1919 to ask if the Wells–James letters could be published, Wells declined, aware that he had made a poor case and that, in the present climate, publication would probably fix him in the mind of the race as a middlebrow philistine.

Wells found some of the new literary experiments rewarding – praising not only the work of Joyce but that of Wyndham Lewis and of Elizabeth von Arnim's cousin Katherine Mansfield – but on the whole judged the modernist tendency to be a force encouraging elitism and political reaction. He was by no means a traditionalist himself, but his experimentation lay in mixing genres, in foregrounding a point of view to encourage critical reading and in violating realism with fantastic events or outlandish ideas in order to open up startling new perspectives. To Wells, individuals did not fully make sense unless their experiences had been recontextualized as part of a greater historical-cosmic process. While contriving closure for the individual story, he was also luring the reader into an ongoing debate about wider issues.

The difficulty Wells faced in pursuing this approach, other than its decreasing fashionability for the next few years, was that the more thought he gave to the historical context and the issues for debate, the less feeling he seemed to retain for the development of characters and story, particularly since he had now pretty much exhausted his formative experiences as subject matter. Reversing Yeats's formula, we may say that players and painted stage took less of his love than those abstract things that they were emblems of.[26] *Joan and Peter* and *The Undying Fire* were by no means bad books, but to discerning readers they seemed ill-proportioned, preachy and, in view of the thirty plus books of fiction Wells had already produced, superfluous.

With characteristic ingenuity, however, Wells came up with a way to outflank his critics, moving into a genre in which he could put his storytelling skills to an unexpected new use. In April 1919 he contributed an article to *John O'London's Weekly* in Britain and the *Saturday Evening Post* in the USA, subsequently printed as a booklet in New York. It was called 'History Is One'. In it he argued that 'a saner teaching of history means a better understanding of international problems, a saner national policy, and a happier world'. The time had come for a Wellsian history of the world.

14
HISTORIAN
1919–1922

The idea of a global history seems to have been simmering at the back of Wells's mind for many years, perhaps since his student days when he kept a notebook of his historical reading. During his League of Nations phase, while trying to get the Great War into perspective, he made similar notes and was frustrated to find there was no book that traced globalization as a central theme of human development. He accordingly proposed that one should be sponsored by the League of Nations Union. Despite the involvement of Gilbert Murray and Leonard Woolf, the project got nowhere. Academic historians with reputations to lose were nervous of venturing outside their specialisms. If Wells really wanted to read such a book, he was going to have to write it himself.

A history of the world was not a project to be undertaken lightly, however – not least because it looked unlikely to bring in much money. Fortunately, *Britling*'s success had boosted Wells's finances to the point where he could stand the loss of income that a lengthy period of research and writing would entail. More than that, as he admitted a quarter of a century later, his success had been accompanied by a guilt which drove him towards the project: 'My wife and I were distressed to think we had made a good thing out of a war that had hurt so many of our friends.'[1]

This may be an understatement. Wells had prospered by depicting the war as the means to a lasting peace, and many of those who had read and believed what he had written had been destroyed. Though Wells had acted in good faith, he might reasonably have wondered whether he did not have blood on his hands. At the very least he must have feared that, in championing the war to end war, he had been part of the problem as well as the solution.

If Wells could not change the dismaying outcome of the Great War, he could at least make a contribution towards preventing a sequel. History was becoming, as he would soon inform readers of the *Outline*, 'a race between education and catastrophe'.[2] The teaching of nationalistic history had fuelled the conflagration – in Germany, most of all, but everywhere to some degree. If an alternative account of history, emphasizing human unity, could be put into the hands of teachers and general readers around the world, it might have the reverse effect and help create a culture for future peace.

Sacrificing income in the process of writing amounted to a form of penance, a larger- scale version of the tithe Wells already paid by producing socialist articles when he might have been working on higher-return fiction. Lest this makes Wells sound saintly, he himself thought his guilt feelings were less of a motivator than the gargantuan vanity and self-belief he had acquired thanks to his runaway success as an unorthodox writer and unrepentant adulterer.

Not all the zeal for the project came from Wells, however. Before committing himself, he had to go through the family finances with Jane, guardian of their joint account. She not only agreed that a year could be devoted to the writing but undertook much of the work herself: typing drafts, checking references, finding quotations, locating illustrations, keeping the material organized and offering constructive criticism. For Jane, it must have been a bit like the old days in Mornington Road, and she resumed the role of collaborator with enthusiasm and indeed love. As the project brought Jane closer, so it distanced Rebecca who found Wells's analytical approach to history unappealing, thought he should stick to creative writing and hated Jane, whom she wished to supplant as the third Mrs Wells.

In October 1918 Wells and Jane settled down to their labours. The *Encyclopaedia Britannica* gave them initial guidance, along with other basic texts such as Winwood Reade's *Martyrdom of Man.* Detailed, specialized knowledge came from books in the London Library (a private lending library) and experts whom Wells consulted. Once each section had been researched and drafted, it was sent to a team of advisers for comment and correction, chief among them Ernest Barker, Harry Johnston, E. Ray Lankester and Gilbert Murray. The sections were then rewritten and circulated for further discussion until Wells judged that they had reached a satisfactory standard. Finally, Gregory, Guedella, Bennett and others reviewed the proofs. J.F. Horrabin designed the maps and many of the others illustrations, ensuring they reinforced the text to maximum effect.

In November 1919, after a gruelling year, the *Outline of History* was completed. It began to appear in the shops almost simultaneously, for Wells had come up with the idea of initial publication in part-work format in order to make purchase easier for ordinary readers. These twenty-four fortnightly parts, published by Newnes, contained forty-seven colour pictures and hundreds of photographs, plus Horrabin's drawings, maps and timelines. Each part sold around 100,000 copies. The unsold parts were then bound into two volumes, together constituting the Library Edition.

A single volume Reader's Edition in September 1920 omitted much of the illustration but added revisions, many of them in response to readers' comments. Further revised editions followed over the years. By the end of 1921 150,000 copies had been sold in Britain and 500,000 in the USA; by the end of 1922 English-language sales were up to a million; ten years later (partly owing to book club editions) two million. There were soon translations into Japanese and Swedish, followed by numerous other languages and also Braille. Far from reducing Wells's income, as he had supposed it would do, the book became an intellectual status symbol everyone wanted to own, and it earned him a fortune.

The story Wells tells is as clear in its outline as his title suggests but deftly filled in with memorable details. It is a story of evolution: first of the earth, then of living creatures, including human beings. Over time the human species has diverged into an array of different cultures. Time and again prophets have expressed a vision of human unity and military leaders established empires, only for division to reassert itself. Now through science and improved communications the world's cultures have at last begun to converge into a global system but with a resulting friction that is generating persecution, religious revivals and warfare. The Great War showed the need for a world polity that would enable all the peoples of the earth to live together in effective harmony, addressing common issues such as economic inequality and, a topic Wells himself far-sightedly singles out, the need to conserve animal species.

A number of historians, naturally, quibbled at Wells's selections and emphases, while ideological opponents condemned his value judgements and interpretations, the former best represented by A.W. Gomme's booklet *Mr Wells as Historian*, the latter by many articles from the Catholic apologist Hilaire Belloc. Wells answered both in an article in the *Fortnightly Review*, reprinted separately in 1921 as *The New Teaching of History*. He continued debating, as Borges puts it, 'politely and mortally' with Belloc, replying to the latter's 1926 attack, *A Companion to Mr Wells's Outline of History*, with the dismissive *Mr Belloc Objects* the same September, though not so mortally that it prevented Belloc returning to the fray before the end of the year with *Mr Belloc Still Objects*.[3]

The overwhelming consensus, however, was that Wells had pulled off a remarkable feat and done the public an important service. That everyone had minor reservations was inevitable, but the reservations were minor, the achievement major. To E.M. Forster it was a masterpiece, to Beatrice Webb 'a gallant achievement', good enough to prompt a reconciliation with the author. Carl Becker and John Harvey Robinson, pioneers of the New History movement in the USA, hailed Wells as a formidable ally. Half a century later A.J.P. Taylor thought the book was still the best general survey of history. As late as the 1990s another notable historian, Norman Stone, wrote admiringly of how Wells had avoided the Eurocentric and racist attitudes of his time.[4]

To many twenty-first-century academics a world history is absurd by definition. All such large-scale narratives – histories, religions, theories of progress – are phoney constructs and the only response possible for an educated person is to embark on a laborious, jargon-heavy and patronizing deconstruction of them. Wells's project is resistant to such stock responses, however. After all, it claims only to be an outline, not a definitive account, and it also has the merit of being largely accurate, at least in its descriptive aspect.

Wells remains open to criticism at a detailed level, for he sometimes regresses to a teleological nineteenth-century conception of progress, with the human race personified into one being that is gradually learning lessons and moving to its inevitable destiny. Some of this can be defended as rhetoric, but Wells's conclusion to his history, proclaiming the fairly immediate goal of a world state and reintroducing his favourite image of the human race as a child on a footstool, certainly underplays the scale of the challenge. He is sufficiently affected by the imperial perspective of his day to assume the world can be modernized and rationalized from above quite swiftly, if only fair-minded administrators take up the task.

These moments of Whiggery and glibness are, however, scrupulously offset by other features. As in his novels, Wells includes a measure of 'irrelevant' material to create a sense of contingency. He cites the chief books he has consulted so that readers can look them up and form their own perspectives, and he includes many of his advisers' comments as footnotes. Sometimes these elaborate Wells's ideas, but at other times they flatly contradict them or turn into arguments that remain unresolved, even though Wells usually allows himself the last word. In their resistance to closure, in fact, the early versions of the *Outline* may be judged intellectually tougher than the later ones, where Wells adopts a more conventional format, deleting the footnotes and removing the adviser credits. (Barker asked for his name to be removed when Wells condemned the British authorities over the Amritsar massacre of 1919.)

Wells acknowledges dozens of advisers and sources, yet one person felt hard done by because she received no mention: Florence Deeks, a Canadian feminist, who claimed the *Outline* was based on a manuscript she had submitted to Macmillan in Toronto. Her case went through the Supreme Court of Ontario, the Appelate Court in Toronto, the Privy Council in London and a petition to the King. Deeks lost on every occasion, but Wells still wound up paying more than £3,000 in legal fees. Despite his consistent success in the courts, a recent book has revived the Deeks claim and Wells is now assumed by some to be a notorious plagiarist.

In point of fact, Deeks made no claim that Wells copied a single passage or even sentence from her book. The allegations refer merely to cumulative similarities of structure, selection and phraseology, some of them frankly negligible. For example, discussing silks from China, Deeks refers to 'silks from China' and Wells to 'silks ... from China'.[5] If Wells somehow drew on Deeks's book, he did not siphon off her theories or her style, only historical points already in the public domain which she herself had taken from previous books. Plagiarism seems a strong word for cherry-picking information from a secondary text, even if there was some structural influence on the early part of the *Outline*. However, there is no evidence that Deeks's manuscript was seen by Wells, and the similarities are likely to come from common sources and overlapping outlooks.

If the *Outline* remains in many respects relevant and valid, it has none the less dated to some degree, as Wells himself foresaw it must. The earlier sections have suffered the worst, since continuing scientific research has drastically modified our knowledge of prehistoric times. For more recent periods, the issue is not so much accuracy as bias – the assumptions of an Englishman of 1920 being significantly different from those of a modern reader. Wells tries hard to think globally and build a cultural consensus, insisting that science and religion share a common vision of human unity and that narrow religious beliefs, often superstitious additions to the original teachings, will gradually be abandoned. Inexperienced in multiculturalism, however, he addresses believers with considerably less sensitivity than his goal of reconciliation requires, describing the Prophet Mohammed, for example, as 'evidently lustful and rather shifty' and siding with Sunni Muslims against Shiites.[6] It is not surprising that the book provoked protest marches and letters to the press.

In a world less interlinked and multicultural than today, such condemnation was a minority pastime; no fatwas ensued. Instead, the *Outline* took Wells to new heights of celebrity, feted and quoted everywhere. When Christopher Isherwood and W.H. Auden encountered Napoleon's tomb as schoolboys on a trip to France in 1922, their automatic reaction was to recite Wells's negative verdict on its occupant. Dashiell Hammett's 1930 crime classic *The Maltese Falcon* could refer to 'Mr Wells's history', and Sidney Greenstreet repeat the allusion to Humphrey Bogart in the 1941 film version in confidence that many would recognize it. To George Orwell, Wells's influence now became such that 'Thinking people who were born about the beginning of this century are in some sense Wells's own creation.'[7]

Wells was not complacent about the success of the *Outline*. Suspecting that many purchasers had never managed to finish the book, he followed it up with *A Short History of the World*, written in 1921 and brought out in October 1922. More assimilable, it was designed to be taken in 'almost as a novel is read'.[8] Wells's insistence that it was not an abridgement of the *Outline* is true enough, though his claim that it was 'planned and written afresh' is an exaggeration as there are many identical passages. Like the *Outline*, the *Short History* was revised several times over the years and remains in print today.

It is hardly surprising that, after his colossal labours, Wells felt the need for recreation. One of the most vivid and amusing accounts of an Easton weekend comes from Cornelia Otis Skinner in July 1920.[9] By this time the Ball Game had evolved into the even more manic 'Wells Game'. To their embarrassment, one of the visitors hit a 'Great Educationist' with the ball at close range (perhaps Sanderson of Oundle). The victim was penalized by Wells for hitting the ball twice in succession, the second time using his face. Throughout the weekend Wells was overflowing with vitality, speaking incessantly, taking an interest in everyone.

Among his other guests was Margaret Sanger, a leading American birth-control campaigner with whom he was enjoying a discreet but intense affair and who would remain his lifelong friend and supporter. She admired the way Wells's presence combined jocularity, brilliance, flirtatiousness and profundity and noted that, to be equal to his company, 'you must pull yourself up, keep alive every second'.[10]

Driving tours included one to Cornwall with Rebecca in April when, while visiting a friend's cottage, she slipped into an open cistern and gashed her arm clambering out. The wound turned septic, causing her to be placed in a nursing home in Redruth. Perhaps under the influence of the medication she was given, she experienced hallucinations and came to believe ever after that she had second sight. It all sounds remarkably like *The Soul of a Bishop.*

A trip abroad in June 1920 demonstrated the full extent of Wells's new fame. Accompanied by Gip, who was now almost twenty and preparing to study science at Trinity College, Cambridge (which Frank would also attend), he visited Czechoslovakia, a country created by the peace settlement. The pair were greeted at the Prague railway station by a brass band, newsreel cameramen and officials who made speeches in several languages, then driven to their hotel through cheering crowds. President Masaryk, a keen follower of British fiction, was eager to get advice from Wells on the latest books to read.

A more controversial trip followed in late September 1920 – to the Soviet Union, at the invitation of a member of the Russians' Trade Delegation. Until recently Britain had been backing the anti-Communists in the warfare that followed Lenin's coup. Churchill was still leader of a faction implacably hostile to the Reds, but the Prime Minister, Lloyd George, was minded to rebuild trading relations. Since Wells was a socialist and an enthusiast for Russian culture, who had been corresponding with Gorky about how he might best support Russian intellectuals through the crisis, he seemed likelier than most to give a sympathetic hearing to the Soviet regime, and as a popular commentator he might be able to swing public sentiment behind the normalization of relations, which was sought as eagerly in the Kremlin as in Downing Street.

Having secured a deal with Beaverbrook to publish his findings in a series of articles, Wells set off via Copenhagen and Stockholm. He was again accompanied by Gip, who – at his father's insistence – had received Russian lessons at Oundle, plus some home tuition by the editor and translator S.S. Koteliansky. The Wells expedition spent just over two weeks in Russia, mostly based at Gorky's apartment in Petrograd, the former St Petersburg. (Like the British royal family, the city had switched names during the war to avoid the embarrassment of sounding German.) Gip records their daily routine as a late breakfast, excursions until the early afternoon, further visits or rest after lunch, then dinner at seven, followed by trips to the theatre or vodka-fuelled discussions lounging about on divans. These discussions were mostly with the surviving members of the Petrograd intelligentsia who had taken refuge at Gorky's.[11]

They included Yevgeny Zamyatin, who was lecturing on writing techniques and editing English translations, Wells's books among them. He would supervise an edition of Wells's works published between 1924 and 1926, personally translating *The Time Machine, The Sleeper, The War in the Air* and *The Undying Fire.* Zamyatin's appreciative essay 'Herbert Wells' displays a comprehensive knowledge of Wells's work and notes how the scientific romances, with their mix of intellectual content and populist story, offer new possibilities to fiction.[12]

In his satirical dystopia *We,* which seems to have been drafted by 1920, Zamyatin took up the challenge of reconciling Wellsian machinery and modernist form. His book is set in a distant future in which human beings are reduced to numbers in a social equation calculated by the Benefactor and his secret police. The narrator, D-503, despite his efforts to conform, is led to challenge the system by his own divided nature and his love for a mysterious female rebel. His conflicting feelings are rendered vividly in an ironic first-person narrative that uses imagery from science, geometry and mathematics to take us into an alien mindset and defamiliarize both the uniformities of industrial civilization and the tyranny of Communism.

While in the West a gulf was opening between Wells's way of writing and modernism, in the East one of the most original literary talents of the century was demonstrating how to cartwheel confidently across it. Wells seems never to have read Zamyatin's maverick masterpiece, which was suppressed in its native land, though he possessed Zamyatin's translations of his own works. Orwell would read *We* in a French translation and copy much of the plot, minus the adventurous style, for his own dystopia, *Nineteen Eighty-Four.* (The plot was not quite original to Zamyatin, however, who seems to have assembled it from the *Sleeper* and, improbably, a short story by Jerome K. Jerome.)

Another significant presence at Gorky's was Wells's official guide and interpreter whom he describes in his account of the visit but does not name – Moura Benckendorf. Her claim that she was educated at Newnham College, Cambridge, was the first of many falsehoods to which the most enigmatic of his mistresses would subject him.

She had been born in 1892 and had married Count Benckendorf in 1911, later giving birth to two children, or possibly three if, as some suspect, her niece was actually a secret daughter. While her husband was away fighting in the Great War Moura threw parties at their estate that drew many officials from the British embassy. Wells reports that he had glimpsed her at a dinner party during his 1914 visit but had no actual recollection of this, only her word for it, which may simply have been a chat-up line. By 1918 Benckendorf was back home in Estonia with the children, while Moura was off in Petrograd and Moscow, engaged in clerical work for the

British and a love affair with the master spy Robert Bruce Lockhart. When someone passed all the Allies' cipher codes to the Bolsheviks, the finger of suspicion pointed at Moura.

During 1918 Benckendorff was shot dead at his estate, while a plot to assassinate Lenin proved to be a sting by the Russian security service that led to the arrest of large numbers of the regime's opponents, hundreds of whom were executed. Lockhart and Moura were among the more fortunate ones rounded up and released. She later claimed to have been pregnant with Lockhart's child and to have suffered a miscarriage. Those who believe she was a Soviet spy interpret her arrest as a cover for liaison with his interrogators. After Lockhart had been expelled from Russia Moura found a job in (or was assigned to) Gorky's group, where she had an obvious use to the authorities, ensuring that visitors received a favourable view of the Communist regime and that Gorky's reservations about it were kept in check. She certainly made an impression on Wells, who quickly invited her into his bed and records, in defiance of her reputation, 'I believed she loved me and I believed every word she said to me.'[13]

While it is unlikely that Moura could have survived the revolution without aiding the authorities, she also had to look after her own interests. In showing Wells around, she may have put a patriotic spin on the state of the nation, but, like many other women, she found Wells genuinely engaging and his potential use to her as an influential foreign contact would have done nothing to diminish his charm. When the couple parted at the Petrograd railway station they promised never to forget each other.

With Moura's help, Wells and Gip – sometimes exploring separately – sampled the sights of Petrograd, including schools, a hospital, the zoo and the two refuges for Russia's leading minds, the House of Literature and Art and the House of Science. Here lived such distinguished figures as the scientist Pavlov and the composer Glazunov, looking distinctly careworn and pallid compared to their British counterparts. Petrograd itself was more wrecked than London had been in *The War of the Worlds*. Wells was fascinated by the ruins, supplying both descriptions and photographs in his book, not least because he could imagine Britain similarly devastated if history delivered a second world war.

At the start of October Wells and Gip managed to get to Moscow, where Wells spent about ninety minutes at the Kremlin talking to Lenin in English. Wells arrived with a dim view of the Russian leader, whom during the war he had compared to the hated Sidney Webb, adding, 'He and the Kaiser ought to be killed by some moral sanitary authority.'[14] Lenin made a more favourable impression in person, though he was no more ready to embrace Wells's version of socialism than Roosevelt had been. This time it was Wells who spoke up for the reform of capitalism, while Lenin proclaimed the need for apocalyptic transformation. Wells was impressed by Lenin's willingness to think outside the little red box of Marxist doctrine but remained sceptical about what he would achieve. According to Trotsky, Lenin's comment on Wells was 'What a narrow petty bourgeois! Ugh! What a Philistine!'

A couple of days later Wells was back in the building where he had seen the Duma in session in 1914. It was now occupied by the Petrograd Soviet, which was noisily debating a peace deal with Poland. After the terms had been agreed, Wells was invited to address the gathering. He had been warned by Moura that this was standard practice, with the guest introduced in such a flattering way that he would feel obliged to reply in kind. His words would then be translated into extravagant praise of the Communist regime, published in *Pravda* and telegraphed as a press release to the rest of the world before the hapless speaker realized he had been tricked into an endorsement. Having been tipped off in advance, Wells not only had a measured speech ready for the occasion but Moura's translation of it as well. It stated that he was a collectivist but not a Marxist or a Communist; he believed that Russia should be allowed the freedom to follow its political programme but did not think it likely that the West would emulate it.

Wells knew a thing or two about propaganda. Having been fooled into reporting the Somme offensive as a famous victory, and having helped concoct disinformation at Crewe House, it is hardly surprising that he was alert to attempts at manipulation. After a visit to a Petrograd school where the pupils rated him as the greatest English author of all time, he insisted on being taken to another school where, it turned out, no one had heard of him.

Contrary to the impression sometimes given, therefore, Wells was not duped into naïve praise of Russian Communism. He took a firm line against Marxist theory, informing astonished Bolsheviks that the only class-conscious proletarians in Britain appeared to be 'a small band of mainly Scotch workers kept together by the vigorous leadership of a gentleman named MacManus'.[15] He insisted that the Russian revolution had no Marxist basis except in the minds of the revolutionaries, who were now going to have to construct a new society by trial and error, though whether, after their bloody and misguided beginnings, they would succeed remained in doubt. Wells suggested to his Western readers that the regime should be recognized meanwhile as the *de facto* government and a policy of détente adopted. Trade would bring a measure of stability to Russia and allow the West to dip into its collectivist experiments, which might turn out to have more links with the practices of big business in advanced capitalism than was generally realized.

Wells's stand seems a sensible one, yet the claim that he was 'soft on Communism' does have a foundation. He consistently legitimizes Lenin's regime by calling it the only possible Russian government, ignoring its rejection at the polls. Worse, Wells even defends the Red Terror since 'Apart from individual atrocities it did on the whole kill for a reason and to an end.'

By 1920 atrocity stories about the German army had been widely discredited, making it easy to believe that atrocity stories about the Reds were similarly exaggerated, especially as those who spread them were those opposed to the government. None the less, Wells's impression that most Russians supported the present regime was, we now know, wrong. Nor were its policies anything like as benign as he was led to believe. The Terror was not a regrettable passing phase in the restoration of order. By the end of 1920 Lenin's secret police had murdered 13,000–50,000 of their fellow citizens (exact figures are naturally hard to come by) and put a comparable number in prison camps, from which they were taken to be shot or drowned whenever reprisals were judged necessary.

On his return to Britain Wells arranged for some up-to-date books to be sent to the beleaguered Russian scientists and wrote a series of articles about his visit that were published in the *Sunday Express* during October and November 1920, producing a reported rise of 80,000 in the newspaper's circulation. A slightly fuller account appeared in book form as *Russia in the Shadows.* In general reviewers appreciated the reportage but questioned the analysis. Anti-Bolsheviks were outraged. In December Churchill laid into Wells in the *Daily Express*, castigating him for giving comfort to fanatics and murderers. Wells retaliated with the accusation that Churchill himself was a menace to world peace. He should be removed from public office so that he could put his talents to better use as a painter.[16]

Wells and Churchill were seasoned journalists whose professional abuse of each other had little impact on their friendship. Wells enjoyed a similar Bob-and-Bing-style relationship with Shaw and Chesterton, both sides benefiting from the publicity that their exchanges brought. This was not the case with the hard-line Catholic Belloc, any more than it had been with Henry James, nor with the socialism-hating playwright Henry Arthur Jones, whose letters to the press about Wells and Russia appeared in book form in 1921 as *My Dear Wells: A Manual for the Haters of England.* As its subtitle suggests, Jones was not so much engaged in political argument as a patriotic rant. Wells was particularly annoyed by Jones's habit of putting choice phrases in inverted commas as though they were incriminating quotations from himself. He eventually came to see Jones as afflicted and ceased to respond to him. This drove Jones to greater lengths of vituperation. Articles from Belloc, legal documents concerning the Deeks case and letters from Jones rained down upon Wells in the 1920s, but the latter's diatribes were probably the least welcome items in his post. He commented, 'A special thud in the morning always represented another bomb from Jones.'[17]

At the end of 1920 Wells moved to a new London base at 120 Whitehall Court. A year earlier Rebecca had moved to Queen's Gate Terrace, just over the road from Wells's old college in South Kensington, and he now joined her there for 'long intimate half-days and evenings'.[18] He also took her on further motoring holidays.

Yet their relationship remained a rocky one. As Rebecca's biographer Victoria Glendinning comments, while the pair had much in common, including a shared sense of humour and an outsider's view of the world, they also shared a self-assertion and lack of emotional discipline that led to constant angry outbursts. To Rebecca, enjoying Wells's company was 'on a level with seeing Nureyev dance or hearing Tito Gobbi sing', but she badly needed financial security and a father for her child.[19] Wells knew of no companion so appealing, but knew, too, that he could not indefinitely sacrifice their relationship to his messianic ambition to change the world, particularly since in doing so he relied on her emotional support. 'God has no thighs and no life,' he told her. 'When one calls to him in the silence of the night he doesn't turn over and say, "What is the trouble Dear?"' [20]

An admission to Rebecca that he had slept with Moura suggests he may have felt the relationship to be becoming expendable, as does the curious holiday arrangement they made for January 1921. While Jane was recuperating from a hysterectomy her husband and his lover decided they ought to go abroad for their own health, but they travelled semi-independently. The anaemic Rebecca went to Capri to stay with Compton Mackenzie's wife, falling out with her when the latter found she had been gossiping about her husband's infidelities. Wells, suffering from congestion of the lungs, travelled via Paris to Amalfi, where Rebecca met up with him at the Hotel Cappucini. They stayed there for a month, but their attempt at tranquillity was disturbed by their own repeated rows and by a drunken major who objected to the presence in the hotel of unmarried subversives. When Wells returned to London Rebecca moved on to Florence, where she remained for several weeks, meeting D.H. Lawrence.

While his parents were working at their relationship in the sun, six-year-old Anthony had been boarded at school. Wells added a codicil to his will acknowledging Anthony as his child and leaving him £2,000, upped the following year to £5,000. Concerned that Anthony was a poor reader, Wells also decided to move him from the Montessori establishment to a conventional preparatory school, from which he could perhaps follow his brothers to Oundle. Eventually he chose St Piran's, between Marlow and Maidenhead, but Anthony's problems were more the fault of his parents than his teachers, and he remained a troubled youngster.

Wells had been hoping to follow up the success of the *Outline* by going on a lecture tour of the USA. Thwarted by his lung trouble, he instead published the lectures in May 1921 as *The Salvaging of Civilization*. The book might better have been called 'The Salvation of Civilization', since it assumes that the world state necessary for future peace can be sustained only by a quasi-religious faith. Just as Jews, Christians and Muslims have their holy books, so cosmopolitans today need a compilation of texts for guidance.

To propose an arbitrary set of books as the bible for a world civilization was a project doomed to failure, because, though Wells had come to see the future as polyglot and multiracial, the canon he chose to aim at his American audience was heavily English-orientated. By the time he started to debate what to include – bits of Henley were in, but all of Shakespeare would have had to be relegated to the apocrypha – it became obvious that he was engaged in a private fantasy rather than a serious proposal. In 1922 Anatole France would declare Wells to be 'the most intelligent of the English', but it is unlikely that he had this project in mind.[21]

After the huge success of the *Outline*, Wells was again in danger of repeating himself with diminishing returns. A reminder that the greater part of his life was now behind him came with the death of his college friend Tommy Simmons on 19 August 1921. After pursuing a less spectacular but similarly constructive career to Wells – teacher, educational journalist, author of textbooks, school inspector – Simmons had been cut down by pneumonia at the age of fifty-six. Wells sent his widow £600. He also paid for her sons to go to Oundle. An unobtrusive tribute to his old friend would be worked into *Men Like Gods*.[22]

Despite the fragmented and problematic nature of his own family, Wells was trying to do his best by them, too. In August 1921, while Jane was off in her beloved Swiss Alps, he took Rebecca and Anthony on a seaside holiday in Norfolk. He paid fatherly attention to Anthony, producing stories, rhymes and picshuas about their excursions together. 'Oh, if only I could have married him,' recalled Rebecca half a century later, 'if Jane had died *then*, he was the best I ever got.'[23] The following month the couple took advantage of Wells's celebrity to meet Charlie Chaplin, who came to stay at Easton and took part in a charade as Noah. (He had second billing: Gip was God.)

Wells also kept up with Amber and Anna Jane. A postcard shows a performance of *Puss in Boots* at a dancing and painting school in Chelsea with an arrow pointing to 'A.J., aged 12'. The following year Anna Jane herself wrote to her mummy's friend, thanking him for a book (probably *A Short History of the World*, since she thought her history teacher would like it) and reciprocating with a stylized painting of a tree, fields and clouds.

Wells sent Amber payments to help support Anna Jane and also continued to fund Isabel, partly by paying her to do some of his typing. She now had a daughter, Joy (short for Joyce), and supplemented her husband's income with jobs of her own, briefly doing some probate work at Somerset House while the regular clerk was in the military, then buying a laundry in Kimpton, Hertfordshire, with £650 from her ex-husband. Though this was supposed to be a final subsidy, she would continue to benefit from Wells's guilt and affection.

In October 1921 Wells's reputation as a global historian at last won him a chance to go to the USA, not as a lecturer but as a special correspondent of the *New York World*, covering the Washington Naval Conference. This was the first-ever international disarmament conference. The ensuing treaties helped the Pacific live up to its name for the rest of the decade. Wells met President Harding, but was more interested in renewing his acquaintance with Margaret Sanger. He wrote that he wished to have as much 'sweet access' to her as possible, preferably without others around and in the scanty 'costume of a tropical island' – even though he was at the same time writing 'devotedly' to Rebecca.[24] Wells was delighted by the growth of his fame in America and told Rebecca that, when he went to see an African-American play, he got a standing ovation from the audience.[25]

Wells's twenty-nine articles on the conference were syndicated in many newspapers during November and December. In Britain the *Daily Mail* carried the first thirteen, but, after censorship from Northcliffe, Wells switched publication to the *Daily Express, Manchester Guardian* and *Glasgow Herald.* The book, *Washington and the Hope of Peace,* failed to impress the *Saturday Review,* which commented that few other journalists would have produced reports so self-centred, desultory and unconsidered.[26] Actually what Wells was doing was positioning himself as a reporter with a specific point of view, instead of claiming his ideas were unproblematically correct. Compared to Norman Mailer's antics in Washington forty-seven years later he seems a model of self-restraint.

None the less, like many a modern artist or politician, Wells had become rather cut off from everyday life and at times was in danger of disappearing up his own fundamental assumptions. Rebecca claimed he was vain, eccentric and boorish when they met up in Gibraltar in January 1922. He had sailed over from New York and now accompanied her to the Maria Cristina hotel, Algeciras, causing scenes and 'whining and nagging like a spoilt child'.[27] They spent February in Seville, where he worked on his next book, *Men Like Gods,* a science-fiction tale he had dreamed up in the USA. They then travelled to Granada, where she claims he walked out in the middle of a party organized in his honour by the composer Manuel de Falla. If so, this may well have been because he was tired and ill. They returned home via Madrid and Paris, arriving in Britain mid-March.

Wells himself showed some awareness of character deterioration in *The Secret Places of the Heart,* written early in 1921 and published in April 1922 to largely negative reviews. Its protagonist, Sir Richmond Hardy, a leading member of an international agency called the Fuel Commission, is struggling to conserve fossil fuels, fearing they will be exhausted before atomic energy can be harnessed. Despite this forward-looking role, it is difficult to warm to him, given his self-importance and contempt for others, including his wife and his mistress, the latter a political cartoonist with an unmistakable resemblance to Rebecca West, who rejoices in the *nom de plume* Martin Leeds.

Like his creator, Hardy is a serial adulterer who needs female attention to bring his experiences to life and make his work seem worth while. He cannot decide whether this has made him a pathological case, exploiting woman after woman by forcing them into the role of 'mistress-mother', or whether his promiscuity is an inescapable part of the romantic quest for the ideal, which has made him an exceptional achiever.[28] Though his name recalls Richard Gregory, Hardy is clearly a Wells surrogate and so is Dr Martineau, the psychologist to whom he goes for advice. Their dialogues – surely among the first in the English novel to allude to Freud – read like a Woody Allen script without the jokes.

Hardy and Martineau embark on a tour of some of the places Wells had visited with Rebecca and Anthony, combining scientific rationalism with a preoccupation with ancient sites and mythology that hints at the deeper sources of Wells's imagination. Anthony makes a guest appearance at Stonehenge. Along the way, to Martineau's distaste, Hardy has an affair with one V.V. Grammont, an American visitor with some resemblance to Margaret Sanger. Lacking a plot, the novel ends with Hardy's abrupt death, followed by emotive testimonials to his greatness from his wife and from Martin Leeds, who weeps over his coffin burbling, 'Speak to me!'[29]

Whatever its interest to biographers of Wells, *The Secret Places of the Heart* was a vanity project incapable of interesting the reading public. It is difficult to imagine it being published had its author not been so famous. Wells himself blew hot and cold about its merits, eventually concluding it was 'the worst bale of writing I ever committed'.[30] Published in the same year as the excellent *A Short History of the World*, the novel confirmed that an outstanding fiction writer with a sideline in social comment had now become a social commentator with a sideline in heavy-handed discussion novels. Wells's conversion into a historian had been a fabulously successful gamble but looked likely to mark the end of his career as an artist.

15
GODFATHER
1922–1926

On 15 June 1922 Wells was at University College, London, in the Botanical Theatre chairing what should have been a routine meeting of the National Union of Scientific Workers. Sanderson was due to speak on 'The Duty and Service of Science in the New Era'. Such was Wells's regard for the Oundle headteacher that he had persuaded Shaw and Bennett to enrol their nephews at his school. All three authors had turned out in March 1919 to see the pupils perform Shaw's *Arms and the Man*, with Gip in the very Wellsian role of Captain Bluntschli.

Sanderson, who was eleven years older than Wells, seemed very tired before and during his speech but agreed to take a few questions at the end. As Wells began introducing the discussion session, however, there was a commotion behind him. Sanderson slid down from his chair breathing hoarsely. Several medical men on the platform hastened to his aid, but in a few moments he was dead of a heart attack. Stunned, Wells closed the meeting and took upon himself the disagreeable task of informing Mrs Sanderson. As he was flagging down a taxi outside the Euston Square tube station, an earnest-looking man accosted him to ask if his friend's death had given him 'new views of immortality'. 'None whatever!' Wells replied firmly.[1]

In due course he agreed to help compile a biography of Sanderson to raise money for the school. Unfortunately, just as he had clashed with the Gissing family in his attempts to help them under similar circumstances, so he fell out with Mrs Sanderson. She expected a book that would emphasize her husband's achievements and stature. Instead, Wells seemed to be remaking him in his own image, stressing his humble origins, outsider mentality, religious doubts and youthful zeal for corporal punishment. Like many biographers, Wells also adopted a slightly critical tone towards his subject, which gave extra credibility to his passages of judicious praise but was not perhaps the ideal approach for a memorial volume. In December 1922 Wells withdrew from the official biography, published anonymously in 1923 as *Sanderson of Oundle.* His minority report, *The Story of a Great Schoolmaster,* followed in 1924.

Coming after Tommy Simmons's death, that of Sanderson was a further reminder of mortality. At a time when, by his own reckoning, average male life expectancy was 51.5 years, Wells's late fifties naturally became a period of consolidation.[2] He reread and amended his books for a collected edition, then penned his longest novel as a summation of his world-view. In a sense – in two senses – Wells could be said to have been marking time during this phase of his life, going back over existing achievements and also preparing himself for the milestone of his sixtieth birthday. Even so, his next half-decade would prove more eventful than most people's entire lives.

Having reflected on education in the Sanderson biography, Wells considered a book devoted to that subject, but nothing came of it. Instead, he produced a pair of hybrid scientific romance/novels, raising the story-to-discussion ratio in an attempt to win back the novel-reading public whose needs he had been neglecting for the previous seven years.

Men Like Gods, published in January 1923, dedicated 'to Florence Lamont, in whose home at Englewood the story was christened', concerns a demoralized journalist named Barnstaple who sets off in search of a rest cure. Thanks to a kink in the fabric of space-time, he instead enters another dimension, accompanied by a number of familiar-looking figures: Rupert Catskill (Churchill), Freddy Mush (Edward Marsh), Cecil Burleigh (Balfour), Lord Barralonga (possibly Beaverbrook) and Father Amerton (just possibly Belloc). Finding themselves in a pastoral world populated by beautiful nudes with names like Lion and Greenlake, and horrified at the socialistic immorality of it all, the other Earthlings attempt an armed coup. The utopians destroy them, then restore Barnstaple to his native era with his spirit renewed by the vision of paradise he has glimpsed. Admittedly the book was more entertaining than anything Wells had produced in the recent past, but, unguarded by the philosophical framework of *A Modern Utopia*, his vision of a perfect world as a snake-free Garden of Eden cum nudist colony inevitably looked rather preposterous.

The Dream, which followed in April the next year, was arguably more effective. Here, one of the utopians, Sarnac, has a dream in which he becomes a twentieth-century Englishman. His life story recycles material familiar from Wells's previous novels, but, presented from the anthropological perspective of a far-off Utopia, the first third of the book gives particularly powerful expression to Wells's anger at the narrow lives that entrap so many people. Unfortunately, as *The Dream* progresses, the narrative voice diminishes into nagging and the plot into melodrama, but the book was still welcomed by reviewers as something of a return to form and sold 15,000 copies before the first month was out.

Wells kept up his journalism with weekly articles for the McClure Syndicate. These were published in newspapers from September 1923 to September 1924 and collected as *A Year of Prophesying*. Considering their topical origin, the views they take have worn surprisingly well. Wells predicts an eventual war between the USA and Japan; he is disappointed by Labour's brief stint in power; he attacks the gold standard, Italian Fascism, the French occupation of the Ruhr and the lenient sentence handed out to Hitler after the Munich putsch; he advocates compulsory schooling to at least the age of sixteen, nursery provision for four-year-olds and global conservation policies to protect whales, gorillas and elephants.

From October 1924 the seal was placed on Wells's stature as a man of letters by the publication of his works in a limited edition of twenty-eight volumes. In publishing terms this made him the equal of Hardy and, more pointedly, James. All the novels and scientific romances were included, plus the bulk of the short stories. Many non-fiction books were featured in their entirety; others abridged or covered through extracts. Charles Scribner's Sons distributed a thousand sets of this Atlantic Edition in the USA, along with fifty presentation copies; Fisher Unwin released six hundred in Britain, plus twenty presentation copies. Wells signed the first volume of each set. He also supplied a preface for each volume and revised all the texts, correcting errors and tidying awkward phrases.

Wells was now at the height of his reputation, and despite his squeaky voice, thinning hair, short stature and increasingly stout shape, he remained irresistible to the literary 'groupies' of the 1920s. By their nature the brief episodes of casual sex that he called '*passades*' went largely undocumented. The most notable exception is his involvement with an Austrian journalist in her late twenties called Hedwig Gatternigg. She contacted him during the winter of 1922–3 to discuss developments in her native country, which was in such a dreadful economic state that it had had to be taken under the control of the League of Nations. He sent her a draft of his Sanderson biography, and, when she came to England in the spring and visited Wells and Jane at Whitehall Court, she volunteered to translate the book into German.

Though the job was eventually done by someone else, the proposal led to further visits in Jane's absence, and, as Wells found Hedy 'an extremely appetizing young woman', one thing soon led to another.[3] Before long he was worried that her obsession with him was out of control, but by his own account he could not resist her advances. A less generous interpretation could be that he was exploiting a disturbed woman for his own ends. Eventually he gave her the fare back to Austria and a letter of introduction to Anatole France, hoping she would transfer her activities to the Continent, but before long she was proclaiming her return to London over the phone. Wells told her he was very busy and directed her to Rebecca West, explaining that she was an eminent author who would soon be visiting central Europe.

One reason that Wells had let the affair get so out of hand was that his relationship with Rebecca was in terminal decline. Their annual driving tour of the West Country in the summer of 1922 had ended in tears and mutual accusations of intolerable behaviour. Wells had retaliated against her criticisms of his historical writing by telling her that her novel *The Judge* was an utter waste of her talent. It was clear to him that a break between them was overdue, yet the magnetic pull remained.

The list of self-accusations and tributes that follows, with its emotional swerves and abrupt laying of cards on the table, is reminiscent of the letters he had written Amber as their liaison disintegrated.

> Do realize that though I can curse you, be unfaithful to you as I was in Russia, goad you and scold you, abuse your work, bring fantastically absurd (self tormenting) charges of unfaithfulness against you and so [on] and so on – you have the catalogue – nevertheless I love you intensely. You have the most wonderful brain I have ever met, the sweetest heart, the most loving and delightful humour, wit abounding, on ten thousand occasions you have been supremely beautiful to me –
>
> None the less I think you are wise to disentangle the rest of your life from mine.[4]

In March 1923 Rebecca had declared she was indeed going to leave him – unless, that is, he divorced Jane and married her. Wells replied that the practical consequences of a divorce were unthinkable. Separation terms were not clinched, however, and, bound together by their responsibilities to Anthony, the couple continued to meet on a decreasingly amicable basis, Wells complaining in April that when Sinclair Lewis and his wife came to visit, Rebecca had cheapened herself by letting the American author 'slobber his way' up her arm.[5]

It was in this disgruntled context that Wells enjoyed the attentions of Hedy Gatternigg, then sent her off to meet Rebecca. Perhaps he hoped that encountering his sharp-tongued mistress would deter Hedy, while Rebecca would realize how much she must have been neglecting her Jaguar if he had to resort to such a dubious source of consolation. Rebecca would later claim that she had no glimmering of the relationship. Hedy's response is evident in her actions.

Having called on Rebecca on the morning of 20 June – the day after the Wells family celebrated Gip's graduation – Hedy turned up at Whitehall Court that evening in a determined mood. Wells had left instructions that she was not to be admitted, but, with a relief housemaid on duty, she managed to get through to his study. When Wells entered the room he found her stretched out on the hearth rug in a waterproof mac, which she flung open to reveal herself naked except for stockings and shoes. She demanded that he make love to her then and there or she would kill herself and produced a razor from her pocket to emphasize the point.

For once Wells did not rise to the occasion. Not only was she armed and dangerous, he was about to go for dinner with the Secretary of State for India. Feeling a need for witnesses, he opened the door wide and shouted for the maid to get the hall porter. While his back was turned Hedy began to slash the razor into her wrists and armpits.

Wells claimed that he managed to disarm her. Anthony West, who presumably heard earlier, oral versions of the tale, reports that it was the porter, a former sergeant major, who had the expertise and presence of mind to do the disarming.[6] Either way, the hapless Hedy – yelling 'Let me die!' and 'I love him!' – was soon bundled off to Charing Cross Hospital by the porter and two policemen. The bloodstained Wells, having recovered sufficiently from the shock, contacted his solicitor Haynes, who had her swiftly and discreetly transferred at his client's expense to a private ward at the Westminster Infirmary, then to a nursing home, where she was minded by Jane's friend Nancy Astor, Britain's first woman Member of Parliament, until she could be sent home. The doctors reported to Wells that this was not the first time Hedy had done her suicide act. She had previously pulled the same stunt on a British attaché in Vienna and seemed to have enough medical knowledge to avoid doing herself permanent harm. This must, at least, have lifted some pressure from his conscience.

With Hedy safe, Wells's next task was to silence the press before a scandal erupted. A version of the story appeared in the *Evening Star* on 22 June, whence it made its way abroad to newspapers such as the *New York Times.* By 23 June several British newspapers were carrying notices and the *Star* had a follow-up article. However, Wells and Rebecca had many influential friends in Fleet Street. Lords Beaverbrook, Rothermere and Riddell all requested fellow-members of the Newspaper Owners' Association to exercise discretion, and the matter was soon buried. By July Wells felt secure enough to lie to the critic Desmond McCarthy that he was a random victim and that the incident might have happened to any prominent man.[7]

As for Hedy, she eventually married and was able to introduce her husband to Wells. She last contacted him in June 1942, by which time she had become a widow. Still haunted by the image of his bloodied rug, Wells noted nervously on the bottom of the letter, 'Sounds more dangerous this time'.[8]

Back in 1923, shaken by the episode into a show of solidarity, Wells and Rebecca spent all of the following day together, taking in lunch at the Ivy in Covent Garden, followed by a theatrical first night. While touring Europe the following month, Wells scheduled a week with Rebecca at the Hotel Klinger in Marienbad where she was taking the waters for her anaemia. For her, however, the presence of 'Mr West' ruined an otherwise peaceful break, while for him their once stimulating relationship had competition from higher things – literally so.

Wells was keen to travel around Europe using the new airline services, better still to spend some time in the open cockpit of a small plane. Even if his aircraft 'danced like a kite on its string' and, hitting turbulence, 'dropped a few score feet', he revelled in the exhilarating, swooping perspectives that he had only been able to imagine when writing *The Sleeper, Tono-Bungay* and *The War in the Air.*[9] Unfortunately, Wells's desire to soar across Europe that summer was repeatedly brought down to earth.

An oil leak caused his initial flight from London to stop at Lympne – the least eventful place in the world, according to *The First Men in the Moon.*[10] When he finally got to Amsterdam the connecting flight failed to show up and Wells had to complete his journey to Berlin by train. Reduced to rail travel for most of his holiday, he compensated himself by three glorious days of flying over the mountains of Slovakia. He paid a call on President Masaryk in Topolcany at the start of August, then found the only way to return west was by yet another train, from Prague. Setting off for the capital by car, he twice ran into ditches, cutting his forehead. Fortunately, he managed to reach an aerodrome and get a plane for Prague the next day. However, his return flight across the Channel was delayed, then suffered a loss of power in one engine that required a return visit to Lympne. Wells got an old friend from Sandgate days to put him up for the night; the other passengers went in search of a slow train to London. If international flight was a key development for globalization, Utopia was clearly some way off.

In September, while Jane and Gip were in Zermatt, Wells belatedly took Rebecca and Anthony for their annual summer holiday, visiting Eastbourne and Swanage. However, by now Rebecca's mind was on Lord Beaverbrook as a potential new sugar daddy and Jaguar's attempts to sweet-talk Panther ('Wants his Black Pussy. His *dear* Black Pussy') fell on deaf ears.[11] On 20 October, in what they both recognized as a decisive break in their relationship, Rebecca set off on the *Mauritania* for a lecture tour of the USA. Wells occupied himself with 'a few minor infidelities'[12] and, more usefully, by setting up a trust fund for Anthony and opening Children's House, a day nursery designed by Voysey in the working-class London district of Bow, a community resource that remains in use to this day.

Wells suffered from bronchitis over the Christmas. On the advice of Bennett he sailed south to the warmer air of Portugal early in January 1924. He remained until March at the Hotel Mirimar, near Estoril, working on the Atlantic edition and a novel provisionally entitled *Sargon: King of Kings.* He also socialized with the Galsworthys, who were staying at an adjacent hotel, and in Rebecca's absence enjoyed a leisurely affair with a 'very pleasant red-haired widow' whose name, according to Wells's appointment diary, was Dorothy Petrie. After the *amour fou* of Hedy, her companionship was refreshingly civilized, and he remained in touch with her for many years.

In March Wells returned home via Paris, where he rendezvoused with Jane, who had again been in the Swiss Alps, this time with both Gip and Frank. Rebecca returned from America around the same time, satisfied that she had managed to step out from under Wells's shadow as an author in her own right but dismayed that in her absence Anthony had taken to cutting up his sheets and talking of conversion to Catholicism. What would Sarah have said? The two parents did their best, such as it was, to approximate a normal family, reconvening for trips to the cinema and other outings with Anthony. Perhaps remembering the comfort he had obtained from Surly Hall, Wells took Anthony for lunches at hotels on theThames.

To judge from his latest novel, however, the member of his family most troubling him at this point was Anna Jane. She had turned fourteen just before he set off for Portugal and was well on the way to becoming an intelligent and attractive teenager. In an undated letter from the early 1920s Amber assures Wells:

> you would like A.J. She is such a darling – and oh, thank heavens, not ugly! In fact I went down to the bathing cliffs at Cap d'Antibes one day this summer and found her posing for a series of posters for the town of Antibes to the disgust of some Gaumont film stars. The camera man said that mademoiselle was a lovely diver and perfectly made and with perfect movements and she patted my shoulder and seemed to consider it all in a day's work. She thinks she manages me very well, and I rather think so too. Our sideboard is covered with her swimming cups. She has your buoyant way of tackling life – in fact I am very grateful to you for her. One cannot feel old & dejected with such a sunny, generous creature about.[13]

Given Wells's need for female approval and his emotional investment in the younger generation as the world's potential saviours, Anna Jane must have seemed to him like the most enchanting of timebombs. For now she was oblivious to her true identity, but, if and when the secret came out, how would she react? Would she be delighted or disgusted to find that she was a love child of the famous H.G. Wells?

Christina Alberta's Father, as *Sargon* became when published in book form in 1925, is a tale of two daddies. One is Preemby, whom Christina Alberta has been told is her parent; the other is Devizes, her biological father. Devizes is Wells as he would like others to see him: a tough-minded progressive thinker meriting trust and admiration. Preemby is Wells as he fears being seen, perhaps most of all by himself: a fantasist whose dreams of changing the world are without rational foundation. In essence the story elaborates an observation Wells makes of himself in one of the Atlantic prefaces: 'Temperamentally he is egotistic and romantic, intellectually he is clearly aware that the egotistic and romantic must go.'[14] Fortunately for the reader, temperament is in the ascendant here, and, despite the author's apparent intentions, it is the crankily imaginative spirit of Preemby that dominates the book.

From childhood Preemby resists his fate through a 'general habit of living a little askew from actual things', epitomized by his Polly-like habit of mispronunciation and his interest in myth.[15] Set free from responsibility by retirement and the death of his wife, Preemby becomes convinced during a seance that he is the reincarnation of the King Sargon lauded by Wells in the *Outline* and sets about inaugurating a golden age by ending war, the exploitation of women and the unjust distribution of wealth.

Deep down Preemby has doubts about his role as prophet, but he dares not acknowledge them. To admit the truth would be to admit that there is no unseen order sanctioning his idealism and self-respect. Rather than abandon the Sargon project, he is willing to undergo martyrdom in an insane asylum. Eventually Preemby is rescued by a young writer called Bobby and 'resurrected' to a type of new life. Devizes persuades Preemby, who is now dying, that his idea of Sargon (and by implication all religions) symbolizes a real truth – that the human race is collectively a king of kings who can save and rule over the world. At the same time Christina Alberta discovers her biological father is actually Devizes, who thus replaces Preemby as the eponymous hero of the book, neatly shifting the basis of its radicalism from imagination to reason.

As he approached sixty Wells became increasingly attached to the notion that he was a Devizes rather than a Preemby, that science underwrote his utopianism and that his fiction was different in kind from that of a James or a Conrad because, with whatever reservations, it was a revelation of truth. Inevitably, the more he cast himself as a prophet of science, the less he was able to recognize the imaginative origin of his ideas and subject them to appropriate discipline. *Christina Alberta's Father* escapes the problem because it gives the characters a chance to dissent from the author's script. Christina Alberta is too much like Anna Jane and Amber to submit to the wishes of her literary godfather. At the end of the book she refuses to take on the messianic role Wells has inscribed in her name. Speaking for the residual dissident within Wells himself, she dismisses 'Sargonism' as a piece of male theology just like all the other religions and isms. 'It is an intellectual game that men have played to comfort themselves. It makes no real difference. Tragedy *is* tragedy, failure *is* failure, death is death . . . I don't want to serve – anything or anybody.'[16]

The acknowledgement of conflict between individual and collective aspirations is restated from the other side when Bobby abandons his attempts to be a novelist to go and help some birds in the garden, leaving his blank manuscript to be blown 'suggestively' on to the unlit fire.[17] This, the book's concluding image – possibly borrowed from Dos Passos's *Three Soldiers* – tacitly accepts that the prophetic political commitment espoused by Wells can only damage his artistry; as proof of which, he then went on to write *The World of William Clissold.*

Christina Alberta's Father was well received but as a minor work; *Clissold*, in contrast, was a big, ambitious novel, published in three volumes and unmistakably intended as a major event in Wells's career. After three books in a row in which he had made some effort to prioritize storytelling, it was time for a grand statement of his opinions. Volume I was published in September 1926 to coincide with his sixtieth birthday, with Volumes II and III following at monthly intervals. There was also a signed, limited edition for collectors. Reviewers were scathing. To L.P. Hartley it was 'thin, flaccid and unorganized', to Lawrence 'a mouse's nest', not to be spoken of in the same breath as *Tono-Bungay*.[18] Even to those who enjoyed the book (a small but distinguished group, including Keynes, Shaw and Mencken) it was valuable as a compendium of ideas, not as a novel.

Unlike *Tono-Bungay, Clissold* really does use a scientifically trained narrator as an excuse for an artistically incoherent monologue. Unlike *The New Machiavelli,* it does rely for interest on polemic, disguised autobiography and guest appearances by well-known contemporaries. And, just like *The Secret Places of the Heart,* it ends with the pompous hero's death, followed by praise of his Wellsian qualities. Many reviewers, having rightly trashed the novel as all talk and no do, took the chance to reflect on how its vices typified Wells's work. More and more the early Wells was being read through the lens of the later, reclassified from a gifted novelist to a commentator who artlessly fictionalized his ideas. The literary talents that had first brought him to fame, and which had enchanted his critics back in their childhoods, were not only being taken for granted but discounted.

One reader who understood that beneath Wells's intellectual generalizations lurked artistic strengths that were intuitive and mythopoeic, and still occasionally capable of breaking through the closed system of his ideology, was Carl Jung. The great psychologist, who had met Wells during 1924, was flattered to find he made a guest appearance in *Clissold* and praised *Christina Alberta's Father* in an 'outburst of enthusiasm'.[19] Wells intuitively understood that religious awareness needed to be updated for the era of science and that this could best be done through a deeper understanding of psychology. It is likely that Wells did not recognize how much of his own mentality he had put into Preemby, but Jung certainly did, slyly commenting, 'one almost imagines you had seen such a good fellow . . . from very close quarters'.

A comparison of Jung's ideas about persona and prophecy with those of Wells is extremely revealing, as we shall see in Chapter 17, but Jung had no intention of making such a critique himself. He was much more interested in winning his famous associate's backing, requesting an article of endorsement for a Swiss newspaper in order to raise his status and help him get funding for an assistant. Wells obliged with a letter of praise, which – when published alongside the *Clissold* extract – seems to have done the trick.

Having attained an eminence few men of letters could equal, Wells was able to play the role of 'godfather' for many individuals and causes – not least the Labour Party, which he joined early in 1922. The Liberals were now in decline, their reduced share of the vote spread too thinly across the country to carry weight in the British electoral system. (If they had listened to Wells and introduced proportional representation while they had the chance, British political history might have been very different.) Labour had grown to be the leading anti-establishment party, and, despite some reservations, Wells now threw his considerable reputation behind it. In May 1922 he stood for Labour as Rector of Glasgow University, and in the General Elections of November 1922 and December 1923 as parliamentary candidate for London University. Since most students of the period had privileged backgrounds, it is not surprising that Wells came bottom in each of these polls (truth to tell, he would have been horrified to have won), but standing gave him the opportunity to make speeches and issue pamphlets in the Labour interest.

In taking on the role of elder statesman, it would have been prudent to put his bed-hopping days behind him. The Gatternigg episode had been a timely warning. Now the end of the affair with Rebecca created an opportunity to put his love life into more conventional order. Being Wells, he did not do so. He felt, as his contemporary Yeats did, a deep connection between literary and sexual potency. His creativity was intimately bound up with his ability to attract and win the admiration of the women he valued.

After the companionship they had enjoyed while writing the *Outline,* Wells and Jane had by now resumed semi-independent lives. He joined her at Easton most weekends, but spent the weekdays at Whitehall Court. On the principle of 'If you can't beat 'em, join 'em', Jane, too, had a London flat, in Bloomsbury, where she could have private time for her own thinking and writing. Wells continued to love and support her, as he did his first wife, who spent three weeks at Easton recuperating from an illness in March 1923. Later in the year Isabel sold her laundry and persuaded Wells to lease a house in Roundwood Lane, Harpenden, Hertfordshire, where she could live as his tenant. He continued to make her frequent gifts of money, covering, for example, her daughter's school fees.

But Jane and Isabel, however congenial they might be, were known quantities. Wells yearned for the exotic and unpredictable. In particular, his thoughts kept returning to Moura. With the help of Gorky, she had succeeded in escaping from Russia in 1921 and made a brief marriage of convenience to a Nicolai Budberg, paying off his gambling debts in return for entitlement to an Estonian passport. Throughout the 1920s Moura travelled around Europe as literary and business assistant to Gorky, who had been forced into exile by Lenin for his criticisms of Bolshevik tyranny. Every so often Wells would receive a letter from her, never quite explaining what she was up to, never quite arranging to meet him. On at least two occasions he tried to find her in Paris but without success. 'It is a big town to look for someone in it,' she commented teasingly. 'And then – one must know so well that someone's tastes and – do you know mine?'[20]

With Moura elusive and Rebecca hostile, Wells had an urgent vacancy for a paramour of comparable qualities: a strong-minded woman with progressive attitudes, someone who could supply him with observations and stimulating ideas and who could challenge his thinking yet in the end be won over by the force of his arguments and personality. By September 1924, when he visited the League of Nations Assembly in Geneva, he was in a state of desperation. Every dark-haired woman he saw turned into Rebecca. Hallucinations of her appeared across rooms or on balconies. He fired off a telegram suggesting a trial reunion for the winter, for Anthony's sake, but Rebecca was having none of it. Yet, even as he fretted, a new lover was homing in on him with the resolution of a heat-seeking missile.

Her name was Odette Keun and she was a socialist travel writer, a profession admirably suited to her restless, combative personality. The daughter of a Dutch diplomat and his Italian–Greek wife, she had been born and raised in Constantinople (present-day Istanbul). After studying there and in the Netherlands she entered a convent in Tours, but, proving temperamentally ill-suited to be a nun, she found an alternative vocation writing novels and articles in Paris. She become the mistress of a law professor and accompanied him to North Africa, where she continued to write, did humanitarian work in the Algerian desert and transferred her affections to a French army officer. He subsequently dropped her, but her love life gave her the material for a novel, *Une Femme Moderne,* which she dedicated to Wells.

Like any other free-spirited young woman of her era, Odette was a Wells enthusiast. She took a copy of the *Outline* with her when she set off for Georgia to report on the fighting between the Mensheviks and the Bolsheviks. Along the way she married a Georgian prince, though not in a form recognized by Dutch law. After the defeat of the Mensheviks she relocated to Constantinople, only to be arrested by the British as a possible Russian spy and deported to the Crimea. The Russians in turn suspected she was a British spy, but after much hardship she managed to get to Moscow and obtain permission to return to Paris, thoroughly disillusioned by her experiences. 'Just as once the Catholic religion had robbed me of a god,' she wrote, 'so, now, had the Bolsheviks robbed me of Communism.'[21] She wrote up her adventures in French as *Sous Lénine,* then in an English version, *My Adventures in Bolshevik Russia.*

Wells wrote an appreciative notice of her book in the *Adelphi,* June 1923. This resulted in a series of letters from Odette, urging him to come to Paris and 'take her'. Hearing he was in Geneva, she moved into a hotel there and phoned him with a further invitation. On arrival he was shown up to a dimly lit room, where a 'dark slender young woman in a flimsy wrap and an aroma of jasmine . . . flung herself upon me with protests of adoration'.[22]

Wells's visit to Geneva left him unimpressed with the League of Nations, which looked just as ineffectual as he had feared; in contrast, Odette made a very positive impact indeed. She was not only passionate about her literary hero but, once he got a good look at his stalker in the light, she turned out to be an animated, eccentric and entertaining character, well suited to taking his mind off Rebecca. Within two weeks they were living together in France at a farmhouse called Lou

Bastidon, near Grasse. This soon became Wells's winter residence, and it was here that he wrote *Clissold*, which he dedicated to Odette and in which she features as Clementine.

Wells certainly cared for Odette, but he never seems to have loved her as wholeheartedly as he loved Jane, Amber or Rebecca, and he soon realized that her outrageous turns of phrase and splenetic temperament were a potential source of embarrassment, especially where visitors were concerned. Yet the generous dash of spice she brought into his life was oddly pleasing, and he liked the idea of having a wife in England and a mistress in France.

Towards the end of 1926 Wells purchased a farmhouse to the south of Lou Bastidon as the site for a new, larger home with a well-appointed kitchen, six bedrooms, six bathrooms and a garage for two cars. Maurice and Félicie Goletto would be his principal servants, with Maurice doubling as chauffeur. Wells roughed out a plan and hired a Dutch architect and a local builder to implement it. The new home, which was completed during 1927, became known as Lou Pidou, a contraction of *le petit dieu* – the little god – Odette's mocking nickname for her messianically inclined partner.[23]

The publication of the Atlantic edition had offered affluent readers what was effectively the Wells canon, as the writings of his later years would never match his early work in impact. Common readers now got an equivalent in Benn's Essex edition, which appeared in twenty-four volumes during 1926–7 with a range of titles more selective than the Atlantic's. Benn also reissued the bulk of the short stories and *The Time Machine* in 1927 as a single volume called *The Short Stories of H.G. Wells*, later known as *The Complete Short Stories*.

Many authors would have seen this moment in their career as the time to retire, or at least slow down, glad of the opportunity to write at leisure and produce more considered books. As a model from within the family there was Fred Wells, who had returned to Britain in 1921, married his cousin Edith Neal and settled at Southbourne. Having left the drapery business behind in South Africa, Fred proceeded to enjoy his retirement for the next thirty-three years. Brother Bertie, however, had no such retirement plan. Outside the utopian enclaves of Lou Pidou and Easton, the world was in a dangerous state. If it was determined to stagger into political catastrophe, economic recession and war, then it would certainly not be because *le petit dieu* had failed to offer it the chance of salvation.

16
LIFE AFTER JANE
1927–1930

It is a peculiar feature of the Wells story that his mistresses make so much more of a showing than his wife. While Dorothy, Violet, Amber, 'little e', Rebecca and Odette sported on a rollercoaster of conspicuous emotions, Jane quietly cultivated her garden. One can only speculate whether she felt resentment at her husband's intense companionship with other women. Though she was on friendly terms with Odette, surely she must have experienced some sense of rejection when her husband dedicated *Clissold* to his latest flame.

Meanwhile: The Picture of a Lady – written during 1926, published in 1927 – features a heroine whose quiet courage and lucidity recall Jane and may therefore represent some acknowledgement of her. Unfortunately, it is not a successful novel. A number of dull characters convene at an Italian villa, share predictable views about the state of the world and engage in token romantic entanglements. Aldous Huxley, grandson of Wells's old professor, had recently been making a reputation for himself doing this sort of thing in a much livelier fashion. The book did nothing for Wells's literary standing, though its critique of current events had substance.

In Britain, as one character reports in a series of letters, the left had fumbled the mid-1920s recession and backed itself into a so-called 'General Strike', actually an ill-thought-out gesture against pay cuts in Britain's biggest industry, coal mining. Having offered false comfort to the miners and false hope to Marxist revolutionaries, the strike soon ended, leaving the public resentful and the miners worse off than ever. In Italy the left had made an even worse job of the Fascist challenge, delivering not only a general strike but riots, looting, factory occupations and a refusal to cooperate with centre parties, all of which helped bring about Mussolini's ascent to total power. The heroine of *Meanwhile*, Cynthia Rylands, has to intervene to rescue a former government minister from gun-toting blackshirt thugs. For the inclusion of this episode both Wells and his book were banned from Italy.

His stand was a bold one when *Il Duce* had been given an honorary knighthood for being a political role model – compare Ceauşescu and Mugabe in more recent times – and could claim such weighty admirers as Shaw and Churchill. The latter, now no longer a Liberal but Conservative Chancellor, was pilloried in Wells's novel for his inflammatory interventions in the General Strike.

When the Fascist-quelling Cynthia is upset to discover her husband philandering with one of their guests, a male friend explains to her, ostensibly in a modern spirit of frankness, actually from a regressively Victorian perspective, that 'the role of a wife is not to compete and be jealous, but to understand and serve and by understanding and serving rule'.[1] Perhaps Wells was feeling uncomfortable about installing his latest mistress in a second home in France, virtually reprising the escapade with Amber that had caused so much distress nearly twenty years earlier. If, through Cynthia, Wells was belatedly paying a covert tribute to Jane, then he was also tagging on to it a defensive message about his adulterous behaviour.

During March 1927 Wells made a point of meeting up with Jane in Paris for a week and taking her to a prestigious lecture he was giving at the Sorbonne. Realizing that she would have to talk to celebrities such as Marie Curie, she secretly took lessons to improve her French and was able to surprise everyone, including her husband, with her unexpected fluency in the language.

In his lecture 'Democracy Under Revision' Wells notes that Communism, Fascism and the Kuomintang in China all resemble the samurai of *A Modern Utopia*. Though he despises the three movements, they may be a sign that it is time for the moderate left to organize itself along the lines he had advocated. The lecture was published as a booklet by Leonard and Virginia Woolf, then included in a collection of Wells's articles, *The Way the World Is Going*. This book opens with reflections on the increase in the human life span, indicating that, having put his sixtieth birthday behind him, Wells was again looking to the future.

After accompanying a now exhausted Jane to London, he headed back across the Channel, as did Gip, who on 20 April had married his father's secretary, Marjorie Craig, at the Strand Register Office and planned a walking tour in central France by way of a honeymoon. Frank, too, was due to marry his fiancée, Peggy Gibbons, in October. However, all their plans were about to be broadsided. On 10 May Wells received a telegram from Frank telling him that an exploratory operation to investigate Jane's ongoing ill health had revealed her to have inoperable cancer. She would be dead within six months. He wrote to her at once. 'My dear, I love you much more than I have ever loved anyone else in the world & I am coming back to you to take care of you now & do all I can to make you happy.'[2]

Jane, being Jane, already had the situation in hand. She quizzed the doctors until they gave her a clear statement that she had cancer of the peritoneum, reassured them that they bore no blame, then set about methodically putting her affairs in order. There is no reason to think that she reproached her husband for any aspect of his past conduct, though Wells's friends knew that this would very much be on his mind. One of the closest, Christabel McLaren (formerly Christabel Aberconway), wrote to him as soon as she heard the news:

> People who think that 'taking liberties with life' means that one doesn't care, – and care deeply and with tender love – for a husband or wife, are just unimaginative

fools. – You won't in these coming months let the thought of those 'liberties' worry you or allow them to become over-important, will you? It would spoil the last months for you both; and I am certain she has always known that if you had been different in one way you would have been different in all ways. She has loved you very much and been proud of you – *that* is what you must remember.[3]

Jane was given X-ray treatment in London to check the spread of the cancer, but it seemed to do more harm than good. Thereafter the family concentrated on palliative care, turning down suggestions for miracle cures from Shaw and Bennett. Though weakened by her radiation therapy, Jane was able to remain on her feet for a few more weeks. Even after she had to use a wheelchair, so long as she could endure car journeys she visited friends, and in August, a month after her fifty-fifth birthday, she went to a hotel in Felixstowe for a final holiday by the sea. Friends also visited her at Easton where she talked to them of her gardening and reassured them with white lies that she was making progress. When there were no visitors, she read and listened to records. Wells recalled,

We would sit about together in the sunshine listening to Beethoven, Bach, Purcell and Mozart, and later, as she grew weaker and less capable of sustained attention, we would sit side by side in silence in the dusk and find loveliness and interest in watching a newly-lit wood fire burn up from the first blue flickerings.[4]

With her pain regulated by an opiate, Jane slept more and more. Though she was shrinking away, she kept up appearances as best she could, spending a whole hour one September day with her hairdresser. She also kept up her concern for others, ordering the felling of a tree that was darkening the servants' bedroom, posting a birthday present to a niece and ordering the breakfast for Frank's wedding, which was scheduled for 7 October. By 6 October her sleep was terminal. She woke briefly around 5.30 p.m. when Frank came home from work, then her eyes closed on the world for the last time. An hour later she ceased to breathe.

The family decided to go ahead with Frank's wedding at the Dunmow parish church, pulling it forward to 9 a.m. to keep the occasion private and low key. Jane had left instructions that she wished to be cremated, and this was arranged for 11 October at Golders Green Crematorium, where Wells had taken the boys out of curiosity almost twenty years before, not thinking that they would one day return with this more sombre purpose.

Following Jane's wish, nearly all those who attended avoided funereal black. Shaw had an amber handkerchief; Wells himself arrived in a dark blue overcoat. Virginia Woolf exclaimed in her diary, 'Poor Jane! It was desperate to see what a dowdy shabby imperfect lot we looked.'[5] Wells had put together a secularist service for the occasion, beginning with the organist playing Franck's 'Pièce Héroïque'. With the exception of Wells himself, who was already sobbing his heart out, everyone sat silently while the classical scholar T.E. Page read the tribute from a desk facing the coffin. The eloquent address emphasized that behind the public face of 'Jane' there always remained an unknowable Catherine, quite separate from her life with her husband. Towards the end the congregation stood while the pale grey coffin slid through the doors into the furnace chamber. The final words were read, commending 'charity, faithfulness, and generosity of living' (one need not be cynical to note that 'faithfulness' here cannot have had quite the conventional sense); the organ played the Bach 'Passacaglia' that Jane had loved, and the people began to file out.

Shaw advised Wells to take his sons and follow the coffin. 'I saw my mother burnt there. You'll be glad if you go.' He was right. V.S. Pritchett once remarked that in Wells's most characteristic fiction there are always fires.[6] From the forest fire that destroys Weena in *The Time Machine* through the Beltane festival of *In the Days of the Comet* to the burning house that liberates Mr Polly, flames burst out to challenge, destroy and cleanse. However terrible its effects, fire ends the stasis and paralysis that are its author's worst fear. So it was now.

> The coffin was pushed slowly into the chamber and then in a moment or so a fringe of tongues of flame began to dance along its further edges and spread very rapidly. Then in another second the whole coffin was pouring out white fire. The doors of the furnace closed slowly upon that incandescence.[7]

Wells reports that he went home relieved that there was no lifeless corpse left to moulder in the ground.

The funeral eulogy was incorporated in the introduction to *The Book of Catherine Wells*, Wells's selection of his wife's stories and poems which was published in May 1928. These show Catherine to have been a sensitive author whose subjects and style were almost programatically distinct from her husband's, focused not on issues and action but on relationships and some rather heavy-handed ironies of fate.

'I do not know what I would have been without her,' Wells admits in his introduction. 'She stabilized my life. She gave it a home and dignity.' Now it was over. Jane had timed her departure to perfection, doing her duty up until the moment that Gip and Frank had found wives. The great literary project begun in Mornington Road by 'Mr Binder' and 'Bits' had run its course and – seventy books later – was essentially done. Wells's supportive home vanished almost overnight.

He remained – albeit in an odd, Wellsian fashion – a family man. He kept an eye on the welfare of Jane's mother Pinnie, sending her flowers and presentation copies of his books. She wrote to him ten days after her daughter's death: 'You really are being an *affectionate son* to me dear H.G. and I value it with all my heart.'[8]

Gip, thwarted of his French honeymoon, had gone to the USA on a study tour during August. While there he told an American interviewer that he had no political or literary ambitions but was spending his time on the 'fascinating study' of clams' gills.[9] He would eventually become Professor of Zoology at University College, London, the institution where Griffin had researched invisibility and where Sanderson had died.

Frank took up work as a freelance designer and writer for stage and cinema. He, too, visited the USA, working as an extra while he studied lighting techniques at the Famous Players–Lasky studio in New York. In the summer of 1928 his father supplied him with scripts for three short films, *Bluebottles, The Tonic* and *Daydreams,* which were made in 1929 by Ivor Montagu with Charles Laughton in the cast. Later Frank tried to arrange options on some of his father's famous books, writing a scenario for *The War of the Worlds,* for example, and carrying out model work and location research before the project was shelved.

While Gip continued the scientific and Frank the artistic sides of Wells's legacy, Anna Jane looked likely to take up the political activism, enlisting, like her mother before her, at the London School of Economics, where she helped run the student branch of the Labour Party as well as the swimming club. In the distant future Anthony would pick up his father's literary legacy, becoming a novelist and critic, but for the time being the youngest remained the most troubled of his four children.

The move to St Piran's had been only a limited success. Forbidden to tell the truth about his parents, Anthony had concocted stories that led to his being ridiculed and bullied. Just as his father had palled up with Bowkett, so Anthony managed to find friends among marginalized Jewish pupils. His circumstances improved when Rebecca arranged a move to the more liberal Hall School in Hampstead, but he still saw very little of his parents and had to call his mother his aunt. She in turn referred to him as 'H.G.'s brat'.[10] At least from 1926 she took him for an annual summer holiday on the Riviera. In December 1927, when Anthony visited Easton for Christmas, Wells set up a trust that would pay him money at the ages of eighteen, twenty and thirty, the value of the pay-outs raised at the insistence of Odette.

In 1928, aged fourteen, Anthony moved on to a top private school, Stowe, but was soon diagnosed with tuberculosis and sent to a sanatorium in Norfolk. Wells paid him a visit and took him to a nearby holiday spot, Wells-next-the-Sea, where inevitably they posed beside a signpost. His illness reclassified as pneumonia, Anthony began again at Stowe in 1929. He cherished a letter from Wells declaring he was proud to be his father, and he was delighted when his father visited the school and acknowledged him openly, something that he could do now with no fear of embarrassing Jane.

Rebecca became so alarmed at the growing bond between Anthony and his father that she feared Wells might attempt to gain custody and took moves legally to adopt the boy herself. This removed the stigma of illegitimacy from his official papers. When Wells raised doubts about her fitness as a mother, the judge found in her favour but stipulated that Wells had a right to be consulted over Anthony's education and holidays and that, in the event of Rebecca's death, he would become a joint guardian.

Without his family, Wells spent less and less time at Easton. He took two apartments, one in Paris at 124 Quai d'Auteil (now Quai Bleriot), in which Odette set up a salon, the other in London at 614 St Ermin's Hotel, Caxton Street, near the Houses of Parliament. By 1930 he had resolved to get rid of Easton completely and at the same time he swapped St Ermin's for 47 Chiltern Court, Baker Street, where he would be a neighbour of Arnold Bennett.

For now his main residence remained Lou Pidou, but life with Odette was becoming less and less congenial. Jane's death had unbalanced their relationship by opening up a possible vacancy for a third Mrs Wells. Rebecca was out of the running, her affairs with wealthy men culminating in marriage to a banker in 1930. Odette remained keen to secure the post. However, her outrageous behaviour, which had once made her such an entertaining foil to Jane, would scarcely be an asset in the wife of a public figure. Aldous Huxley's brother Julian, who saw the couple at close quarters, characterized her as 'articulate, unreticent, explosive' and noted how their relationship alternated fierce quarrels with passionate reconciliations.[11]

Anthony experienced this all too clearly on his first visit to Lou Pidou. He was insecure and self-conscious as only a fourteen-year-old boy can be and as subject to adolescent feelings of homosexuality as his father had been at a similar age. As Wells was driving him to Grasse with Odette, she decided to put their visitor at his ease by chatting about this and that, mentioning along the way how she and his father had first met when she seduced him in a darkened hotel room. If she noticed Anthony's discomfort it must have meant little to her, for a few days later she returned to the topic of sex while they were having lunch with several visitors, including the Aga Khan. Fifty-five years later Anthony could still recall her words vividly (in a striking accent which reminded him, appropriately, of a French farce). 'Loooook! Anthonee is blushing . . . Can it be that you know nothing of these theeengs, that you are still a virgin?'[12]

Wells's attempts to make her desist were useless. On a further car journey, while Wells did his best to evade a series of trucks carrying the lavender crop to the local perfume factories around blind bends, Odette quizzed their young guest relentlessly about potential mates, male and female, and advocated an affair with an older woman as the best way for him to start on an activ e sex life. Unable to stop her, Wells pulled the car over and dragged her off for a blazing row in which she blamed him for neglecting Anthony and leaving him to grow up with too much female influence. Eventually the two made up and returned to the car laughing, Wells assuring his son, 'We have these little tiffs'.

In fact Wells was frequently aghast at her antics, which included recounting intimate details of their sex life to visitors, saying 'fuck' in polite company – then blaming him for teaching the word to her – and violently scolding the servants. (As the son of a servant Wells was especially sensitive on this score.) On good days she was a delightful companion, but the good days were now in a minority. Wells reports that she was positively 'deranged' for a day or two every month, possibly implying she was a victim of premenstrual tension.[13] The thought of letting her loose in London horrified him. The impact on his gardener, maids and secretaries, let alone his friends and acquaintances, would be catastrophic. While in her eyes she was the third Mrs Wells in waiting, the role he thought fittest for her remained that of a mistress or, as he later put it bluntly, a 'prostitute-housekeeper'.

By 1928 Odette had developed a sinus inflammation that required two very painful operations to fix. She was angry that, while she was suffering and in need of support from her partner, Wells went off to write in London and Easton. Her attitude is understandable, but Wells, from his point of view, was determined to produce needful books in whatever span of years remained to him and presumably felt he had done his duty by paying for the operations. Jane, he must have reflected, would have understood his position and maintained a stiff upper lip.

Odette sought revenge by having an affair with her doctor and mentioning it frequently to Wells, though the effect of this was weakened when the doctor dumped her. Wells claims that she was so enraged she bought a pistol and talked of shooting the philandering physician – plausibly enough, given that she had previously issued similar death threats against General Charles Harington, whom she blamed for her deportation in 1921, purchasing a Browning pistol for two hundred francs and proposing to blow him away before turning the gun on herself. On this occasion Wells tried to quell her 'feverish disorder' by driving her round Brittany and Switzerland and forcing himself to take an interest in the novel she was working on, *La Capitulation*.

In the circumstances it seems unlikely that the Wells–Odette liaison could have gone on for many more years, but it was about to receive a mortal blow. Wells was asked by Antonina Vallentin, who would later write a biography of him, to contribute to a series of talks by distinguished foreigners at the Reichstag. In April 1929 Wells left Odette in France, fearing her casual conversation might cause an international incident, and set off for Berlin to deliver 'The Common Sense of World Peace' on the 15th. The lecture was published shortly afterwards by the Woolfs (and in a German edition translated by Vallentin) and was later included in Wells's 1932 collection, *After Democracy*. Among the many who gathered to hear him read it out was the woman of his dreams, the elusive Moura Budberg.

She had been at large in Europe for eight years, working for Gorky, though the French secret service suspected her of spying for the Russians and perhaps even for the Germans, too, presumably by reporting on the activities of Russian exiles. Historians of espionage have suggested that she renewed contact with Wells because the Kremlin wanted to influence Western opinion-formers, but it seems equally likely that, a decent time having now elapsed since the death of Jane, she genuinely wished to resume the love affair she had begun in Moscow a decade earlier.

Like the liaison with Odette, it began with a letter at Wells's hotel. Moura wanted to see him; she would try to get a ticket for the lecture. When the rest of the audience dispersed, he saw her waiting, an attractive *femme fatale* still, though with novel streaks of grey in her hair. For the rest of his stay in Berlin they were lovers, and they spent all the time they could with one another, confiding solely in the diplomat and biographer Harold Nicolson. Wells would remain with Odette for four more years but was secretly in ever closer contact with Moura.

What Wells concealed from Odette, however, was as nothing to what he had been concealing from his first biographer – named, improbably enough, G.H. Wells. Presumably Geoffrey Wells had been partly drawn to his subject by the lexical resemblance, but, as a long-term admirer of his namesake's work who had left school at fourteen and turned to authorship because of ill health, he had other points of identification, too. In the past Wells had grumbled about G.H. getting articles published by allowing editors to think he was his son; none the less, he gave the *Sketch for a Portrait* his cooperation, granting the author detailed interviews, putting him in touch with numerous sources and ultimately supplying an introduction. This involvement enabled Wells to have considerable control over what came to light and ensure the biography presented him in a way with which he was reasonably comfortable.

In return for this cooperation Wells was able to enforce a distancing change of name on G.H., who obliged from 1927 by adopting the pen name Geoffrey West. Now Wells was hoist with his own petard. Having concealed his links to Rebecca and Anthony, he had no grounds to object to the new name, though in fact it added to the confusion, continuing the suggestion that G.H. was his son – just removing his legitimacy.

The *Sketch* appeared in 1930, dedicated by West 'to Catherine Wells, a most gracious memory'. Notwithstanding the limited amount of information available to its author, it remains one of the best-written, most perceptive books in the field, as well as the one closest to the events it recounts. Keeping his nerve in the presence of the great man, West manages to combine a sympathetic account of the life with a firm critical assessment of the work. He concludes that at least a dozen of Wells's books will continue to be read into the twenty-first century, powered by their author's imagination and the quality of his best prose, but that Wells's achievement is finally limited by a mismatch between intuition and intellect. Unable to commit fully to either, Wells can neither face up to life in a realistic way nor come to terms with the spiritual aspects of human experience. Instead, he offers a future-oriented identification with the species as an unsatisfactory substitute for both.[14]

Wells ducks this well-made point in his introduction, characterizing himself as a 'journalist', denying any 'inner conflicts' and claiming that he has never put much effort into the art of writing. He is 'the absolute antithesis of Mr James Joyce', a remark prompted by a meeting with the latter in Paris during 1928. Initially Wells had offered Joyce some kind of financial or promotional support, but he soon thought better of it. In a follow-up letter he explains to Joyce, 'I've an enormous respect for your genius dating from your earliest books and I feel now a great personal liking for you but you and I are set upon absolutely different courses.'[15] He praises the 'extraordinary experiment' that would eventually become *Finnegans Wake* but can see no justification for the effort Joyce is demanding from his readers. He ends: 'My warmest good wishes to you Joyce. I can't follow your banner any more than you can follow mine. But the world is wide and there is room for both of us to be wrong.'

In querying the accessibility of Joyce's work in progress, Wells was speaking for most readers then and since, but his claim to be Joyce's antithesis is a stronger and stranger statement. Downplaying the years of work he had put into becoming a writer, Wells presents himself as a peculiarly artless artist, a scientifically trained analyst of current affairs whose thinking is disciplined and rational yet who happens to possess intuitive literary skills. Wells wanted to be feted as the author of past masterpieces, yet to evade literary assessment of his present work, just as he wanted to be received on equal terms with creative artists yet to outgun them by evoking the authority of science.

During the 1920s he pressed Richard Gregory to find some way in which he could become a Fellow of the Royal Society. Though he was offered honours by the British state, and even shortlisted for the Nobel Prize for Literature (being nominated by Sinclair Lewis, who had named his son Wells), FRS was the only title he coveted. Its award would convert his literary career into an impressive digression, wipe out the guilt of his undergraduate failure and make him, at least in his own eyes, an incontestable champion of truth.

Needless to say, Wells still remained keenly interested in literature and the other arts. He wrote letters to the press defending Stravinsky's 'Les Noces', calling for a new edition of Tolstoy's works (he subsequently supplied an introduction to *Resurrection*) and deploring the police seizure of Radclyffe Hall's lesbian novel *The Well of Loneliness*, an action masterminded by his old antagonist Joynson-Hicks. He sent Wyndham Lewis fan letters in praise of *The Childermass* and *The Apes of God*, went to a clinic in Vence, near Nice, to pay his respects to the dying D.H. Lawrence and hailed the advent of a new author, J.B. Priestley. 'Beware of "dissertations",' he warned him. 'That fellow Wells has always had a tendency to let his dissertations get out of hand.'[16]

Wells's greatest claim on the scientific world in this period was *The Science of Life*, a massive project on which he worked between 1925 and 1929 in collaboration with Julian Huxley and Gip. In 1927 Julian actually resigned his professorship in Zoology at King's College, London, in order to focus on the writing. Collaboration did not come naturally to Wells, but it was reasonably successful in this instance because there was a clear division of labour. Julian supplied the bulk of the first draft, Gip the rest; Wells edited, rewrote and managed the overall perspective. Even so, it was not an easy process, with Wells threatening to cut Julian's pay or even cancel the whole project if he did not speed up and produce better drafts.

The Science of Life appeared in fortnightly parts during 1929–30, and in three volumes in 1930. As its mode of publication suggests, it was intended to be a companion piece to the *Outline of History*, but, though it sold well, it could not match the earlier book's success. Given its subject, it was impossible to duplicate the narrative momentum of the *Outline*, and, despite Wells's heroic efforts as editor, there remained rather too much detail. None the less, *The Science of Life* was a formidable achievement, fulfilling Wells's ambition from his University Correspondence College days to make the discipline of biology, in its widest sense, available to all comers. Subsequent growth of knowledge has overtaken the book, though it is not quite as dated as one might suppose. There is even a section on 'The Ecological Outlook', discussing the growing impact of the human species on the environment, its destruction of other species and the importance of alternative power sources.

Before the project was over Wells had already embarked on a third outline, investigating what he provisionally called *The Science of Work and Wealth*. He meanwhile restated his views on changing the world in a shorter book called *The Open Conspiracy*, dedicated to Odette's brother-in-law Daniel Gerbault whose idea it was. Revised several times and also reconceived as *What Are We to Do with Our Lives?*, it calls for educated people of goodwill to create a better world rather than accept the bias of the institutions in which they work. This call to arms was somewhat vague in application. Wells's enemies have denounced it ever since as a call for world domination by an anti-democratic elite; his supporters have interpreted it as a boost for a civil society realized today by bodies such as Greenpeace and Amnesty International. Beatrice Webb caught its cloudy Fabianism nicely when she told Wells it was 'a magnificent introduction to the work of the Webbs'.[17]

In his effort to make his ideas more widely understood, Wells now turned to the new medium of broadcasting. The BBC had tried to lure him on to the radio for four years but had no luck until they made it clear he would not be censored and sent their offer via a female representative. For the first talk they paid him 50 guineas (later the fee became 100 guineas) and threw in a pre-broadcast meal for guests including Leonard and Virginia Woolf, plus a bottle of whisky to revive his spirits after the ordeal. Wells's first half-hour talk, 'World Peace', which incorporated some of his Reichstag address, went out on 10 July 1929. Like most of his radio speeches, it was printed in the BBC's journal the *Listener*, and, together with four of his other pieces, a version of it appeared in the *After Democracy* collection. As a speaker Wells was no match for Shaw or Churchill. His faint, slightly prissy voice, carefully enunciating its way through the text, adds nothing to its impact. Nevertheless, the broadcasts kept his ideas before the public and helped maintain his reputation.[18]

In the midst of all this didacticism, Wells unexpectedly came up with his most entertaining piece of fiction since *Mr Polly*, dedicated 'to the Immortal Memory of CANDIDE' and published in 1928 under the slightly cumbersome title, *Mr Blettsworthy on Rampole Island*. Arnold Blettsworthy is brought up by his rector uncle in an apparently secure liberal environment, but after his uncle dies disillusioning experiences lead him to a nervous breakdown. He goes on a therapeutic sea voyage, only to become trapped on Rampole Island among its fantastically unjust and savage inhabitants. Those who break taboos are subject to the 'reproof', a blow on the head from a two-hundredweight club set with sharks' teeth. The resulting corpses, euphemistically known as the 'Gift of the Friend', are the islanders' chief source of food, though they regard cannibalism as the greatest vice of their enemies.

As the tribe's Sacred Madman Blettsworthy tries vainly to become the prophet of a more straightforward and generous way of life but cannot persuade others there is an alternative to the island's wilful squalor. His status as a tolerated eccentric is used by Chit the soothsayer as a way to overcome obstructive customs, but only in order to practise warfare more efficiently, rather as Wells felt the liberal views of writers like himself had been exploited for propaganda purposes during the Great War. Eventually Blettsworthy escapes in a highly unexpected way. He comes to realize that he has been living in a delusion and the island he is on is really Manhattan. The stone goddess brandishing a threatening club is the Statue of Liberty; a cage of patriarchal sloths appears to represent the US constitution and a council of hairless old men the Supreme Court.

All minds have to select and interpret experience, but in his trauma Blettsworthy's mind has gone one step further and set up a protective fiction, locating the unbearable aspects of reality in a remote fantasy world. The full horror of existence is revealed when Blettsworthy becomes a soldier in the Great War and loses a leg in battle, then returns to the USA to be demoralized by the Sacco and Vanzetti trial, against which Wells had campaigned in *The Way the World Is Going*.

The book is an engaging piece of satire, but from a biographical point of view the most interesting feature is the equation of artist and madman. The fear of losing touch with reality and becoming trapped in one's own creation is a recurrent theme in Wells's fiction, starting in *The Desert Daisy* with Buss locked away in an asylum. In Wells's adult work we encounter the time traveller swallowed up by the fourth dimension, Griffin lost in invisibility, Cavor attaining the Moon only to be imprisoned there for ever, Chatteris dragged beneath the sea by the irresistible mermaid, Wallace passing through the door in the wall to his death. The obsessive recurrence of the situation suggests that Wells feared his powerful imagination might overwhelm him and cut him off from the scientific and political developments that another part of his mind thought vital for guidance. Hence his resolve, recorded in the last chapter, that 'the egotistic and romantic must go' and his retreat from the vivid particularities of the early work to the abstractions of the later.

In *Blettsworthy*, as in *Christina Alberta's Father*, enough of the 'egotistic and romantic' is retained to allow some uninhibited creativity, but when Wells goes into his preaching mode artistic integrity quickly fails. It is hard to believe that the man who wrote *Blettsworthy* could follow it up the next year with *The King Who Was a King*. This scenario for an imaginary film is a clunkingly patronizing piece of propaganda with an uninteresting plot and cardboard characters.

The Autocracy of Mr Parham, published the following year, with illustrations by the cartoonist David Low, is a more spirited affair, revisiting the theme of self-delusion. An academic historian named Parham dreams he becomes the British Mussolini. His supporters' team includes Joynson-Hicks (very thinly disguised as Jameson Jicks) and Lord Beaverbrook (Bussy Woodcock), a newspaper owner who finally turns against him. Another opponent, ironically, is Oswald Mosley (Osbert Moses) who had been a notable player of the Ball Game at Easton and was currently a Fabian Labour MP but who two years later would found the British Union of Fascists. If Mosley read the book he certainly missed the point. Parham, unlike Mosley, soon takes control of the country but provokes a second world war by a stupid decision to invade Afghanistan. The book has its striking moments – notably the surrealistic bombing of Trafalgar Square – but is underdeveloped because Wells fixes on Parham to the detriment of the other characters yet does not empathize with him sufficiently to round him out. This unacknowledged ambivalence would inhibit further novels as he moved into the 1930s and the worst economic upheavals of the century.

Even before the Great War Germany had overtaken Britain in manufacturing, while the USA was out-producing Britain, Germany and France combined. The war, which wrecked all the European economies, made the USA into the world's wealthiest nation, until in the autumn of 1929 its investment bubble burst and the country toppled straight from the Jazz Age into the Great Depression. The other capitalist nations swiftly followed it down, adding to the disaster by competitive devaluations and trade barriers. The long-running financial crisis that ensued also devalued liberal democracy. In Britain the normal party political system was quickly replaced by a coalition government. In less stable countries people turned to dictators, who delivered a degree of order, prosperity and self-respect but at a shockingly high price.

With his usual foresight Wells had tackled economic issues as early as 1928 through the third volume of his educational trilogy. He had again enlisted two collaborators, Edward Cressy and Hugh P. Vowles, and harassed them to raise their game, making clear that if they couldn't take his criticism they should get out of the study. When it became evident during 1929 that they couldn't, he paid them off and paused to rethink the book.

Cressy accepted the settlement, but Vowles complained to the Society of Authors. Instead of mediating, its secretary G. Herbert Thring decided to back Vowles. Wells reacted with fury, producing a 74-page booklet to set out his case, *The Problem of the Troublesome Collaborator*. Eventually, during 1930, despite bloody-mindedness on both sides and with much urging of restraint by Shaw, the affair was settled. Wells had to do some paying out and apologizing but also had the final word with another booklet, *Settlement of the Trouble Between Mr Thring and Mr Wells*.

Needing more compliant collaborators, Wells turned to his womenfolk. Amber took over much of the drafting, Odette the kind of researching and editing role that Jane had performed on the *Outline*. Graham Wallas also helped with some of the writing and editing.

The Work, Wealth and Happiness of Mankind was published in the USA in two volumes during 1931 and in a single volume in Britain in 1932. It was packed with information and ideas, from harrowing descriptions of imperialist atrocities to speculation about whether the gigolo would make a good role model for the liberated woman. (Wells rather thought he might.) Lacking a unifying story or argument, Wells found it difficult to bring his wide-ranging material into an effective shape. The world depression does not appear until page 393 of the British edition, and Wells's advocacy of Bretton Woods-style international institutions to regulate global trade and finance does not discuss how they might be established against national self-interest. An impressive compendium, the book lacked the focus to make an impact comparable to the *Outline*.

In the new decade of confrontation, cynicism and glib ideology-mongering, Wells looked like an anachronism. True, he would call his 1932 collection of articles and speeches *After Democracy* and include a talk to a Liberal summer school calling for 'Liberal Fascisti . . . enlightened Nazis', but the emphasis clearly falls on the adjectives rather than the nouns.[19] Wells does not want Liberals to emulate their enemies' vile policies, only to be equally purposeful and united. His aim is to get beyond the limits of party politics, unequal opportunities and press barons who control the news agenda in order to achieve a more effectively open society, not to replace it with what, with reference to Russia, he scathingly sums up as an 'ego-centred autocrat, with a political party disciplined to death, a Press bureau, and a secret police'.[20]

To the extremists Wells's desire to discard class conflict and nationalism was petty-bourgeois nonsense. To those at the political centre, patiently waiting for market forces to restore equilibrium, his idealism was irrelevant. Sidelined as a thinker, Wells fared little better as a writer. Literary fashion may have swung back towards socio-political engagement, but Wells's best work was now behind him and his prose style seemed dated alongside the more streamlined, modernist-tinged work of Huxley, Waugh, Maugham, Orwell and Greene, let alone adventurous American authors such as Steinbeck, Dos Passos and Faulkner. Wells's utopianism seemed ever more irrelevant in a world moving towards a second world war.

17
AN INFLATED PERSONA
1930–1934

Hunger marches, Nazi rallies, the bombing of Guernica, the Munich peace conference: these are the newsreel images that define the 1930s. Wells followed such events closely but at the same time inhabited a privileged world on which the Great Depression and deteriorating international relations had little direct impact. From the biographical point of view, at any rate, the most interesting events in Wells's life during the early 1930s are his peculiar, sometimes outrageous, personal relationships.

While Wells was collaborating with Amber on *The Work, Wealth and Happiness of Mankind*, he was also becoming closer to their daughter, enjoying a series of meals and outings with Anna Jane from the summer of 1930. Wells decided he would bestow some money on her for her twenty-first birthday, but, unimpressed by her boyfriend Eric Davis – or, more likely, jealous of him – he worded the settlement so that even after marriage she alone would have access to it. On 6 March 1931, prompted by her plans to set off with Eric for South Africa once she had obtained her Economics degree, he sat down to compose a letter breaking the news to her that he was her biological father (quite possibly she knew this already) and asserting his parental authority. Their correspondence, which has not previously been published, repays a detailed look.

> My dear,
>
> I think that you and I have to come to perfectly frank dealings with each other. Let us clear up the situation.
>
> For nineteen years I have been doing my best to ignore your existence because of various humiliating and baffling things that occurred when you were born. Now I have met you I love you very much. I do not know how much you may have felt or guessed in the past year but the fact is you are my daughter, half your genes are mine, and you are bone of my bone and flesh of my flesh. Gip and Frank Wells and also Mr Anthony P. West are your half brothers as well as your half brother and your half sister on your mother's side. So you have a very much wider family than you used to think. It's all very good stuff, I can assure you. And I want to see you have a pleasant and happy life *and* play a part of some importance in the world.
>
> Everybody who knows about you says you have a very good fine mind. Lasky [*sic*] talks of you in superlatives. You've got to take care of that mind and make the

utmost use of it and I want to standby you *for that.* I don't in the least mind your having a lover. Considering your parentage that was to be expected. I understand all about that. But I don't want all this lovely physical recreational stuff to dominate your life or stand in the way of you realizing your individual possibilities. And it seems to me that following Eric Davis to S. Africa will just about smash up all that.

I don't know for sure. I'm quite ready to take in new aspects of the matter but that is how I feel about it.

Let us be quite clear about what you propose to do. You are going to put your career in a secondary relation to Eric's. Well, before I rejoice in that I want to ask some questions about him. (You are quite free to show what I am writing here to him. The questions I am asking are quite as much for him to answer as you.)

First, *what sort of love is it that allows him to accept the sacrifice of your very considerable possibilities?*

What is he? He didn't impress me when I met him as a very outstanding personality. What is there in him that justifies his taking you out of your proper work? Lasky tells me he is intelligent but no great wonder. A.P. is of the same opinion. K[?] thinks very little of him. If it is put to him, what can he say on his own behalf, that he should use up your very promising and delightful life? If he is really good stuff and sure of himself he ought to follow his own career and let you follow yours wherever it may lead you. He would know you were there in the world for him so soon as he made good.

I won't multiply questions. What I have asked goes to the root of the matter.

I don't think this objection to Eric as your 'object in life' is a matter of pride with me. You are I think of a very good strain and I want to see you all that you might be. But you do not understand what weak things you women are and how you need to be protected. There was once a lovely and beautiful woman who married Pember Reeves and he enclosed her, thwarted her and deadened her. Your mother was a flame at twenty and now she's just a memory of what she was then. (I'll make her work and come alive again if I can.) Now here you are at twenty one proposing to adapt all your living to a young man, who as far as I know, has shown no trace of moral or intellectual initiative or distinction. I put it to you. Still more do I put it to him.

I shall be back in London early in April and then we must talk. After all it is a long time yet before anything positive is to be done. Anyhow you must do a good degree. You owe that to yourself and everyone.

I'm getting better of my flue [*sic*] – slowly, but Odette Keun who lives with me here has been in bed for four weeks and is still very ill. I'm distressed about her.

Very much love my dear,

Yours, H.G.[1]

It is understandable that, having had no hand in Anna Jane's upbringing, Wells was eager to intervene before she made decisions she might later come to regret. Even so, the letter catches him close to his worst. Surely the paternity information would have been enough trauma for one piece of post to carry, without attempting to revise Anna Jane's life as though it was a draft from Vowles. In trying to show concern, he not only patronizes her but insults her boyfriend and her family, projecting on to them all his anxiety about the damage he himself might have done to Amber's career.

After six days had passed without a reply Wells penned a more conciliatory card. To his relief Anna Jane was prepared to maintain friendly relations, but she had no intention of giving up her trip to South Africa or her Eric. Safely back at Lou Pidou in May, Wells tried again, with a rather more reasoned tone. Perhaps a bit of financial support and some caring words about her mother's sacrifices would give him leverage.

My dearest Anna Jane,

Very well. I wish I could spend an hour inside your nice little brain and find out whether it is love or wanderlust or what is driving you south. You are making this journey against my doubts and questionings. I enclose a cheque for fifty pounds which will make your journey easier. I want you to go second class, so make the transfer straight away please. I shall arrange that there shall be a credit for you at some Bank in Cape Town for fifty pounds. This you are to use *only* if you want to return. It is to keep your line of return open. There are a score of reasons why you may want to come back. It will not be cheap to come back, but it may be liberation.

Be very careful how you behave in Cape Town. It is a small place compared with London, a place of aged ideas and ruthless intolerance. Don't lay yourselves open to indignities. Be pedantically correct in your outward lives. You have no idea how dangerous a spiteful press or some academic scandalmonger can be, and how impossible it is to clean up a publicity mess once it has begun.

I don't like to think of your career beginning with even the appearance of following someone else about the world. If you do not return almost immediately, it seems to me you will have to marry Eric. This means that the scale and quality of your life will have to be determined by the scale and quality of his. You break altogether with any possibility of a career as my brilliant god-daughter in London, who has fought the world on her own. You can't have a double alliance. You will have to start in at his level. I don't know enough of Eric to gauge him, but I can't for the life of me see that he is, as you call him, a 'generous creature'. He seems to me to have grabbed something very lovely, with a considerable risk of spoiling it.

If things go wrong, if the unexpected meets you at Cape Town, at once *or later,*

> cash in this credit and come home to your mother and to me. We are letting you experiment very freely with your life. Amber Pember made great sacrifices to get you and to give you as good a training and education as possible. Neither of us wants you to be anything but happy, but you *do* owe *her* a certain measure of success in your life. You were not born and framed and loved to be a handy little wife for Eric.[2]

Anna Jane's reply was robust. Having thanked him for the cheque and agreed to upgrade her boat travel to second class, she put him firmly in his place:

> I happen to regard my life as something entirely my own; it would be of little use if I could not. I have chosen to go south, and the action is not mere whim. Please do not think that you are 'letting me experiment freely'. I have chosen and you cannot interfere.
>
> I cannot help it, that you should dislike my marrying Eric. I am fully aware of its implications. I regret that you should so misunderstand my relationship with him. I am satisfied about it, and that is all that is relevant to this discussion, I think.
>
> I would like to thank you also for placing money in Cape Town for me. I do not expect to touch it. I will do so only upon the conditions you lay down, but I do not want it to put me under any obligations when I return.
>
> Do give me advice, but let me decide. Sorry to hear you've been ill.[3]

Sure enough, she never touched his cheque, which remains to this day in pristine condition in the Wells Archive, drawn from the account at the Westminster Bank in Wandsworth which he had opened on his marriage in 1891.

Wells knew he was beaten. He could square up to dictators like Lenin, denounce Church and King and, when the mood was on him, shout down virtually anybody, but there was one person whom he simply dared not cross because her good opinion meant so much to him. 'Very well,' he wrote to his daughter. 'I accept my dismissal as a parent.'[4] Not daring to contradict Anna Jane, he had to make do with venting his frustration in a brief postcard to Amber in which he went so far as to call their daughter 'a pig headed little bitch'.[5]

Yet if Wells's overbearing approach was typical of him, so was the swiftness with which he put away his vexation. Even after Anna Jane perkily announced, 'I married Eric the other day – the authorities were most surprised when we stated we were not Christians,'[6] he was less angry at being thwarted than sorrowful at losing a daughter. A father rarely finds it easy to hand over his princess to a young man who cannot possibly be worthy of her, and to part with Anna Jane after enjoying her company so briefly must have been a sad wrench. Wells summed up his feelings when she postponed her return in 1932:

> I'm sorry (and much more so is our Amber) that you're going to be away from us for so much longer. Life moves fast at your age and when you and I meet again you'll be a different person and you'll approach me at such a different angle that I shall be a different person too. But all the same we are agreed you are right in taking that job.[7]

The job was lecturing in Economic History at the University of the Witwatersrand in Johannesburg. She was also working for change in South Africa through the Joint Council of Europeans and Bantu. She stressed to Wells the importance of engaging with manual workers, hinting that his version of socialism was too remote from the struggles of ordinary people.[8] Anna Jane and Eric returned to England during 1933. From 1934 to 1936 she lectured at the University College of the South West of England (later Exeter University), while he became Director of Education for the western region of the BBC.

While Anna Jane had got her life well under control, Anthony's progress remained uncertain. He disliked his stepfather and was not really flourishing at Stowe, where he lost several friends to expulsions. When he left the school in 1930 he was unqualified in Latin and, even with help from a private tutor, could not meet the entry requirements for Oxford. In any case, he had no real wish to stay in the education system.

Thanks to Rebecca, his next move was to sign up with a psychoanalyst. Anthony followed the therapist to Harvard, but eventually returned to Britain and became an art student. This seems to have been the cure he really needed, as thereafter, despite a lifelong hatred of his mother, he became more at ease with himself. In March 1936 he married a fellow artist, Kitty Church. He was incredulous at this point to receive a 'sermon' from his father on the importance of monogamy and fidelity.[9] The speech sounded like hypocrisy but possibly represented Wells's judgement that Anthony needed a greater degree of stability than he had done.

Despite the conflicts with Anna Jane and Anthony, the greatest personal challenge for Wells in the early 1930s came from his rival mistresses, Odette and Moura, between whose charms he continued to writhe, rage and reposition himself. He managed to resume his relationship with Moura when she visited Britain during 1929, but once he had disposed of Easton her presence became harder to conceal from Odette, so in the spring of 1930 he executed a manoeuvre of adroit immorality by sending the latter at his own expense to investigate Egypt and the Sudan. While she was recuperating from pulmonary congestion in the sun and writing *A Foreigner Looks at the British Sudan*, he was otherwise occupied with Moura.

Odette was too much a woman of the world to be entirely taken in, though she did not yet appreciate the identity of her rival. In a letter to Amber, she noted of Wells:

> He looks tired and pale after his stay in London. I don't know whether it was too much work or too much pleasure; I don't enquire too closely into his morals when he's away from me, but that man is like a cat; he'd wilt if he wasn't petted. I've never met anybody who liked so much to be liked! It's not very deep, but it's frightfully promiscuous ...[10]

Despite his fixation on Moura, on whom he had settled £200 per year, Wells could not bring himself to leave Odette and their life at Lou Pidou. When Chaplin visited them in 1931 and commented on the inscription above the fireplace, 'Two Lovers Built This House', Wells spun him a yarn which summed up the relationship, claiming that the local mason had repeatedly been hired to remove the stone when he and Odette quarrelled and restore it when they made up, so that he now refused to touch the token of their love at all. And yet Wells was compulsively carrying on not only with Moura but other women, as unable to commit to a single direction as a lump of iron wobbling around between powerful magnets.

His position began to shift in August 1931 when he was diagnosed as a mild type 2 diabetic. Since his treatment required a stay in London, Odette seized the opportunity to break through the exclusion zone he had imposed on her and take some training in diabetic nursing at King's College Clinic. Her actions were prompted by love but infuriated their recipient, who was ashamed at the outlandish, exhibitionistic figure she cut in the reserved world of London society. He managed to return her to Lou Pidou before the month was out, but such loyalty towards her as he had felt was evaporating, and, with his insulin deficiency remedied by diet changes, he was regaining the energy he needed to redirect his life.

On 7 October he escaped domestic pressures by setting out for the USA to oversee the publication of *Work, Wealth and Happiness,* observe the latest economic developments across the Atlantic and be guest of honour at a birth-control campaign dinner organized in New York by Margaret Sanger. In January 1930 he had become a founding vice-president of Britain's National Birth Control Council – later the Family Planning Association. Ever since his reading of the *Malthusian* as a teenager, he had been aware how much contraception might do to curb misery, poverty and ill health, and he remained keen to promote it against the opposition of conservatives and fundamentalists.

In addition to his work in New York, Wells travelled to Boston, Washington, Chicago and Detroit, along the way meeting Henry Ford, Walter Chrysler and President Hoover. He left the USA on 13 November. With his educational trilogy completed, Wells was momentarily tempted by thoughts of retirement. None the less, when his chauffeur picked him up at Cannes, he returned to Lou Pidou and resumed his writing and his strained relationship with Odette.

Come April he managed to sneak a few days with Moura at Fothergill's Hotel,

Ascot. The following month, he went to Madrid to deliver a talk on economic affairs at the Residencia des Estudiantes, pointedly leaving Odette in Grasse. He later relented and, along with car and chauffeur, she joined him at Barcelona for a scenic tour that took in Valencia, Alicante, Granada and Córdoba. They quarrelled less than normal since Wells no longer cared enough about her to mind what she said, and she sensed that he was slipping away from her.

Returning home via Madrid, they dined with the Romanian ambassador and his wife, Asquith's eldest daughter Elizabeth, a celebrated society hostess and author in her own right, much admired by Proust. Odette's outrageous conversation so shocked the family that the governess removed their daughter from the room. After all his efforts to turn himself into a classless man accepted at all levels of society, Wells was mortified that yet again Odette had made a fool of him. He refused to travel home with her, dispatching her by train from Barcelona while he drove the car back on his own, vowing he would henceforth keep her under control.

During the rest of the year he spent more time in Britain with Moura, giving her a key to Chiltern Court. Odette meanwhile undertook nursing training in Geneva for a projected philanthropic expedition to Africa. By now she had no doubt that she was being cold-shouldered for a rival, and in the spring of 1933 she started opening Wells's mail in search of evidence. (Christabel McLaren seems to have been her prime suspect.) Inevitably Odette discovered some derogatory remarks about herself. When she confronted Wells, he told her that he was not prepared to live with someone who opened his letters and he would therefore leave her. On 22 May he went. Whether he departed at his own choosing or she threw him out depends on whose version you credit.

For all the show of firmness he gives in his own accounts, he did not find the break easy. He had intended Lou Pidou to be his final home. A paragraph of his autobiography is devoted to how he went around the grounds, taking a last look at his domestic Utopia, feature by treasured feature, not least his beloved cat, before sloughing it all off 'as a snake casts its skin'.[11] He set off for Ragusa (Dubrovnik) where he was to preside over a meeting of the International PEN Club, promoting writers' freedom of speech. At the end of the conference he took a train to Salzburg to spend some time with Moura.

He had not, however, seen the last of Odette. Before he returned to London she had taken up residence at the Berkeley Hotel – Wells reluctantly agreed to pay her bill for one month – where she was working on a book about the English and on her projected expedition to Uganda. She tried to rekindle the relationship, but Wells was not to be budged. Odette therefore went on the attack, circulating allegations about her ill usage to a network of feminist supporters including Lady Rhondda, owner of the weekly literary and political magazine *Time and Tide*.

Odette had not been left as destitute as she liked to suggest. To help her through the Great Depression she was receiving about £1,000 a year from Wells and she also had the right to live at Lou Pidou. According to Wells, whenever they met to discuss a more detailed settlement she erupted into an impenetrable volubility.

At a meeting in the Queen's restaurant, Sloane Square, she told Wells that if he did not agree to her terms (essentially, full ownership of Lou Pidou plus a hefty annuity) she would write a book exposing his private life and/or publish the hundreds of letters he had sent her, often indecent. Though inwardly disturbed, Wells shrugged off the threats. If the book found a publisher he would sue. If the letters appeared in print, he would rather enjoy his reputation as a lady's man. Her bluff called, Odette went upstairs and was sick into the toilet, then allowed herself to be escorted to her lodgings at 46D Tite Street, changing tactics in the taxi and trying once more to charm him into submission.

In the event, the articles that were to form the basis of the book were rejected by the publishers Lane and Cape who, Wells tells us, had lost money before over Odette's libels. The editorial staff of *Time and Tide* enjoyed the proposal – Vera Brittain told Winifred Holtby that Odette's delightfully frank accounts of Wells really should be published some day – but they declined to follow through. For all his claims of indifference, Wells made a point of contacting Holtby to head off possible publication. The whereabouts of Odette's extraordinary treasure trove is now unknown, making it the unholy grail of Wells biographers. The present writer for one would be very grateful for any information on the subject.

Amidst the ongoing battles with Odette, Wells at least had the consolation of taking as his new partner the woman she dismissed as 'the Countess Bedbug', though the relationship did not turn out quite as he had imagined. He had hoped to make Moura the third Mrs Wells, but she was the ultimate Wellsian woman in every sense, as footloose and independent as he was. Far from wishing to be married to her 'Aigee', she preferred to remain a free agent.

One reason may have been that her deepest love was reserved for another agent, Bruce Lockhart. His secret service memoirs, published in 1933, gave her the leading romantic role in his life, unsurprisingly, as she had rewritten those parts herself before publication. In the extremely free 1934 film adaptation, *British Agent*, directed by Michael Curtiz and starring Leslie Howard, Kay Francis played Moura under the name 'Elena' as a woman torn between her love for a British spy and her loyalty to her evil boss, Stalin. Moura's public reputation as a glamorous, mysterious figure was assured.

Even after she had become his chief mistress Wells found Moura elusive and full of disturbing surprises. A letter of July 1933 from somewhere in Germany announced that she would be able to join him in Portmeirion for only two weeks of a promised four because she had discovered she was pregnant with his child and had arranged an abortion:

> I will 'disappear' the day after to-morrow and in a fortnight will be ready to do everything all over again! I don't want of course to attract any attention to this, so I am not telling anybody where I go and one also has to be very careful so as not to harm anyone else involved, so you can't write there, but please do to the Kobinger address and I will arrange to fetch the letters, but perhaps there will be a little delay.[12]

One wonders whether Wells had any qualms about her decision to kill their baby without consulting him, let alone telling him where she was going. Andrea Lynn, who has made a thorough study of Wells's later love affairs, is highly sceptical about the pregnancy and suggests it was a cover story for one of Moura's clandestine journeys.[13] The story also resembles Dorothy Richardson's miscarriage of 1907. Could Wells have confided his suspicions about Dorothy to Moura only to plant in her head the idea of pulling a similar trick on him? With Moura, anything is possible, including of course a genuine pregnancy. Whatever the case, Wells found himself slipping into the unfamiliar role of 'exploited partner', worrying where Moura was and who she was seeing, longing for the security of marriage, while she, in the 'man of the world' role, went her self-possessed way.

By now many of Wells's closest friends were going out of his life for good. Isabel died in a diabetic coma in September 1931. Arnold Bennett died in March of the same year, Graham Wallas in August of the next. In January 1933 it was John Galsworthy's turn, followed on 5 May by Wells's brother Frank, victim of a heart attack. Perhaps most shocking was the death of Sidney Bowkett. After twenty years without contact, a letter arrived from Dorking County Hospital in September 1935. The companion who had shared Wells's childhood dreams and the adventure of authorship had, it turned out, been overwhelmed by his addictions. He had been found unconscious several times and three times charged with the rather odd crime of attempting suicide by chloroform. Now he was pleading for money, desperate to escape the prospect of a sordid death. Wells sent him £5, but Bowkett was a lost cause. By June 1936 he was arrested for begging in the street. In October he was found dead in his lodgings. Perhaps without the work ethic and commitment to a better world instilled in him by Sarah, Wells might have succumbed to such demons. A tragic figure in his own right, Bowkett figures in the margin of Wells's story as a disturbing foil to his better-known schoolfellow.

Forced to reflect on his career by Geoffrey West's biography, and released to write candidly about his love life by the death of Jane, Wells decided it was time to present his own account of himself, a notion that prompted him to get back in touch with surviving friends such as Elizabeth Healey and Adeline Roberts. He started the autobiography during 1932 but gave it up owing to depression over the Odette–Moura impasse. He had wanted to show how he became an 'originative intellectual worker' with a message that could save the world, but his literary intuitions warned him that he was planing against the grain of the story.[14]

By January 1933, with a growing conviction about where he was heading in his private life, he had gained the confidence to resume the project without imposing his conclusions so rigidly. His claim to be an important thinker working for human salvation was, he admitted,

> not even the beginning of a statement of what I am, but only of what I most like to think I am. It is the plan to which I work, by which I prefer to work, and by which ultimately I want to judge my performance. But quite a lot of other things have happened to me, quite a lot of other stuff goes with me and it is not for the reader to accept this purely personal criterion.[15]

This openness paid artistic dividends, freeing him to recreate his life in a series of vivid descriptions and reflections, supported by letters, extracts from his books and thirty of his best picshuas. Wells gives a spirited account of his political goals and philosophy, but it is the human interest that compels us to read on and makes the *Experiment in Autobiography*, published in September 1934 in two volumes, by far the best of his later books. Samples of it are liberally scattered through the present work; anyone with an interest in Wells needs to read it right through.

Those who do will find that some aspects of the book actually work against his programme for combined world- and self-reconstruction. There is, for example, his discomfort with twentieth-century science, recalling the horror of particle physics he had put into the mouth of George Ponderevo. This disquiet is not surprising. If science was not, after all, a straightforward account of reality, a kind of organized common sense, but a bewildering tale of subatomic quanta and space-time curvature, it made it much harder to argue that a global society could best be run by scientific experts.

A more important self-contradiction can be seen in Wells's ideas on psychology. Having questioned his identity as an 'originative intellectual worker', he reinstates his self-image using a version of Jung's persona theory. If his view of himself is not comprehensive, neither is it bogus. It is a constructive simplification. He compares himself to the 'happy hypocrite' of Max Beerbohm's fable, who temporarily adopts a virtuous mask then discovers his face has taken on its shape.

To bring out the full implications of this apparently straightforward claim, we need to look carefully at *The Science of Life*, which notes that for such a persona to function, impulses, desires and even memories that are incompatible with it must be suppressed. They remain active in the unconscious, however, and together constitute what *The Science of Life* calls the 'anima'.[16] Jung prefers to call this inferior splinter personality the 'shadow', though its contents do seem to overlap with the 'anima', which is the feminine element in a man's unconscious. Wells differs from Jung in more than terminology, however. Where Wells sees the adoption of a persona as a chance for redemption, Jung regards it as a necessary but dangerous evil, encouraging shallow, stereotyped behaviour.

Geoffrey West had noted that the key element of the Wellsian persona is identification of the individual with the human race. Wells reaffirms this commitment in his autobiography, tracing his career from his beginnings as a baby in the basement of Atlas House upward and outward through his quest for personal fulfilment to an eventual recognition of, identification with and contribution to, the course of human history, which at last frees him from his limitations and gives him such immortality as a human being can attain. The persona of *le petit dieu* is an 'inflated' persona, something like the Victorian higher self.

To Jung this type of aspiration is little better than self-deception. If you pretend the unwanted part of your identity has somehow been destroyed, you merely surrender to its power, since it can then function unregulated. At best an inflated persona results in an exaggerated self-importance, undercut by secret feelings of inferiority; at worst it produces full-scale delusions like those of madmen who believe themselves to be Jesus or Napoleon.

The Science of Life concedes all this – and more. In the inflation process, it explains, there is a danger of the individual confusing his true self with the human race or God. The persona may then develop inconsistencies in attempting to rationalize behaviour that originates in the anima. It follows logically that inflation of the persona is less likely to be the constructive response that Wells claims, demoting egotism and subjectivity to their rightful place, than a turning away from reality, which allows egotism to run amok.

Worse, if we turn back to the previous chapter of *The Science of Life* we encounter the related danger of 'mind-splitting . . . between inner and outer, self and reality, wish and experience'.[17] The full-blown schizophrenic lives in a dream world; lesser cases can function more normally or, if their ideas are in tune with the times, develop into prophets or reformers.

Back in the 1890s, when he was on better terms with his imagination, Wells had praised 'eccentric and innovating people' who sought to change the world.[18] Having successfully become one, he now questioned their sanity. Yet there is logic in his position, for how can we be sure that an attack on conventional thinking will not sweep aside the good with the bad? Even Wells's most attractive heroes are dangerous troublemakers, powered by primitive energy and imagination. From the time traveller to Mr Polly, they escape charges of egotism and insanity only because Wells legitimizes their behaviour by supplying them with his own version of a transcendent referent, an alternative world of which they are pioneering representatives: a 'fourth dimension' in the science fiction, a just society in the social fiction.

Read by an unsympathetic Jungian analyst, Wells's books would present a worrying picture. All the best ones are rooted in seriously 'schizoid' conflicts. Several early stories, written during Wells's most intense period of social mobility, allude to a feeling of extreme detachment that Jung notes as a symptom of persona failure and links to fantasies featuring mythological and religious motifs, flight through space and the sensations of enormous speed and movement, the ingredients of many of Wells's best-known books.[19] *When the Sleeper Wakes* lets loose a persona inflation so extreme that the whole fate of the human race becomes dependent on one man.

Wells was not, of course, a victim of his imagination but an artist who steered it with considerable skill, consciously controlling the interplay between the realistic and the fantastic, sometimes deliberately polarizing stories around a pair of characters who embodied the imaginative and rational antithesis in his temperament. Unfortunately, his desire to believe he had overcome his divided temperament meant that he could no longer make effective use of it. Instead, he hobbled it by trying to prioritize the rational over the imaginative.

This may sound like a restatement of the obvious. Wells's critics have been telling us for a century that he was a potentially great artist who sold his birthright for a pot of message. However, the standard criticism of Wells's views is that they are wrong or impossible to incorporate into a work of art, and both of these allegations are contestable. There is nothing foolish in advocating ecological awareness, social planning, a global perspective or even the creation of a world state. Books such as *Tono-Bungay* or *The War in the Air* integrate ideas and art at least as effectively as *Brave New World* or *The Grapes of Wrath.* Wells's problems come when he refers us to an imaginary Utopia and claims it is somehow equivalent to a political argument. Having declared he was a journalist rather than an artist, Wells actually remained an artist, producing little journalism in the ordinary sense but a great deal of inferior art, in the process ironically becoming precisely what he sought to escape: a prisoner of his imagination.

Odette grasped the point (though by the wrong end) when she reviewed the autobiography for *Time and Tide* in October 1934 under the title, 'H.G. Wells – The Player'. She questioned Wells's sincerity in opposing capitalism while so spectacularly benefiting from it. She noted that his involvement with organizations including the Fabian Society and the League of Nations movement was always temporary. His political interventions looked suspiciously like an irresponsible game played for his own amusement then left behind, just as he left behind his homes and those who loved him. Though intellectually unfair, this criticism of him as two-faced and in denial was psychologically astute. From where she stood the flaw in his self-conception looked very like hypocrisy.

Wells himself had tackled the issue in *The Bulpington of Blup*, a novel published at the end of 1932. As a tribute to a volatile relationship, the book carried an unprecedented second dedication to 'the critic of the typescript, ODETTE KEUN gratefully (bless her)'. Its protagonist, Theodore Bulpington, is loosely based on Ford Madox Ford. Wells had sent his old friend 2,000 francs in July 1930 to help him weather the Depression, only to receive a request for a repeat subsidy the next month. Wells regarded Ford as a gifted author but also as a textbook example of a self-deluding persona compounded by shell shock. The novel traces the life of Bulpington, who lacks Ford's talent and has a much coarsened version of his mentality, from a reactionary High Church upbringing, through shallow flirting with art school socialism, cowardly service in the Great War and half-hearted dabbling in avant-garde poetry, to a retirement enlivened by ludicrous reminiscences. A caricature of the right-wing aesthete, Bulpington is repeatedly contrasted with the Broxteds, a family of Wellsian scientists.

The novel is more densely imagined than *The Autocracy of Mr Parham* but has the same flaws: lack of effective comic detail and lack of sympathy for its protagonist. Wells is not prepared to acknowledge that Bulpington's neuroses are a projection of his own quite as much as a caricature of Ford's. Bulpington, representative of Wells's 'romantic' side, becomes a straw man to be incinerated by satire, while the smug Broxteds, representatives of Wells's 'scientific' side, escape unscathed. Wells was convinced the novel was as good as *Kipps*; reviewers found it decidedly patchy.

Posterity has taken more interest in *The Shape of Things to Come*, published in September 1933. This return to science fiction seems to have been partially prompted by Aldous Huxley's bestselling *Brave New World*, which was itself inspired by *The Science of Life*. While Gip and Julian Huxley were collaborating on the latter at a chalet in Diablerets during the winter of 1927–8, Aldous had joined them and installed his friend D.H. Lawrence across the way. Having done so, he then had to endure his brother enthusing over eugenics and behaviourism, Lawrence ranting about liberating the instincts and the two of them laying into each other.[20] It is surely no coincidence that his dystopian novel first takes eugenics and behaviourism to a satirical extreme, then introduces an unbalanced romantic savage to criticize them, letting the two misguided sets of beliefs clash until both are thoroughly discredited.

Wells, too, was sceptical about Julian's more extreme views. He forbade any references to a 'submerged tenth' of the population in *The Science of Life* and warned his collaborator against endorsing the American scientist J.B. Watson's simplistic brand of behaviourism.[21] None the less, he could not bear seeing the idea of a scientific Utopia mocked, and Huxley's later admission that his book began as a parody of *Men Like Gods* confirms that he did have the limits of Wells's ideals in his sights.[22] Wells's retaliatory book features a similar echo of Shakespeare in its title and a glancingly derisive reference to *Brave New World* in its text.[23] Wells drew positive inspiration from the work of his admirer Olaf Stapledon, particularly his future history, *Last and First Men*, and dedicated *The Shape of Things to Come* to another radical thinker, the Spanish philosopher 'José Ortega y Gasset, Explorador'.

An anatomy combining satire, prediction, storytelling and discussion, supposedly revealed to one of Wells's friends in a series of dreams, *The Shape of Things to Come* sets up a potentially complex interaction of voices and genres but delivers Jung's prognosis for an inflated persona: overconfidence undercut by doubt. The future historian may pity the 'divided mind' of the twentieth century, but his own story lacks coherence and is highly derivative of the past.[24] After civilization has been destroyed in a second world war, a new world order is imposed by an Air Dictatorship, also known as the 'Puritan Tyranny'. This totalitarian world government, as wedded to a single version of reality as Plato or Stalin, abolishes all games, suppresses all unorthodox books, eliminates promiscuity and confers a habitually unironic expression on the human face.

Some people assumed this shrunken life was Wells's own ideal. The Nazis knew better; in 1933 his books were burned across Germany. While part of Wells's mind does seem to have been excited by his dictatorial fantasy, which, in a curious mixture of self-indulgence and self-loathing, destroys everything reminiscent of his own character, he remains clear about its monstrosity. Critical detachment is supplied through the notebooks of a twenty-first-century dissident artist, and, once the possibility of significant backsliding is past, a revisionist coup introduces a measure of perestroika. None the less, the book fails to come to terms with its political themes or with Wells's personal ambivalence. Its subject matter of totalitarianism, warfare and catastrophe, coupled with Wells's reputation for prescience, were enough to make it a compellingly alarming read in the 1930s. In retrospect, it is an interesting misfire.

Fortunately, Wells's reputation with new generations of readers still had support from his earlier work. In 1933 *The Scientific Romances of H.G. Wells* collected eight of his books into one volume, four others appeared as *Stories of Men and Women in Love*, and the *Daily Mail* offered a twelve-volume edition of Wells as part of the Fleet Street circulation wars. The 'talkies' found Wells as promising a source of material as had the silent cinema of the 1920s. In 1933 Paramount turned *Doctor Moreau* into the widely banned horror movie *Island of Lost Souls*, with Charles Laughton as Moreau and Bela Lugosi as the leader of the Beast People, and the expatriate English director James Whale made *The Invisible Man* for Universal, scripted by R.C. Sherriff and starring Claude Rains, who shot to stardom even though he barely appeared on the screen. Wells was impressed by the potential of the sound cinema and, as we shall see, had ideas of his own about how his work might translate to the new medium.

He continued to make good use of his fame by working for a number of important causes. As well as his ongoing commitment to the international network of PEN clubs and the National Birth Control Association, he was co-founder, and from March 1934 first president, of the British Diabetic Association. Not a man simply to bestow his name on a letterhead, he drummed up support, chaired meetings and wrote letters to the press, raising funds for a holiday home for deprived children with diabetes.

During the 1930s his admirers – among them Olaf Stapledon, Vera Brittain and Sylvia Pankhurst – founded an H.G. Wells Society. Wary of disciples, Wells insisted on a name change. The organization became the Open Conspiracy, then Cosmopolis and by 1937 had merged into the Federation of Progressive Societies and Individuals.

In the spring of 1934 Wells had the idea of visiting F.D. Roosevelt and Stalin to compare the attitudes of the top capitalist and Communist leaders. No doubt he sincerely wished to hear the opinions of these two contrasting exponents of state intervention, but the interviews would also make a perfect climax to his autobiography. Roosevelt already knew of Wells as a major opinion-former; he had taken the trouble to write to him in response to a sceptical article about the Democrats' New Deal policies. When Wells told Roosevelt that he would be in the USA at the end of April, FDR was happy to see him in the hope of winning him over.

Stalin was at least as keen. It probably helped that Wells was friendly with the Soviets' foreign minister, who had married the daughter of Walter Low, but the effective broker of the deal was Hitler. Since the arrival in power of the German leader, who made no secret of his desire to invade Russia, Stalin had been busy signing treaties with other major powers, arranging to join the League of Nations and ordering Western Communists to form a 'Popular Front' with anti-Fascist parties. Perhaps Wells could be added to the supporters' club. Having been given the Kremlin experience in 1931, Bernard Shaw was now defending Stalin's every policy, from the disastrous agricultural schemes of Lysenko to the wholesale murder of former Communist leaders.

Wells was not to be so easily persuaded. Though his imagination was haunted by New Republics and Air Dictatorships, he was inclined to believe that in practice the world state would arrive by the gradual evolution of international agencies rather than by revolutionary militancy. Moreover, he had never met an actual existing elite he did not despise. Shortly before he left for the USA, for example, he took a look at a blackshirt rally at the Albert Hall. At a time when Yeats was penning marching songs for the Irish blueshirts, Wells found Mosley laughable and judged his followers to be a bunch of losers who urgently needed to read the *Outline.* Bizarrely, Mosley had hoped to make a convert of Wells, assuring him he was responding to his call for 'liberal Fascisti', even if he could not guarantee the liberal part of the deal.[25]

Hoping there were more promising political developments in the USA, Wells set sail from Southampton on 26 April. Entering New York harbour through fog, he was startled by a surge of voices near by and, looking through his porthole, saw several faces unaccountably sliding past. They were passengers on a German liner that had almost run down his own vessel. It seemed symbolic of the 'large dangerousness' of the times, not least in the way everyone soon shrugged off the incident and went on as though nothing had happened.[26]

Wells spent about two weeks in the USA, collecting views on the New Deal. He had some sympathy for radicals such as Clarence Darrow, but in the end could not share their distrust of big government. The members of FDR's Brains Trust seemed as much like open conspirators as anyone he had encountered. Franklin and Eleanor Roosevelt made a very favourable impression. If Roosevelt was not consciously working towards world socialism, his efforts to build welfare and justice through collective action might be a significant step along the way. This was precisely the fear of his enemies. To Wells, however, it was inspirational, and he praised the US leader to the skies in the final section of his autobiography. When Roosevelt read the book he replied in kind, calling the *Experiment in Autobiography* 'an experiment in staying awake' instead of putting out his light.[27]

By 21 July Wells was on his travels again. He and Gip flew from Croydon aerodrome and, after passing through appropriately ominous thunderstorms, spent the night in Nazi Berlin. By the next evening they were in Moscow, ready to see how the Soviet Union was progressing. Many in the West were convinced it was doing superbly. While capitalism was in depression, the USSR was industrializing so rapidly that it would soon account for almost one-fifth of the world's manufactures. What was not apparent through the haze of secrecy and propaganda was the human cost. The USA may have had 22 per cent unemployment and a 'Dust Bowl' caused by over-farming, but the USSR had lost 4 million people to a famine caused by collectivization, had another million in forced labour camps and millions more in prisons, deportation camps and resettlement areas. While Roosevelt was contemplating legislation to protect workers' rights and create more jobs, Stalin was planning the Great Terror.

In addition to interviewing the dictator, Wells was taken to meet the science-fiction and historical novelist Alexei Tolstoy, a second science-fiction writer Aleksander Belaev, Moscow's Chief Architect, the People's Commissar for Enlightenment, the workers of the First Ball Bearing Factory and his old acquaintances Pavlov and Gorky. Pavlov showed Wells around his Physiological Institute outside Leningrad and spoke with remarkable freedom about the failings of Communism. In contrast, Gorky, who had been lured back to Russia in 1928, spoke up firmly in favour of state control of literature, the same argument that Wells had previously heard from Nazi and Fascist spokesmen at PEN conferences. In Russia, it seemed, the revolution had revolved one hundred and eighty degrees and come up with 'the worst vices of the right'.[28] Wells argued for free speech and for contraception, handing over proposals for a Russian PEN Club, but had no illusions about the likely response. Gorky, he reflected with disgust, had become a state-sponsored Great Man, wielding much the same arguments for conformity as Americans had turned on him in 1906. The distaste was mutual. In a letter to the French author Romain Rolland, Gorky called Wells 'a self-important cockerel'.[29]

Stalin, perhaps surprisingly, made a more favourable impression, his friendly, unpretentious demeanour banishing for the moment the sinister allegations Wells had heard. Asked what he was doing to change the world, Uncle Joe replied disarmingly, 'Not so very much.'[30] However, no meeting of minds followed. The two men simply talked past each other. Every time Wells put forward the idea that Russia and the USA were working towards the same goal by different means and that Russia could therefore afford to become a less defensive, more open society, Stalin simply reasserted the primacy of the class struggle.

The conversation was printed two months later in the *New Statesman*. Subsequent issues carried commentaries by well-known intellectuals. In December the debate was published as a booklet called *Stalin–Wells Talk*, with portraits by David Low. Shaw ridiculed Wells for his impertinence in questioning the wisdom of Stalin. Keynes alone sided with him, arguing that capitalism had moved on since the days of Marx, revolution was a bad answer to an obsolete question and subtler economic theories were now needed.

In a letter to *Nature* of December 1934 Wells bracketed the Soviet Union and Nazi Germany together, as nations deformed by violent concentration of power. While he was not above occasional praise of the Soviet experiment, his residual sympathy with the revolution did not make him a credulous fellow-traveller in the style of Dreiser, Shaw and the Webbs. Yet the allegation that he nose-dived at Stalin's throne is still made by critics whom one cannot imagine telling Stalin to his face he should permit free speech, as Wells had the guts to do.

When he had finished his Russian travels at the end of July, Wells took the Red Arrow train to the former St Petersburg and Petrograd, then known as Leningrad. From there he flew to Estonia and joined Moura at her long-term base in Tallinn, where twice a year she returned from her travels to bestow a little quality time on her children. He finished his autobiography in the mornings, using the afternoons to swim in the lake and literally make hay while the sun shone. In her memoir, Moura's daughter, Tania Alexander, recalls that Wells offered to pay for some improvements, including a supply of electricity, but the family had no wish for these.[31]

On the surface 1934 seemed to have gone wonderfully. At an age when most men of his generation were deceased or decrepit, he had brought off two historic interviews, written one of his most compelling books and taken his reputation to new heights. Yet all was not well. At Tallinn he had taken Tania to one side and asked her whether her mother had ever been Gorky's mistress. Tania naturally could shed no light on the question.

The fact was that, though Wells had learned little about Communism while he was in Russia, he had learned something very significant about Moura. She had refused to accompany him on the journey, claiming she would face serious, perhaps fatal, consequences if she entered the Soviet Union. However, when Wells mentioned to Umansky, his interpreter for the Stalin interview, that he intended to go home by way of Estonia and stay a while with the Baroness Budberg, Umansky let drop that she had been at Gorky's the previous week. Wells's guide, Andreychin, quickly intervened in Russian and Umansky corrected himself: perhaps he was mistaken. But the cat was out of the diplomatic bag. Pressed by an agitated Wells, Andreychin admitted Moura was a regular visitor to Russia and her visits were kept secret because of the likely reaction of her friends in Estonia and London.

We now know that Moura had been visiting Gorky every year, that through him she was personally acquainted with Stalin and that she was also in touch with the intelligence chief Yagoda, one of the architects of the Gulag. Given this set-up, it is hard not to believe that she was passing the Soviets information about Russian exiles and prominent Westerners such as Wells.

Wells was so devastated he could only express his feelings in a series of stunned declaratives.

> I never slept for the rest of my time in Russia. I was wounded excessively in my pride and hope. I was wounded as I had never been wounded by any human being before. It was unbelievable. I lay in bed and wept like a disappointed child. Or I prowled about in my sitting-room and planned what I should do with the rest of my life, that I had hoped so surely to spend with her. I realized to the utmost that I had become a companionless man.[32]

Next day he struck her out of his will and cancelled the overdraft he had arranged for her. He intended a showdown in Estonia, but she had endless glib excuses for the secret visit and denied all her previous trips to Russia. They patched up their relationship, and she joined him in rain-lashed Oslo and Bergen in late August and early September, then accompanied him to Britain on a North Sea ferry. She stayed below seasick; he paced the deck alone. They would remain a couple after all – he was too smitten to let her go – but depression would afflict him for the rest of his life.

18
THE MAN WHO CONTINUED TO WORK MIRACLES
1935–1939

At Christmas 1934 Wells was back on the Riviera. He and Moura had planned a holiday in Palermo, but Ostia airport was flooded and, unable to face the long train journey, they decided to spend time with friends such as Somerset Maugham and 'little e'. Naturally a stopover with Odette was out of the question.

Moura soon headed back to England, where her children were staying, but Wells remained in France working on a film treatment of 'The Man Who Could Work Miracles'. In her absence, he was able to assert his independence by getting involved with an American heiress and racehorse owner called Constance Coolidge. She was the same age as Moura and, as he noted with pleasure, similarly tall, dark and charming, though a refreshing contrast in her slenderness and plain-dealing. Constance had already enjoyed a varied love life – three husbands, three dozen lovers – and had a special penchant for literary men. An enthusiast for Wells's writings, she drew the line only at *God the Invisible King*.[1]

Wells began his liaison with Constance by dining at her hotel and discussing her current reading: a higher cortex work-out comprising J.W. Dunne, A.N. Whitehead, Bertrand Russell, Katherine Mansfield and T.S. Eliot. Wells was not keen on Eliot, formulating *Prufrock* as 'a classical dictionary . . . raped by *The New Yorker* in the extremely dirty gutter of an extremely disgusting back street in Paris'.[2] When it was time for Wells to return to his hotel, the two book-lovers sealed the evening with such an enthusiastic kiss that his departure was delayed by a good hour. Thereafter they enjoyed a week of exploring the region's mountains, restaurants, cinemas and each other.

When Moura returned, she was characteristically unfazed, though such was her reputation as an international woman of mystery that a friend jokingly cautioned Constance about poisoned drinks. No matter how much Wells might be captivated by other women (and the relationship with Constance continued through two years of occasional intimacy, plus another eight of letters), Moura remained confident of her supremacy.

Wells tried to rationalize his promiscuity in an elaborate 'Postscript' to the *Experiment in Autobiography*, though his best explanation is probably the simple statement he made to Constance, 'I am afraid as a child of being lonely.'[3] Writing an account of his love affairs took him from late 1934 to May 1935. He then tried to set them in the context of his wider philosophy. From 1936 to 1942 he continued the book as a looseleaf diary of additional notes, sometimes pithy, sometimes naïvely self-reassuring, almost in the manner of *Krapp's Last Tape*. The project was intended to appear posthumously, which it did in 1984, edited by Gip, as *H.G. Wells in Love.* Some passages intended for the middle section were incorporated into a less risky and less risqué book, *The Anatomy of Frustration*, published in summer 1936.

Like a number of earlier works, the *Anatomy* tries to set up a critical perspective through the interaction of two voices, author and editor, but in this case the result is little more than a fragmentary rant. The protagonist, William Burroughs Steele, is a device for loosening Wells's usual persona and letting us glimpse someone disappointed with himself. Steele's death by overdose at the end of the book is ominous, especially given Wells's then fascination with Harry Crosby, a former lover of Constance who had wanted to kill both himself and her, but – thwarted by her refusal to cooperate – who had eventually shot himself and another woman instead. Wells considered that this cracked icon of the 'Lost Generation' embodied a widespread yearning for a more fulfilling life and considered writing a novel based on him.

As well as acting as an outlet for his depressive side, Steele is also Wells's device for expressing sweeping views unsupported by proper argument. The nadir is an attack on Jewish culture as not only the provoker but the model for the messianic delusions of the Nazi movement. This argument needed more thorough development to be worth making, and in the context of the mid-1930s, when the concentration camps were filling with people who would never return, its casual inclusion is repellent. Unfortunately the ageing Wells would repeat the claim over the next eight years, his insensitivity offending Jews and Gentiles alike. As ever, his point, such as it was, concerned culture, not race. He spent much of the year enthusiastically collaborating with the film-making Korda brothers, the kind of assimilated Jews he admired.

In both the *Anatomy* and the 'Postscript', Wells returns, more productively, to Jung's idea of the 'anima', retitled the 'lover shadow'. Every person, he argues, needs a counterpart, a complementary other who will make them whole. In down-to-earth terms Wells compares himself to a drunken sailor who wants physical satisfaction but also some kind of mutual affirmation: 'He'll talk to the bitch; he'll show off; he'll hear about her and sympathize.'[4] He ruefully concludes that his own ultimate ideal is 'Jane plus Moura plus fantasy – a being made up of a dead woman, a stimulating deception and the last dissolving vestiges of imaginative hope.'[5] If no one person can incarnate the lover shadow, it is not surprising that a man of sufficient energy becomes promiscuous. Perhaps, he suggests, most men and women would be promiscuous if they had the opportunities he had enjoyed.

Wells found himself casting a new lover shadow when he returned to the USA in March 1935, though his motive in travelling was not a complementary other but

$12,500 from *Collier's Weekly* for four articles on the New Deal. He sailed to New York, then flew to Washington, DC, where he again met with Roosevelt. At the Senate he encountered the left-wing demagogue Huey Long (just six months before he was assassinated) and found him even more of a real-life Ostrog than the fascistic broadcaster Father Coughlin. If democracy meant cynical media personalities manipulating ignorant masses, how could the open conspiracy for a socialist world state ever prevail? In a letter to Constance he complains that the New Deal is a mess and that Americans 'drink too much, talk too much & they think at odd times in taxicabs when the radio isn't on'.[6] Yet in his reports, published in book form in June as *The New America: The New World*, he was forced to conclude that the energy, intelligence and free speech of the USA represented the only hope left in a world that was sliding into totalitarianism and war.

And what of his new love? Martha Gellhorn was an ambitious journalist, and also a fine-looking blonde, currently being paid by the government to write up the stories of people on relief. She was a mere twenty-six but so confident and outspoken that she had gone directly to the Roosevelts to complain about the way some of the unemployed were treated. She had no trouble attracting Wells's interest and he soon found himself 'making love' to her, perhaps using the term in its older sense of 'flirting', perhaps not.[7] He thought her letters were highly entertaining and, before the end of the year he would head back to the USA, determined to 'grapple' with her.

In the meantime, it was back to Britain and to Moura. He had hoped that the breadth of the Atlantic would put her into perspective, but throughout the trip she remained his imaginary companion. The fixation angered him – if he was going to be obsessed by her she should at least be his permanent partner. Perhaps he could then settle down and stop chasing women like Martha, who was, after all, forty-two years younger than him. He told Moura to meet him at Southampton in submission or send back the key to his flat. The ultimatum was futile. On his return she simply rang him to say she was ill and requested a visit. By paying it, he instantly relegated himself to the number two role; the next day she mysteriously recovered. He made another attempt at escape during August, when she was in Estonia, again by letter, in fact several letters, setting out the reasons they should break up. Yet when she appeared at an Institute of Journalists reception he was giving as PEN president, he found himself welcoming her with open arms.

Their relationship is epitomized by an ambiguous event held at the Quo Vadis restaurant, Soho, apparently in November 1933, though Anthony West places it in 1935. Invitations went out to many eminent acquaintances, including Violet Hunt, Maurice Baring, Harold Nicolson, Enid Bagnold and David Low, announcing a dinner party to celebrate Wells's and Moura's union. The recipients were expecting an engagement party but discovered the event merely marked the permanence of the open liaison. It seems that Wells himself had not realized this: in some versions he actually proposed to Moura in front of the whole company and was ignominiously refused.

Wells wanted to recruit Moura to the role that Jane and Odette had occupied, looking after his home base, assisting him in his work and social life and being there for him when he returned from his travels. This was not Moura's idea of fulfilment. She told Enid Bagnold bluntly that she had no intention of marrying him and would leave his housekeeping to Gip's wife Marjorie.[8] In fact Marjorie was far more than a housekeeper to Wells, effectively substituting for Jane as his typist and confidante.[9] With her help he kept himself busy during 1935, working on his cinematic projects and paying occasional visits to Europe, in particular taking refuge in Paris at the start of May to escape George V's silver jubilee.

On 8 November he returned to the USA, intending to investigate how films were made in Hollywood and to enjoy the company of 'Stooge', as Martha had now nicknamed herself. The date of return was left open. He stayed a few days in New York with the president of Macmillan, meeting Sinclair Lewis among others, before joining Martha in a house in Connecticut. They stayed together for a week, 'making love, talking, reading over her second book'.[10] Here 'making love' seems to have shifted decisively to its more modern meaning. He continues, 'Martha in skiing trousers with her shock of ruddy golden hair in disorder, her brown eyes alight and her face rosy with frost, is unforgettable'.

On 25 November Wells took a plane west. The aircraft began to ice up over the Adirondack Mountains, and, since there were blizzards ahead, Wells caught a train from Kansas City to Albuquerque. Here he was able to get a second plane, which carried him across the Grand Canyon and brought him at last to Los Angeles, where he spent a 'rejuvenating' five weeks staying with Charlie Chaplin and Paulette Goddard at their home on Summit Drive, Beverly Hills.[11] Frequent visits to film studios were interspersed with expeditions to such glamorous locations as Palm Springs, Cecil B. de Mille's ranch and William Randolph Hearst's kitsch castle at San Simeon. Chaplin talked of offering Wells $30,000 for the movie rights to *Mr Polly*, but in the event it was John Mills who took the title role in a British version fifteen years later.

At Christmas Wells headed back east. His plane again afflicted by ice, he switched to a train in Dallas, proceeding via Washington, DC, to New York, where he moved into the Ambassador Hotel and resumed his affair with Martha. Wells recollected that they gave serious thought to their future together.

> We both felt the manifest incompatibility of our ages. There was no sense in her becoming my kept-mistress and we both were divided between the desire and inclination to marry and a realization of the impossibility of marriage.[12]

Decades later Martha professed horror when Gip wanted to publish such passages in *Wells in Love*. While conceding that Wells had proposed to her, she was adamant she had never reciprocated his passion, even claiming that she had got so fed up with him in November that she telegraphed Chaplin, whom she had never met, asking him to invite Wells over. She claimed she enjoyed the great man's company only as a serious, if sometimes boring, conversationalist. To Rebecca West's biographer Victoria Glendinning, she put the indignant question: why would she sleep with a little old man when she could have any number of attractive young men?[13] To this there is an obvious answer: a taste for literary celebrities with publishing clout. She had already been the mistress of the political economist Bertrand de Jouvenal, and her husbands would later include the editor of *Time* magazine and Ernest Hemingway. On their break-up the latter accused her of depending on his writing advice for her success.[14]

On the subject of their relationship, should we believe Wells, a man whose reminiscences contain occasional inaccuracies but never lies and delusions, or Gellhorn, whose best known work is a fabricated 'eye-witness' account of a lynching and who professed to be shocked at Wells's claims of intimacy, even though his letters to her at the time contain repeated references to sharing her bed? Readers may review the evidence and draw their own conclusions.

In January 1936 Wells returned to Britain, taking with him the manuscript of Martha's short-story collection, *The Trouble I've Seen*. Her previous book had not been a success, but this one would have more impact, endorsed as it was in an enthusiastic preface by one of the world's most famous writers. Within days of his return, Wells had started a bidding war between Hamish Hamilton and Putnam. In May Martha came to Britain and stayed three weeks with her patron. This time there was definitely no hanky-panky. She told Wells that she had resumed a violent love affair on the voyage with a man named Willert, with the emotional consequence that she could now offer merely caressing. She continued to send him flattering letters, at least, for the rest of his life.

Towards the end of May it was Moura's turn to become enigmatic, bursting into tears and expressing an urgent desire to be in Paris. When the newspapers announced Gorky was mortally ill, she left Paris for Moscow to nurse him on his deathbed. Needless to say, she had known of Gorky's condition and meant to go to Moscow all along. Aware of Wells's feelings about her past visits to Russia, she had provided her daughter with a cover story about being in a nursing home, but Tania persuaded her to come clean.

In recent years the Russian intelligence service has suggested the deception went much further and that Moura was actually implicated in the murder of Gorky, for which Yagoda and two doctors were executed in 1938.[15] The general view, however, is that Gorky died from natural causes and the murder charge was a standard excuse for Stalin to eliminate a former ally. Moura's descendant Dimitri Collingridge has done a good job of discrediting the murder allegation in his television documentary *My Secret Agent Auntie.*[16]

During May, amidst his slightly bewildering dealings with Stooge and Moura, Wells made a long-contemplated house move, to 13 Hanover Terrace, one of a row of twenty luxury homes designed by Nash overlooking the Outer Circle of Regent's Park. It was the part of London where Wells had spent his early years with Isabel and Jane. Now he was back, in another century, ageing, famous and positioned on the affluent west side. He had begun negotiations with the previous owner, the poet Alfred Noyes, back in January 1935, telling him he was 'looking for a house to die in'.[17] Perhaps it was this awareness that made him delay the move. Along the way, while inspecting the house in September 1935, he acquired a black eye from a fire-escape ladder. The incident was followed by prolonged and painful neuritis, though Wells came to the conclusion that this did not originate from the accident but from a vitamin deficiency caused by adopting too strict a diabetic diet.

The furnishing of the house was handled by Frank and Peggy, with input from top interior designer Sybil Colefax. Key features were a four-poster bed, a photograph gallery of principal lovers, with Jane in pride of place, and a Tang dynasty terracotta horse. Wells was keen to add a bust of Voltaire, commenting in the 'Postscript' that it symbolized his ideal of being an old gentleman, pronouncing upon the world from a comfortable retirement.[18]

Presumably it was in imitation of Voltaire's *Candide* that he published four slender fables during 1936–8. *The Croquet Player* (dedicated to Moura) tells of a fatuous young man who learns that an evil spirit, representing the bestial element in human nature, is gradually spreading over the world. *Star Begotten* (dedicated, mischievously, to Churchill) discusses whether cosmic rays from Mars are mutating selected human beings into open conspirators. A disembodied voice in *The Camford Visitation* denounces the traditional university system as reactionary and irrelevant. Finally, and presumably inspired by contemporary events in Spain, *The Brothers* (dedicated to the illustrator of the *Outline*, J.F. Horrabin) concerns a civil war between left and right that leads to the mutual destruction of the siblings who lead the rival factions. Wells sent Stapledon a copy inscribed 'Damn the Left and Damn the Right'.[19]

While several critics have argued that the first two short books of the period mark a return to the darker, more poetic approach of the 1890s – and John Huntington has interpreted the second of them as a subtle meditation on the borderline between vision and madness – most readers have found the quartet a negligible addition to the canon.

In the opinion of the present writer, there is a stronger case to be made for the merits of *Brynhild*, a longer work of fiction published in 1937 which offers a systematic meditation on the issue of personal identity. The story is focused through a set of carefully drawn characters: Rowland Palace, an author who discovers that he needs to cultivate an image in order to flourish in mass society; Immanuel Cloote, the public relations consultant he hires to build his career; Alfred Bunter, a rival author whose slightly Lawrentian persona conceals a desperately troubled former life; and finally, the presiding intelligence of the piece, Palace's wife Brynhild, who secretly bears Bunter's child. In the words of Robert Bloom, it is 'the most Jamesian of Wells's novels', a maverick creation that does not fit easily into the Wells canon (except in so far as the male characters may represent aspects of Wells himself).[20] While the book lacks the stylistic flair or depth of characterization necessary to qualify it as a lost classic, it demonstrates clearly that even in his early seventies Wells could manage impressive new tricks.

His other memorable novel of the period was one provoked out of him by Odette. Not content with her dismissive review of the autobiography, she had tackled Wells below the belt in her next book, *I Discover the English.* The Englishman, she reported, 'will not give enough time, trouble or attention to the sexual act, and thereby makes it as flat, stale and deadly as a slab of one of his own cold suet puddings. In brief: in bed, he's boring.'[21] No one who knew them can have had any doubt whom she had in mind.

Relations were no friendlier in private communications. A typical letter starts amiably enough, 'Dear Pidoo', but works itself up to a salvo of denigration.

> Curse and blast and shit the day on which we decided to live together, you swine, and the house you built, and what you did and what you are. Can't that diabetes of yours carry you off at last! The time and nervous energy you make me waste! God damn you everlastingly.[22]

Anthony West reports that on one occasion Odette turned up at Amber's house with her revolver and proposed the pair of them set off for Hanover Terrace to avenge themselves on the man who had wronged them. Most likely this was a theatrical gesture intended to give Wells a nasty shock. Amber impounded Odette's gun and handed it in to the police, claiming she had found it on Hampstead Heath. Wells laughed off the episode with the comment 'And to think she has the nerve to call me a comedian.'[23]

Wells risked occasional visits to Lou Pidou in Odette's absence. As he still loved the house and was upset at the condition it was in, he offered to buy it back, but Odette would never agree to the deals he proposed. In March 1937, while she was in the USA seeking treatment for an illness she feared might be cancer, Wells stayed for a couple of weeks, along with Marjorie and her children, Catherine and Oliver.

Odette returned in fury, convinced he had been using the house to canoodle with Moura. She made her views on the matter clear in her inimitable style:

> Your pleasant little plan of removing my furniture and boarding up two houses which you dream are yours, has gone phut – you can shove it up your arse, where I hope it will constipate you for good . . . You, and your slatternly breed, and your Bedbug, will never set foot in Lou Pidou as long as I live . . . I send you in parting my pious hope that your neuritis, your diabetes, your sclerosed lung and your one kidney will soon combine to put a definitive stop to the diarrhetic deluge of drivelling works with which you persist in swamping a long-suffering public – and so I end a mortally boring association.[24]

Wells could give as good as he got. In the summer of 1937, not long after he received the above letter, he started one of his Saul Bellow-type first-person novels in which a publisher called Stephen Wilbeck ends his association with his outrageous wife Dolores, not with curses but by giving her an overdose of painkillers. Methuen received the manuscript in April 1938 but suspected a potentially libellous resemblance between Wilbeck's trouble-and-strife and the combative Mademoiselle Keun. *Apropos of Dolores* was instead picked up by Jonathan Cape, who published it in October, presumably reasoning that even Odette was unlikely to appear in court claiming she was the original of the repulsive Dolores. As several critics have noted, the book is written with a verve that makes it stand out among Wells's later works. Yet Wilbeck, for all his evident intelligence, has a blind spot about himself. He never explains clearly why he was attracted to Dolores in the first place and he shows little genuine capacity for self-criticism, even after he has 'accidentally' disposed of her. Like so many Wellsian narrators he is also wearyingly prone to opinions.

Those who knew Wells and Odette were amused by the opening disclaimer that the book was not based directly on life. Even the characters' cars were recognizable. Wilbeck drives Wells's Voisin; a beautiful woman glimpsed towards the end travels in Constance's distinctive Hispano Suiza. Given this autobiographical basis, the book is disturbing, not only for its homicidal resolution but because of the way Wilbeck's daughter is depicted. Like Anna Jane, she has been raised as another man's child, but she grows up to be a dullard, and Dolores repeatedly suggests that Wilbeck's relationship with her is incestuous. His denials are convincing enough, yet he does admit to some degree of sexual feeling for her.

Surely Anna Jane and Amber must have been taken aback when they read this section of the novel, yet it does not seem that they expressed any disquiet. Perhaps they had come to accept that Wells was now an elderly eccentric whose troublesome side had to be balanced against his kindly qualities. Perhaps the world's drift towards war put mere novels into perspective. In August 1939 Amber would assure Wells, 'What you gave me all those years ago – a love that seemed perfect to me, the influence of your mind, and Anna Jane – have stood by me ever since. I have never for a moment felt that they were not worth the price.'[25]

Anna Jane and Eric visited Wells frequently during this period. On 26 May 1937 a grandson, Anthony, was born. 'I shall try to help him learn to be a star-begotten human being,' Anna Jane wrote. 'Just now he is a normal greedy baby.'[26] Motherhood did not stop Anna Jane remaining busy as an open conspirator, lecturing and organizing events for the Workers' Educational Association. She followed in her father's footsteps in the summer of 1938 by visiting the USA (Wells helped with the fare), where she enjoyed the skyscrapers, the union campaigns and the variety of people but hated segregation. On 1 February 1939 she gave birth to another child, Anne, of whom Anthony proved 'very fond'.[27] Since the infant Anne could not pronounce the word 'Anthony', he ended up being called by his middle name, Michael, an amendment that would confuse his grandfather's biographers. A photograph that both David Smith and Michael Foot present as Rebecca and Anthony West, because it carries the name 'Anthony', is in fact Anna Jane and son.

In 1939 Anna Jane helped start a film club in Bristol and arranged the screening of one of Wells's silent movies, *Bluebottles*. She had reported to him three years earlier that his most ambitious film project had run locally for two whole weeks, though to mixed reactions. *Things to Come* was based loosely on *The Shape of Things to Come*. The book of the film was published in 1935; the film itself premièred at Leicester Square on 21 February 1936.

Wells worked hard at the movie between 1933 and 1935, not only producing several drafts of the script but spending considerable time at the studios in Isleworth and Denham. He had realized that in an era of mass communication the book was no longer the chief vehicle for storytelling, but, like many other well-known writers who acted on the observation, he then found himself caught up in a process where others called the shots: namely, the director William Cameron Menzies, who had considerable flair as a designer and second unit director but who was out of his depth at the helm of such an innovative project, and the producer Alexander Korda, who wanted to curtail Wells's discursiveness and deliver an accessible crowd-pleaser. Though Wells was credited with masterminding the film and Moura was on hand to translate his discussions with the Korda brothers, his artistic control was limited. Raymond Massey, the leading actor, dryly recalled that, having little else to do, Wells solaced himself by adjusting the actresses' garments 'with the touch of a costumier and much more enthusiasm'.[28]

Wells did succeed in commissioning some outstanding soundtrack music from Arthur Bliss, but his wish that the visuals be edited to the music rather than vice versa seems to have been followed only in the 'rebuilding of civilization' sequence, arguably the best part of the film. Even though his son Frank was assistant art director, attempts to enlist notable modern artists to do design work were unproductive. Le Corbusier was uninterested, Léger was unsatisfactory, Moholy Nagy's work appeared only fleetingly. The film's influential designs and special effects, supervised by Vincent Korda, have none the less earned it a place in cinema history.

In contrast, the crude script and ham acting, which coarsen Wells's ideals and art in a misconceived attempt to reach the masses, have made it something of a laughing stock. Wells defended the film in public but was disappointed in private. He complained that the film-makers had sidelined him, cut half the scenes he had envisaged (the final script was the work of Lajos Biro) and had damaged his prestige with the half-educated audience he was trying to influence.[29] However, there is nothing to suggest that the film would have turned out any better if Wells had exercised greater control.

In February 1937 the Kordas released a second Wells film, *The Man Who Could Work Miracles,* which had actually been shot before the first one. Wells's conception of the movie, elaborated from his classic short story, was published as a book in 1936, but again the script was Biro's. Wells judged the director Lothar Mendes to be even worse than Menzies and found the result dull. It was a considerably less pretentious, and therefore rather more satisfactory, film than its predecessor, but by the same token it had less impact on the box office or cinema history. Wells worked on two more treatments for the Kordas, neither of which reached production: *The Food of the Gods* and a version of 'Elvesham' known as *The New Faust,* published in *Nash's Pall Mall* in December 1936.

If Wells's ventures into the cinema were artistically disappointing, their educational effect may have been worse. His Utopia motivated no one. Who would want to live in the vacuous world of big white buildings depicted in *Things to Come* or be under the control of the fanatical – not to say fascistic – airmen who created them? On the other hand, his depiction of air raids and gas bombings in the near future was terrifyingly credible, reinforcing Stanley Baldwin's warning that the bomber would always get through, a consideration that inhibited the British public from standing up to Hitler as he tore up the Versailles settlement piece by piece and resumed the expansion of Germany by force. It was a sign of the times that when the Crystal Palace burned down in November 1936 it was widely believed that the government had torched it so it would not be a landmark for German bombers if and when they came to destroy London.

Like international relations, Wells was starting to fall apart. He had lost all his teeth, his painful neuritis continued for several months, he was sure now Moura would never marry him, and he was troubled by recurrent thoughts of suicide. In November 1937 he told Margaret Sanger – and himself:

> Last spring I had neuritis very badly & had my doubts whether the fag end of life was worth living. But people like you & I have so many people getting a sort of courage to live out of us, weak as we may be in reality, that we cannot afford to do anything but live with the utmost apparent stoutness to the end.[30]

The following year, drinking whisky late into the night with C.P. Snow in a Cambridge hotel, he suddenly asked his protégé whether he had ever thought of suicide, confessing that the idea had been in his own mind ever since he turned seventy.[31]

As a public figure Wells continued to champion racial equality, diabetic treatment, contraception and free speech, though he handed over the presidency of PEN to Priestley in November 1936. Privately he gave much-needed allowances to many relatives, friends and lovers, adding Elizabeth Healey (now Elizabeth Bruce) to his payroll from 1936 after the death of her husband and Dorothy Richardson from 1937. But such individual efforts were a tiny breakwater against the tide of history.

Time and again Japan, Italy and Germany were invading their neighbours in defiance of treaties and sanctions. For Britain the lowest point in the process was the Munich Conference of September 1938. The blurb to the 1922 Czech translation of *A Modern Utopia* had noted that 'the existence of our state depends on gaining the help and affection of Great Britain'. By 1938 many Britons were willing to harden their hearts and see Czechoslovakia dismembered if it would put an end to Hitler's demands. When the Nazis went on to take over the rest of the country six months later, their disillusionment and humiliation were complete.

Wells wrote an open letter to the Czech president Eduard Beneš at the time of the Munich sell-out, having met Beneš in June 1938 on a trip to a PEN Club meeting in Prague. He condemned the settlement as a shameful setback in the war for a liberal, democratic civilization.[32] Through Ritchie Calder, science correspondent of the *Daily Herald*, he had been receiving secret reports from inside Germany on anti-Nazi resistance and was disgusted that the British government paid these no heed. He suspected that, faced with consistent opposition from the democracies, Hitler would have long since backed down, lost face and fallen from power. Now, as totalitarianism fed on the weakness of its opponents, all Wells could do was cling to the mission that had inspired the *Outline of History* to promote public access to truth and to a vision of human unity.

Having decided against synthesizing his three outlines into one volume, he made proposals for a fresh encyclopaedia compiled by a group of progressive thinkers. This grew into a more fluid concept: not a book but an organization that would update and distribute sound information and ideas. He floated the notion in a series of lectures and articles, notably talks to the Royal Institution in November

1936 (published in various formats, including a booklet from the Woolfs), the Congrès Mondial de la Documentation Universelle in Paris in August 1937 and the British Association for the Advancement of Science at University College, Nottingham, in September 1937. Some of the talks and articles were collected in a book called *World Brain*. His ideas had little impact at the time, but since the creation of the internet and online databases they seem suddenly and characteristically prescient, even if they raise unanswered questions about the coherence of the 'brain' and who controls it.[33]

Wells publicized his World Brain concept on a lecture tour of the USA, sailing to New York early in October 1937, returning five weeks later. He spoke in Philadelphia, Kansas City, Boston, Detroit, Chicago, New York and Washington, DC, meeting up with Roosevelt for a third time over lunch in the capital. In general he enjoyed the tour, though not the mass hand-shaking it entailed. As well as a parade of arm-pumping Americans, he saw Niagara Falls from the air, watched the foundations for the 1939 World's Fair being laid at Flushing Meadows, New York, and caught Rodgers and Hart's satirical Broadway musical *I'd Rather Be Right*.

He also spent a day with Henry Ford at Dearborn, Michigan. Wells didn't agree with all Ford's views, particularly regarding Jews and trade unions, but was impressed by his experiments with soya beans as an ecologically sound source of food and material and felt that his imaginative genius should somehow have been brought more into the running of the nation. In contrast, he was unimpressed by the trade-union boss John L. Lewis and the US labour organizations, judging that the workers' representatives had settled for a sectional interest role within the capitalist system instead of working for a more just and liberal alternative. Wells was, however, impressed by the students he met at Harvard and Yale and by the general American capacity for 'scrapping and starting again'.

This visit was considerably more businesslike than his last. After all, Margaret was hospitalized through a gall-bladder operation (Wells called on her, but she was unable to receive visitors), and Martha was in Spain with Hemingway, reporting on the Civil War. However, this does not necessarily imply that Wells went without female company altogether, as there are rumours, as yet unconfirmed, of a liaison in Detroit.

Wells had always regarded the USA as a land of potential and surprise, and, along with many Americans, he got a particularly big surprise in October 1938 when a radio adaptation of *The War of the Worlds*, broadcast by Orson Welles' Mercury Theatre on Halloween Eve, convinced at least a million people that their country was being invaded. Thousands of listeners jammed the switchboards of the emergency services, phoned their loved ones to say goodbye for the last time, gathered in churches to pray for deliverance, fled into the night with towels over their heads and handkerchiefs to their faces or simply leaped into their cars and put as much space as they could between themselves and the Martians' supposed bridgehead in New Jersey.

Wells was horrified at the adaptation and considered asking for damages, though in the long run he was reconciled by the boost given his book sales. In fact the Mercury Theatre's low-budget jape proved cannier than his unwieldy films in reinventing his work for a mass medium. Dependent on their radios for coverage of news stories such as the Nazi takeover of Austria and Czechoslovakia, listeners retuned to CBS after a popular comedy show, missed the opening credits and encountered not a conventional play but a cunningly timed *audio vérité* mix of overlapping voices, interruptions and background noises that approximated a live broadcast running out of control. They did not stay to reflect on the semiotic niceties but made straight for the garage, in many cases assuming the invaders were Germans.[34]

Nor were Americans uniquely gullible. According to Reuters and Associated Press dispatches of February 1949, an attempt to recreate the broadcast a decade later in Ecuador led to a similar panic, followed by the burning of the radio station and riots in which fifteen people died. Where Orson Welles's broadcast earned him the chance to make *Citizen Kane*, the directors of the second version, unprotected by the traditions of Halloween, found themselves under arrest.[35]

The panic made it clear how much power resided in Wells's earliest works. It is difficult to imagine anyone rioting over a broadcast of *Star Begotten*, however ingeniously dramatized. Wells none the less persevered in his role of ideological agitator, making the most of the time left before war broke out by taking his gospel to the southern hemisphere.

At the start of December 1938 he flew from Croydon to Marseilles and boarded the SS *Comorin*, bound for Australia via Aden, Bombay and Colombo. The journey took over three weeks, something of a trial for a man of Wells's impatient temperament. Throughout the subsequent tour his writings fizzed with a splenetic impatience that makes them among his most entertaining later works. In the first of his articles for the *News Chronicle*, he dubbed the ship the 'SS *Pukka Sahib*' and made it a metaphor for Britain: slow, ill-equipped and full of idiots doing the Lambeth Walk. Conversations in Bombay (now Mumbai) confirmed his view of the Indians as a highly civilized people whose potential was being diverted into nationalism by the racist treatment they received from the British. 'I had imagined that non-cooperation was a device of Gandhi's, but it seems to be an established British method.'[36]

Having finally arrived at the port of Fremantle, Wells flew a short distance to the University of Western Australia in Perth to be the guest of honour of the Australian and New Zealand Association for the Advancement of Science (ANZAAS) and also of the West Australian Federation of Writers. He then flew to Adelaide, where he gave the first of a series of talks broadcast by the Australian Broadcasting Company. On 3 January 1939 he arrived by car in Melbourne where he gave another radio talk, plus lectures and interviews. A private plane to Canberra gave him a bird's-eye view of the bush fires, which – in a temperature of 114°F (46°C) – were raging through the outback.[37]

Things were hotting up in the press, too. In a widely syndicated article, 'A Forecast of 1939', Wells had referred to Germany's leaders as 'certifiable lunatics . . . suffering from delusions of grandeur and a contagious form of homicidal mania'. The only benefit of Hitler's antics that he could see was that they might awaken the British people to a new radicalism. While Wells felt uncharacteristically positive about the short-lived monarchy of Edward VIII (Wallis Simpson was a friend of Constance's, and Wells was unaware of Edward's pro-German leanings), he thought the King had no part to play in the coming crisis. His comments provoked widespread indignation. The *Sunday Dispatch* sprang to the defence of royalty; the Nazi newspaper *Attack* said Wells's remarks only confirmed the importance of the Axis fight against Bolshevism. Behind the scenes the British government pressured the *News Chronicle* to restrain Wells. Even the Australian Prime Minister, Joseph Lyons, joined in, rebuking Wells for stirring up 'international misunderstanding'.

Now Wells was in his element. He hit back at the British press in an article on 'Discussing Royalty' and, since no one in Britain or America would print it, put it into a book defiantly titled *Travels of a Republican Radical in Search of Hot Water.* Lyons received his comeuppance in the following chapter, 'Mr Lyons Protects Hitler, the Head of a Great Friendly Power, from My "Insults"'. Wells compared Lyons to Neville Chamberlain as an appeaser: both suffered 'delusions of sagacity'. For his discomfort with free speech Lyons was also like the head of the BBC, Lord Reith: both were 'inspired by a fear of life'. The controversy that raged in the Australian newspapers may or may not have contributed to Lyons's death of a heart attack three months later.

In Canberra, Wells made two further broadcasts and several contributions to an international conference organized by ANZAAS on 'The Place of Science in World Affairs'. The most notable of these was 'The Poison Called History', which restated somewhat more ferociously the thinking behind the *Outline,* that nationalistic history foments racism and war. Before leaving Canberra, Wells accompanied Governor General Gowrie to inspect the bush fires at closer quarters. Just as he had turned the ship into a metaphor for Britain, so he took this 'fiery contagion' as a metaphor for Axis expansion, requiring a programme of 'aggressive prevention'.

He gave further speeches in Sydney – one on 'The Human Outlook' concluded, to Wells's disgust, with the audience singing 'God Save the King' – and gave interviews in Brisbane and Darwin before setting off for home on 26 January on a Dutch airliner via Bali, Rangoon, Jodphur, Baghdad, Istanbul and Athens, where he met up with Moura and visited Sunium and Delphi. A ship from Greece got him home on 20 February, ill with shingles and a spastic colon that he attributed variously to the germs of Baghdad and the wrath of God – though Anthony West says the underlying problem was viral pneumonia caused by sleeping near an open window on his last night in Canberra.[38] Wells was depressed by the state of the world, but satisfied that his tour had made an impact.

Controversy was still rife about his views, not only of royalty and Nazis, but also of Jews. In an article of December 1938 Wells had tried to speak up for the Jews, declaring that their extermination by the Nazis would be followed by the murder of nation after nation unless everyone banded together now. At the same time he condemned Zionists for their treatment of Palestinians and suggested that the price of human unity was for everyone to abandon their claims to be special. He concluded, 'The future of the Jews is like the future of the Irish, Scotch, Welsh, English, Germans and Russians, and that is common humanity in one large and varied world order, or death.'[39] While many people agreed, others assumed his agenda was anti-Semitic. To Wells's disappointment, even Eleanor Roosevelt courted the Jewish vote with an article called 'Mr Wells Is Wrong'.

His critics might have been surprised to learn that during April and May 1939 Wells was making a considerable effort to help the Jewish literary translator Pavel Eisner and his family escape from Czechoslovakia. Thanks to a mix-up by the British Consulate, however, the Pavel Eisner whom Wells succeeded in freeing was not the one he had intended but a lucky namesake. The translator did survive the war, though as a prisoner in the Terezin concentration camp, and later settled in the USA.[40]

Wells had been taking a sympathetic interest in another Jewish refugee, Sigmund Freud. Though he despised irrational Freudians like Wilhelm Reich and A.S. Neill, and thought that psychoanalysis might profitably be reversed into 'psychosynthesis', Wells admired Freud himself for his willingness to defy traditional beliefs.[41] When they met in November 1938 the dying Freud spoke enthusiastically about his forthcoming book *Moses and Monotheism* and argued that religious faith was incompatible with being fully adult. Wells demurred, admitting in so doing that he was 'an essentially religious person'.[42]

To take on simultaneously the Nazis, the royal family and the Jewish lobby may have been foolhardy, but Wells was also under fire from an antagonist with more immediate power to damage him – the taxman. Considering his public arguments for collectivization of wealth, Wells was remarkably reluctant to hand over his own earnings to the state. He noted in the 'Postscript' that he had always tried to evade income tax when he could, arguing with a neat dovetailing of idealism and self-interest that

> I have thought it better, not only for myself but for my world, to live easily and work amply than to overtax myself for fools who build bombers and battleships and for the extravagances of incompetent administrators and officials.[43]

Faced with the need to rearm against Germany, the British government took the contrasting view that they had a good use for Wells's overdue tax on 'income retained in America'. Wells was forced to hand over a massive £23,000 in March 1939.

Fortunately, his fame was such that he could command impressive advances from publishers who wanted his prestigious name in their catalogues, even if they then struggled to recoup their outlay. His latest victim was Michael Joseph, publisher of his 1939 novel, *The Holy Terror.* A superior remake of *Mr Parham*, the book takes off from an observation in Wells's autobiography that his immature fantasies at the age of thirteen are embodied in Hitler.[44] The Wellsian protagonist, Rud Whitlow, is an angry young man in search of a cause who eventually seizes control of the extremist political party of Lord Bohun, a delightfully vicious caricature of Mosley as a self-obsessed, sadomasochistic snob. The early parts of the book are pacy and satirical, but, once Whitlow has taken over the world, the book reverts to the *Things to Come* syndrome: a recognition that its Utopia is tyrannical, set against an evasive claim that the problem can be readily fixed by a change of leadership. We seem to be reading an unhinged psychodrama concerning Wells's own yearnings for extremes of discipline and freedom, rather than a focused political debate.

Outside the pages of his fiction, Wells continued to do his best to bring sanity to the world, in July 1939 putting his name to an appeal for an amnesty in Spain, where the victorious forces of the right were executing their enemies, and at the end of August setting off for Sweden to deliver a defiant speech on 'The Honour and Dignity of the Human Mind' to the Annual Congress of the International PEN Club at Stockholm. The speech was never made. On 1 September Nazi Germany and Communist Russia, having struck a deal, carved up Poland between them. At this point the British government realized appeasement was through. They had left it very late. Poland could not be aided meaningfully as Czechoslovakia might have been. None the less, on 3 September Britain declared war on Germany.

Wells found himself trapped on the Continent. Accompanied by Moura, who had come from Estonia, he managed to get a plane west as far as Amsterdam. A week of suspense ended on the 17th when the couple caught the last boat to Britain. As they arrived, they passed the aircraft carrier HMS *Courageous*, the kind of converted Great War vessel on which Britain was still relying for its defence. That night it was torpedoed by a German submarine and went down with the loss of more than five hundred lives.

After a lifetime of advocating a liberal-socialist world state, Wells had to watch as the world plunged into another war that would kill and maim millions, driven by the totalitarian states that had banned his books and looked likely now to replace the comparatively open society in which he had thrived with authoritarian empires that gloried in violent uniformity. A few days short of seventy-three, Wells could have been forgiven for quietly throwing in his hand and relocating to neutral territory, but it is doubtful the option even occurred to him. He had the enemy in his sights.

19
DECLARATIONS
1939–1943

To the American critic Malcolm Cowley in an article of November 1939 – in imagery recalling the early chapters of the *Outline* – Wells was like a mighty survivor from prehistoric times, imperfectly adapted to the present Ice Age, yet overshadowing the tinier creatures of today.[1] Four months later T.S. Eliot delivered less qualified praise, bracketing Wells with Churchill, who was now back in government as First Lord of the Admiralty.[2] Churchill may have had delusions about the permanence of the empire and the class system, but the public cherished him for his determination to fight Fascism to the death. To Eliot, Wells was similarly archaic yet equally far from obsolete. The sad fact, he concluded, was that there was no one in the current generation who could offer the conviction and leadership possessed by these two 'furious' codgers.

Wells's early work showed great imaginative gifts. As a commentator he had outshone most other intellectuals, while managing to address a constituency vaster than they could muster. His beliefs and arguments might be crude, but in wartime subtlety was not the weapon of choice. Like Churchill, Wells was capable of a bluntness that was 'more endearing, in the long run, than the cautious, diplomatic politeness of the people who are so careful never to put their feet into anything'. Though Eliot was an American-born Anglo-Catholic, he declared that Wells's hostility to Catholicism was refreshing and his intemperate attacks on American neutrality 'worth all the suave palaver and exasperating preachments to which other publicists treat that country'.

One must question Eliot's superior tone. Spelled out, his own Utopia was a closed society whose aristocratic rulers forbade education to the masses and purged subversives such as free-thinking Jews. [3] Having seen uncomfortably similar ideas put into practice by Mussolini and Hitler, Eliot – unlike his old partner in crime, Ezra Pound – had somewhat modified his attitude to liberal democracy. But what had Wells been doing lately to make such an impression on this repentant enemy?

Following his experiments in cinema, Wells had found a new means to address a mass audience in the growth of paperback books, specifically Allen Lane's Penguin imprint. Wells's most recent hardcover, *The Fate of Homo Sapiens*, had been a rather tired reaffirmation of his ideas, including another clumsy attack on Judaism, though its publication date of August 1939 caused it to be unusually well received. In contrast, *In Search of Hot Water*, published in November as a Penguin Special, felt like a new stage in his career. He sent a copy to Beatrice Webb, telling her delightedly that there was an initial print run of 50,000 copies and that fan mail was coming in from all over the world.[4]

To go with the new medium, Wells was developing a new message. Drawing on his experience of the previous world war, he had begun by pressing for war aims that would commit the Allies to some kind of global federation. He sent letters to the press calling for a debate on the topic. By late October, however, his thinking had moved on a step. 'I've been hit by a great idea,' he wrote to the left-wing journalist and MP Vernon Bartlett; '. . . what of Magna Carta over again? Why not a *Declaration of Right* – something of the sort I send you herewith?'[5] He put his moral wants list into another letter to *The Times,* which ignited considerable public attention, and incorporated it into his latest call to arms, published in January 1940, *The New World Order*.

From February 1940, prompted by Ritchie Calder, the *Daily Herald* devoted a page every day for a month to the 'Great Debate'. Contributions flooded in from all over the world, and, in an unintended tribute, the project was denounced on the front page of Mussolini's newspaper *Il Popolo d'Italia* and for a full week by Hans Fritzsche on German radio. Wells chaired a committee to revise his draft in the light of the more constructive comments he had received. Calder and the *Herald*'s editor Francis Williams were members, along with the internationally renowned journalist Sir Norman Angell, Britain's first woman Cabinet Minister Margaret Bondfield, the country's top physician Lord Horder, the politician Lord Lytton, the nutritionist Sir John Boyd Orr, the former Lord Chancellor Lord Sankey, the sociologist Barbara Wootton and, meeting the need for an eminent scientist, Wells's old college pal Sir Richard Gregory.

Wells's opening article for the *Herald* contained an attack on the leading Conservative appeasers, Chamberlain and Halifax. While Lord Sankey entirely agreed with Wells's view of them, he felt that to express it in this context made the human rights campaign look party political and that this obliged him to resign. Others seemed likely to quit along with him, not least Horder who was both Wells's and Chamberlain's doctor. Called to account by a phone call from Calder, Wells chuckled and agreed to turn over the chairmanship to Sankey. Thus the final document, though largely Wells's work, became the Sankey Declaration. Thirty-five years after the Fabian débâcle, Wells had not mellowed into a committee man. On one occasion when he refused to break for lunch until he got his way, Horder had to call a halt at 3 p.m. and propose they leave Hanover Terrace for a Lyons Corner House before Wells finally gave in.

The Sankey Declaration appeared in the *Herald* on 20 April 1940 and was presented more fully in a bestselling Penguin Special by Wells, *The Rights of Man, Or What Are We Fighting For?*, its title adapted from Tom Paine. Despite all the heated debate, the Sankey Declaration varied little from Wells's original draft, though some clauses were reordered and elaborated to make them clearer and more logical. It proclaimed that people, whatever their race or skin colour, were entitled to such goods as health, education, mobility, work, property and equality of opportunity and were also entitled to freedom from impositions such as intrusion, torture, slander and false imprisonment. The revised version added comments on the growing government power that necessitated the declaration and noted the implications for national laws. Between 1939 and 1944 Wells produced six versions, each time trying to remove ambiguities and make the points more internationally applicable.

Wells's *Rights of Man* book entirely jettisons the tact of Sankey and Calder, marrying support for human rights to controversial causes such as the bombing of Berlin. Wells repeats his attack on Chamberlain, at one point comparing him unfavourably to Hitler ('Hitler anyhow has the prestige of being in his rough way a successful man').[6] He also gives a drubbing to the papacy and to those products of 'Catholic education', the IRA, whose wartime terrorist campaign had recently killed five people in Coventry.[7]

Wells's human rights agitation filled newspaper columns during the period known as the Bore War or Phoney War, but inevitably as fighting began in earnest the debate dropped away. In April 1940 the Nazis invaded Denmark and Norway. In May, on the same day that Churchill took over from Chamberlain as Prime Minister, they began to blitz their way across the Netherlands, Belgium and France. By June the British army was fleeing from the Continent at Dunkirk, and it was clear that the next stage of the conflict would be the Battle of Britain. These historic calamities buried the human rights issue, though, as it turned out, only as a seed that would later bear fruit.

The Sankey Declaration was translated into ten languages and published in forty-eight countries. Roosevelt praised the original version in a letter to Wells of November 1939.[8] When FDR went on to proclaim his Four Freedoms in 1941, and when in 1946 Eleanor Roosevelt began the campaign that would lead to the United Nations Universal Declaration of Human Rights, neither of them mentioned Wells, but they were certainly following his example. While it is possible that they would have adopted the language of rights without him, it is undeniable that here, as so often, his energetic intervention contributed considerably to the global climate of opinion. The human rights lawyer Geoffrey Robertson has called Wells's *Rights of Man* one of the twentieth century's most influential books.[9]

This view of Wells's influence may well have been shared by the Nazis, though with less enthusiasm. In July 1940 they drew up a list of key people to round up when they invaded Britain. In the alphabetical catalogue Wells appeared two places below Chaim Weizmann, nine above Rebecca West. Fortunately, during the summer of 1940 the Luftwaffe failed in their attempt to secure control of the English skies, the prerequisite for an invasion. In September they switched to a bombing campaign that went on for ten nightmare months, leaving 43,000 civilians dead, half of them killed in raids on London. By the time Wells celebrated his seventy-fourth birthday there 100–200 bombers were flying overhead every night, raining down explosives.

The birthday party had to be held a day early because, on 21 September, Wells was setting off on what would prove to be his last lecture tour of the USA. Moura accompanied him as far as Liverpool, where his liner was held up during three nights of bombing until a protective convoy could be assembled. As Britain's lifeline to America, the port of Liverpool and the ships that sailed in and out of it were prize targets. On the 21st and 22nd, while Wells was waiting on the Mersey, narrowly missing destruction by a delayed-action bomb, U-boats were attacking a convoy in the Atlantic, sinking eleven ships. The trip to America was a risky business.

On 24 September Wells finally set off for New York. Precautionary depth charges were dropped along the way, but no U-boat attack materialized. Between the danger of the voyage and having to share a cabin with two other men, Wells was in a tense, bad-tempered state throughout the journey. Even his unease about Jews became overt in the letters he sent Moura. 'I think the way Germans treat Jews is scandalous but after five days on a mainly Yiddish boat, I realize there is a slight but perceptible strain of Teuton in my composition.'[10] On the night of the 25th he had to go to the saloon and sleep on a sofa to avoid the sound of people being seasick in adjacent cabins. He was highly relieved to reach his destination on 3 October.

He stayed in New York for a week with his old friends the Lamonts, then set off on the tour, which took in Birmingham, San Antonio, Dallas, San Francisco, Los Angeles, Phoenix, Denver, Detroit, Toledo, Connecticut and Florida. The exact sequence of his itinerary is unclear – after flying more than 24,000 miles it may have been unclear to Wells himself – and his appointment book also lists Austin and Tuscaloosa among his destinations. Forced to break off in the run-up to the presidential election, which took place on 5 November, he was able to relax a while in California, taking it easy with the Hollywood in-crowd on Santa Monica beach.

Remembering his experiences in the Great War, Wells had refused to accept guidance from the Ministry of Information, and questions were now being asked in Parliament about the effects his maverick interventions were having on Anglo-American relations. One official with a realistic turn of mind noted in Wells's file that, whatever the authorities' indignation, no power on earth was going to prevent him speaking his mind.[11]

Wells delivered his principal lecture 'Two Hemispheres or One World?' thirteen times. He had not been a strong public speaker even in his prime, and he struggled now to make an impact on those who assembled to hear him. Maugham observed he was looking 'old, tired and shrivelled'. People couldn't hear him and walked out in large numbers.[12] Yet even if he was played out as a platform speaker he still had lead in his pencil. Praising his tour agent, the writer and lecturer Harold Peat, Wells reported, 'Wherever he goes, accommodating young ladies appear at his call, and he is mindful of the needs of his client.'[13]

Other highlights of the tour, perhaps not quite so exciting, included the première of Chaplin's movie *The Great Dictator* in New York on 15 October and an on-air conversation with Orson Welles on 28 October, broadcast on station KTSA, San Antonio.[14] H.G. had been addressing the Brewers Association when he was invited to take part in the programme. In this good-natured meeting, skilfully hosted by Charles T. Shaw, both men professed indignation at Hitler, who had seized upon public reaction to the Mercury *War of the Worlds* broadcast as a sign of democratic decadence. Wells invited Orson to do some pre-publicity for his latest project, *Citizen Kane*, which had been completed only a few days before. When H.G. eventually saw the film, he sent Orson a telegram hailing it as 'magnificent'. [15]

He also used the Texan interview to publicize his own latest piece of fiction, a return to the full-length novel called *Babes in the Darkling Wood*. The book's preface is one of Wells's firmest ripostes to the James gang. He denies the existence of *the* novel and *the* short story and argues for a range of sub-genres of which the discussion novel is a valid member. Unfortunately, *Babes* itself is a notably poor example of dialogue fiction, bludgeoning the reader with almost 400 pages of heavy-handed discussion, including an ungrateful denunciation of T.S. Eliot.

Babes was published in November. By the end of the month Wells had returned to New York. He remained there during December and dined with his old flame Martha and her new husband Ernest Hemingway. It may have been around this time that he attended a variety show at Loew's State Theatre on Broadway, enjoying such entertainers as the Ritz Brothers, one of whom came off the stage and landed in his lap.[16]

A biography based on Wells's writings naturally tends to memorialize him as a thinker, but, as the Ritz Brothers anecdote reminds us, on a day-to-day basis he was a more colourful character than this suggests, something like a hybrid of Albert Camus and Robert Benchley or, if that is too hard to picture, a seriously clued-up version of Mr Polly. Wells's appointment book records that, between delivering a lecture to the Royal Institution in September 1941 and publishing it in booklet form as 'Science and the World Mind' in 1942, he attended the première of a less earnest but more enduring work, Disney's *Dumbo*. Frank Wells's son Martin recalls that around this period his grandfather was prone to teach him and his sister 'unsuitable games'. These included climbing around the room without touching the floor and turning every object in the room, including those in cupboards, upside down, leading to considerable breakages.[17]

At the end of his visit to the USA the mischievous old-timer took a Pan American Airways flight south to Bermuda, where he had a well-earned rest in the sunshine, before sailing to Lisbon and, after some delay, returning to England on 4 January 1941. Travelling on a ship out of neutral Portugal, rather than taking the direct route from New York to Liverpool, made it much less likely that he would end up as a statistic in the Battle of the Atlantic.

Anthony reports that on Wells's return from America those who knew him were shocked by his physical deterioration. His clothes hung on him like 'reach-me-downs'.[18] American groupies notwithstanding, Moura would later confide that even the fabled Wells libido was flagging by the 1940s. To keep work and love life separate, he would arrange his assignations with her in a flat he owned in the mews behind Hanover Terrace. 'And my dear, at his age,' she would conclude, 'by the time he had walked there, I don't know why he bothered.'

Wells's 1940 schedule was already a busy one for a man of his years, but he managed to fit in two further books. A rather scrappy Penguin Special, *The Common Sense of War and Peace*, chews over the realignment of the left and stresses the importance of opposition in a democratic system, but fails to explain how the new global institutions he advocates might guarantee such opposition. The book is perhaps most notable for its classic statement of Wells's intended relationship with his readers:

> Read me, I would say, use all I have to give you, assimilate me to yourself (and assimilation may very well mean a digestive change and improvement) and we will go on together in fraternal co-operation, but please, please, do not imagine you are being invited to line up behind me. You have a backbone and a brain; your brain is as important as mine and probably better at most jobs; my only claim on your consideration is that I have specialized in trying to get my Outlines true.[19]

In *All Aboard for Ararat* Wells returns to *Candide*-length fiction with some success. A series of comical debates between God and Noah Lammock leads to the unwilling Noah piloting a new ark into unknown waters. Graham Greene, reviewing the book in the *Spectator*, praised the residual creative drive and humour that had once made Wells a novelist of genius.[20]

Wells must have retained some concern for his literary reputation because in August 1941 he replied to the American critic, Edward Wagenknecht, commenting on a draft chapter for the latter's *Cavalcade of the English Novel*. Wagenknecht was more catholic in his admiration for Wells's fiction than most critics since but reaches the same conclusion as everyone else: namely, that Wells's gift for storytelling enabled him to produce some fine books and extend the scope of fiction, especially in the earlier part of his career, but latterly distrust of the non-rational had inhibited his artistry.

Readers with long memories may recall that at the height of that career Wells had given encouragement to the African–American author Mary Church Terrell. The two had continued to correspond and occasionally meet up, most recently in 1937 at Hanover Terrace. She had now found a publisher for an autobiography, who, among several requirements, seems to have stipulated that the book needed a preface by Wells to guarantee sales. He obliged at the start of April 1940. He also suggested she change the title from *Confessions of a Colored Woman* to the more confrontational *A Colored Woman in a White World,* under which name the book was published later that year.

In June 1940 Wells wrote to another protégé, J.B. Priestley, praising his hugely popular wartime radio 'Postscripts'. Though these pulled in sixteen million listeners, the BBC ceased to broadcast them later in the year, after many Conservatives, not least Winston Churchill, protested that their tone was too socialistic. The following year Wells gave some cautious support to Priestley's 1941 Committee, a kind of left-wing think tank that involved such Wellsian figures as Vernon Bartlett, Ritchie Calder, Michael Foot, Victor Gollancz, Kingsley Martin and David Low and which later gave birth to the short-lived Common Wealth Party, of which Wells disapproved.

Perhaps Wells's truest disciple – not least in being a rebel with a backbone and brain of his own and a consequent disinclination to follow leaders – was the man known to his parents as Eric Blair but familiar to most people by the last of the three pseudonyms he had come up with for his first book: Kenneth Miles, H. Lewis Allways and George Orwell. All three names, as Patrick Parrinder has pointed out, sound like covert variations on 'H.G. Wells'.[21] Among Orwell's novels, *Keep the Aspidistra Flying* can be regarded as a remodelling of *Love and Mr Lewisham* and *Coming Up for Air* a jaundiced update of *Mr Polly* incorporating a sly parody of *Men Like Gods.*[22] *Nineteen Eighty-Four,* based on Zamyatin's *We,* also derives directly from the *Sleeper* and, like *Brave New World,* implies a principled repudiation of Wells's utopianism. (A cruder attack would come in 1945 from C.S. Lewis in the form of *That Hideous Strength,* where Wells is caricatured as the Cockney journalist Jules.)

It was perhaps fortunate that *Nineteen Eighty-Four* did not appear until after Wells's death. When the two authors crossed swords it was over a mere article of Orwell's, 'Wells, Hitler and the World State', published in the August 1941 issue of *Horizon.* Orwell praises Wells's work up to 1914 but contends that his utopianism has blinded him to the perversities of human nature. Orwell does not deny that something like the Wellsian world state may come into existence in the long term, but for now science and technology have put power into the hands of crazed war lords rather than men of peace.

In some ways the attack is unfair. As John Partington has pointed out, Orwell simplifies Wells's message and is plain wrong in implying that Wells equates scientific and social progress.[23] In fact Wells had repeatedly warned of the dangers of science and the need for its power to be controlled by a sane polity. One might add that Orwell's own version of socialism, damagingly rooted in upper-middle-class guilt and entailing a naïve hope that the war would end in a workers' uprising, was infinitely sillier than Wells's. Even so, many readers have felt that Orwell had a point. Something had gone decisively wrong with Wells's vision around the time of the Great War. The storytelling gift praised by Wagenknecht had been overwhelmed by an obsessive idealism. Wells's fiction had become solipsistic and top-heavily discursive, his political writings focused too narrowly on a pseudo-religious dream of the future. The contingent world appeared as little more than an annoying obstruction.

Orwell was a particularly annoying obstruction into whom Wells seemed fated to run. They had previously met through a mutual acquaintance, the novelist Inez Holden, and Wells had agreed to have dinner with her, Orwell, Orwell's wife Eileen and the poet and critic William Empson. The meal took place on 30 August 1941 at the Orwells' flat in Abbey Road, St John's Wood, shortly after the offending article was published. When Holden arrived she found Orwell looking like an embarrassed schoolboy.[24] Both men produced copies of *Horizon*, slapped them on the table like duellists offering their weapons for inspection and fell to arguing point by point about what Orwell had said. They fought to a draw, agreeing that they wanted an essentially similar world, with Wells focused more on its nature and Orwell on how it might be achieved. They parted amicably enough, but hostilities broke out again six months later when Orwell's radio talk, 'The Rediscovery of Europe', was published in the *Listener* on 19 March 1942.

This time Orwell's hostile points were made as part of an argument that the best modern authors, for all their ideological shortcomings, at least escaped the provincial English mentality of their late-Victorian counterparts because of the disillusionment caused by the Great War. As so often with Orwell, the argument has a basis in truth and is expressed persuasively, but many of its details dissolve on inspection, not least because modernism was well under way before the Great War broke out.

Orwell's particular criticism of Wells is that his vision of life rests on a reductive belief in scientific progress. Outraged to be so circumscribed and, worse, to be told he belonged to an era that had passed almost thirty years before, Wells fired off a letter to Orwell the following week, the text of which has not survived save for the words, 'I don't say that at all. Read my early works, you shit.'[25] This reference to 'early works' gives the game away. Wells's early fiction was broader in scope than Orwell allowed, yet Orwell was right to suggest that most of Wells's later fiction was unbalanced by a superficial vision of redemption, rationalized by often illegitimate appeals to science.

Shortly after the second dispute with Orwell, Wells was confined to bed with bronchitis and exhaustion. At seventy-five he was flagging physically, but continued to devise new writing projects. He managed two books in 1941, another human rights primer called *Guide to the New World* and a novel, *You Can't Be Too Careful.* The latter is a spirited satire on reaction and timidity, tracing the life story of a man hopelessly devoid of idealism, though in the end its one-note negativity becomes wearing. The book is dedicated to the American novelist Christopher Morley 'who richly deserves it', which sounds ironic but is actually not, as Wells admired his writings.

You Can't Be Too Careful would be Wells's last novel. The three books he produced in 1942, a year during which he was confined indoors much of the time by his health, were all reiterations. *The Conquest of Time* was designed to replace *First and Last Things* in Watts' Thinker's Library. *The Outlook for Homo Sapiens* was a combined revision of *The Fate of Homo Sapiens* and *The New World Order. Phoenix* was a discussion of revolution that might better have been called 'Ashes', since – despite the requests of the publisher – no practical suggestions emerged from the burning topics discussed. A chapter called 'A Short History of War and Human Inequality' may preserve something of *A Baiting of Warriors,* which Wells had been drafting at the end of 1941. Another cancelled project was an atlas of natural resources for war materials, mooted in October 1942.

From October 1942 to early 1943 Wells helped the BBC's Lance Sieveking develop an eight-part radio adaptation of *Mr Polly* into a film scenario. According to Wells, he made £4,000 on the deal to Sieveking's £1,250 but expected most of it to go in tax.[26] The script was partially filmed by RKO, it seems, but scrapped once the Hollywood studios switched to war films. Wells also advised Sieveking on a radio adaptation of one of his lesser short stories called 'Mr Ledbetter's Vacation' and warned him off attempting *The Wheels of Chance,* as the story was rooted in an age long past.

One notable Wells film did get made during this period: the 1941 version of *Kipps* (known in the USA as *The Remarkable Mr Kipps*), scripted by Sidney Gilliat with uncredited aid from Frank Launder and directed by Carol Reed. Elizabeth Healey, now Elizabeth Bruce, was impressed by how much Michael Redgrave as Kipps had been made to physically resemble the young Wells.[27] Wells himself was disgruntled to find his didactic prologue cut from the script.

The project closest to Wells's heart in this period was a doctoral thesis on human identity, which he hoped would get him the Fellowship of the Royal Society he had long desired, but his most interesting production may well have been an article called 'What a Zulu Thinks of the English', incorporating a letter he had received in August 1942 from Lance-Corporal Aaron Hlope, who had been serving with the Allies in Cairo.

South African troops were fighting alongside British ones in the war, despite hostility to Britain among the former Boers, so Wells's attack on South African racism was controversial. The BBC and *The Times* were among those that prudently declined to take a piece that might damage Allied solidarity. It eventually appeared in the London *Evening Standard* of 16 March 1943 and at greater length in Wells's book *'42 to '44*, renamed 'The Rights of Man in South Africa'.

Hlope had targeted Wells because of the latter's stand on human rights. Wells replied to him sympathetically, though disavowing Hlope's view that he should be ranked alongside Jesus Christ.[28] He told Hlope that his daughter and her husband had investigated the 'colour question' during their time in South Africa and had developed 'the utmost contempt and indignation for the unfairness of the handicaps put upon men of colour'.

For all his cosmopolitanism, Wells was proud to quote the following passage from Hlope's letter in his article:

> What has shocked every black man from South Africa is the behaviour of your English tommies . . . They shake hands with us, they talk to us, they sit next to us in cinemas, they drink beer with us, they smoke cigarettes with us. Even when one goes to the British Hospital, he gets the same food with them, he lines into one line with them, he is given a bed in the ward same to other beds and blankets, he is sent to the ward according to the nature of his sickness . . . It is the first time in life that we have seen people of that kind.

Wells's article highlights the uncomfortable contradiction between the Allies' liberal war aims and this racist segregation that in a few years' time would be formulated into 'apartheid'. Anticipating (perhaps inspiring) Harold Macmillan's 'wind of change' speech by seventeen years, and Bob Dylan's song 'Blowin' in the Wind' by twenty, he declares:

> The breath of freedom is blowing round the world, and it will blow into your Dominion as elsewhere . . . If you let up these poor devils now, you will get a civilized deal. If not, race rebellion . . . I ask you, when all the rest of the world is made equal and free, how can the petty tyranny of your system escape a convulsion?

Anna Jane had returned to South Africa during 1940, where she noted that some of the 'more Afrikaans members' of the University of the Witwatersrand were indeed 'proud to call themselves Nazis'.[29] She made the journey because in July of that year Eric had been offered the job of director of the Singapore radio station, which was intended to broadcast news, entertainment and propaganda to much of the Far East, including Japan and China. Planning to wait for Eric in the relative safety of the Cape, Anna Jane sailed with the children from Glasgow during August and put up at a seaside hotel, where she occupied herself with a secretarial course. Eric was going to tour several Far Eastern countries before taking up his post. Intending to travel via Canada, he set out from Liverpool on the *City of Benares*, bound for Montreal.

He left Liverpool a few days before his father-in-law and faced the same risks as Wells had on his crossing of the Atlantic. At about 10 p.m. on 17 September the *Benares* was hit by a torpedo from a U-boat. There were 406 passengers and crew aboard; 245 of them drowned, including 77 out of 90 children who were being evacuated to safety. [30] Eric helped many people reach lifeboats, several times refusing a place for himself. He eventually got on to a raft carrying a second engineer with a head wound and also managed to haul aboard an eight-year-old boy called Jack Keeley. After a grim night the trio were picked up in the early hours by HMS *Hurricane*. After returning to Britain, Eric twice visited Jack and his family with cheering food and gifts.

In Eric's absence, Anna Jane and the children completed the journey to Singapore on 15 December, where the family were then reunited. During the following year Anna Jane did some scriptwriting and broadcasting but mainly worked for the Economic Research Bureau. Singapore was supposed to be an impregnable fortress, but to those stationed there it felt increasingly vulnerable. Aerial bombing and radio threats about the fate of white females who fell into enemy hands eroded morale, as did the knowledge that a history of arrogant, racist treatment by upper-class British had made many of the locals sympathetic to the Japanese cause. In late 1941, when Eric was recalled to England, Anna Jane sent the children to Australia, and, together with many other English women, she quit Singapore during January 1942.

Eric put up for several weeks at Hanover Terrace before flying back from Dublin, via Sudan, India and Java. 'Passed Eric in mid-air,' Anna Jane informed her father, 'maddening'.[31] She would now be based in Delhi, researching pamphlets and running a library for the Ministry of Information. Eric had been given the option of remaining in India or in Batavia (present-day Jakarta), where he was setting up an alternative radio station in case the Singapore transmitter went down, but he was determined to return and support his colleagues, no matter what the danger.

On 9 February, the day the Japanese invasion force landed, one colleague, Giles Playfair, wrote a vivid pen portrait of him:

> he has remained immune from the prevailing malaise of hopelessness . . . he thrives on responsibilities . . . He is quite fearless in his approach to problems and quite ruthless in smashing down opposition. He is no respecter of position. He has considerable personal magnetism, but while I imagine he is capable of charming a cheerless landlady into serving him with a drink after hours, he is not averse, when

> crossed, to being witheringly rude to a pundit. Everything he does – even little things – he does in a big way – with Cyrano's panache.[32]

And this is the man Wells had once judged to be an unimpressive personality. Twelve years on the pundit of Hanover Terrace surely knew better.

Eric switched broadcasting to the Batavia station but could not get permission to destroy the Singapore transmitter before it fell into enemy hands. On 11 February, with the Japanese forces advancing ever closer, he ordered his men to evacuate while he awaited the authorization. In the event the job was done by others, and he was able to rejoin his party and lead it on the hazardous escape route to Batavia. Behind them, on 15 February, in the worst defeat in British military history, 80,000 Allied troops surrendered to just 30,000 Japanese, permanently destroying Britain's military credibility in the Far East.

Eric remained in Batavia to cover the war for the BBC. When the station ceased to broadcast on 19 February his own fate went unreported. The Japanese landed in Java on 28 February; the Allied forces surrendered on 8 March. Throughout Indonesia millions would soon perish under a regime of forced labour, famine and massacre.

Wells sent Anna Jane a telegram:

> COURAGE ERIC MAY BE PRISONER OR HIDING FIGHTING ADVISE STICK IT AT DELHI CHILDREN SAFER WHERE THEY ARE I HAVE HAD COLLAPSE THROUGH OVERWORK AND STILL HORS DE COMBAT SEEING ONLY HOUSEHOLD AND DOCTORS. LETTER WILL FOLLOW. LOVE MY DEAR.[33]

Anna Jane knew that her chances of seeing either husband or father again were low. In November she told Wells she had been homesick, thinking of the sound of ducks in Regent's Park at dawn, then him breakfasting in his Jaeger suit, contemplating piles of letters.[34] Ten months later, writing on his birthday, she told him:

> I saw a picture, in one of the BBC publications, I think it was, of people by the side of Regent's Park, and if I imagined a little, there among them was a nice not too tall and not too slim man with a felt hat and a stick, looking at the water.[35]

A letter from Amber to Marjorie reports that Anna Jane had been suffering from anaemia and malaria.[36] She and her colleagues had been turned out of their billets at the Hotel Cecil and put into a hostel with inadequate bathing and sanitary arrangements. Could H.G. pull strings with the Ministry of Information or the BBC to remedy the situation? With or without his help, Anna Jane eventually transferred to Economic Intelligence in Ceylon.

In October 1945, a month before she returned to Singapore, she was able to confirm that Eric had perished in 1942 trying to escape on a ship out of Surabaya that had been hit and sunk – one of the 50 million or more individuals whose lives were squandered in the war.[37]

Surrounded by death, Wells anticipated his own in a partly fictional 'Auto-Obituary', originally published in *Coronet* in 1937 but reprinted for a wider audience in the *Strand Magazine* in January 1943. He summed himself up as a liberal democrat in his commitment to free speech but a socialist in his 'antagonism to personal, racial, or national monopolization'.[38] His novels, films and 'repetitive' essays had pointed the way to a new civilization but, according to his forecast, lacked the distinction to be preserved by posterity. He was injured in a brawl with Fascists in 1948, then imprisoned in a concentration camp during the brief Communist dictatorship of 1952. A civil-list pension helped him linger on until 1963, an obese figure hobbling around Regent's Park with the aid of a stick and muttering to himself.

'Some day,' he would be heard to say, 'I shall write a book, a *real* book.'

20
EXASPERATIONS
1943–1946

Wells was indeed slowing down: going out less, dozing more. Weather permitting, he tried to walk a mile or so every day, to the Zoo, to Queen Mary's Gardens, to the Savile Club in Brook Street, sometimes calling in at the Baker Street branch of W.H. Smith's to see what was on the bookshelves. When Margaret Sanger invited him to come over and take it easy in the sunshine of Tucson, he told her he would wait until he was 'really old & worn out'. He declined a similar offer of refuge in Kansas from the radical publisher Emanuel Haldeman-Julius.[1] He did not want people to think he had run away to lecture at others from a privileged position of safety. Lesser writers might flee to the other side of the Atlantic; Wells was made of sterner stuff.

He was scornful of the V1 'doodlebugs', 2,500 of which fell on London from June 1944 onwards, joined from September by the more powerful V2 missiles. 'Robot bombs break a lot of windows and so forth but are quite ineffective from a military point of view,' he reassured Sanger, 'and they are nothing to those of us who went through the hard times of 1941.' His front door had been blown in repeatedly during the Blitz, and he estimated that incendiary bombs would have burned down the house a dozen times if those around him had not tackled them promptly. One such bomb, if it had fallen twenty yards nearer and on hard road instead of mud, would probably have brought the building down on top of him.[2]

The V-weapons, which killed more than 6,000 people, were Hitler's last resort. By 1944 Germany was threatened from all directions. The project that had begun around the time of Wells's birth, to make Prussia Europe's dominant power, was coming to its terrible conclusion. Even Italy, the birthplace of Fascism, had switched sides. While the vengeful Russians drove Hitler's army back through Eastern Europe, Western Europe was being overrun by a huge Allied invasion force while from above bombers inflicted destruction on German cities, incinerating men, women and children in a campaign that even at the time struck some as morally and militarily dubious. In the Far East the Americans were moving slowly but relentlessly across the Pacific islands towards Japan.

Wells's thoughts were, as ever, on the longer term. In February he informed Anna Jane that he was getting his declaration of rights translated into every key language so that it could become a fundamental law for the whole world. Translation was imperative because, if left in English, the declaration might look like propaganda for a 'new Imperialism'.[3] In October 1944 Wells asked London University's School of Oriental and African Studies to revise the Urdu, Hindi and Arabic translations they had already made and to add several others.[4] Aaron Hlope must have been in his mind when he received the Zulu version. 'Why should the world play the nigger driver to a fine upstanding eloquent people like the Zulus?' he asked in a letter. 'Are they to be forced into slavery to compete with workers elsewhere and earn dividends for the appropriating classes?'[5]

Wells's terminology is unusually Marxist here. Like many people in Europe he did tend to move left during this period. The Russians won sympathy for the shocking magnitude of their losses (seventy times those of the USA, forty times those of Britain), people were getting used to a society in which virtually everything was controlled by the government for the public good, and there was an obvious need for a meeting of minds with the Communists in building a post-war order – but Wells's willingness to reach out the hand of friendship did not imply uncritical acceptance of the Kremlin's ideology or actions. He continued to regard the Soviets as pioneers of socialist revolution who were mostly of value in demonstrating its pitfalls.

In their backward-looking dogmatism and sectarian conspiracies, Communists were, in his view, the exact counterparts of the Catholics who obstructed progress to socialism more openly. He declared, 'The Roman Catholic Church is my *bête noire* and the Communist Party my *bête rouge*.'[6] If the Russian war record had caused him to adopt a more positive tone towards Communism, the recent policies of the Vatican renewed his hostility to Catholicism, which he had once seen as a possible vehicle for the spiritual unity of mankind. In his old age Sarah's anti-Catholic teaching seems to have taken belated effect.

The sole book Wells produced during 1943 was a controversial Penguin Special called *Crux Ansata: An Indictment of the Roman Catholic Church.* Wells explained to a puzzled Margaret Sanger that the title referred to the plain cross on the book's front cover, in opposition to the triple cross of the Papacy.[7] As a former Catholic turned birth-control campaigner, Sanger encouraged Wells to write the book and proofed it for him. Unable to find an American publisher, Wells gifted her the US rights, though her edition was delayed when Catholic printworkers refused to bind it.

There was, of course, no shortage of ammunition for an attack on the Church, even in those days before widespread sexual abuse by priests had come to light. Pope Pius XI supported Franco and accommodated Mussolini, announcing that *Il Duce* had survived an assassination attempt because he enjoyed divine protection. Pius XII, who succeeded to the papal throne in 1939, decided that the best policy for the war years was not a firm moral stand but defensive neutrality. Urged to condemn the extermination of 10 million people in Nazi death camps, he produced disappointingly vague rebukes and studiedly never mentioned the Jews who constituted more than half the victims, though he did help Jews behind the scenes. (It must be said that his record was better than that of many Protestant leaders and, arguably, no worse than Wells's.)

Wells does not mince his words, insisting on Pius XII's 'profound ignorance and mental inferiority'.[8] It could be argued that such a tone was wantonly divisive at a time when everyone on the Allied side, including Christians and Communists, needed to be brought together, but Wells could have retorted that in 1940s Britain truth was one of the few commodities that did not have to be rationed. Writing shortly afterwards, Orwell would struggle to find a publisher for his similarly controversial *Animal Farm*, though, ironically, the Soviets whom he satirized soon became the enemy and his fable was a runaway bestseller. In *Nineteen Eighty-Four* Orwell went on comprehensively to satirize Communism, Fascism and all religions, particularly Catholicism, as orthodoxies that promise to take away anxiety, guilt and weakness in return for a fateful sacrifice of individual judgement.

Orwell's books were written at the height of his powers, but *Crux Ansata*, which Wells put on to paper in a mere three weeks, is an undisciplined mess. Wells hardly engages with recent events, preferring to devote most of his diatribe to warmed-over material from the *Outline*, plus digressions on Chaucer, Langland, Milton and Shakespeare. Even the belligerently topical heading of his first chapter, 'Why Do We Not Bomb Rome?', lacked force by October 1943 when the book was published, as the Allies had actually bombed Rome in July. *Crux Ansata* had no impact on the world except to give notice that Wells was in decline.

Further evidence followed a year later when Wells began a campaign against one of his neighbours, Sir Thomas Moore, a Conservative MP with links to the Right Book Club, distributors of Odette's meditation on recent history, *And Hell Followed . . .* Moore had allowed his London residence at 1 Hanover Terrace to be used as a Salvation Army Club. Wells objected violently to the signboards displayed outside, arguing that their positioning breached the terms of the residents' contract and insinuating that they were a device for lowering property values so that the whole terrace could be bought up cheaply. In addition to abusive letters to Moore, questioning whether he was part of some Catholic conspiracy, and complaints to the Crown authorities, Wells pursued the matter in the letter pages of the *Daily Mail*, *New Leader*, *The Times*, *Star* and *New Statesman*, making an unfortunate exhibition of himself.

While baiting Catholics, Wells paradoxically decided it was time to make up with the Jews and stop repeating his painfully ill-timed claim that their persecution was self-provoked. In a letter to the Jewish leader Chaim Weizmann, he admitte:,

> In many ways, and largely I am afraid, through my own ready irritability and tactlessness, I have aroused the resentment of Jews who are essentially at one with me in their desire for a sane equalitarian world order . . . I have girded at Jews as

> Johnson used to gird at Scotchmen, and some of them are among the best of my friends. In these urgent days there is a need for a fundamental solidarity in creative work that should rule out these minor resentments.[9]

Wells even tried to accommodate himself to Zionism, accepting that there should be historic Jewish centres around the world, though 'you can no more put the Jews back into Palestine than you can put the English back into Schleswig Holstein and Saxony'.

Weizmann was clearly unconvinced by this argument, as six years later he became the first President of Israel. Determined after the Holocaust to establish a nation state of their own in which they would not be a vulnerable minority, thousands of Jews set off for Palestine to drive out the Arabs who were already living there and see off the British who were trying to balance the interests of both parties. Sixty years later the ensuing conflict shows no real sign of ending. All round the world Wells's dream of nationalist rivalries becoming obsolete after the war has proved wholly unrealistic.

Crux Ansata had been extracted and elaborated from a record of Wells's wartime reflections. The remainder of the project, including 'The Plain Truth About the Communist Party', became available in March 1944 in a limited edition of 2,000 copies, priced at two guineas and entitled *'42 to '44: A Contemporary Memoir Upon Human Behaviour During the Crisis of the World Revolution.* The book was dedicated to the dissident fourteenth-century priest and leader of the Peasants' Revolt, John Ball, whom Wells saw as both role model and local hero. Forget the German and Russian socialists; it was in Kent that democratic collectivism first found clear expression. An epigraph taken from Nietzsche declares life to be fragmentary and accidental but man to be 'a poet and a solver of riddles and the saviour of accidents'.

The book has little new to offer but is a vigorous miscellany, containing a fulsome tribute to the recently dead Beatrice Webb and four pages of quotations from Thomas Jefferson, whom Wells had been reading in an edition presented to him years before by the former presidential candidate William Jennings Bryan. Despite Jefferson's input, Wells had still not grasped the importance of accountability, arguing that human rights need not entail General Elections and that focus groups might be a more effective way of finding out public opinion.

An appendix contains Wells's Ph.D. submission, 'A Thesis on the Quality of Illusion in the Continuity of the Individual Life in the Higher Metazoa, with Particular Reference to the Species *Homo Sapiens*', for which he had been awarded a doctorate in science by the University of London in June 1943. (It had awarded him an honorary Doctor of Literature in 1936.) A shortened version of the thesis appeared in the April 1944 issue of *Nature* and as a pamphlet. The thesis restates Wells's conviction that the individual human being has no unitary identity but is made up of disparate 'behaviour systems'. What enables people to function with a degree of consistency is a set of ongoing stories about themselves. Full coherence cannot be achieved by individuals, only by the species of which the individual is an experiment, though occasionally the individual experiment will make a positive difference to the species – in effect, Wells's core story about himself.

Despite the numbered paragraphs, academic citations and specialist jargon, the thesis is not a scientific formulation but a secularized recasting of sin and salvation. The academics of London University were stretching a point in awarding him a doctorate on the strength of it. Since the thesis was submitted with the *Outline* trilogy and *Phoenix*, they presumably judged it was a valid reward to bestow on someone who had done outstanding work as a public educator. Though Wells did not gain the Fellowship of the Royal Society, the prize for which he yearned most of all, he had at least made good his youthful ambition to become a learned doctor.

That ambition had been voiced in 1885, when the future lay open before him. By the time of the publication of *'42 to '44* his life was drawing to a close. In March 1944 Anthony told Rebecca that Wells had been diagnosed with liver cancer. Anthony was now living near his father, keeping an eye on him. He had used money from his trust fund to buy a farm for himself, his wife and their two children near Newbury. However, as a pacifist, he had been raided by the police, who confiscated many of his personal possessions including the toy soldiers that had inspired *Floor Games* and *Little Wars*. Anthony had then moved to London, found a job as a sub-editor for the BBC and moved into 'Mr Mumford's', the flat behind Hanover Terrace. There he learned of his father's illness from Lord Horder.

Horder advised Gip, Frank and Anthony not to tell their father the bad news, but after thinking through the consequences they decided they must so that his affairs could be put in order, even if it meant losing Horder's services as physician. Wells himself records the outcome in the final chapter of *Exasperations*, an uncompleted collection of articles reviewing his life and ideas.

> When they told me about it I wept like a child from whom some treasure had been snatched, because I had been counting on at least four years before my natural expectation of life ran out. And I had got so very much to do that I had set my heart on doing. I confess that I wept with vexation at this sudden, harsh truncation of my future. I blubbered with disappointment, and so did my family.[10]

Having composed himself for death, Wells then went into remission and felt better than he had done for months. He told himself that he had been misdiagnosed and might go on for ten years or more. Eventually, however, it became clear that the reprieve was only temporary, and in February 1945 he finalized his will, naming

Marjorie as the executor. The final sentence recorded 'the good and sane behaviour of all my offspring towards me and each other and the abundant interest and happiness with which they have enriched my life . . . I leave them my benediction.'[11]

In the same month Wells published *The Happy Turning*. This had started out as the penultimate chapter of *Exasperations* but was extracted and elaborated into a separate book, recalled from the literary agent Curtis Brown in October 1944 for final revisions and cuts. The end result was a slim volume of fifty pages, describing the dreams and reveries of Wells's old age. Many of the dreams in *The Happy Turning* are conversations with Jesus, who at some point in the last 2,000 years seems to have swapped his Jewish beliefs for Wellsian ones. '*Never* have disciples,' Jesus warns his successor: revolutions must emerge from the work of many people over time, not the preachings of a Messiah and a bunch of hangers-on. When Wells asks him if he follows terrestrial affairs, Jesus replies that he has the gist: 'They crucify me daily.'[12] Wells abuses his biblical knowledge further by taking a 900-word curse from Deuteronomy 28 and unleashing it against the nearest epitome of life's ills, the sycamore tree of an absentee neighbour that had sent some of its seeds into his garden.

The editor of the *Countryman* was so impressed by this piece of vituperation that he persuaded Wells to take part in a photoshoot for an article called 'H.G. Wells: Back Gardener'. The photographer Ronald Proctor, calling in the second week of March 1945, found Wells a frail old man recovering from an attack of bronchitis who had to be helped on with his cloak and assisted downstairs. Wells could only remain outside for a couple of minutes before going back in, completely exhausted. Proctor took a picture of Wells glowering at some sycamore seeds and another of him brandishing his fist at the offending tree.

Exactly two months after the photoshoot, Victory in Europe was declared, triggering the end of coalition government in Britain. Despite his professed scepticism about elections and the fact that he was confined to bed for several weeks, Wells made a determined effort to reach a polling station, hoping to put in a cantankerous vote for the Communists. Unable to locate a suitably revolutionary candidate in his Marylebone constituency, he had to settle for the Labour Party representative, Dr Elizabeth Jacobs, the granddaughter of his old friends W.W. and Nell Jacobs. She assured him that she wished to cooperate with Russia and to let the Communist Party affiliate to Labour; Wells sent her a donation of 2 guineas. On 5 July Gip and Marjorie drove him to the polling station. As he was too ill to get out of the car the returning officer brought the ballot paper out.

Despite his efforts, the Conservatives won the seat. Nationally, however, the result was a landslide victory for Labour, delivering the nearest things to a Wellsian government that Britain has seen. Under Clement Attlee's leadership Britain would withdraw from India, Burma, Ceylon and Jordan. There would be nationalization of the Bank of England, the coal mines, the electricity and gas industries, railways, aviation and canals. National Insurance and a National Health Service would be introduced, entitlement to old-age pensions extended. But in the end there would be no irreversible swing away from capitalism and the marketplace towards a comprehensive system of socialist planning. Even if Labour had thought out its nationalization policies properly, the time was hardly ripe for utopian experiments, for Britain was massively in debt to the USA, which severed its financial support as soon as Japan had been defeated. Replacement loans, when they came, were not calibrated to keep Britain in business as a rival world power. With the major exception of the health service, the Attlee years would not be remembered as an era of revolutionary reforms but an age of austerity: rationing, shortages, unemployment, wage freezes and high taxes.

Victory in Japan day came on 14 August, after atomic bombs slaughtered 100,000 innocent people at Hiroshima and Nagasaki. Leo Szilard, who had come up with the idea of the nuclear chain reaction in 1936, was a lifelong Wells enthusiast, inspired by *The World Set Free* to carry out his research but also to fear its consequences. He had originally assigned his patent to the British admiralty to ensure it stayed secret.[13] A few years later, faced by the danger of Fascism, Szilard changed his mind and called for an American nuclear research programme but tried to persuade the US authorities not to drop the resulting bombs directly on to Japanese cities. He did not succeed. The world was entering an era in which the new spirit of prophecy was to think the unthinkable, and Wellsian idealism looked old-fashioned, even if Wells's foresight could not be denied him.

Martha Hemingway wrote to tell Wells that he was the greatest man in the world, but, since he seemed to have influence with history, she wished he could foresee something positive.[14] He did his best, starting work on a film scenario that would update *Things to Come* for the atomic age. None the less, without quite saying as much, his open letter about the proposed film seems to assume that the human race faces extinction, especially in the light of the growing hostility between the USA and the USSR.[15]

A similarly negative view of the human prospect lies behind his final book, *Mind at the End of Its Tether*, a slim volume at which he worried from the summer of 1944 to January 1945. The first three chapters announce the likely extinction of the human race, yet despite a reference to the 'uranium-led riddle' they do not specify atomic warfare as the source of danger.[16] Eternity and the human mind, once parallel, have now parted. Events no longer follow predictably. Facts can no longer be analysed. Space is shrinking. 'Our doomed formicary is helpless as the implacable Antagonist kicks or tramples our world to pieces.'[17]

Eliot had formerly noted that, by pinning his hopes on the near future, Wells was risking despair.[18] Had he now lost that hope because of fear that the USA, so far the only nation with the atomic bomb, might unleash it on the Russians? Or had the splitting of the atom plunged Wells back into George Ponderevo's nightmare vision of a crumbling subatomic world? Or was Wells's mind simply overwhelmed by the approach of his own death? To complicate matters, the last five chapters of *Mind at the End of Its Tether* were adapted from the 1946 revision of *A Short History of the World* (which was made at the end of 1944) and are more positive in attitude, leaving the book fundamentally incoherent. Those who claim it represents Wells's realization that socialism is naïve and impossible are reading a more precise statement into the fears of a dying man than the evidence will support.

Six months after the book was published Wells flatly denied reports that he had plunged into despair, telling Elizabeth Bruce that he was simply bored with human folly and found little satisfaction in the opportunity to say 'I told you so.' His outlook remained the same as ever: 'Take what comes to you & help the weaker brethren to endure.'[19] An accompanying note from Marjorie added that if his old friend could see him she would find Wells had aged considerably recently, requiring a day and a night nurse now to mind him. He spent most of his time in the windowed balcony of the drawing-room, venturing down into the garden only in really warm weather.[20] One visitor was told, 'Don't interrupt me. Can't you see I'm dying?'[21]

He was often joined in the sun lounge by Anthony. Depressed by the ongoing break-up of his first marriage, Anthony longed to talk with his father but was forced to wait through long, drowsy periods for Wells to surface into occasional attentiveness. When he did there was little meeting of minds. Ever since the summer of 1944 Wells had believed that Anthony was working for a pro-Nazi faction at the BBC who were blackmailing him in some way. Anthony suspected that Rebecca was to blame for planting this idea in the old man's head, though senility seems a likelier culprit. Convinced he would never get through to Wells, Anthony buried his face in his hands, eventually raising his gaze to find Wells looking lucidly at him and saying quietly, 'I just don't understand you.'[22] It was the last time the two would communicate.

On the morning of 13 August 1946 Wells was contrastingly bright, cheerful and active, going through his letters with Marjorie and making an attempt at the crossword in *The Times*. It looked as if he would soon be able to come downstairs and be in reasonably good form for his eightieth birthday, just five weeks away. In the afternoon he decided to take a rest. He rang the bell for the nurse shortly after 4 p.m. and asked her to help him off with his pyjama jacket. When she had done so he sat thoughtfully on the edge of the bed a moment, then asked her to replace the jacket and climbed back in. 'Go away,' he told her. 'I'm all right.'[23] When she looked in ten minutes later to see how he was she found a corpse.

Wells had predicted he would die from the weak heart that ran in his family. Most reports have blamed liver cancer, but the official certificate sides with Wells, listing the immediate causes of his death as heart failure, myocardial degeneration and diabetes mellitus, presumably aggravated by the cancer.[24] So it was that Wells kept his record as a prophet to the end.

Obituaries were soon sounding out around the world. 'I do not think of H.G. as dead at all but as going into a far country,' confessed Richard Gregory. 'He is as alive to me as ever he was, & his spirit remains to encourage mankind to high endeavour for many generations.' 'Without men like Wells,' warned the Sydney *Morning Herald*, 'we should be much poorer. . . . When they are dead, the world is left to the mercy of the bookburners, the Communists, the Fascists, the Ku Klux Klan, the extremists of all kinds . . .' 'He was so big a figure,' reflected Orwell, 'he has played so great a part in forming our picture of the world, that in agreeing or disagreeing with his ideas we are apt to forget his purely literary achievement.' Borges concurred, championing the scientific romances but recognizing the impressive range of his other writings from *Mr Polly* to the *Outline*. In his view Wells was not so much an author as a whole literature.[25]

Not only the eminent gave testimonials. On 14 August Edie Rutherford, a Sheffield housewife, noted in her diary:

> So H.G. Wells is dead at last. Roman Catholics will be pleased. He was a highly gifted mind, and courageous, and he has left behind enough testimony to that for all time. Wells was what I call a God man, for all his atheism.[26]

Three days after Wells's death his body was cremated in a private ceremony. (A public commemoration followed on 30 October.) Gip, Frank and Anthony went to the Golders Green Crematorium, along with their Uncle Fred and a select band of mourners, including Gregory, Arthur Morley Davies, Winifred Simmons, Frank Swinnerton and Rebecca West. J.B. Priestley gave a moving address. Readings included an extract from the conclusion of *Tono-Bungay* – 'We are all things that make and pass, striving upon a hidden mission, out to the open sea' – which gave Gip the idea that the ashes of the man who had always hated urns, obelisks and permanent homes should be distributed across the waves.

Just over a year later he took his father's ashes down to the coast to be scattered, not, as legend has it, from an aeroplane – though this would have been an appropriately Wellsian flourish – but from a boat called the *Deidre*, chartered by Anthony.[27] Starting from Poole Harbour, the half-brothers intended to go some way out to sea, but, having run into choppy water, they instead emptied out the ashes just off Studland.

The contents of Wells's house, valued with precision at £3,679 and 12 shillings, were auctioned off item by item to the highest bidders. His archive of books, letters and papers, unable to attract a reasonable offer in austerity Britain, was snapped up by Professor Gordon N. Ray of the University of Illinois for $40,000. Wells left £59,811 to family and friends in his will, though £13,721 of it was promptly claimed for the greater good by the taxman. The sum was smaller than that left by comparable writers because Wells had given so much away during his lifetime. Most of the royalties went to the Wells Estate to be shared out among named recipients. Gip and Frank were among those who received a share of the residue of Wells's property. Frank, who found a niche for himself working for the Children's Film Foundation, also had the rights to film and stage adaptations, while Gip received the rights to the *Outline* and *Science of Life*. Gip continued his career as a professor of biology, achieving the coveted Fellowship of the Royal Society, and also edited several of his father's books. Frank lived on until 1982, Gip until 1985.

Moura received a lump sum of £1,000, plus £3,000 with which to purchase an annuity, was allowed to buy items from Hanover Terrace before the public auction and got a share of the residue in trust for life. She lived on until 1974 as a well-known hostess, literary adviser and London character – talking, drinking and smoking copiously, watching the children's television show *Pinky and Perky* and on at least one occasion shoplifting. At a party in August 1950 she told her secret-service minder 'Klop' Ustinov, father of the actor Peter Ustinov, that the former intelligence officer Anthony Blunt was a spy for the Russians. It would take the security services fourteen years to realize she was right and twenty-nine years before the treachery became public knowledge. Having amassed a huge number of reports on Moura over the years, the security services decided in 1951 that she was not after all a threat to national security, noting gallantly that she was 'an unusually intelligent and amusing woman – a quite outstanding personality'.[28]

Odette had been in England when the war started and, after being bombed out of the Mount Royal Hotel, London, took up residence on the south coast of England at Torquay. She eventually sold her rights in Lou Pidou to the Wells family and spent her last years in Worthing, where she died in 1978. Her books retain a select band of admirers. Amber lived until 1981, and had a successful career as a lecturer and author. She stood for Parliament three times for Labour, but, disillusioned by the development of socialism after Attlee, she voted Conservative in 1970.

Martha's writings continue to be widely admired, particularly her war reporting, though for many her prejudice against Arabs devalues her work on the Middle East. She killed herself in 1998 when the quality of her life in old age became unendurable to her. A US postage stamp was issued in her honour. Rebecca, who also became a highly admired writer, though with a similarly contentious dimension in her support for McCarthyism, died in 1983, a Dame of the British Empire.

Anthony became a successful author, though not so eminent a one as his mother, from whom he remained estranged, the more so after the publication in 1955 of *Heritage*, an autobiographical novel about his upbringing in which she appears as

Naomi Savage, Wells as Max Town and Odette as Lolotte. The book did not appear in Britain until 1984, when Rebecca's death removed the threat of legal action, and it was followed by a long-meditated biography of his father, *H.G. Wells: Aspects of a Life*, a final putting to rest of the past before his own death in 1987.

Anthony's most significant intervention on his father's behalf, however, was an essay of 1957, called simply 'H.G. Wells'. Emphasising the pessimistic character of the early science fiction, this essay decisively challenged the assumption that had grown up over the years that Wells was a simple-minded utopian propagandist and so cleared the way for Bernard Bergonzi's influential study of 1961, *The Early H.G. Wells.* With the scientific romances reinstated in the literary canon, a series of essays by David Lodge – '*Tono-Bungay* and the Condition of England' (1966), 'Reassessing H.G. Wells' (1967) and 'Utopia and Criticism' (1969) – set out the case for some of the mid-period novels as accomplished works of fiction that brokered ingenious deals between Wells's inner conflicts. Wells might have been surprised to find his reputation rebuilt by two critics with Roman Catholic backgrounds, but perhaps the interplay of faith and scepticism in his work was something they were particularly well equipped to understand.

While Anthony adopted a high profile, Anna Jane, or Annajane as she later preferred to be known, carefully avoided publicity. In 1948 she married one of Eric's broadcasting colleagues and for many years worked for the Governor General in Malaya and North Borneo and as an archivist for the *Straits Times* press, coming back to Britain every three years. At the time of writing she is Wells's only surviving child, preparing for her hundredth birthday on the last day of 2009. She and her son Michael have encouraged and supported me in the writing of this biography, as has Catherine Stoye, the daughter of Gip and Marjorie, establishing living connections between past and present that I hardly anticipated when I began the project.

Critical appreciation of Wells has grown during the past half-century, sustained by the tireless efforts of such devotees as Patrick Parrinder and the founder of the H.G. Wells Society, John Hammond. Yet enthusiasm for Wells remains a minority pastime. Many still think of him as a lightweight writer who clumsily confounds serious and popular genres, violates the illusion of art with authorial interruptions and disturbs the texture of his stories with extravagant scientific and global perspectives. Now that all these vulgar lapses have become the postmodern norm, almost compulsory for any author who seeks a prestigious literary prize, one might have expected some re-evaluation of Wells's place in the scheme of things. Instead, the grounds for dismissal have shifted, and he has been put down as an exemplar of the twentieth-century intellectual whose irreligious, revolutionary ideas lead in practice to nihilism and genocide.

If I have dented either of these views by bringing them into abrasive contact with the facts, our trip through time will have been worth while. Returning to the present, we inevitably find ourselves living another kind of life from Wells's, one with significantly different assumptions and opportunities, yet there is much in his picture of the world that we can continue to recognize as we try to fashion our raw experience into meaningful stories of our own. Wells's writings and life cannot provide us with any kind of blueprint, and arguably this was never really his aim, but they do offer a combination of entertainment and intellectual provocation that, contrary to his own self-effacing forecast, seem likely to inspire new generations of readers for a considerable distance into the future.

NOTES

Since there is no single authoritative edition of Wells's works, references for these are normally cited by chapter and section (§) rather than page number.

Chapter 1. Family and Childhood, 1851–1880

1. Thomas Carlyle, 'Signs of the Times', 1829.
2. All quotations from Sarah Wells are from her diary, preserved in the Wells Archive in the Rare Book Room and Manuscript Library of the University of Illinois at Urbana-Champaign. A microfiche copy is held in the Wells Collection at Bromley Central Library.
3. Letter of 7 November 1852 from Joe Wells to Sarah Neal, quoted in Norman and Jeanne MacKenzie, *The Time Traveller*, London, Weidenfeld and Nicolson, 1973, p. 8.
4. Jane Austen, *Pride and Prejudice*, 1813, Ch. 37.
5. William Baxter's papers are preserved in the Wells Collection at Bromley Central Library, along with Geoffrey L. Eames' 1970 typescript, 'Joseph Wells: Father of "H.G." and of the Bromley Cricket Club'.
6. Letter of 23 August 1940 from HGW to Mark Benney, quoted in HGW, *The Desert Daisy*, Gordon N. Ray (ed.), Urbana, Beta Phi Mu, 1957, p. viii.
7. HGW, *Experiment in Autobiography*, Ch. 2, §4.
8. HGW, *The Happy Turning*, Ch. 2.
9. HGW, *Experiment in Autobiography*, Ch. 2, §4.
10. HGW, *First and Last Things*, Bk III, Ch. 1.
11. HGW, *Experiment in Autobiography*, Ch. 3, §2.
12. Geoffrey West, *H. G. Wells: A Sketch for a Portrait*, London, Howe, 1930, p. 25.
13. Draft letter of 12 July 1944 from HGW to unknown recipient, in *The Correspondence of H.G. Wells*, Vol. 4, David C. Smith (ed.), London, Pickering and Chatto, 1998, p. 498.
14. Christoph Christian Sturm, *Reflections on the Works of God*, 1740–86.
15. HGW, *Experiment in Autobiography*, Ch. 3, §1.
16. HGW, *Experiment in Autobiography*, Ch. 2, §5.
17. HGW, *Experiment in Autobiography*, Ch. 3, §4.
18. Anthony West, *H.G. Wells: Aspects of a Life*, London, Hutchinson, 1984, p. 198.
19. HGW, *Experiment in Autobiography*, Ch. 2, §4.
20. Quoted in A. H. Watkins (ed.), *The Catalogue of the H.G. Wells Collection in the Bromley Public Libraries*, Bromley, London Borough of Bromley Public Libraries, 1974, p. ix.

21. HGW, *Experiment in Autobiography*, Ch. 2, §4.
22. HGW, *Experiment in Autobiography*, Ch. 3, §1.
23. HGW, *Experiment in Autobiography*, Ch. 3, §4.

Chapter 2. Five False Starts, 1880–1884

1. HGW, *Experiment in Autobiography*, Ch. 3, §5.
2. HGW, *The Happy Turning*, Ch. 2.
3. HGW, *Experiment in Autobiography*, Ch. 3, §5.
4. Wells refrains from naming Edith in the autobiography, though his statement that she was the youngest daughter identifies her clearly enough. After publication of the book, in a letter of 7 July 1935, now in the Illinois Wells Archive, she wrote to him complaining about how she and her father had been depicted and suggested he might like to buy her a house in compensation. It does not seem that Wells responded to this suggestion favourably.
5. HGW, *Kipps*, Bk I, Ch. 2, §3.
6. HGW, *Experiment in Autobiography*, Ch. 4, §2.
7. HGW, *Experiment in Autobiography*, Ch. 3, §7.
8. HGW, *First and Last Things*, Bk III, Ch. 23.
9. Undated letter from HGW to Frank Wells, in *Correspondence*, Vol. 1, pp. 13–14.
10. Undated letter from HGW to Sarah Wells, reproduced in HGW, *Experiment in Autobiography*, Ch. 4, §2.
11. Undated letter from HGW to Sarah Wells, in *Correspondence*, Vol. 1, p.27.
12. HGW, *H.G. Wells in Love*, G.P. Wells (ed.), London, Faber, 1984, p. 215.
13. Henry George, *Progress and Poverty*, 1879, Ch. 26.
14. W.E. Campbell in the *Catholic World* (May 1910), quoted in William J. Scheick and J. Randolph Cox (eds), *H.G. Wells: A Reference Guide*, Boston, G.K. Hall, 1988, p. 46.
15. HGW, *Experiment in Autobiography*, Ch. 4, §4.
16. Geoffrey West, *Sketch for a Portrait*, p. 45.
17. HGW, *Experiment in Autobiography*, Ch. 4, §4.
18. Letter of 1860 from T.H. Huxley to Frederick Dyster, quoted in Ronald W. Clark, *The Huxleys*, London, Heinemann, 1968, p. 59.

Chapter 3. Student, 1884–1887

1. HGW, *Experiment in Autobiography*, Ch. 5, §1.
2. HGW, *Experiment in Autobiography*, Ch. 5, §6.
3. HGW, 'Professor Graham Wallas: In Memoriam', *The Literary Guide*, September 1932.
4. Undated letter from HGW to Fred Wells, in *Correspondence*, Vol. 1, p. 41.
5. HGW, *Experiment in Autobiography*, Ch. 5, §4. The phrase 'moral desperadoes' occurs in a letter of 23 September 1849 from Thomas Carlyle to A. H. Clough. Wells's affinity with Arnold is noted in Van Wyck Brooks, *The World of H.G. Wells*, London, T. Fisher Unwin, 1915, p. 15.
6. Letter of 22 November 1802 from William Blake to Thomas Butts.

7. HGW, *Experiment in Autobiography*, Ch. 5, §4.
8. Undated letter from HGW to A. T. Simmons, in *Correspondence*, Vol. 1, p. 44.
9. The picshua appears as illustration 12 in MacKenzie, *The Time Traveller*.
10. Letter of 9 September 1886 from HGW to A. T. Simmons, in *Correspondence*, Vol. 1, p. 49.

Chapter 4. 'In the Wilderness', 1887–1890

1. Letter of 6 November 1895 from HGW to Grant Richards, in *Correspondence*, Vol. 1, p. 249.
2. HGW, *Experiment in Autobiography*, Ch. 6, §1.
3. Letter of 23 August 1887 from HGW to A.M. Davies, in *Correspondence*, Vol. 1, p. 61.
4. HGW, *Experiment in Autobiography*, Ch. 6, §1.
5. Wells describes the game simply as 'football' in his letters and in *Experiment in Autobiography*, Ch. 6, §1. However, the foul he received at Holt has all the appearance of a rugby tackle, and in *The Invisible Man*, Ch. 12, the word 'football' denotes rugby football rather than soccer.
6. Undated letter from HGW to Sarah Wells, in *Correspondence*, Vol 1, pp. 63–4.
7. Undated letter from HGW to A.M. Davies, in *Correspondence*, Vol 1, p. 66.
8. Letter of 22 February 1888 from HGW to A.M. Davies, in *Correspondence*, Vol. 1, p. 80.
9. Letter of 23 February 1888 from HGW to Elizabeth Healey, in *Correspondence*, Vol. 1, p. 82.
10. Letter of 29 March 1888 from HGW to Elizabeth Healey, in *Correspondence*, Vol. 1, p. 97.
11. HGW, *Experiment in Autobiography*, Ch. 6, §2.
12. Undated letter from HGW to A. M. Davies, in *Correspondence*, Vol. 1, pp. 102–3.
13. HGW, *Experiment in Autobiography*, Ch. 6, §2.
14. Deuteronomy, 32: 48–52.
15. Undated letter from HGW to A. M. Davies, in *Correspondence*, Vol. 1, pp. 102–3.
16. Letter of 24 September 1889 from HGW to A.T. Simmons, in *Correspondence*, Vol. 1, p. 130.
17. Letter of 28 April 1888 from HGW to Elizabeth Healey, in *Correspondence*, Vol. 1, p. 98.
18. Letter of 18 September 1889 from HGW to A.T. Simmons, in *Correspondence*, Vol. 1, p. 129.
19. Letter of 5 September 1888 from HGW to Elizabeth Healey, in *Correspondence*, Vol. 1, pp. 111–12.
20. Undated letter from HGW to A.T. Simmons, in *Correspondence*, Vol. 1, p. 117.
21. See John S. Partington, 'H.G. Wells: A Political Life', *Utopian Studies*, 19: 3, 2008, pp. 518–19. The article, pp. 517–76, is a masterful summary of Wells's political views over his lifetime.

Chapter 5. An Attempt at Conformity, 1890–1893

1. Letter of 1 June 1890 from HGW to A.T. Simmons, in *Correspondence*, Vol. 1, p. 150.
2. Letter of 21 August 1946 from T. Ormerod to the *Manchester Guardian*, quoted in MacKenzie, *The Time Traveller*, p. 83.

3. Geoffrey West, *Sketch for a Portrait,* p. 90.
4. 'The Universe Rigid' was never published, but some of it was incorporated into the version of *The Time Machine* serialized in the *New Review* January–May 1895. Relevant extracts from this and the whole of 'The Rediscovery of the Unique' are reprinted in Robert Philmus and David Y. Hughes (eds), *H.G. Wells: Early Writings in Science and Science Fiction,* Berkeley and Los Angeles, University of California Press, 1975. The *New Review* material is also included in HGW, *The Definitive Time Machine,* (ed.), Harry Geduld, Bloomington and Indianapolis, University of Indiana Press, 1987.
5. HGW, *Experiment in Autobiography,* Ch. 6, §6.
6. HGW, *Experiment in Autobiography,* Ch. 6, §5.
7. HGW, *Experiment in Autobiography,* Ch. 7, §2.
8. HGW, *Experiment in Autobiography,* Ch. 7, §2.
9. HGW, *You Can't Be Too Careful,* Bk III, Ch. 11.
10. Nancy Steffen-Fluhr, 'Women and H.G. Wells', in John Huntington (ed.), *Critical Essays on H.G. Wells,* Boston: G.K. Hall, 1991, pp. 148–69.
11. HGW, *Experiment in Autobiography,* Ch. 7, §2.
12. HGW, *Experiment in Autobiography,* Ch. 7, §2.
13. HGW 'Introduction' to Catherine Wells, *The Book of Catherine Wells,* London, Chatto and Windus, 1928.
14. HGW, *Experiment in Autobiography,* Ch. 6, §6.

Chapter 6. Author, 1893–1895

1. HGW, *The Dream,* Ch. 5, §8.
2. Lovat Dickson, *H.G. Wells: His Turbulent Life and Times,* 1969, Harmondsworth, Penguin edition, 1972, p. 75.
3. Letter of 27 December 1893 from HGW to A.M. Davies, in *Correspondence,* Vol. 1, pp. 209–10.
4 HGW, *H.G. Wells in Love,* p. 53.
5. HGW, *Experiment in Autobiography,* Ch 8, §1.
6. HGW, 'Introduction', *The Country of the Blind and Other Stories.*
7. Bernard Bergonzi, *The Early H.G. Wells,* Manchester, Manchester University Press, 1961, p. 166.
8. W.B. Yeats, *Autobiographies,* London, Macmillan, 1980 edition, p. 124.
9. HGW, 'Preface' to Vol. 1 of *The Works of H.G. Wells,* Atlantic edition, London, T. Fisher Unwin, 1924–7.
10. Geoffrey West, *Sketch for a Portrait,* p. 109.
11. John Huntington, 'Wells and Social Class', *Wellsian,* 11, 1988, p. 27.
12. Letter of 10 August 1894 from HGW to Joseph Wells, in *Experiment in Autobiography,* Ch. 6, §7.
13. HGW, *Experiment in Autobiography,* Ch. 8, §2.
14. Undated letter from HGW to A.M. Davies, in *Correspondence,* Vol. 1, p. 214.

15. *H.G. Wells's Literary Criticism*, Patrick Parrinder and Robert Philmus (eds), Brighton, Harvester Press, 1980, p.82.
16. Letter of 22 December 1894 from HGW to Elizabeth Healey, in *Correspondence*, Vol. 1, p. 226.
17. Letter of 2 January 1895 from HGW to J.M. Dent, in *Correspondence*, Vol. 1, p. 228.
18. Quoted in Scheick and Cox (eds), *Reference Guide*, p. 2.
19. Patrick Parrinder (ed.), *H.G. Wells: The Critical Heritage*, London and Boston, Routledge and Kegan Paul, 1972, pp. 33 and 38–9; and HGW, *The Time Machine*, Nicholas Ruddick (ed.), Ontario, Broadview Press, 2001, pp. 261–76.
20. Mark, 15: 34.
21. HGW, *The Time Machine*, Ch. 11 (Atlantic text, Ch. 8).
22. HGW, *The Time Machine* Ch. 14 (Atlantic text, Ch. 11).
23. Parrinder (ed.), *Critical Heritage*, p. 37, and HGW, *The Time Machine*, Ruddick (ed.), p. 267.
24. Patrick Parrinder, '*The Time Machine*: H.G. Wells's Journey Through Death' (1981), in *The Wellsian: Selected Essays on H.G. Wells*, John S. Partington (ed.), Uitgevers, Equilibris, 2003, pp. 31–43.
25. HGW, *The Time Machine*, Ch. 8 (Atlantic text, Ch. 5).

Chapter 7. The Scientific Romances, 1895–1899

1. Robert P. Weeks, 'Disentanglement as a Theme in H.G. Wells's Fiction' (1954), and Anthony West, 'H.G. Wells' (1957), in Bernard Bergonzi (ed.), *H.G. Wells: A Collection of Critical Essays*, Englewood Cliffs, Prentice-Hall, 1976, pp. 8–31.
2. HGW, *Literary Criticism*, p. 61.
3. Letter of 13 October 1895 from HGW to Sarah Wells, in HGW, *Experiment in Autobiography*, Ch. 6, §7.
4. HGW, *Experiment in Autobiography*, Ch. 8, §2.
5. HGW, *The Way the World Is Going*, Ch. 19.
6. Undated letter from HGW to Elizabeth Healey in *Correspondence*, Vol. 1, p. 261.
7. Gene and Margaret Rinkel, *The Picshuas of H.G. Wells*, Urbana and Chicago, University of Illinois Press, 2006, pp. 140 and 174.
8. HGW, *Early Writings*, p. 217.
9. Geoffrey H. Wells, *The Works of H.G. Wells 1887–1925: A Bibliography, Dictionary and Subject-Index*, London, Routledge, 1926, p. 7; and Parrinder (ed.), *Critical Heritage*, pp. 44, 52–3, 61.
10. HGW, *The Wheels of Chance*, Ch. 3.
11. HGW, *The Wheels of Chance*, Ch. 6.
12. HGW, *Early Writings*, p. 218.
13. Arthur H. Lawrence, 'The Romance of the Scientist' (1897), in John R. Hammond (ed.), *H.G. Wells: Interviews and Recollections*, London, Macmillan, 1980, pp. 2–6.
14. Rinkel, *Picshuas*, pp. 179–81 and 195–6.
15. HGW, *H.G. Wells in Love*, pp. 58–61.

16. HGW, *Experiment in Autobiography*, Ch. 8, §3; Gloria Glikin Fromm, 'Through the Novelist's Looking Glass' (1969), in Bergonzi (ed.), *Critical Essays*, pp. 157–77.
17. Dorothy Richardson, *The Tunnel*, 1919, Ch. 6.
18. HGW, *H.G. Wells in Love*, pp. 61–4.
19. David Lodge, *The Novelist at the Crossroads*, London, Routledge and Kegan Paul, 1971, pp. 218–20.
20. Extract from Picaroon, 'Mr H.G. Wells' (1896), in HGW, *The Time Machine*, Ruddick (ed.), pp. 278–81.
21. Undated letter from HGW to Harry Quilter, in *Correspondence*, Vol. 1, p. 333.
22. Quoted in letter of 17 September 1896 from HGW to J.M. Dent, in *Correspondence*, Vol. 1, p. 269.
23. Draft letter of 7 August 1897 from HGW to William Heinemann, in *Correspondence*, Vol. 1, p. 288.
24. Letter of 14 May 1897 from HGW to J.B. Pinker, in Bernard Loing, *H.G. Wells À L'Œuvre*, Paris, Didier Erudition, 1984, p. 435.
25. HGW, *Love and Mr Lewisham*, Ch. 10.
26. George Gissing, *London and the Life of Literature in Late Victorian England: The Diary of George Gissing, Novelist*, Pierre Coustillas (ed.), Brighton, Harvester Press, 1978, entry for 9 January 1897.
27. Royal A. Gettmann (ed.), *George Gissing and H.G. Wells*, Urbana, University of Illinois Press, 1961, p. 242–59; and HGW, *Literary Criticism*, pp. 144–55.
28. HGW, *The World of William Clissold*, Bk I, Ch. 7.
29. Letter of 2 October 1897 from HGW to Edmund Gosse, in *Correspondence*, Vol. 1, p. 290.
30. HGW, *The Invisible Man*, Ch. 20.
31. HGW, *Literary Criticism*, pp. 88–93.
32. Frederick R. Karl, *Joseph Conrad: The Three Lives*, London, Faber, 1979, p. 372.
33. Parrinder (ed.), *Critical Heritage*, p. 60.
34. Undated letter from HGW to the editor of the *Academy*, in *Correspondence*, Vol. 1, p. 297.
35. HGW, *The War of the Worlds*, Bk I, Ch. 10.
36. T.H. Huxley, *Evolution and Ethics*, 1894, London, Macmillan, 1895 edition, pp. 32–3, 161.
37. HGW, *The War of the Worlds*, Bk II, Ch. 2.
38. HGW, *The War of the Worlds*, Bk I, Ch. 1, and Bk I, Ch. 16.
39. HGW, *The War of the Worlds*, Bk I, Ch. 3.
40. Robert Crossley, *H.G. Wells*, Mercer Island, Starmont House, 1986, p. 49.
41. John Huntington, 'H.G. Wells: Problems of an Amorous Utopian', in Huntington (ed.), *Critical Essays*, pp. 136–47; and in Patrick Parrinder and Christopher Rolfe (eds), *H.G. Wells Under Revision*, London and Toronto, Associated University Presses, 1990, pp. 168–80.
42. HGW, *H.G. Wells in Love*, p. 58; Rinkel, *Pichshuas*, p. 189.
43. HGW, *Experiment in Autobiography*, Ch. 7, §4.
44. Peter Kemp, *H.G. Wells and the Culminating Ape*, London, Macmillan, 1982, pp. 119–24.
45. Parrinder (ed.), *Critical Heritage*, p. 66.

46. Parrinder (ed.), *Critical Heritage*, p. 321.
47. Parrinder (ed.), *Critical Heritage*, p. 332.
48. Undated letter and letter of 22 January 1898 from HGW to George Gissing, in *Gissing and Wells*, pp. 69–71 and 76–80.
49. Geoffrey West, *Sketch for a Portrait*, p. 133.
50. Undated letter from HGW to Harry Quilter, in *Correspondence*, Vol. 1, p. 305.
51. HGW, *Experiment in Autobiography*, Ch. 8, §4.
52. Undated letter from Amy Catherine Wells to George Gissing, in *Gissing and Wells*, p. 97.
53. HGW, *Experiment in Autobiography*, Ch. 8, §3
54. Patrick Parrinder, *Shadows of the Future*, Liverpool, Liverpool University Press, 1995, pp. 69–71.
55. HGW, *Experiment in Autobiography*, Ch. 7, §2.
56. Letter of 19 August 1898 from R.A. Gregory to HGW, in the Illinois Wells Archive.
57. Undated letter from HGW to Elizabeth Healey, in *Correspondence*, Vol. 1, p. 323.
58. Quoted in Geoffrey West, *Sketch for a Portrait*, p. 138.

Chapter 8. A New Prospectus, 1899–1901

1. For 'Dumb Crambo', see HGW, *Joan and Peter*, Ch. 7, §5.
2. Letter of 23 June 1899 from HGW to Sidney Low, quoted in Loing, *H.G. Wells À L'Œuvre*, p.447.
3. Bergonzi, *The Early H.G. Wells*, p. 141.
4. Letter of 25 September 1899 from HGW to Arnold Bennett in Harris Wilson (ed.), *Arnold Bennett and H.G. Wells*, London, Hart-Davis, 1960, pp. 43–4; HGW, 'H.G. Wells, Esq., B.Sc.', *Royal College of Science Magazine*, April 1903.
5. HGW, *When the Sleeper Wakes*, Ch. 23.
6. Ford Madox Ford, *Mightier Than the Sword*, London, George Allen and Unwin, 1938, pp. 154–5.
7. HGW, *Literary Criticism*, pp. 190–1.
8. Letter of 12 October 1900 from HGW to the editor of the *Morning Post*, in *Correspondence*, Vol. 1, pp. 362–3, and letter of 9 September 1902 from HGW to Arnold Bennett, in *Bennett and Wells*, p. 84.
9. Letter of 9 November 1943 to Elizabeth Healey, in *Correspondence*, Vol. 4, p. 461.
10. HGW, *Experiment in Autobiography*, Ch. 8, §5.
11. Letter of 6 January 1900 from Joseph Conrad to HGW, in the Illinois Wells Archive.
12. Letter of 1 September 1900 from HGW to Arnold Bennett, in *Bennett and Wells*, p. 52.
13. HGW, *Experiment in Autobiography*, Ch. 8, §5.
14. HGW, *Literary Criticism*, pp. 161–70.
15. Scheick and Cox (eds), *Reference Guide*, pp. 16–18; and Parrinder (ed.), *Critical Heritage*, pp. 78–81.
16. Letters to HGW of 15 June 1900 from A.T. Simmons, of 17 June 1900 from Elizabeth Healey and of 8 June 1900 from Edmund Gosse, in the Illinois Wells Archive.

17. Letter of 17 June 1900 from Henry James to HGW, in Leon Edel and Gordon N. Ray (eds), *Henry James and H.G. Wells*, London, Hart-Davis, 1958, p. 67.
18. Letter of 3 July 1900 from George Gissing to HGW, in *Gissing and Wells*, pp. 142–3.
19. Letter of 15 June 1900 from HGW to Arnold Bennett, in *Bennett and Wells*, p. 45.
20. HGW, *Love and Mr Lewisham*, Ch. 23.
21. Letter of 30 August 1900 from HGW to J.B. Pinker, in Loing, *H.G. Wells À L'Œuvre*, pp. 454–5.
22. Parrinder (ed.), *Critical Heritage*, p. 320. For the complex textual history of *The First Men in the Moon* see David Lake's note in his edition of the book, New York, Oxford University Press, 1995, pp. xxviii–xxxii.
23. Letter of 7 October 1902 from Henry James to HGW, in *James and Wells*, pp. 81–2.
24. HGW, *Experiment in Autobiography*, Ch. 8, §6.
25. HGW, *Anticipations*, Ch. 4.
26. Postcard of 8 December 1900 from HGW to Arnold Bennett, in *Bennett and Wells*, p. 53.
27. Letter of 3 June 1901 from HGW to Arnold Bennett, in *Bennett and Wells*, p. 55.
28. HGW, *The Secret Places of the Heart*, Ch. 4, §2.
29. Undated letter from HGW to J.B. Pinker, in Loing, *H.G. Wells À L'Œuvre*, p. 455.
30. HGW, 'Introduction', *The Book of Catherine Wells*.
31. Letter of 16 November 1925 from HGW to Arnold Bennett, in *Correspondence*, Vol. 3, pp. 203–4.
32. HGW, *Outline of History*, Ch. 26.
33. Anthony West, *Aspects of a Life*, pp. 257–8.
34. HGW, *The Soul of a Bishop*, Ch. 2, §4.
35. Letter of 7 July 1901 from HGW to Elizabeth Healey, in *Correspondence*, Vol. 1, p. 379, but I have adopted the reading 'buster' favoured in Geoffrey West, *Sketch for a Portrait*, p. 123, and most later citations, rather than 'beauty'.
36. HGW, *Anticipations*, Ch. 5.
37. Letter of 21 November 1901 from A.T. Simmons to HGW, in the Illinois Wells Archive.
38. HGW, *Anticipations*, Ch. 8.
39. HGW, *Anticipations*, Ch. 9.
40. Letter of 21 November 1901 from George Gissing to HGW, in *Gissing and Wells*, pp. 195–8; letter of 16 November 1900 from HGW to John Galsworthy, in *Correspondence*, Vol. 1, p. 366.
41. Lovat Dickson, *H.G. Wells*, pp. 112–13.
42. Michael Coren, *The Invisible Man*, London, Bloomsbury, 1993, p. 65.
43. HGW, *Anticipations*, Ch. 9.
44. HGW, *Outline of History*, Ch. 30, §1.
45. Bryan Cheyette, *Construction of 'the Jew' in English Literature and Society*, Cambridge, Cambridge University Press, 1993, pp. 123–49.

46. An example is A.N. Wilson, *After the Victorians*, 2005, London; Arrow edition, 2006. On p. 67 Wilson claims that for Wells, 'genocide is the only answer to the problems of world overpopulation'. He has plainly not read *Anticipations*, which does not deal with overpopulation as such, but instead relied on the discussion of the book in John Carey's *The Intellectuals and the Masses*, London, Faber, 1992, which he reports with small but fatal simplifications.
47. Parrinder (ed.), *Critical Heritage*, p. 85.
48. Letter of 29 December 1901 from HGW to R.A. Gregory, in *Correspondence*, Vol. 1, p. 391.

Chapter 9. Annexing the Future, 1902–1905

1. HGW, 'Herbert George Wells, Esq., B.Sc.', *Royal College of Science Magazine*, April 1903.
2. Letter of 22 March 1899 from HGW to J.B. Pinker, in Loing, *H.G. Wells À L'Œuvre*, p. 445.
3. George Orwell, 'Wells, Hitler and the World State' (1941), in *Collected Essays, Journalism and Letters*, Vol. 2, Harmondsworth, Penguin, 1971 edition, p. 171.
4. Patrick Parrinder, 'Introduction' to HGW , *The Discovery of the Future*, London, PNL Press, 1989, p. 9.
5. Wells's views are in Francis Galton, 'Eugenics: Its Definition, Scope and Aims', *Sociological Papers* Vol. 1, pp. 58–60; also published in *Nature*, 70: 82, and the *American Journal of Sociology*, 10: 1–6, and accessible in facsimile on the website http://galton.org. See also HGW, *First and Last Things*, Bk III, Ch. 4.
6. Rinkel, *Picshuas*, p. 162.
7. HGW, *Experiment in Autobiography*, Ch. 7, §3, and HGW, *H.G. Wells in Love*, p. 61.
8. HGW, *Anticipations*, Ch. 4.
9. David C. Smith, *H.G. Wells: Desperately Mortal*, New Haven and London, Yale University Press, pp. 197–8.
10. Letter of 19 March 1902 from HGW to Graham Wallas, in *Correspondence*, Vol. 1, p. 396. I have substituted 'between' for 'below'.
11. Letters of 18 and 21 January 1904 from HGW to Elizabeth Healey, in *Correspondence*, Vol. 2, pp. 4–5.
12. HGW, *Experiment in Autobiography*, Ch. 7, §2.
13. HGW, *The Future in America*, Ch. 11.
14. Letter of 2 October 1903 from Florence Popham to HGW, in the Illinois Wells Archive.
15. Undated letter from HGW to the editor of the *Daily Chronicle*, in *Correspondence*, Vol. 1, pp. 427–8.
16. Letter of 8 February 1902 from HGW to Arnold Bennett, in *Bennett and Wells*, pp. 72–5.
17. Arnold Bennett, 'H.G. Wells and His Work' (1902), in *Bennett and Wells*, pp. 260–76.
18. John S. Partington, *Building Cosmopolis*, Aldershot, Ashgate, 2003, pp. 36–7.
19. Undated letter from HGW to Amy Catherine Wells, in *Correspondence*, Vol. 1, pp. 423–4.

20. HGW, *Experiment in Autobiography*, Ch. 8, §3.
21. Undated letter from HGW to Edmund Gosse, in *Correspondence*, Vol. 3, pp. 215–16. 'George Gissing: An Impression' is reprinted in *Gissing and Wells*, pp. 260–77.
22. Letter of 17 March 1904 from HGW to Edward Pease, in *Correspondence*, Vol. 2, p. 13.
23. HGW, *A Modern Utopia*, Ch. 2, §2.
24. Letter of 10 May 1905 from HGW to A.J. Balfour, in *Correspondence*, Vol. 2, pp. 71–3.
25. Letter of 9 October 1906 from Winston Churchill to HGW, in the Illinois Wells Archive.
26. HGW, *A Modern Utopia*, Ch. 9, §5.
27. Letter of 19 November 1905 from Henry James to HGW, in *James and Wells*, pp. 102–7.
28. Letter of 9 November 1905 from Arnold Bennett to HGW, in *Bennett and Wells*, pp. 126–9.
29. Letter of 25 October 1905 from A.T. Simmons to HGW, in the Illinois Wells Archive.
30. HGW, *H.G. Wells in Love*, p. 64.
31. HGW, *Kipps*, Bk II, Ch 3, §8.

Chapter 10. Fabianism and Free Love, 1905–1909

1. Letter of 17 June 1905 from HGW to Amy Burgess, in *Correspondence*, Vol. 2, p. 76; HGW, *Experiment in Autobiography*, Ch. 4, §6.
2. HGW, *Experiment in Autobiography*, Ch. 7, §1.
3. HGW, *H.G. Wells in Love*, p. 64.
4. Letter of 6 May 1906 from HGW to Amy Catherine Wells, in *Correspondence*, Vol. 2, p. 98.
5. Quoted in Anne M. Windholz, 'Ella D'Arcy', *Dictionary of Literary Biography, Vol. 135: British Short-Fiction Writers, 1880–1914: The Realist Tradition*, Detroit, Gale Research, 1994, pp. 85–95. See also Patricia Stubbs, *Women and Fiction*, 1979, London, Methuen, 1981 edition, pp. 106–7.
6. Barbara Belford, *Violet Hunt*, New York, Simon and Schuster, 1990, p. 102.
7. HGW, *H.G. Wells in Love*, p. 65.
8. HGW, *In the Days of the Comet*, Bk III, Ch. 2, §4.
9. Undated letter from HGW to the *Daily Express*, published 19 September 1906, in *Correspondence*, Vol. 2, pp. 105–6.
10. Letters of 13 February and 3 March 1905 from Florence Popham to Amy Catherine Wells, in the Illinois Wells Archive.
11. Letters of 29 January 1907 from J. Ramsay MacDonald to HGW and 13 June 1906 from Kier Hardie to HGW, cited in MacKenzie, *The Time Traveller*, pp. 223 and 204; undated letter from HGW to the *Christian Commonwealth*, published 12 May 1909, in *Correspondence*, Vol. 2, p. 239.
12. Letter of 7 March 1907 from John Galsworthy to HGW, cited in MacKenzie, *The Time Traveller*, p. 223.
13. Eric Hobsbawm, *The Age of Empire 1875–1914*, 1987, London, Abacus, 1994 edition, p. 273.
14. MacKenzie, *The Time Traveller*, p. 223.

15. See Krishan Kumar, 'Wells and "the So-Called Science of Sociology"', in Parrinder and Rolfe (eds), *H.G. Wells Under Revision*, pp. 192–217; also Wolf Lepenies, *Between Literature and Science*, Cambridge, Cambridge University Press, 1988, pp. 131 and 150.
16. *Boon* manuscripts, Illinois Wells Archive.
17. Beatrice Webb, *The Diary of Beatrice Webb*, Norman and Jeanne MacKenzie (eds), Vol. 3, London, Virago, 1984, p. 31.
18. Letter of 19 September 1906 from HGW to the Borough Librarian of Bromley, in *Correspondence*, Vol. 2, p. 109.
19. Quoted in Ingvald Raknem, *H.G. Wells and His Critics*, London, Allen and Unwin, 1961, p. 59.
20. Letter of 26 November 1904 from HGW to Edmund Gosse, in *Correspondence*, Vol. 2, pp. 57–8. The letter also appears in Vol. 1, p. 442, where it is dated as 1903.
21. HGW, *The Future in America*, Ch. 10, §1.
22. Undated letter and letter of 15 November 1907 from Mary Church Terrell to HGW, in the Illinois Wells Archive.
23. Letter of 6 May 1906 from HGW to Amy Catherine Wells, in *Correspondence*, Vol. 2, p. 98.
24. Letter of 26 April 1906 from Amy Catherine Wells to HGW, in *Correspondence*, Vol. 1, p. 456.
25. HGW, *The Future in America*, Ch. 3, §6.
26. HGW, *The Future in America*, Ch. 3, §7.
27. HGW, *The Future in America*, Ch. 14, §1.
28. HGW, *H.G. Wells in Love*, p. 65.
29. HGW, *The Future in America*, Envoy.
30. Anthony West, *Aspects of a Life*, pp. 335–44.
31. Letter of 14 September 1906 from Bernard Shaw to HGW, in J. Percy Smith (ed.), *Bernard Shaw and H.G. Wells*, Toronto, University of Toronto Press, 1995, pp. 37–40.
32. Oaths of allegiance 1837–1907, East Kent Archive.
33. Sessions papers, East Kent Archive.
34. HGW, *First and Last Things*, Bk III, Ch. 4.
35. Letter postmarked 9 March 1907 from HGW to Violet Hunt, in *Correspondence*, Vol. 2, p. 141. For further information on the Bland affair, see MacKenzie, *The Time Traveller*, pp. 225–66 and 246–7, HGW, *H.G. Wells in Love*, pp. 68–9, and Ruth Brandon, *The New Women and the Old Men*, 1990, London, Macmillan, 2000 edition, pp. 172–82.
36. Brandon, *The New Women and the Old Men*, p. 180.
37. Letter of 26 January 1929 or 1930 from Rosamund Sharp to HGW, in *Correspondence*, Vol. 3, pp. 327–8.
38. HGW, letter to the *Daily Mail*, published 21 April 1908, in *Correspondence*, Vol. 2, pp. 214–17.
39. Letter of 10 March 1908 from Bernard Shaw to HGW, in *Shaw and Wells*, p. 63.

40. Letter of 30 March 1907 from HGW to 'Maurice Browne', cited in MacKenzie, *The Time Traveller*, p. 221; also included in *Correspondence*, Vol. 2, but with minor differences of transcription, dated as April and addressed to 'Lewis Browne'.
41. HGW, *First and Last Things*, Bk III, Ch. 29.
42. HGW, *First and Last Things*, Bk I, Ch. 8.
43. HGW, *H.G. Wells in Love*, p. 73.
44. John R. Hammond, *An H.G. Wells Companion*, London, Macmillan, 1979, p. 106.
45. Undated letter from Amber Reeves to HGW, in the Illinois Wells Archive.
46. HGW, *H.G. Wells in Love*, pp. 74–6.
47. Undated letter from Amber Reeves to Amy Catherine Wells, in the Illinois Wells Archive.
48. Letter of 31 August [1908] from Amy Catherine Wells to Amber Reeves, in the Illinois Wells Archive.
49. Beatrice Webb, *Diary*, Vol. 3, pp. 98–9.
50. Letter postmarked 18 October 1908 from HGW to 'Mrs Graham Wells' (Amber Reeves), in the Illinois Wells Archive.
51. Undated postcard and letter from HGW to Amber Reeves, in the Illinois Wells Archive.
52. Undated letter from HGW to Amber Reeves, in the Illinois Wells Archive.
53. Extract from Compton Mackenzie, *My Life and Times* (1965), in Hammond (ed.), *Interviews and Recollections*, p. 33.
54. Virginia Woolf, *Carlyle's House and Other Sketches*, David Bradshaw (ed.), London, Hesperus Press, 2003, p. 5.
55. HGW, *H.G. Wells in Love*, pp. 79–80.
56. Letter postmarked 18 October 1908 from HGW to 'Mrs Graham Wells' (Amber Reeves), in the Illinois Wells Archive.
57. Undated letter from HGW to Amber Reeves, in the Illinois Wells Archive.
58. Undated letter from 'Peter Wells' (HGW) to Amber Reeves, in the Illinois Wells Archive.

Chapter 11. Novelist, 1909–1911

1. 'The Contemporary Novel' in HGW, *An Englishman Looks at the World*, reprinted in *James and Wells*, pp. 131–56, and in HGW, *Literary Criticism*, pp. 192–206.
2. HGW, *Tono-Bungay*, Bk I, Ch. 1, §1.
3. HGW, *Tono-Bungay*, Bk IV, Ch. 3, §1.
4. HGW, *Tono-Bungay*, Bk I, Ch. 2, §4.
5. Virgilio Marchi wrote of 'a machine for living in' in 1920 (www.futurism.org.uk), and in 1914 Antonio Sant 'Elia stated that 'The Futurist house must be like a gigantic machine' (www.unknown.nu/futurism/architecture.html). Listening to Marinetti reciting to the Poetry Society, Wells was repelled by what he later recognized as the

spirit of Fascism. See HGW, *The Way the World Is Going*, Ch. 3, and Maria Teresa Chialant, 'H.G. Wells, Italian Futurism and Marinetti's *Gli Indomabili (The Untamables)*', in Patrick Parrinder and John S. Partington (eds), *The Reception of H.G. Wells in Europe*, London and New York, Thoemmes Continuum, 2005, pp. 205–21.

6. Edward Mendelson, 'Introduction' to HGW, *Tono-Bungay*, London, Penguin edition, 2005, p. xxiii.
7. HGW, *The Time Machine*, Ch. 4; *The War of the Worlds*, Bk I, Ch. 16; *A Modern Utopia*, Ch. 2, §2.
8. HGW, *Tono-Bungay*, Bk II, Ch. 4, §10.
9. HGW, *Tono-Bungay*, Bk III, Ch. 4, §5.
10. HGW, *Tono-Bungay*, Bk IV, Ch. 3, §3.
11. Letter of 20 December 1902 from Gilbert Murray to Bertrand Russell, quoted in Jonathan Rose, *The Edwardian Temperament 1895–1919*, Athens, Ohio University Press, 1986, p. 29.
12. Patrick Parrinder, *H.G. Wells*, Edinburgh, Oliver and Boyd, 1970, p. 78.
13. HGW, *Tono-Bungay*, Bk I, Ch. 3, §1.
14. Parrinder (ed.), *Critical Heritage*, pp. 154–6 and 146–7.
15. Letters of 6 March 1909 and 8 May 1909 from D.H. Lawrence to Blanche Jennings, in Harry T. Moore (ed.), *D.H. Lawrence: Collected Letters*, London, Heinemann, 1962, pp. 51 and 54.
16. Mendelson, 'Introduction', *Tono-Bungay*, pp. xxv–xxvii.
17. For Masterman, see David Lodge, '*Tono-Bungay* and the Condition of England', in his *Language of Fiction*, 1966, London, Routledge, 2002 edition, especially pp. 227–58; also included in Bergonzi (ed.) *Critical Essays*, pp. 110–39. For Eliot, see Bryan Cheyette, 'Introduction', HGW, *Tono-Bungay*, New York, Oxford University Press, 1996, p. xl–xli.
18. Chris Baldick, *The Modern Movement*, Oxford, Oxford University Press, 2004, pp. 2–5, questions the narrow definition of 'modernity' in the study of English literature. Cheyette, 'Introduction', *Tono-Bungay*, pp. xviii–xli, suggests the anomalous nature of *Tono-Bungay*. Rose, *Edwardian Temperament*, pp. 27–39, gives examples of synthesis versus conflict in the culture of the period, and Jefferson Hunter, *Edwardian Fiction*, Cambridge, Mass., Harvard University Press, 1982, pp. 245–55, stresses *Tono-Bungay*'s open form.
19. Letter of 19 October 1908 from Frederick Macmillan to HGW, quoted in Dickson, *H.G. Wells*, pp. 196–7.
20. Parrinder (ed.), *Critical Heritage*, pp. 169–72.
21. Quoted in Arnold Bennett, *Books and Persons*, 1917, London, Chatto and Windus, 1919 edition, p. 134.
22. Rinkel, *Picshuas*, pp. 40, 163 and 171.
23. Sylvia Hardy gives an intelligent survey of the feminist response in her 'Introduction' to HGW, *Ann Veronica*, London, Dent Everyman, 1993, pp. xxix–xlv. The most substantial feminist account of Wells's fiction is in Stubbs, *Women and Fiction*.

24. Letter of 14 October 1909 from Henry James to HGW, in *James and Wells*, pp. 121–3.
25. Letter of 13 October 1909 from Edmund Gosse to HGW, reprinted in Hardy (ed.), *Ann Veronica*, pp. 265–6, and HGW, *Experiment in Autobiography*, Ch. 7, §4.
26. Quoted in MacKenzie, *The Time Traveller*, p. 252.
27. HGW, *.G. Wells in Love*, p. 81–2.
28. Undated letter from HGW to Amber Reeves, in the Illinois Wells Archive.
29. Undated letter from HGW to Amber Reeves, in the Illinois Wells Archive.
30. HGW, *Experiment in Autobiography*, Ch. 7, §2.
31. HGW, *H.G. Wells in Love*, p. 84.
32. HGW, *H.G. Wells in Love*, p. 84.
33. Beatrice Webb, *Diary*, Vol. 3, pp. 120–1.
34. Undated letter from HGW to Amber Blanco White, in the Illinois Wells Archive.
35. Letter of 8 January 1910 from HGW to Amber Blanco White, in the Illinois Wells Archive.
36. Undated letter from HGW to Amber Blanco White, in the Illinois Wells Archive.
37. Anthony West, *Aspects of a Life*, p. 17.
38. HGW, *H.G. Wells in Love*, pp. 81–2.
39. For suggestions about the origins of the name Polly, based on the manuscript of the novel, see Christopher Rolfe, 'From Puttenhanger to Polly', *Wellsian*, 5, 1982, pp. 33–5. My own suspicion is that the name derives from Huxley's description of the new lower-class voters as 'of the poll, polly', but I have to confess that I cannot locate this quotation.
40. HGW, *The History of Mr Polly*, Ch. 3, §1.
41. HGW, *The History of Mr Polly*, Ch. 9, §1.
42. Walter Allen, *The English Novel*, 1954, Harmondsworth, Penguin, 1982 edition, p. 316.
43. Parrinder (ed.), *Critical Heritage*, p. 180.
44. HGW, *Experiment in Autobiography*, Ch. 4, §6.
45. HGW, *The New Machiavelli*, Bk II, Ch. 4, §4.
46. Letter of 21 June 1910 from Sir Frederick Macmillan to HGW, in Dickson, *H.G. Wells*, p. 215. There is a detailed account of the novel's publication at pp. 211–43.
47. M.M. Meyer, *Wells and His Family*, Edinburgh, International Publishing, 1956, pp. 66–8, and Jane Wells's diary for 1910, in the Illinois Wells Archive. See also D. Gert Hensel, 'July–August 1910', *Wellsian*, 27, 2004, pp. 13–22.
48. Letter of 22 September 1910 from Amber Blanco White to HGW, in the Illinois Wells Archive.
49. Undated letter from HGW to Edwin Pugh, in *Correspondence*, Vol. 2, p. 314.
50. Letter of 20 January 1911 from Joseph Conrad to HGW, in the Illinois Wells Archive; Upton Sinclair, quoted by Dennis Poupard, *Twentieth Century English Literary Criticism*, Vol. 12, Detroit, Gale Research, 1984, pp. 4–5; letter of 26 April 1913 from D.H. Lawrence to A.W. McLeod, in Lawrence, *Collected Letters*, p. 203; Beatrice Webb, *Diary*, Vol. 3, p. 147, also in Parrinder (ed.), *Critical Heritage*, pp. 181–2

51. Bennett, *Books and Persons*, pp. 210–13.
52. Letters of 3 March 1911 from Henry James to HGW and 25 April 1911 from HGW to Henry James, in *James and Wells*, pp. 126–31.
53. John S. Partington, 'Notes', HGW, *The New Machiavelli*, Penguin, London, 2005, p. 468.
54. Letter of 10 May 1948 from George Orwell to Julian Symons, in *Collected Essays, Journalism and Letters*, Vol. 4, pp. 478–9.
55. Frank Swinnerton, *The Georgian Literary Scene*, 1938, London, Dent, 1951 edition, p. 50.
56. Meyer, *Wells and His Family*, p. 63.

Chapter 12. Journalist, 1911–1916

1. See Meyer, *Wells and His Family*, pp. 45–65, and Swinnerton, 'Wells as Seen by His Friends', in Hammond (ed.), *Interviews and Recollections*, pp. 38–41.
2. See HGW, *Floor Games*, Barbara A. Turner (ed.), Cloverdale, California, Temenos Press, 2004.
3. Letter of 8 July 1911 from Arnold Bennett to Amy Catherine Wells, in *Bennett and Wells*, pp. 177–8. See also Bennett, *Books and Persons*, pp. 233–4.
4. Quoted in Hammond, *H.G. Wells Companion*, p. 163.
5. Letter of 18 October 1912 from Henry James to HGW in *James and Wells*, pp. 165–8; letter of 1 October 1912 from Edmund Gosse to HGW, in Illinois Wells Archive.
6. HGW, *First and Last Things*, revised 1917 edition, Bk III, Ch. 11.
7. MacKenzie, *The Time Traveller*, p. 274.
8. Frances, Countess of Warwick, *Afterthoughts*, London, Cassell, 1931, p. 182. For more on Easton, see Meyer, *Wells and His Family*, pp. 93–104. Further accounts are noted in Smith, *Desperately Mortal*, p. 525.
9. Brooks, *The World of H.G. Wells*, p. 164.
10. Letter of 17 September 1913 from A.T. Simmons to HGW, in the Illinois Wells Archive.
11. HGW, *Wells in Love*, p. 89.
12. HGW, *A Modern Utopia*, Ch. 2, §2.
13. Anonymous reviewer in the New York *Nation*, April 1914, quoted in Scheick and Cox, *Reference Guide*, p. 62.
14. HGW, *Wells in Love*, p. 71.
15. Letters of 28 June and 10 July 1916 from Eleanor Jacobs to Amy Catherine Wells, in the Illinois Wells Archive.
16. Parrinder (ed.), *Critical Heritage*, p. 220.
17. Parrinder (ed.), *Critical Heritage*, pp. 203–8.
18. HGW, *Wells in Love*, pp. 94–6.
19. Undated letter from HGW to Rebecca West in Gordon N. Ray, *H.G. Wells and Rebecca West*, London, Macmillan, 1974, pp. 45–6.
20. Parrinder and Partington (eds), *Reception in Europe*, pp. 3 and 48.

21. Vladimir Nabokov, *Strong Opinions*, 1973, London, Weidenfeld and Nicolson, 1974 edition, p. 104; HGW, *Star-Begotten*, Ch. 2, §3.
22. HGW, *Wells in Love* p. 84.
23. Letter postmarked 14 April 1914 from HGW to Rebecca West, quoted in Andrea Lynn, *Shadow Lovers*, New York, Perseus Press, 2001, p. 71.
24. Rebecca West, *Henry James*, London, Nisbet, 1916, p. 41.
25. Letter of 25 March 1912 from HGW to Henry James, in *James and Wells*, p. 160.
26. HGW, *The Way the World Is Going*, Ch. 5.
27. Letter of 26 March 1912 from Henry James to Edmund Gosse, in *James and Wells*, pp. 163–4.
28. Janet Gebler-Hover, 'H.G. Wells's and Henry James's Two Ladies', in William J. Scheick (ed.), *The Critical Response to H.G. Wells*, Westport, Conn., Greenwood Press, 1995, pp. 145–64.
29. Letter of 5 August 1914 from HGW to Rebecca West, in Ray, *Wells and West*, p. 54. Ray states that Anthony was born on 4 August, apparently on the authority of Rebecca. Everyone else, including Anthony himself, records the birth as having occurred on 5 August. See Anthony West, *Aspects of a Life*, p. 3.
30. Jon Stallworthy, *Wilfred Owen: A Biography*, 1974, Oxford, Oxford University Press, 1977 edition, pp. 104 and 109.
31. HGW, *Wells in Love*, pp. 97–8.
32. HGW, *Boon*, Ch. 4, §2.
33. HGW, *Boon*, Ch. 4, §4. West, *Sketch for a Portrait*, p. 210, notes that 'The Spoils of Mr Blandish' is based on an uncollected story by Wells, 'The Rajah's Treasure', since made available in John R. Hammond (ed.), *Complete Short Stories*, London, Dent, 1998, pp. 745–54.
34. Letter of 6 July 1915 from Henry James to HGW, in *James and Wells*, pp. 261–3.
35. Letter of 8 July 1915 from HGW to Henry James, in *James and Wells*, pp. 263–4.
36. Letter of 10 July 1915 from Henry James to HGWin *James and Wells*, pp. 265–8.
37. Letter of 13 July 1915 from HGW to Henry James, quoted in *James and Wells*, p. 267.
38. Hardy is quoted in Malcolm Bradbury, *The Modern British Novel*, 1993, London, Penguin, 1994 edition, p. 29; E.M. Forster, *Aspects of the Novel*, 1927, Harmondsworth, Penguin, 1968 edition, pp. 163–4.
39. HGW, *Boon*, Ch. 5, §1; Wells's review 'James Joyce' was originally published in the *Nation*, February 1917, and *New Republic*, March 1917, and is collected in HGW, *Literary Criticism*, pp. 171–5. See also letters of 1916 from Wells to Ezra Pound and James Joyce, in *Correspondence*, Vol. 2, pp. 484–5.
40. Nabokov, *Strong Opinions*, p. 139.
41. For an informed placing of the Wells–James dispute in literary history, see Baldick, *The Modern Movement*, pp. 155–69.
42. Arthur Marwick, *Britain in the Century of Total War*, London, Bodley Head, 1968, p. 76.

43. Peter Buitenhuis, *The Great War of Words*, London, Batsford, 1987, pp. 14–15. In consulting this book beware both its anti-British bias and the photograph purporting to show Wells, which is actually Eden Phillpotts.
44. Undated letter from HGW to Amy Catherine Wells, in *Correspondence*, Vol. 2, p. 468. Wells praises Joffre in the opening section of his *War and the Future*, 'The Passing of the Effigy'.
45. HGW, *War and the Future*, Ch. 3, §3.
46. HGW, *Experiment in Autobiography*, Ch. 9, §5.
47. Rose Tilly, 'The Search for Wells's Ropeways', *Wellsian*, 9, 1986, pp. 18–21.
48. Fortunately for the present writer, his grandfather was one of the survivors.
49. Undated letter from HGW to E. Haldeman-Julius, in *Correspondence*, Vol. 4, pp. 509–10.
50. HGW, *Boon*, Ch. 8, §5.

Chapter 13. Prophet, 1916–1919

1. Letter of 2 October 1916 from Richard Gregory to HGW, in the Illinois Wells Archive.
2. HGW, *Mr Britling Sees It Through*, Bk I, Ch. 4, §3.
3. HGW, *Mr Britling Sees It Through*, Bk III, Ch. 2, §11.
4. Beatrice Webb, *Diary*, Vol. 3, p. 372.
5. Arnold Bennett, *Journals*, Frank Swinnerton (ed.), London, Penguin, 1954, p. 109.
6. Letter of 19 May 1917 from HGW to Rebecca West, in Ray, *Wells and West*, p. 78.
7. West, *Sketch for a Portrait*, p. 217.
8. Letter of 20 May 1917 from A.T. Simmons to HGW, in the Illinois Wells Archive.
9. For the sense of being part of a greater consciousness, see *The War of the Worlds*, Bk I, Ch. 7, *The First Men in the Moon*, Ch. 19; *The New Machiavelli*, Bk III, Ch. 1, §5, and 'Under the Knife'.
10. Undated letter from HGW to Frederic Harrison, in *Correspondence*, Vol. 2, p. 535.
11. HGW, *Experiment in Autobiography*, Ch. 9, §6.
12. Victoria Glendinning, *Rebecca West: A Life*, London, Weidenfeld and Nicolson, p. 63.
13. 'Master Anthony and the Zeppelin' appeared as pp. 13–16 of *Princess Marie-Joe's Children's Book*, London, Cassell, 1916.
14. Ray, *Wells and West*, p. 82.
15. A.J.P. Taylor, *English History 1914–1945*, 1965, Harmondsworth, Penguin, 1973 edition, p. 149.
16. Parrinder (ed.), *Critical Heritage*, pp. 244–7.
17. Geoffrey H. Wells, *Bibliography*, pp. 16–17.
18. Alan Wykes, *H.G. Wells in the Cinema*, London, Jupiter, 1977, p. 58.
19. Glendinning, *Rebecca West*, p. 68.
20. Bennett, *Journals*, p. 307.
21. Letter of March 1919 from HGW to Marie Stopes, in *Correspondence*, Vol. 3, p. 9.
22. Quoted in Buitenhuis, *Great War of Words*, p. 61.

23. Ernest Hemingway, *A Farewell to Arms*, 1929, Harmondsworth, Penguin edition, 1969, pp. 143–4 and 201–2.
24. This 'relevance theory' of modernism comes from David Trotter, *The English Novel in History 1895–1920*, 1993, London, Routledge, 2006 edition, pp. 62–70.
25. Bennett, *Books and Persons*, p. 203.
26. W.B. Yeats, 'The Circus Animals' Desertion' (1939).

Chapter 14. Historian, 1919–1922

1. HGW, *Exasperations* typescript, in the Illinois Wells Archive. Wells's chief accounts of the writing of the *Outline* occur in the 'Introduction' to the fifth 'Popular' edition, London, Cassell, 1930, and in his *Experiment in Autobiography*, Ch 9, §7.
2. HGW, *Outline of History*, Ch. 41, §4.
3. Parrinder (ed.), *Critical Heritage*, p. 332. For Wells's debate with Belloc, see Vincent Brome, *Six Studies in Quarrelling*, London, Cresset Press, 1958, pp. 170–89.
4. Parrinder (ed.), *Critical Heritage*, p. 248; Webb, *Diary*, Vol. 3, p. 371; William T. Ross, *H.G. Wells's World Reborn*, London, Associated University Presses, 2002, pp. 39–41; Huntington (ed.), *Critical Essays*, p. 133; Norman Stone, 'Introduction'. HGW, *A Short History of the World*, London, Penguin, 2006 edition, p. xvii.
5. A.B. McKillop, *The Spinster and the Prophet*, London, Aurum Press edition, 2001, p. 161.
6. HGW, *Outline of History*, Ch. 32, §3, and Ch. 32, §6.
7. Christopher Isherwood, *Lions and Shadows*, 1938, London, New English Library, 1974 edition, p. 18; Dashiell Hammett, *The Maltese Falcon*, 1930, London, Orion, 2002 edition, p. 120; George Orwell, *Collected Essays, Journalism and Letters*, Vol. 2, pp. 170–1.
8. HGW, 'Preface', *A Short History of the World*.
9. Lynn, *Shadow Lovers*, pp. 79–80; Cornelia Otis Skinner and Emily Kimborough, *Our Hearts Were Young and Gay*, 1944, Leicester: Ulverscroft edition, no date, pp. 113–27.
10. Quoted in John R. Reed, *The Natural History of H.G. Wells*, Athens, Ohio University Press, 1982, p. 235.
11. Undated letters from G.P. Wells to Amy Catherine Wells, in the Illinois Wells Archive.
12. Parrinder (ed.), *Critical Heritage*, pp. 258–74. See also Mark R. Hillegas, *The Future as Nightmare*, 1967, London, Feffer and Simmons, 1974 edition, pp. 99–109, 123–32, and Robert Russell, *Zamiatin's 'We'*, London, Bristol Classical Press, 2000, pp. 11–14 and 29–30.
13. HGW, *H.G. Wells in Love*, p. 164. On Moura Benckendorf, see Andrea Lynn, *Shadow Lovers*, pp. 105–211.
14. Undated letter from HGW to Upton Sinclair, in *Correspondence*, Vol. 3, p. 3. MacKenzie, *The Time Traveller*, p. 328, records the embarrassment Wells suffered when his slur on Webb was picked up and published by H.A. Jones but seems to be wrong in naming the recipient of the letter as Sinclair Lewis.
15. HGW, *Russia in the Shadows*, Ch. 3.
16. Brome, *Six Studies*, pp. 58–62. See also David C. Smith, 'Winston Churchill and H.G.

Wells', in *Cahiers Victoriens et Edouardiens*, 30, 1989, pp. 93–116, and Richard Toye, 'H.G. Wells and Winston Churchill: A Reassessment', in Steven McLean (ed.), *H.G. Wells: Interdisciplinary Essays*, Newcastle, Cambridge Scholars Publishing, 2008, pp. 147–61.

17. Quoted in MacKenzie, *The Time Traveller*, p. 327.
18. HGW, *H.G. Wells in Love*, p. 103.
19. Rebecca West, 'The Real H.G. Wells', *Sunday Telegraph*, 17 June 1973, cited in Glendinning, *Rebecca West*, p. 84.
20. Letter of November 1920 from HGW to Rebecca West, in Ray, *Wells and West*, p. 106.
21. Geoffrey West, *Sketch for a Portrait*, p. 237.
22. HGW, *Men Like Gods*, Bk I, Ch. 7, §3. I owe this point to Smith, *Desperately Mortal*, p. 282.
23. Diary entry quoted in Glendinning, *Rebecca West*, p. 75.
24. Letter of 7 December 1921 from HGW to Margaret Sanger, in *Correspondence*, Vol. 3, p. 78–9, and Glendinning, *Rebecca West*, p. 76.
25. Letter from HGW to Rebecca West, quoted in Ray, *Wells and West*, p. 113.
26. Review in the *Saturday Review*, January 1922, quoted in Scheick and Cox, *Reference Guide*, p. 124.
27. Letter of 22 January 1922 from Rebecca West to Lettie Fairfield, quoted in Glendinning, *Rebecca West*, p. 77.
28. HGW, *The Secret Places of the Heart*, Ch. 4, §6.
29. HGW, *The Secret Places of the Heart*, Ch. 9, §8.
30. HGW, *Exasperations* typescript, in the Illinois Wells Archive.

Chapter 15. Godfather, 1922–1926

1. HGW, *The Story of a Great Schoolmaster*, Ch. 8, §4.
2. The figure of 51.5 comes from HGW, *The World of William Clissold*, Bk I, Ch. 1.
3. HGW, *H.G. Wells in Love*, p. 104.
4. Undated letter from HGW to Rebecca West, in Ray, *Wells and West*, p. 127.
5. Letter of April 1923 from HGW to Rebecca West, in Ray, *Wells and West*, p. 135.
6. Wells's account is in HGW, *H.G. Wells in Love*, pp. 103–7; Anthony West's in *Aspects of a Life*, pp. 94–100.
7. Letter of 9 July 1923 from HGW to Desmond McCarthy, in *Correspondence*, Vol. 3, p. 148.
8. Letter of 21 June 1942 from Hedy Gossman to HGW, in *Correspondence*, Vol. 4, p. 330.
9. HGW, *A Year of Prophesying*, Ch. 2; HGW, *The Way the World Is Going*, Ch. 11.
10. HGW, *The First Men in the Moon*, Ch. 1.
11. Undated letter from HGW to Rebecca West, in Ray, *Wells and West*, p. 146
12. HGW, *H.G. Wells in Love*, p. 108.
13. Undated letter from Amber Blanco White to HGW, in the Illinois Wells Archive.
14. HGW, 'Preface' to Vol. 5 of the Atlantic edition.
15. HGW, *Christina Alberta's Father*, Bk I, Ch. 3, §1.
16. HGW, *Christina Alberta's Father*, Bk III, Ch. 4, §5.

17. HGW , *Christina Alberta's Father*, Bk III, Ch. 4, §7.
18. L.P. Hartley in the *Saturday Review*, September 1926, quoted in Scheick and Cox, *Reference Guide*, p. 14; D.H. Lawrence, quoted in Brian Murray, *H.G. Wells*, New York, Continuum, 1990, p. 69.
19. Letter of 11 September 1926 from C.G. Jung to HGW, in the Illinois Wells Archive.
20. Letter dated '10 Feb' from Moura Budberg to HGW, in the Illinois Wells Archive.
21. Odette Keun, *My Adventures in Bolshevik Russia*, London, Bodley Head, 1923, p. 313.
22. HGW, *H.G. Wells in Love*, p. 125.
23. On Lou Pidou, see Bernard Loing, 'H.G. Wells at Grasse' (an interview with Félicie Goletto), *Wellsian*, 7, 1984, pp. 32–7, and Gareth Davies-Morris, 'Looking for Lou Pidou', *Wellsian*, 18, 1995, pp. 23–8.

Chapter 16. Life After Jane, 1927–1930

1. HGW, *Meanwhile*, Bk 1, Ch. 11.
2. Undated letter from HGW to Amy Catherine Wells, in *Correspondence*, Vol. 3, pp. 235–6.
3. Letter of 16 May 1927 from Christabel McLaren to HGW, in the Illinois Wells Archive.
4. HGW, 'Introduction', *The Book of Catherine Wells*.
5. Virgina Woolf diary entry, quoted in *Shaw and Wells*, pp. 134–5.
6. V.S. Pritchett, 'The Scientific Romances' (1946), in Bergonzi (ed.), *Critical Essays*, p. 32.
7. HGW, 'Introduction', *The Book of Catherine Wells*.
8. Letter of 16 October 1927 from Pinnie Robbins to HGW, in the Illinois Wells Archive.
9. Newspaper clipping in Amy Catherine Wells's Garden Book, in the Illinois Wells Archive.
10. Glendinning, *Rebecca West*, pp. 102–7.
11. Julian Huxley, *Memories*, London, George Allen and Unwin, 1970, p. 166.
12. Anthony West, *Aspects of a Life*, pp. 109–12.
13. HGW, *H.G. Wells in Love*, p. 127.
14. West's views are summarized in G.H. Wells, 'The Failure of H.G. Wells', in Parrinder (ed.) *Critical Heritage*, pp. 290–9.
15. Letter of 23 November 1928 from HGW to James Joyce, in *Correspondence*, Vol. 3, pp. 276–7.
16. Undated letter from HGW to the editor of the *Dancing Times*, in *Correspondence*, Vol. 3, pp. 213–14; letter of 21 February 1922 from HGW to the editors of several literary journals, pp. 96–7; letter of 22 November 1928 from HGW to Desmond McCarthy; p. 278; letter of 24 September 1928 from HGW to Wyndham Lewis, pp. 260–70; undated letter from HGW to the Arthur Press, p. 359; letters of 6 August 1930 and 20 July 1932 from HGW to J.B. Priestley, pp. 360–1 and 430–1.
17. Letter of 25 May 1928 from Beatrice Webb to HGW, quoted in Smith, *Desperately Mortal*, p. 292.

18. In 2006 the British Library issued the surviving recordings of Wells's BBC broadcasts on a compact disc entitled *The Spoken Word: H.G. Wells.*
19. HGW, 'Liberalism and the Revolutionary Spirit', in *After Democracy.*
20. HGW, 'Russia and the World', in *After Democracy.*

Chapter 17. An Inflated Persona, 1930–1934

1. Letter of 6 March 1931 from HGW to Anna Jane Blanco White, in the Illinois Wells Archive. 'Lasky' is Harold Laski, Professor of Political Science at the London School of Economics, a leading Fabian and Labour intellectual.
2. Letter of 23 May 1932 from HGW to Anna Jane Blanco White, in the Illinois Wells Archive.
3. Letter of 26 May 1931 from Anna Jane Blanco White to HGW, in the Illinois Wells Archive.
4. Letter of 30 May 1931 from HGW to Anna Jane Blanco White, in the Illinois Wells Archive.
5. Postcard of 1 June 1931 from HGW to Amber Blanco White, in the Illinois Wells Archive.
6 Letter of 28 July 1932 from Anna Jane Davis to HGW, in the Illinois Wells Archive.
7. Letter of 16 August 1932 from HGW to Anna Jane Davis, in the Illinois Wells Archive.
8. Letter of 4 January 1933 from Anna Jane Davis to HGW, in the Illinois Wells Archive.
9. Anthony West, in Bergonzi (ed.), *Critical Essays,* p. 22.
10. Letter of 18 May [1930?] from Odette Keun to Amber Blanco White, in the Illinois Wells Archive.
11. HGW, *Experiment in Autobiography,* Ch. 9, §8.
12. Letter of 28 July 1933 from Moura Budberg to HGW, in *Correspondence,* Vol. 3, p. 358. Based on my own transcript of the letter in the Illinois Archive, I have substituted 'Kobinger' for 'Vobarger', but I think we're both guessing.
13. Lynn, *Shadow Lovers,* p. 165.
14. HGW, *Experiment in Autobiography,* Ch. 1, §1.
15. HGW, *Experiment in Autobiography,* Ch. 1, §2.
16. HGW, Julian Huxley and G.P. Wells, *The Science of Life,* Bk VIII, Ch. 8, §2.
17. HGW, Huxley and Wells, *The Science of Life,* Bk VIII, Ch. 7, §13.
18. HGW, *Early Writings,* p. 218.
19. For feelings of extreme detachment, see *The First Men in the Moon,* Ch. 19, *The War of the Worlds,* Bk I, Ch. 7, *The New Machiavelli,* Bk 3, Ch. 1, §5, *The World of William Clissold,* Ch. 1, §2, and 'The Crystal Egg'.
20. Julian Huxley, *Memories,* p. 160; also in Hammond (ed.), *Interviews and Recollections,* p. 79.
21. Julian Huxley, *Memories,* p. 169, and letter of 12 February 1928 from HGW to Julian Huxley, in *Correspondence,* Vol. 3, p. 258.
22. Kay Dick (ed.), *Writers at Work,* Harmondsworth, Penguin, 1972, p. 158. For links between *Brave New World* and Wells, see Hillegas, *The Future as Nightmare,* pp. 110–23.

23. HGW, *The Shape of Things to Come,* Bk III, Ch. 7.
24. HGW, *The Shape of Things to Come,* Bk I, Ch. 2.
25. Letter of 31 August 1932 from Oswald Mosley to HGW, quoted in W. Warren Wagar, *H.G. Wells and the World State,* New Haven, Yale University Press, 1961, p. 196.
26. HGW, *Experiment in Autobiography,* Ch. 9, §9.
27. Letter of 13 February 1935 from F.D. Roosevelt to HGW, quoted in MacKenzie, *The Time Traveller,* p. 384.
28. HGW, *Experiment in Autobiography,* Ch. 9, §9.
29. Lynn, *Shadow Lovers,* p. 159.
30. HGW, *Stalin–Wells Talk,* p. 4.
31. Tania Alexander, *A Little of All These,* London, Jonathan Cape, 1987, p. 102.
32. HGW, *H.G. Wells in Love,* p. 176.

Chapter 18. The Man Who Continued to Work Miracles, 1935–1939

1. The information on Constance Coolidge and Martha Gellhorn is largely taken from Chapters 4 and 5 of Lynn, *Shadow Lovers.*
2. Undated letter from HGW to Constance Coolidge, quoted in Lynn, *Shadow Lovers,* p. 280. Also in *Correspondence,* Vol. 3, p. 652, in a slightly different transcription.
3. Letter of 12 March 1935 from HGW to Constance Coolidge, in *Correspondence,* Vol. 4, p. 11.
4. HGW, *H G. Wells in Love,* p. 54.
5. HGW, *H.G. Wells in Love,* p. 200.
6. Letter of 19 March 1935 from HGW to Constance Coolidge, in *Correspondence,* Vol. 4, p. 12.
7. HGW, unpublished material from the 'Postscript', in Lynn, *Shadow Lovers,* p. 336.
8. Enid Bagnold, *Enid Bagnold's Autobiography,* 1969, London, Century, 1985 edition, p. 132.
9. See Catherine Stoye, 'My Mother, Marjorie Craig Wells', in *Wellsian,* 21, 1998, pp. 14–17.
10. HGW, unpublished material from the 'Postscript', in Lynn, *Shadow Lovers,* p. 337.
11. HGW, *H.G. Wells in Love,* p. 208.
12. HGW, unpublished material from the 'Postscript', in Lynn, *Shadow Lovers,* p. 338.
13. Letter of 29 September 1987 from Martha Gellhorn to Victoria Glendinning, quoted in Lynn, *Shadow Lovers,* p. 363.
14. Letter of 5 August 1946 from Ernest Hemingway to Martha Gellhorn, possibly unsent, quoted in Lynn, *Shadow Lovers,* pp. 421–3.
15. Lynn, *Shadow Lovers,* pp. 187–8.
16. 'My Secret Agent Auntie', broadcast 7 May 2008 on BBC4 television.
17. Quoted in MacKenzie, *The Time Traveller,* p. 389.
18. HGW, *H.G. Wells in Love,* p. 211.
19. Wells and other writers, *Authors Take Sides on the Spanish War,* London, Left Review, 1937. In his contribution to a booklet called *Authors Take Sides on the Spanish War* he expressed his sympathy with the republican government but declined to align himself himself to

the mix of views represented by its left-wing supporters and, misleadingly therefore, was placed by the editors in the neutral section alongside Eliot and Pound.

20. Robert Bloom, *Anatomies of Egotism*, Lincoln, University of Nebraska Press, 1977, p. 87.
21. Odette Keun, *I Discover the English*, London, Bodley Head, 1934, p. 188.
22. Letter of 16 April 1936 from Odette Keun to HGW, in the Illinois Wells Archive. Also included with a different transcription, dated 12 September 1936, in Lynn, *Shadow Lovers*, p. 98.
23. Anthony West, *Aspects of a Life*, p. 142.
24. Letter of 10 June 1937 from Odette Keun to HGW, in the Illinois Wells Archive. Transcribed more fully in Lynn, *Shadow Lovers*, p. 99.
25. Letter of 25 August 1939 from Amber Blanco White to HGW, in the Illinois Wells Archive. Published more fully, but in a slightly different transcription, in *Correspondence*, Vol. 4, p. 233.
26. Letter of 17 July 1937 from Anna Jane Davis to HGW, in the Illinois Wells Archive.
27. Letter of 1 July 1939 from Anna Jane Davis to HGWin the Illinois Wells Archive.
28. Quoted in Christopher Frayling, *Things to Come*, London, British Film Institute, 1995, p. 24.
29. HGW, *H.G. Wells in Love*, p. 212.
30. Letter of 4 November 1937 from HGW to Margaret Sanger, quoted in MacKenzie, *The Time Traveller*, p. 404. A fuller version, with transcription differences, appears in *Correspondence*, Vol. 4, pp. 173–4.
31. C.P. Snow, *Variety of Men*, 1967, London, Readers Union edition, 1968, p. 61.
32. Letter of 22 October 1938 from HGW to Eduard Beneš, in *Correspondence*, Vol. 4, pp. 202–4. The letter was signed by thirty-nine prominent Britons but drafted by Wells and produced at his initiative.
33. See Alan Mayne's introduction to his edition of *World Brain*, London, Adamantine Press, 1994, but see also W. Boyd Rayward's article, 'HGW's idea of a World Brain: A Critical Re-Assessment', first published in the *Journal of the American Society for Information Science*, 50, 15, May 1999, but widely available on the internet.
34. See Hadley Cantril's investigation, *The Invasion from Mars*, Princeton, Princeton University Press, 1940. The incident has been dramatized in a notable television movie, *The Night That Panicked America* (1975), directed by Joseph Sargent and scripted by Nicholas Meyer. To date, the film has not been distributed on DVD or any similar format. Meyer went on to write and direct the more widely available satirical science-fiction thriller *Time After Time* (1979) in which Malcolm McDowell as Wells gives battle to David Warner as Jack the Ripper. Both are superior to the run of films derived more directly from Wells's work.
35. The Ecuador incident was reported in *The Times*, 15 February 1949. For discussion of *The War of the Worlds* as a modern myth, see Michael Draper, 'The War Against Little Green Men', in the *Times Higher Education Supplement*, 11 November 1988, p. 13.
36. HGW, *In Search of Hot Water*, Ch. 1.

37. My account of Wells's Australian tour is indebted to Smith, *Desperately Mortal*, pp. 338–51.
38. Anthony West, *Aspects of a Life*, p. 151.
39. HGW, *in Search of Hot Water*, Ch. 5.
40. Parrinder and Partington (eds), *Reception in Europe*, pp. 170–1.
41. Undated letter from HGW to A.S. Neill and letter of 24 May 1940 from HGW to R.A. Gregory, in *Correspondence*, Vol. 4, pp. 422 and 264.
42. HGW, *H.G. Wells in Love*, p. 222.
43. HGW, *H.G. Wells in Love*, p. 222.
44. HGW, *Experiment in Autobiography*, Ch. 3, §2.

Chapter 19. Declarations, 1939–1943

1. Malcolm Cowley, *The New Republic*, November 1939, quoted in Scheick and Cox, *Reference Guide*, p. 187.
2. T.S. Eliot, 'Wells as Journalist', reprinted in Parrinder (ed.), *Critical Heritage*, pp. 319–22.
3. T.S. Eliot, *After Strange Gods*, London, Faber, 1934, p.20. Eliot later withdrew the book from circulation.
4. Letter of 5 January 1940 from HGW to Beatrice Webb, in *Correspondence*, Vol. 4, p. 253.
5. Letter of 24 October 1939 from HGW to Vernon Bartlett, in *Correspondence*, Vol. 4, p. 245.
6. HGW, *The Rights of Man*, Ch. 1.
7. HGW, *The Rights of Man*, Ch. 5.
8. Letter of 9 November 1939 from Franklin D. Roosevelt to HGW, in Teru Hamano, 'H.G. Wells and the Universal Declaration of Human Rights', *Wellsian*, 24, 2001, pp. 31–46.
9. Quoted in Partington, *Building Cosmopolis*, p. 139.
10. Letter of 26 September 1940 from HGW to Moura Budberg, in *Correspondence*, Vol. 4, p. 281.
11. Robert Calder, *Beware the British Serpent*, Montreal, McGill–Queen's University Press, 2004, p. 108.
12. Quoted in Vincent Brome, *H.G. Wells*, London, Longmans, Green and Co., 1951, p. 220.
13. HGW, *H.G. Wells in Love*, p. 224.
14. The interview was issued in 1979 on a long-playing record, mostly taken up by a radio version of *The War of the Worlds* from 1955 (Radiola MR-1101). A truncated version is available at http://sounds.mercurytheatre.info.
15. Undated telegram from HGW to Orson Welles, in *Correspondence*, Vol. 4, p. 298.
16. Ed Sullivan, 'Little Old New York' column, *Daily News*, 17 May 1944 – newspaper cutting sent to HGW by Margaret Sanger, in the Illinois Wells Archive.
17. Martin Wells, 'Flashback', *Telegraph Magazine*, 6 December 2008, p. 106.
18. Anthony West, *Aspects of a Life*, p. 151.
19. HGW, *The Common Sense of War and Peace*, Ch. 1.
20. Graham Greene, *The Spectator*, October 1940, quoted in Scheick and Cox, *Reference Guide*, p. 215.

21. Neither I nor Patrick Parrinder has managed to track down this reference, though we both believe him to have published it. The point was previously implied by Vladimir Nabokov in his introduction to the 1959 translation of his novel *Invitation to a Beheading*, where he contemptuously dismisses Blair as 'G.H. Orwell'.
22. Howard Fink, '*Coming Up for Air*: Orwell's Ambiguous Satire on the Wellsian Utopia', in Darko Suvin and Roberts M. Philmus (eds), *HGW and Modern Science Fiction*, Lewisburg, Bucknell University Press, 1977.
23. Partington, *Building Cosmopolis*, pp. 14–15. See also John S. Partington, 'The Pen as Sword: George Orwell, H.G. Wells and Journalistic Parricide', in *Journal of Contemporary History*, 39: 1, 2004, pp. 45–56.
24. Bernard Crick, *George Orwell: A Life*, 1980, Harmondsworth, Penguin, 1982 edition, p. 429.
25. Quoted in MacKenzie, *The Time Traveller*, p. 431.
26. Letter of 5 March 1942 from HGW to Anna Jane Davis, in the Illinois Wells Archive.
27. Letter of 2 August 1941 from Elizabeth Bruce to HGW, in the Illinois Wells Archive.
28. Letter of 24 November 1942 from HGW to Lance Corporal Aaron J. Hlope, in *Correspondence*, Vol. 4, pp. 352–3.
29. Letter of 25 September 1940 from Anna Jane Davis to HGW, in the Illinois Wells Archive.
30. See Tom Nagorski, *Miracles on the Water*, London, Robinson, 2007, especially pp. 113–16 and 156–7.
31. 'Airgraph' of 4 February 1942 from Anna Jane Davis to HGW, in the Illinois Wells Archive.
32. Giles Playfair, *Singapore Goes Off the Air*, London, Jarrolds, 1943, p. 111.
33. Telegram of 7 May 1942 from HGW to Anna Jane Davis, in the Illinois Wells Archive.
34. 'Airgraph' of 6 November 1942 from Anna Jane Davis to HGW, in the Illinois Wells Archive.
35. 'Airgram' of 21 September 1943 from Anna Jane Davis to HGW, in the Illinois Wells Archive.
36. Letter of 15 August [no year given] from Amber Blanco White to HGW, in the Illinois Wells Archive.
37. Letter of 14 October 1945 from Anna Jane Davis to HGW, in the Illinois Wells Archive.
38. HGW, 'My Auto-Obituary', in Hammond (ed.), *Interviews and Recollections*, pp. 117–19.

Chapter 20. Exasperations, 1943–1946

1. Letters of 3 January 1943 and 17 July 1944 from HGW to Margaret Sanger, in *Correspondence*, Vol. 4, pp. 365 and 499–500; undated letter from HGW to E. Haldeman-Julius, p. 509.
2. HGW, *'42 to '44*, Part II, Ch. 5.
3. 'Airgraph' of 1 February 1944 from HGW to Anna Jane Davis, in the Illinois Wells Archive; letter of 17 September 1943 from HGW to C.K. Ogden, in *Correspondence*, Vol. 4, pp. 441–2.

4. Letter of 11 October 1943 from HGW to N.W. Angus, in *Correspondence,* Vol. 4, pp. 445–6.
5. Letter of 19 October 1943 to A.T. Bryant, in *Correspondence,* Vol. 4, p. 451. I have substituted 'forced' for 'forged', suspecting a slip of the pen or a transcription error.
6. HGW, *'42 to '44,* Part II, Ch. 5.
7. Letter of 17 July 1944 from HGW to Margaret Sanger, in *Correspondence,* Vol. 4, pp. 499–500.
8. HGW, *Crux Ansata,* Ch. 21.
9. Letter of 3 August 1943 from HGW to Chaim Weizmann, in *Correspondence,* Vol. 4, pp. 424–5.
10. *Exasperations* typescript, in the Illinois Wells Archive.
11. Hammond (ed.), *Interviews and Recollections,* p. 62.
12. HGW, *The Happy Turning,* Ch. 5, §1.
13. William Lanouette with Bela Silard, *Genius in the Shadows,* 1992, Chicago, University of Chicago Press, 1994 edition, pp. 107, 137 and 179.
14. Letter of 25 August 1945 from Martha Hemingway to HGW, in the Illinois Wells Archive.
15. Undated letter from HGW to various addressees, in *Correspondence,* Vol. 4, pp. 531–2.
16. HGW, *Mind at the End of Its Tether,* Ch. 1.
17. HGW, *Mind at the End of Its Tether,* Ch. 3.
18. Parrinder (ed.), *Critical Heritage,* p. 322.
19. Letter of 28 May 1946 from HGW to Elizabeth Bruce, in *Correspondence,* Vol. 4, p. 532.
20. Letter of 28 May 1946 from Marjorie Wells to Elizabeth Bruce, in *Correspondence,* Vol. 4, p. 533.
21. Brome, *H.G. Wells,* p. 226.
22. Anthony West, *Aspects of a Life,* p. 153.
23. Brome, *H.G. Wells,* p. 226.
24. Copy of death certificate, from 14 August 1946.
25. Letter of 9 September 1946 from R.A. Gregory to Elizabeth Bruce, in W.H.G. Armytage, *Sir Richard Gregory,* London, Macmillan, 1957, p. 206; *Sydney Morning Herald* quoted in Smith, *Desperately Mortal,* p. 480; Orwell quoted in Lynn, *Shadow Lovers,* p. 453; Borges in Parrinder (ed.), *Critical Heritage,* p. 332.
26. Simon Garfield (ed.), *Our Hidden Lives,* 2004, London, Ebury Press edition, 2005, p. 265.
27. Anthony West, *Aspects of a Life,* pp. 153–4. The mythical aircraft can be glimpsed in Smith, *Desperately Mortal,* p. 479. MacKenzie, *The Time Traveller,* p. 447, gives the impression the ashes were scattered from the Isle of Wight.
28. Quoted in John Ezard, 'Security services ignored warning about Blunt', originally published in the *Guardian* on 28 November 2002; available online via www.guardian.co.uk/politics/freedomofinformation.

BIBLIOGRAPHY

Works by Wells

In addition to first editions, I have noted modern critical editions that offer helpful notes and critical perspectives. The Oxford and Penguin series, both supervised by Patrick Parrinder, have sound texts, introduction and notes and so are particularly recommended, as are the two books from the Broadview Press. The Dent/Tuttle editions are more variable in what they provide, so at the risk of inconsistency I have included some and not others. Readers should be warned that the editions edited by Leon Stover are somewhat eccentric and hostile in their approach to Wells, yet scholars may find their commentaries often repay investigation. Wells's books are listed in order of first publication.

Text-Book of Biology, 2 vols, London: W.B. Clive, 1893

(with Gregory, R.A.), *Honours Physiography*, London: Joseph Hughes, 1893

Select Conversations with an Uncle, London: John Lane, 1895; New York: Merriam, 1895

— (ed.) David C. Smith and Patrick Parrinder, London: University of North London Press, 1992

The Time Machine, London: Heinemann, 1895; New York: Holt, 1895

— (ed.) Harry Geduld, Bloomington and Indianapolis: Indiana University Press, 1987

— (ed.) John Lawton, London: Dent, 1995; Rutland: Tuttle, 1995

— (ed.) Patrick Parrinder (with *The Island of Doctor Moreau*), New York: Oxford University Press, 1996

— (ed.) Leon Stover, Jefferson and London: McFarland, 1996

— (ed.) Nicholas Ruddick, Ontario: Broadview Press, 2001

— (ed.) Patrick Parrinder, London and New York: Penguin, 2005

The Wonderful Visit, London: Dent, 1895; New York: Macmillan, 1895

The Stolen Bacillus and Other Incidents, London: Methuen, 1895

The Island of Doctor Moreau, London: Heinemann, 1896; New York: Stone and Kimball, 1896

— (ed.) Robert Philmus, Athens and London: University of Georgia Press, 1993

— (ed.) Patrick Parrinder (with *The Time Machine*), New York: Oxford University Press, 1996

— (ed.) Leon Stover, Jefferson and London: McFarland, 1996

— (ed.) Patrick Parrinder, London and New York: Penguin, 2005

The Wheels of Chance, London: Dent, 1896; New York: Macmillan, 1896

The Plattner Story and Others, London: Methuen, 1897

The Invisible Man, London: Pearson, 1897; New York: Arnold, 1897
— (ed.) Macdonald Daly, London: Dent, 1995; Rutland: Tuttle, 1995
— (ed.) David Lake, New York: Oxford University Press, 1996
— (ed.) Leon Stover, Jefferson and London: McFarland, 1998
— (ed.) Patrick Parrinder, London and New York: Penguin, 2005
Certain Personal Matters, London: Lawrence and Bullen, 1897
Thirty Strange Stories, New York, Arnold, 1897
The War of the Worlds, London: Heinemann, 1898; New York: Harper, 1898
— (ed.) David Y. Hughes and Harry Geduld, Bloomington and Indianapolis: Indiana University Press, 1993
— (ed.) David Y. Hughes, New York: Oxford University Press, 1995
— (ed.) Leon Stover, Jefferson and London: McFarland, 2001
— (ed.) Martin Danahay, Ontario: Broadview Press, 2003
— (ed.) Patrick Parrinder, London and New York: Penguin, 2005
When the Sleeper Wakes, London and New York: Harper, 1899
— (ed.) John Lawton, London: Dent, 1995; Rutland: Tuttle, 1995
— (ed.) Leon Stover, Jefferson and London: McFarland, 2000
— revised as *The Sleeper Awakes*, London: Nelson, 1910
— (ed.) Patrick Parrinder, London and New York: Penguin, 2005
Tales of Space and Time, London: Harper, 1899; New York: Doubleday, McClure, 1899
Love and Mr Lewisham, London and New York: Harper, 1900
— (ed.) Jeremy Lewis, London: Dent, 1993; Rutland: Tuttle, 1993
— (ed.) Simon J. James, London and New York: Penguin, 2005
The First Men in the Moon, London: Newnes, 1901; Indianapolis: Bowen-Merrill, 1901
— (ed.) David Lake, New York: Oxford University Press, 1995
— (ed.) Leon Stover, Jefferson and London: McFarland, 1998
— (ed.) Patrick Parrinder, London and New York: Penguin, 2005
Anticipations, London: Chapman and Hall, 1901; New York: Harper, 1902
The Discovery of the Future, London: Fisher Unwin, 1902; New York: Huebsch, 1913
— (ed.) Patrick Parrinder, London: PNL Press, 1989
The Sea Lady, London: Methuen, 1902; New York: Appleton, 1902
— (ed.) Leon Stover, Jefferson and London: McFarland, 2001
Mankind in the Making, London: Chapman and Hall, 1903; New York: Scribner's, 1904
Twelve Stories and a Dream, London: Macmillan, 1903; New York: Scribner's, 1905
The Food of the Gods, London: Macmillan, 1904; New York: Scribner's, 1904
A Modern Utopia, London: Chapman and Hall, 1905; New York: Scribner's, 1905
— (ed.) Mark. R. Hillegas, Lincoln: University of Nebraska Press, 1967
— (ed.) Krishan Kumar, London: Dent, 1994; Rutland: Tuttle, 1994
— (ed.) Gregory Claeys and Patrick Parrinder, London and New York: Penguin, 2005
Kipps, London: Macmillan, 1905; New York: Scribner's, 1905

— (ed.) Simon J. James, London and New York: Penguin, 2005
In the Days of the Comet, London: Macmillan, 1906; New York: Century, 1906
The Future in America, London: Chapman and Hall, 1906; New York: Harper, 1906
New Worlds for Old, London: Constable, 1908; New York: Macmillan, 1908
The War in the Air, London: Bell, 1908; New York: Macmillan, 1908
— (ed.) Patrick Parrinder, London and New York: Penguin, 2005
First and Last Things, London: Constable, 1908; New York: Putnam's, 1908
Tono-Bungay, London: Macmillan, 1909; New York: Duffield, 1908
— (ed.) A.C. Ward, London: Longmans, Green, 1961
— (ed.) Bernard Bergonzi, Boston: Houghton-Mifflin, 1966
— (ed.) John R. Hammond, London: Dent, 1994; Rutland: Tuttle, 1994
— (ed.) Bryan Cheyette, New York: Oxford University Press, 1996
— (ed.) Patrick Parrinder, London and New York: Penguin, 2005
Ann Veronica, London: Fisher Unwin, 1909; New York: Harper, 1909
— (ed.) Sylvia Hardy, London: Dent, 1993; Rutland: Tuttle, 1993
— (ed.) Sita Schütt, London: Penguin and New York, 2005
The History of Mr Polly, London: Nelson, 1910; New York: Duffield, 1910
— (ed.) Gordon N. Ray, Boston: Houghton Mifflin, 1960
— (ed.) David Y. Hughes, London: Dent, 1993; Rutland: Tuttle, 1993
— (ed.) Simon J. James, London and New York: Penguin, 2005
The New Machiavelli, London: John Lane, 1911; New York: Duffield, 1910
— (ed.) Norman MacKenzie, London: Dent, 1994; Rutland: Tuttle, 1994
— (ed.) Simon J. James, London and New York: Penguin, 2005
The Country of the Blind and Other Stories, London and New York: Nelson, 1911
— (ed.) Michael Sherborne, New York: Oxford University Press, 1996
Floor Games, London: Palmer, 1911; Boston: Small, Maynard, 1912
— (ed.) Barbara A. Turner, Cloverdale: Temenos Press, 2004
The Great State (ed. with Lady Warwick and G.R.S. Taylor), London: Harper, 1912; as *Socialism and the Great State*, New York: Harper, 1914
Marriage, London: Macmillan, 1912; New York: Duffield, 1912
Little Wars, London: Palmer, 1913; Boston: Small, Maynard, 1913
The Passionate Friends, London: Macmillan, 1913; New York: Harper, 1913
An Englishman Looks at the World, London: Cassell, 1914; as *Social Forces in England and America*, New York: Harper, 1914
The World Set Free, London: Macmillan, 1914; New York: Dutton, 1914
The Wife of Sir Isaac Harman, London and New York: Macmillan, 1914
The War That Will End War, London: Palmer, 1914; New York: Duffield, 1914
Boon, London: Fisher Unwin, 1915; New York: Doran, 1915
Bealby, London: Methuen, 1915; New York: Macmillan, 1915
The Research Magnificent, London and New York: Macmillan, 1915

What Is Coming? London: Cassell, 1916; New York: Macmillan, 1916
Mr Britling Sees It Through, London: Cassell, 1916; New York: Macmillan, 1916
The Elements of Reconstruction, London: Nisbet, 1916
War and the Future, London: Cassell, 1917; as *Italy, France and Britain at War*, New York: Macmillan, 1917
God the Invisible King, London: Cassell, 1917; New York: Macmillan, 1917
The Soul of a Bishop, London: Cassell, 1917; New York: Macmillan, 1917
In the Fourth Year, London: Chatto and Windus, 1918; New York: Macmillan, 1918
Joan and Peter, London: Cassell, 1918; New York: Macmillan, 1918
The Undying Fire, London: Cassell, 1919; New York: Macmillan, 1919
The Outline of History, London: Cassell, 1920; New York: Macmillan, 1921
Russia in the Shadows, London: Hodder and Stoughton, 1920; New York: Doran, 1921
The Salvaging of Civilization, London: Cassell, 1921; New York: Macmillan, 1921
Washington and the Hope of Peace, London: Collins, 1922; as *Washington and the Riddle of Peace*, New York: Macmillan, 1922
The Secret Places of the Heart, London: Cassell, 1922; New York: Macmillan, 1922
A Short History of the World, London: Cassell, 1922; New York: Macmillan, 1922
— (ed.) Michael Sherborne, London and New York: Penguin, 2006
Men Like Gods, London: Cassell, 1923; New York: Macmillan, 1923
The Works of H.G. Wells, Atlantic edition, 28 volumes, London: Unwin, 1924–7; New York: Charles Scribner's Sons, 1924–7
The Story of a Great Schoolmaster, London: Chatto and Windus, 1924; New York: Macmillan, 1924
The Dream, London: Jonathan Cape, 1924; New York: Macmillan, 1924
A Year of Prophesying, London: Fisher Unwin, 1924; New York: Macmillan, 1925
Christina Alberta's Father, London: Jonathan Cape, 1925; New York: Macmillan, 1925
The World of William Clissold, London: Ernest Benn, 1926; New York: Doran, 1926
Mr Belloc Objects to the 'Outline of History', London: Watts, 1926; New York: Doran, 1926
Meanwhile, London: Ernest Benn, 1927; New York: Doran, 1927
The Way the World Is Going, London: Ernest Benn, 1928; Garden City: Doubleday, Doran, 1929
The Open Conspiracy, London: Gollancz, 1928; Garden City: Doubleday, Doran, 1928
Mr Blettsworthy on Rampole Island, London: Ernest Benn, 1928; Garden City: Doubleday, Doran, 1928
The Book of Catherine Wells, London: Chatto and Windus, 1928; Garden City: Doubleday, Doran, 1928
The King Who Was a King, London: Benn, 1929; Garden City: Doubleday, Doran, 1929
The Adventures of Tommy, London: Harrap, 1929; New York: Stokes, 1929
The Autocracy of Mr Parham, London: Heinemann, 1930; Garden City: Doubleday, Doran, 1930
With Huxley, Julian and Wells, G.P., *The Science of Life*, London: Amalgamated Press, 1930: Garden City: Doubleday, Doran, 1931

What Are We to Do with Our Lives? London: Heinemann, 1931; Garden City: Doubleday, Doran, 1931
The Work, Wealth and Happiness of Mankind, London: Heinemann, 1932; Garden City: Doubleday, Doran, 1931
After Democracy, London: Watts, 1932
The Bulpington of Blup, London: Hutchinson, 1933; New York: Macmillan, 1933
The Shape of Things to Come, London: Hutchinson, 1933; New York: Macmillan, 1933
— (ed.) John R. Hammond, London: Dent, 1993; Rutland: Tuttle, 1993
— (ed.) Patrick Parrinder, London and New York: Penguin, 2005
Experiment in Autobiography, London: Gollancz and Cresset, 1934; New York: Macmillan, 1934
Stalin–Wells Talk, London: New Statesman and Nation, 1934
The New America: The New World, London: Cresset, 1935; New York: Macmillan, 1935
Things to Come: A Film Story, London: Cresset, 1935; New York: Macmillan, 1935
— (ed.) Leon Stover, Jefferson and London: McFarland, 2007
The Anatomy of Frustration, London: Cresset, 1936; New York: Macmillan, 1936
The Croquet Player, London: Chatto and Windus, 1936; New York: Viking, 1937
— (ed.) John Huntington, Lincoln: University of Nebraska Press, 2004
The Man Who Could Work Miracles: A Film Story, London: Cresset, 1936; New York: Macmillan, 1936
— (ed.) Leon Stover, Jefferson and London: McFarland, 2003
Star Begotten, London: Chatto and Windus, 1937; New York: Viking, 1937
— (ed.) John Huntington, Middletown: Wesleyan University Press, 2006
Brynhild, London: Methuen, 1937; New York: Scribner's, 1937
The Camford Visitation, London: Methuen, 1937
The Brothers, London: Chatto and Windus, 1938; New York: Viking, 1938
World Brain, London: Methuen, 1938; Garden City: Doubleday, Doran, 1938
— (ed.) Alan Mayne, London: Adamantine Press, 1994
Apropos of Dolores, London: Jonathan Cape, 1938; New York: Scribner, 1938
The Holy Terror, London: Michael Joseph, 1939; New York: Simon and Schuster, 1939
Travels of a Republican Radical in Search of Hot Water, Harmondsworth: Penguin, 1939
The Fate of Homo Sapiens, London: Secker and Warburg, 1939; as *The Fate of Man*, New York: Alliance, 1939
The New World Order, London: Secker and Warburg, 1939; New York: Knopf, 1940
The Rights of Man, Or What Are We Fighting For? Harmondsworth and New York: Penguin, 1940
Babes in the Darkling Wood, London: Secker and Warburg, 1940; New York: Alliance, 1940
The Common Sense of War and Peace, Harmondsworth and New York: Penguin, 1940
All Aboard for Ararat, London: Secker and Warburg, 1940; New York: Alliance, 1941
Guide to the New World, London: Victor Gollancz, 1941
You Can't Be Too Careful, London: Secker and Warburg, 1941; New York: Putnam's, 1942
The Outlook for Homo Sapiens, London: Secker and Warburg, 1942
Phoenix, London: Secker and Warburg, 1942; Girard: Haldeman-Julius, 1942
The Conquest of Time, London: Watts, 1942

Crux Ansata, Harmondsworth: Penguin, 1943; New York: Agora, 1944
'42 to '44, London: Secker and Warburg, 1944
The Happy Turning, London and Toronto: Heinemann, 1945; New York: Didier, 1946 with *Mind at the End of Its Tether*
Mind at the End of Its Tether, London and Toronto: Heinemann, 1945; New York: Didier, 1946, with *The Happy Turning*
The Desert Daisy, (ed.) Gordon N. Ray, Urbana, Illinois: Bet Phi Mu, 1957
Hoopdriver's Holiday, (ed.) Michael Timko, West Lafayette: Purdue University, 1964
The Wealth of Mr Waddy, (ed.) Harris Wilson, Carbondale: Southern Illinois University Press, 1969
Early Writings in Science and Science Fiction, (ed.) Robert Philmus and David Y. Hughes, Berkeley and London: University of California Press, 1975
H.G. Wells's Literary Criticism, (ed.) Patrick Parrinder and Robert Philmus, Brighton: Harvester Press, 1980; Totowa, NJ: Barnes and Noble, 1980
H.G. Wells in Love, (ed.) G. P. Wells, London: Faber; Boston: Little, Brown, 1984
The Complete Short Stories, (ed.) John R. Hammond, London: Dent, 1998
The Correspondence of H.G. Wells, 4 vols, (ed.) David C. Smith, London and Vermont: Pickering and Chatto, 1998

Books about Wells

Archer, William, *God and Mr Wells*, London: Watts, 1917
Ash, Brian, *Who's Who in H.G. Wells*, London: Elm Tree Books, 1979
Batchelor, John, *H.G. Wells*, Cambridge and New York: Cambridge University Press, 1985
Bergonzi, Bernard, *The Early H.G. Wells*, Manchester: Manchester University Press, 1961; Toronto: University of Toronto Press, 1961
— (ed.), *H.G. Wells: A Collection of Critical Essays*, Englewood Cliffs: Prentice-Hall, 1976
Bloom, Robert, *Anatomies of Egotism*, Lincoln: University of Nebraska Press, 1977
Brooks, Van Wyck, *The World of H.G. Wells*, New York: Mitchell Kennerley, 1915; London: T. Fisher Unwin, 1915
Brome, Vincent, *H.G. Wells*, London and New York: Longmans, Green and Co., 1951
Coren, Michael, *The Invisible Man*, London: Bloomsbury, 1993; New York: Atheneum, 1993
Costa, Richard Hauer, *H.G. Wells*, Boston: Twayne, 1985
Crossley, Robert, *H.G. Wells*, Mercer Island: Starmont House, 1986
Dickson, Lovat, *H.G. Wells: His Turbulent Life and Times*, London: Macmillan, 1969; New York: Atheneum, 1969
Dilloway, James, *Human Rights and World Order*, London: H.G. Wells Society, 1983
Draper, Michael, *Modern Novelists: H.G. Wells*, London: Macmillan, 1988; New York: St Martin's Press, 1988
Edel, Leon and Ray, Gordon N. (eds), *Henry James and H.G. Wells*, London: Hart-Davis, 1958; Urbana: Illinois University Press, 1958

Foot, Michael, *H.G.: The History of Mr Wells*, London: Doubleday, 1995; Washington: Counterpoint, 1995

Frayling, Christopher, *Things to Come*, London: British Film Institute, 1995

Gettmann, Royal A. (ed.), *George Gissing and H.G. Wells*, London: Hart-Davis, 1961; Urbana: Illinois University Press, 1961

Haining, Peter (ed.), *The H.G. Wells Scrapbook*, London: New English Library, 1978

Hammond, John R., *H.G. Wells: An Annotated Bibliography*, New York and London: Garland, 1977

— *An H.G. Wells Companion*, London: Macmillan, 1979; New York: Harper and Row, 1979

— *H.G. Wells: Interviews and Recollections*, London: Macmillan, 1980

— *H.G. Wells and Rebecca West*, London and New York: Harvester Wheatsheaf, 1991

— *An H.G. Wells Chronology*, London: Macmillan, 1999; New York: St Martin's Press, 1999

H.G. Wells Society, *H.G. Wells: A Comprehensive Bibliography*, 1966, fourth edition, London: H.G. Wells Society, 1986

Hillegas, Mark R., *The Future as Nightmare*, New York: Oxford University Press, 1967

Huntington, John, *The Logic of Fantasy*, New York: Columbia University Press, 1982

— (ed.), *Critical Essays on H.G. Wells*, Boston: G.K. Hall, 1991

Kagarlitski, Julius, translated by Moura Budberg, *The Life and Thought of H.G. Wells*, London: Sidgwick and Jackson, 1966

Kemp, Peter, *H.G. Wells and the Culminating Ape*, London: Macmillan, 1982; New York: St Martin's Press, 1982

Loing, Bernard, *H.G. Wells À L'Œuvre: Les débuts d'un écrivain*, Paris: Didier Erudition, 1984

Lynn, Andrea, *Shadow Lovers*, New York: Perseus Press, 2001

MacKenzie, Norman and Jeanne, *The Time Traveller*, London: Weidenfeld and Nicolson, 1973; New York: Simon and Schuster, 1973; revised London: Hogarth Press, 1987

McKillop, A.B., *The Spinster and the Prophet*, New York: Da Capo Press, 2000, London: Aurum Press, 2001

McLean, Steven (ed.) *H.G. Wells: Interdisciplinary Essays*, Newcastle: Cambridge Scholars Publishing, 2008

Meyer, M.M., *H.G. Wells and His Family*, Edinburgh: International Publishing, 1956

Murray, Brian, *H.G. Wells*, New York: Continuum, 1990

Parrinder, Patrick, *H.G. Wells*, Edinburgh: Oliver and Boyd, 1970; New York: Putnam, 1970

— (ed.), *H.G. Wells: The Critical Heritage*, London and Boston: Routledge and Kegan Paul, 1972

— and Rolfe, Christopher (eds), *H.G. Wells Under Revision*, London and Toronto: Associated University Presses, 1990

— *Shadows of the Future*, Liverpool: Liverpool University Press, 1995

— and Partington, John S., (eds), *The Reception of H.G. Wells in Europe*, London and New York: Thoemmes Continuum, 2005

Partington, John S., *Building Cosmopolis: The Political Thought of H.G. Wells*, Aldershot and Vermont: Ashgate, 2003

— (ed.), *The Wellsian: Selected Essays on H.G. Wells*, Uitgevers: Equilibris, 2003

— (ed.), *H.G. Wells's Fin-de-Siècle: Selections from the Wellsian,* Frankfurt: Peter Lang, 2007
— (ed.), *H.G. Wells in 'Nature', 1893–1946,* Frankfurt: Peter Lang, 2008
Raknem, Ingvald, *H.G. Wells and His Critics,* London: Allen and Unwin, 1962
Ray, Gordon N., *H.G. Wells and Rebecca West,* New Haven: Yale University Press, 1974; London: Macmillan, 1974
Reed, John R., *The Natural History of H.G. Wells,* Athens: Ohio University Press, 1982
Renzi, Thomas C., *H.G. Wells: Six Scientific Romances Adapted for Film,* London and New Jersey: Scarecrow Press, 1992
Rinkel, Gene and Margaret, *The Picshuas of H.G. Wells,* Urbana and Chicago: University of Illinois Press, 2006
Ross, William T., *H.G. Wells's World Reborn,* Selinsgrove: Susquehanna University Press, 2002; London: Associated University Presses, 2002
Scheick, William J., *The Splintering Frame: The Later Fiction of H.G. Wells,* Victoria, BC: University of Victoria, 1984
— and Cox, J. Randolph (eds), *H.G. Wells: A Reference Guide,* Boston: G.K. Hall, 1988
— (ed.), *The Critical Response to H.G. Wells,* Westport, Conn.: Greenwood Press, 1995
Smith, David C., *H.G. Wells: Desperately Mortal,* New Haven and London: Yale University Press, 1986
Smith, Don G., *H.G. Wells on Film,* Jefferson: McFarland, 2002
Smith, J. Percy (ed.), *Bernard Shaw and H.G. Wells,* Toronto and London: University of Toronto Press, 1995
Stover, Leon, *The Shaving of Karl Marx,* Lake Forest, Illinois: The Chiron Press, 1982
— *The Prophetic Soul,* Jefferson and London: McFarland, 1987
Suvin, Darko and Philmus, Robert M. (eds), *H.G. Wells and Modern Science Fiction,* Lewisburg: Bucknell University Press, 1977
Wagar, W. Warren, *H.G. Wells and the World State,* New Haven: Yale University Press, 1961
Watkins, A.H. (ed.) *The Catalogue of the H.G. Wells Collection in the Bromley Public Libraries,* Bromley: London Borough of Bromley Public Libraries, 1974
Wells, Frank, *H.G. Wells: A Pictorial Biography,* London: Jupiter, 1977
Wells, Geoffrey H., *The Works of H.G. Wells 1887–1925: A Bibliography, Dictionary and Subject-Index,* London: Routledge, 1926
Wellsian, The
West, Anthony, *H.G. Wells: Aspects of a Life,* New York: Random House, 1984; London: Hutchinson, 1984
West, Geoffrey, *H.G. Wells: A Sketch for a Portrait,* London: Howe, 1930; New York: Norton, 1930
Williams, Keith, *H.G. Wells: Modernity and the Movies,* Liverpool: Liverpool University Press, 2007
Wilson, Harris (ed.), *Arnold Bennett and H.G. Wells,* London: Hart-Davis, 1960; Urbana: University of Illinois Press, 1960
Wykes, Alan, *H.G. Wells in the Cinema,* London: Jupiter, 1977

Further Sources

Aberconway, Christabel, *A Wiser Woman?*, London: Hutchinson, 1966

Alexander, Tania, *A Little of All These*, London: Jonathan Cape, 1987

Allen, Walter, *The English Novel*, London: Phoenix House, 1954; New York: Dutton, 1954

Armytage, W.H.G., *Sir Richard Gregory: His Life and Work*, London: Macmillan, 1957

Bagnold, Enid, *Enid Bagnold's Autobiography*, London: Heinemann, 1969; New York: Little, Brown, 1969

Baldick, Chris, *The Oxford English Literary History: The Modern Movement 1910–1940*, Oxford and New York: Oxford University Press, 2004

Barker, John, *The Superhistorians*, New York: Scribner, 1982

Batchelor, John, *The Edwardian Novelists*, London: Duckworth, 1982; New York: St Martin's Press, 1982

Belford, Barbara, *Violet Hunt*, New York: Simon and Schuster, 1990

Bennett, Arnold, *Books and Persons*, London: Chatto and Windus, 1917; New York: Doran, 1917

— *The Journals of Arnold Bennett*, (ed.) Frank Swinnerton, London: Penguin, 1954

Berberova, Nina, translated by Marian Schwartz and Richard D. Sylvester, *Moura: The Dangerous Life of the Baroness Budberg*, New York: New York Review Books, 2005

Born, Daniel, *The Birth of Liberal Guilt in the English Novel*, Chapel Hill and London: University of North Carolina Press, 1995

Bradbury, Malcolm, *The Modern British Novel*, London: Secker and Warburg, 1993

Brandon, Ruth, *The New Women and the Old Men*, London: Secker and Warburg, 1990; New York: Norton, 1990

Brittain, Vera, and Holtby, Winifred, *Selected Letters of Winifred Holtby and Vera Brittain, 1920–1935*, London: A. Brown, 1960

Brome, Vincent, *Six Studies in Quarrelling*, London: Cresset Press, 1958

Buitenhuis, Peter, *The Great War of Words*, Vancouver: University of British Columbia, 1987; London: Batsford, 1987

Calder, Robert, *Beware the British Serpent: The Role of Writers in British Propaganda in the United States, 1939–1945*, Montreal and London: McGill-Queen's University Press, 2004

Cantril, Hadley, *The Invasion from Mars*, Princeton: Princeton University Press, 1940

Carey, John, *The Intellectuals and the Masses*, London: Faber, 1992; Gordonsville: St Martin's Press, 1993

Chesterton, G.K., *Heretics*, London: The Bodley Head, 1905

Cheyette, Bryan, *Construction of 'the Jew' in English Literature and Society*, Cambridge and New York: Cambridge University Press, 1993

Clark, Ronald W., *The Huxleys*, London: Heinemann, 1968

Clarke, Peter, *Hope and Glory: Britain 1900–1990*, London and New York: Allen Lane, 1996

Crick, Bernard, *George Orwell: A Life*, London: Secker and Warburg, 1980; New York: Little, Brown, 1980

Delbanco, Nicholas, *Group Portrait*, New York: Morrow, 1982; London: Faber, 1982
Dick, Kay (ed.), *Writers at Work*, Harmondsworth: Penguin, 1972
Eliot, T.S., *After Strange Gods*, London: Faber, 1934
Ford, Ford Madox, *Mightier Than the Sword*, London: George Allen and Unwin, 1938
Forster, E.M., *Aspects of the Novel*, London: Edward Arnold, 1927; New York: Harcourt, Brace, 1927
Fromm, Gloria G., *Dorothy Richardson: A Biography*, Athens: University of Georgia Press, 1994 edition
Fry, Ruth, *Maud and Amber*, Christchurch, New Zealand: Canterbury University Press, 1992
Frye, Northrop, *Anatomy of Criticism*, Princeton: Princeton University Press, 1957
Garfield, Simon (ed.), *Our Hidden Lives*, London: Ebury Press, 2004
Gissing, George, *London and the Life of Literature in Late Victorian England: The Diary of George Gissing, Novelist*, (ed.) Pierre Coustillas, Brighton: Harvester Press, 1978
Glendinning, Victoria, *Rebecca West: A Life*, London: Weidenfeld and Nicolson, 1987; New York: Knopf, 1987
Gomme, A.W., *Mr Wells as Historian*, Glasgow: Maclehose, Jackson, 1921
Hobsbawm, Eric, *The Age of Empire 1875–1914*, London: Weidenfeld and Nicolson, 1987; New York: Pantheon, 1987
— *Age of Extremes 1914–1991*, London: Michael Joseph, 1994; New York, Pantheon, 1994
Hosking, Geoffrey, *A History of the Soviet Union*, London: Fontana, 1985; Cambridge, Mass.: Harvard University Press, 1985, revised edition 1992
Hunter, Jefferson, *Edwardian Fiction*, Cambridge, Mass. and London: Harvard University Press, 1982
Huxley, Julian, *Memories*, London: George Allen and Unwin, 1970; New York: Harper and Row, 1970
Huxley, T.H., *Evolution and Ethics and Other Essays*, London: Macmillan, 1894
Hynes, Samuel, *The Edwardian Turn of Mind*, Princeton: Princeton University Press, 1968
Karl, Frederick R., *Joseph Conrad: The Three Lives*, New York: Farrar, Straus and Giroux, 1979; London: Faber, 1979
Keating, Peter, *The Haunted Study*, London: Secker and Warburg, 1989
Keun, Odette, *My Adventures in Bolshevik Russia*, London: Bodley Head, 1923; New York: Dodd, Mead and Co., 1923
— *I Discover the English*, London: Bodley Head, 1934
Kumar, Krishan, *Utopia and Anti-Utopia in Modern Times*, Oxford: Basil Blackwell, 1987
Lanouette, William, with Silard, Bela, *Genius in the Shadows*, Chicago: University of Chicago Press, 1992
Lawrence, D.H., *Collected Letters*, (ed.) Harry T. Moore, London: Heinemann, 1962; New York: Viking Press, 1962
Lepenies, Wolf, trans. R.J. Hollingdale, *Between Literature and Science*, Cambridge: Cambridge University Press, 1988

Lodge, David, *Language of Fiction*, London: Routledge and Kegan Paul, 1966; New York: Columbia University Press, 1966

— *The Novelist at the Crossroads*, London: Routledge and Kegan Paul, 1971; New York: Cornell University Press, 1971

Lowe, Norman, *Mastering Modern World History*, Basingstoke and New York: Palgrave, revised edition 1997

MacKenzie, Norman and Jeanne, *The First Fabians*, London: Weidenfeld and Nicolson, 1977; New York: Simon and Schuster, 1977

Marwick, Arthur, *Britain in the Century of Total War*, London: Bodley Head, 1968; Boston: Little, Brown, 1968

Meek, George, *George Meek, Bath Chair-Man*, with an introduction by H.G. Wells, London: Constable, 1910

Mercer, Derrik (ed.), *The 20th Century Day by Day*, London and New York: Dorling Kindersley, 2000

Moorehead, Caroline, *Martha Gellhorn: A Life*, London: Chatto and Windus, 2003; New York: Henry Holt, 2006

Nabokov, Vladimir, *Strong Opinions*, New York: McGraw Hill, 1973; London: Weidenfeld and Nicolson, 1973

Nagorski, Tom, *Miracles on the Water*, London: Robinson, 2006; New York: Hyperion, 2006

Orwell, George, *Collected Essays, Journalism and Letters*, 4 vols, London: Secker and Warburg, 1968; New York: Harcourt, Brace and World, 1968

Playfair, Giles, *Singapore Goes Off the Air*, London and New York: Jarrold's, 1943

Poupard, Dennis (ed.), *Twentieth Century English Literary Criticism, Vol. 12*, Detroit: Gale Research, 1984

Reintjes, Monique, *Odette Keun*, Netherlands: privately printed, 2000

Richardson, Dorothy, *The Tunnel*, London: Duckworth, 1919

— *Dawn's Left Hand*, London: Duckworth, 1931

— *Clear Horizon*, London: Dent and the Cresset Press, 1935

Rollyson, Carl, *Rebecca West: A Saga of the Century*, New York: Scriber, 1996; London: Hodder and Stoughton, 1996

Rose, Jonathan, *The Edwardian Temperament 1895–1919*, Athens and London: Ohio University Press, 1986

— *The Intellectual Life of the British Working Classes*, New Haven and London: Yale University Press, 2001

Rosenberg, John, *Dorothy Richardson: The Genius They Forgot*, London and New York: Duckworth, 1973

Russell, Robert, *Zamiatin's 'We'*, London: Bristol Classical Press, 2000

Searle, G.R., *The New Oxford History of England: A New England? Peace and War 1886–1918*, Oxford and New York: Oxford University Press, 2004

Shaw, Valerie, *The Short Story: A Critical Introduction*, London and New York: Longman, 1983

Sinclair, Keith, *William Pember Reeves: New Zealand Fabian*, Oxford: Clarendon Press, 1965

Skinner, Cornelia Otis, and Kimborough, Emily, *Our Hearts Were Young and Gay*, New York: Dodd, Mead, 1942; London: Constable, 1944

Snow, C.P., *Variety of Men*, London: Macmillan, 1967; New York: Scribner's, 1967

Stableford, Brian, *Scientific Romance in Britain 1890–1950*, London: Fourth Estate, 1985; New York: St Martin's Press, 1985

Stallworthy, Jon, *Wilfred Owen: A Biography*, Oxford and New York: Oxford University Press, 1974

Stevenson, John, *The Pelican Social History of Britain: British Society 1914–45*, Harmondsworth: Penguin, 1984; New York: Viking, 1984

Stubbs, Patricia, *Women and Fiction: Feminism and the Novel 1880–1920*, London: Methuen, 1979; New York: Harper and Row, 1979

Swinnerton, Frank, *The Georgian Literary Scene*, London: Heinemann, 1935; New York: Farrar and Rineheart, 1935; revised edition London: Hutchinson, 1938

Taylor, A.J.P., *English History 1914–1945*, Oxford and New York: Oxford University Press, 1965

Terrell, Mary Church, *A Colored Woman in a White World*, with a preface by H.G. Wells, Washington: Ransdell, 1940

Trotter, David, *The English Novel in History 1895–1920*, London and New York: Routledge, 1993

Usborne, Karen, *'Elizabeth'*, London: Bodley Head, 1986

Wagenknecht, Edward, *Cavalcade of the English Novel*, New York: Henry Holt, 1944

Warwick, Frances, Countess of, *Afterthoughts*, London: Cassell, 1931

Webb, Beatrice, *The Diary of Beatrice Webb*, Vol. 3, (ed.) Norman and Jeanne Mackenzie, London: Virago, 1984; Cambridge, Mass.: Harvard University Press, 1984

West, Rebecca, *Henry James*, London: Nisbet, 1916

Wiener, Martin J., *Between Two Worlds: The Political Thought of Graham Wallas*, Oxford: Clarendon Press, 1971

Williams, Raymond, *The English Novel from Dickens to Lawrence*, London: Chatto and Windus, 1970; New York: Oxford University Press, 1970

Wilson, A.N., *After the Victorians*, London: Hutchinson, 2005; New York: Farrar, Straus and Giroux, 2005

Windholz, Anne M., 'Ella D'Arcy', in *Dictionary of Literary Biography, Vol. 135: British Short-Fiction Writers, 1880–1914: The Realist Tradition*, Detroit: Gale Research, 1994

Woolf, Virginia, *Carlyle's House and Other Sketches*, (ed.) David Bradshaw, London: Hesperus Press, 2003

Yeats, W.B., *Autobiographies*, London: Macmillan, 1980 edition

INDEX

All works by H.G. Wells are listed under: Wells, H.G., Works